Re-examining Insolvency Law and Theory

Re-examining Insolvency Law and Theory

Perspectives for the 21st Century

Edited by

Emilie Ghio

Lecturer in Corporate and Insolvency Law, School of Law, University of Edinburgh, UK

John M. Wood

Lecturer in Law, School of Law, Lancaster University, UK

Jennifer L. L. Gant

Senior Lecturer in Law, College of Business Law and Social Sciences, University of Derby, UK

Edward Elgar PUBLISHING

Cheltenham, UK • Northampton, MA, USA

Cover image: Giammarco Boscaro on Unsplash

Published by
Edward Elgar Publishing Limited
The Lypiatts
15 Lansdown Road
Cheltenham
Glos GL50 2JA
UK

Edward Elgar Publishing, Inc.
William Pratt House
9 Dewey Court
Northampton
Massachusetts 01060
USA

A catalogue record for this book
is available from the British Library

Library of Congress Control Number: 2023946857

This book is available electronically in the **Elgar**online
Law subject collection
http://dx.doi.org/10.4337/9781803928760

ISBN 978 1 80392 875 3 (cased)
ISBN 978 1 80392 876 0 (eBook)

EEP

Contents

Contributors

EDITORS

Emilie Ghio

Lecturer in Corporate and Insolvency Law, University of Edinburgh, UK.

John M. Wood

Lecturer in Law, Lancaster University, UK.

Jennifer L. L. Gant

Senior Lecturer in Law, University of Derby, UK.

CONTRIBUTORS

Colin Anderson

Adjunct Associate Professor, Queensland University of Technology, Australia.

Catherine Brown

Senior Lecturer, Queensland University of Technology, Australia.

Laura N. Coordes

Associate Professor, Arizona State University, US.

Jonathan Hardman

Senior Lecturer in Company and Commercial Law, University of Edinburgh, UK.

Jason Harris

Professor of Corporate Law, University of Sydney, Australia.

Lézelle Jacobs

Associate Professor, University of Technology Sydney, Australia.

Alisdair MacPherson

Senior Lecturer in Law, University of Aberdeen, UK.

Stephan Madaus

Professor, Martin-Luther-University Halle-Wittenberg, Germany.

David Milman

Professor, Lancaster University, UK.

Paul Omar

Senior Lecturer, De Montfort University School of Law, UK.

Xenophon Paparrigopoulos

Associate Professor of Law and Philosophy, University of the Peloponnese; Partner at Potamitis Vekris, Greece.

Stathis Potamitis

Partner, Potamitis Vekris, Greece.

John Tribe

Senior Lecturer in Law, University of Liverpool, UK.

Eugenio Vaccari

Senior Lecturer in Law, Royal Holloway, University of London, UK.

Tara Van Ho

Senior Lecturer in Law and Human Rights, University of Essex, UK.

1. Introduction: insolvency theory for a new age

Emilie Ghio, John M. Wood and Jennifer L. L. Gant

Over the last two decades or so, the study and practice of insolvency law have changed significantly. Traditionally, insolvency law was largely perceived as a technical and vocational area of law, with a concentration of academics and practitioners alike focusing on statutory developments and case law rather than seeking to dive into theoretical considerations.[1] Over time, it became apparent that theory has an important role to play in the development of insolvency law and, as such, debates around what insolvency law should strive to achieve and what drivers should be responsible for this change, have greatly increased.

The study of theories and concepts matters, as they are the essential foundation on which the understanding of any topic lays. The term 'theory' comes from the Greek verb θεωρώ (theorw), which means 'considering', 'contemplating', and 'speculating'. Today, theory is defined as 'a formal statement of the rules on which a subject of study is based or of ideas that are suggested to explain a fact or event or, more generally, an opinion or explanation'.[2] Therefore, theories are ways of testing speculative hypotheses with a view to reaching an argument with universal validity. Ben Rosamond notes that 'the process of theorizing is, to a very large extent, a mechanism for the generation and organization of disagreement [...] [B]eing theoretically conscious sharpens the sense in which analysts are aware of their own assumptions'.[3] In short, theories matter.

---

1 For example, in the early years, certainly in the UK, insolvency work after the enactment of the Joint Stock Companies Act 1844 was merely a business opportunity led by accountants and it was due to its development away from legal practitioners that made insolvency laws accountant bias, see J M Wood, 'Assessing the Effectiveness of the UK's Insolvency Regulatory Framework at Deterring Insolvency Practitioners' Opportunistic Behaviour' (2019) 19(2) *Journal of Corporate Law Studies* 333.

2 *Cambridge Dictionary*.

3 B Rosamond, *Theories of European integration* (Palgrave Macmillan 2000) p. 9.

However, the theories underpinning the scope and purpose of insolvency law are somewhat antiquated and couched broadly in economics' dogma. There have since been some notable theoretical advances on the original neo-liberal premise rooted in the idea of the creditors' bargain. This book notes some of the key theoretical influences that have emerged since the beginning of this century and plots the importance of this evolution on the development of insolvency law.

THEORETICAL CONSIDERATIONS TO DATE

Insolvency law theory has been the subject of serious debate since the 1980s. This can be seen from American scholars who collectively focused on an array of issues which gave rise to some of the best-known theories in the field, such as the Creditors' Wealth Maximisation theory and the Creditors' Bargain theory,[4] the Broad-based contractarian approach,[5] the Communitarian vision,[6] the Contractualist approach,[7] the Team Production theory[8] and the Explicit Value approach,[9] to name but a few. In the area of cross-border insolvency, a closer examination of the law led to the development of theories such

---

[4] T Jackson, *The Logic and Limits of Bankruptcy Law* (Harvard University Press 1986); D Baird, 'The Uneasy Case for Corporate Reorganisations' (1986) 15(1) *Journal of Legal Studies* 127; D Baird and T Jackson, 'Corporate Reorganisations and the Treatment of Diverse Ownership Interests: A Comment on Adequate Protection of Secured Creditors in Bankruptcy' (1984) 51(1) *University of Chicago Law Review* 97.

[5] D Korobkin, 'Contractarianism and the Normative Foundations of Bankruptcy Law' (1992) 71(3) *Texas Law Review* 541.

[6] K Gross, *Failure and Forgiveness: Rebalancing the Bankruptcy System* (Yale University Press 1997); E Warren, 'Bankruptcy Policy' (1987) 54(3) *University of Chicago Law Review* 775.

[7] R Epstein, *Simple Rules for a Complex World* (Harvard University Press 1995); D Baird, 'A World Without Bankruptcy' (1987) 50(2) *Law and Contemporary Problems* 173; B Adler, 'A World without Debt' (1994) 72(3) *Washington University Law Quarterly* 811; A Schwartz, 'A Contract Theory Approach to Business Bankruptcy' (1998) 107(6) *Yale Law Journal* 1807.

[8] M Blair and L Stout, 'A Team Production Theory of Corporate Law' (1999) 85(2) *Vanderbilt Law Review* 741; L LoPucki, 'A Team Production Theory of Bankruptcy Reorganization' (2004) 57(3) *Vanderbilt Law Review* 741.

[9] See R Goode, *Principles of Corporate Insolvency Law* (Sweet & Maxwell 2019); V Finch and D Milman, *Corporate Insolvency Law: Perspectives and Principles* (Cambridge University Press 2017).

as universalism,[10] territorialism,[11] modified universalism,[12] contractualism,[13] cooperative territoriality[14] and universal proceduralism.[15]

While worthwhile, these theoretical discussions have all largely emanated from American scholarship, while other parts of the world remained quieter in discussing insolvency law from a theoretical standpoint. Additionally, these theories were developed in the 1990s and 2000s, reflecting issues which emerged at the time. Since then, these theories have been dwelt on and rehashed.

To be effective, it is important that theories that inform insolvency practice are regularly reviewed and updated. There is, therefore, a need to rethink insolvency law theories in response to the growing body of American and

---

[10] J Westbrook, 'A Global Solution to Multinational Default' (2000) 98(7) *Michigan Law Review* 2276; J Westbrook, 'Theory and Pragmatism in Global Insolvencies: Choice of Law and Choice of Forum' (1991) 65(4) *American Bankruptcy Law Journal* 457; J Westbrook, 'Universal Priorities' (1998) 33(1) *Texas International Law Journal* 27; A Guzman, 'International Bankruptcy: In Defense of Universalism' (1999) 98(7) *Michigan Law Review* 2177; L Perkins, 'A Defense of Pure Universalism in Cross-Border Corporate Insolvencies' (2000) 32(3) *New York University Journal of International Law and Politics* 787.

[11] L LoPucki, 'Cooperation in International Bankruptcy: A Post-Universalist Approach' (1999) 84(3) *Cornell Law Review* 696; L LoPucki, 'Universalism Unravels' (2005) 79(1) *American Bankruptcy Law Journal* 143; E Adams and J Fincke, 'Coordinating Cross-border Bankruptcy: How Territorialism Saves Universalism' (2008) 15(1) *Columbia Journal of European Law* 43; A Kipnis, 'Beyond UNCITRAL: Alternatives to Universality in Transnational Insolvency' (2007) 36(2) *Denver Journal of International Law & Policy* 155.

[12] J Westbrook, 'Choice of Avoidance Law in Global Insolvencies' (1991) 17(3) *Brooklyn Journal of International Law* 499; K Anderson, 'The Cross-border Insolvency Paradigm: A Defence of the Modified Universal Approach Considering the Japanese Experience' (2000) 21(4) *University of Pennsylvania Journal of International Law* 679; I Mevorach, *The Future of Cross-Border Insolvency: Overcoming Biases and Closing Gaps* (Oxford University Press 2018) 13.

[13] R Rasmussen, 'A New Approach to Transnational Insolvencies' (1997) 19(1) *Michigan Journal of International Law* 1; R Rasmussen, 'Debtor's Choice: A Menu Approach to Corporate Reorganisation' (1992) 71(1) *Texas Law Review* 51; A Schwartz, 'Contracting about Bankruptcy' (1997) 13(1) *Journal of Law, Economics, & Organization* 127.

[14] LoPucki (n 11).

[15] E Janger, 'Predicting When the Uniform Process will Fail: Article 9, Capture, and the Race to the Bottom' (1998) *83 Iowa Law Review* 569; E Janger, 'Reciprocal Comity' (2011) 46(2) *Texas International Law Journal;* E Janger, 'Universal Proceduralism' (2007) 32(3) *Brooklyn Journal of International law* 819; E Janger, 'Virtual Territoriality' (2010) 48(3) *Columbia Journal of Transnational Law* 401.

non-American literature on insolvency law theories.[16] While theoretical discussions on insolvency law have been published outside the United States, they often only consider insolvency law from a specific viewpoint, such as fundamental principles and recurring goals of insolvency law (such as fairness, economic efficiency, impartiality, and so on). While they have advanced our understanding on the scope and purpose of insolvency regulation, few have created new paradigms. Further, these theories, due to their restrictive scope have left many details unaddressed in light of recent developments in the field.

Recent events such as the Coronavirus pandemic, the war in Ukraine, and the cost-of-living crisis, have shed light on the relevance of insolvency laws and why it is important that they address a range of interests. To that end, as the world changes, so does the role and objectives of laws generally. Insolvency laws in this respect are no exception. While 20 years ago, most national insolvency regimes around the world focused on the liquidation of companies in financial distress, the twenty-first century witnessed a decisive shift towards rescue and restructuring mechanisms. Rescue is a relatively new concept that entered collective consciousness during the 1960s or 1970s, although its meaning has evolved over time. For example, the rescue timeline has changed, with a greater emphasis on upstream measures that are available before functional insolvency at a time when financial distress is merely looming. These developments have produced new theoretical frameworks against which insolvency law can be construed. To address this shortcoming, there is a need, driven by both the academic community and practitioners alike, to review theories in relation to insolvency law.[17]

---

[16] See e.g., J M Wood, *Interpretation and Value of Corporate Rescue* (Edward Elgar Publishing 2022); R Mokal *Corporate Insolvency Law: Theory and Application* (Oxford University Press 2005); G McCormack, 'Universalism in Insolvency Proceedings and the Common Law' (2012) 32(2) *Oxford Journal of Legal Studies* 325; S Etukakpan, 'The Lost Voice in Insolvency: Theories of Insolvency Law and Their Implications for the Employees' (2014) 23 *Nottingham Law Journal* 34; A B Onakoya and A E Olotu, 'Bankruptcy and Insolvency: An Exploration of Relevant Theories' (2017) 7(3) *International Journal of Economics and Financial Issues* 706; S Paterson, 'Rethinking Corporate Bankruptcy Theory in the Twenty-first Century' (2016) 36(4) *Oxford Journal of Legal Studies* 697.

[17] See H Buxbaum, 'Rethinking International Insolvency: The Neglected Role of Choice-of-Law Rules and Theory' (2000) 36(1) *Stanford Journal of International Law* 23, 24, Buxbaum acknowledges the 'dissatisfaction with international bankruptcy theory as an invitation to re-examine [...] theory'; S Paterson, 'Rethinking Corporate Bankruptcy Theory in the Twenty-First Century' (2016) 36(4) *Oxford Journal of Legal Studies* 697, 697, Paterson flags the 'need to rethink corporate bankruptcy theory [in the twenty-first century]'.

RE-EXAMINING THE LAW

The objective of this book is to go beyond the confines of statutes and case law, to ensure that modern and novel corporate practices can be properly addressed. The need to develop distinct and separate theories that go beyond established principles is crucial to ensure that theory does not become circular and is erroneously applied to out-of-date concepts. Global changes have come swiftly, and the traditional theoretical explanations can no longer keep pace with the considerable shifts in economic and social policies that influence legal development. Recent examples of such change vary from the influence of the Coronavirus pandemic that emerged in the early part of 2020, whereby governments around the world rushed through an array of economic and legal measures to help address the financial troubles that many companies faced. These measures altered insolvency laws, with their implications still felt today. More broadly, changes to how companies are financed, how credit is secured, and the type of assets that modern companies possess have all contributed to a need for change to insolvency law theory. Simply put, the essence of the company has changed, and so this means that the theory must also change to accommodate what is happening in practice.

Thus, given that change is perpetual, insolvency frameworks are also in an evolutive phase, and the necessary changes will occur practically and organically, backed by a vast body of supporting literature to meet the emerging challenges of the modern day. Ultimately, this volume aims to produce a repository of modern, contemporary theoretical perspectives on insolvency law, capturing the evolution of the field in the last two decades; and with this, provide credible theories that are responsive to present-day and future insolvency issues across a variety of jurisdictions in the twenty-first century.

STRUCTURE OF THE BOOK

This book is divided into three parts.

In Part I, the philosophical influences on insolvency law are examined from a modern perspective. Topics examined include the morality behind insolvency law by Dr Paul Omar; the liberalisation of bankruptcy law by Professor Milman; the influence of the feminist movement on insolvency law by Dr Lezelle Jacobs; and a study of insolvency law from a Dworkinian viewpoint by Dr Catherine Brown and Dr Colin Anderson, Nietzschean standpoint by Dr John Tribe, and Rawlsian perspective by Stathis Potamitis and Xenophon Paparrigopoulos.

The book then adopts a dual approach to the theoretical study of insolvency law.

Part II proposes an inward-looking investigation of insolvency law, looking at theories which have emerged from within the field of insolvency law. These theories include decision theory and insolvency law by Dr John Wood; reconciling the public and private law goals of insolvency by Professor Jason Harris; successor liability theories by Professor Laura Napoli Coordes; and vulnerability theory by Dr Jennifer Gant. Inward looking theories help *deepen* our understanding of insolvency law and its mechanics.

The last section, Part III adopts an outward-looking perspective. This approach is guided by the belief that external elements, including other legal fields, can enhance our understanding of insolvency law. This section, therefore, considers insolvency law from the perspective of human rights by Dr Eugenio Vaccari and Dr Tara Van Ho; company law by Dr Jonathan Hardman; contract law by Professor Stephan Madaus; property law by Dr Alisdair MacPherson; and psychology by Dr Emilie Ghio. Outward-looking theories *broaden* our appreciation of insolvency law by considering issues outside of insolvency.

The book will conclude with some final remarks from the editors.

PART I

Philosophical considerations and influences on insolvency law

2. Insolvency law and morality

Paul Omar

WHAT DOES MORALITY MEAN?

To be able to figure out what the relationship is between insolvency law and morality, it is first necessary to understand what 'morality' means. For Cicero, the reflection: '*O tempora, o mores*!', uttered against the background of the Catilinian conspiracy,[1] was of the age he found himself in and the morals of those times (of which he disapproved). For Cicero, *mores* (singular *mos*) signified a code of behaviour, the foundation of ethics, a sense of right and wrong, the standards to apply to living in any age, which, though possibly idealistic to begin with, should not cede to the corruption of politics and social discourse. In fact, *mos maiorum* summed up, for the Romans, those customs of the people (or of their genteel betters) that were the essence of society. In fact, extending the observation that Günther Teubner makes about social constructs in reference to the law,[2] it is possible to draw analogies and (confidently) surmise that most cultural, religious, political and even moral constructs are likewise creations of society. Giving a little credence to this is the contemporary linguistic understanding of morality, which defines morality, taking a view point of the structure, as '[a] particular system of values and principles of conduct' but also, drilling down into the system and adopting a functional approach, as '[p]rinciples concerning the distinction between right and wrong or good and bad behaviour'.[3] Combining both ideas, there is the definition that states morality to be: '[a] personal or social set of standards for good or bad behavio[u]r and character, or the quality of being right and honest'.[4] Thus, what seems embedded in morality is the idea of choice, whether of individuals or

1 Marcus Tullius Cicero, *In L Catilinam Oratio Prima Habita in Senatu* (63 BCE).

2 Günther Teubner, 'How the Law Thinks: Towards a Constructivist Epistemology of Law' (1989) 23(5) *Law and Society* 727.

3 *Oxford Languages* (OUP) definitions provided to Google https://languages.oup.com/google-dictionary-en/ accessed 5 May 2023.

4 *Cambridge Academic Content Dictionary* (CUP) https://dictionary.cambridge.org/dictionary/english/ accessed 5 May 2023.

of society, these choices being at the heart of the elaboration of a system of principles based on the accretion of choices over time.

NOTIONS OF DEBT AND FAULT: A MORAL VIEWPOINT?

In understanding how morality may impact on insolvency, it is necessary to appreciate the role of debt in society. Taking the Graeber synthesis in his magisterial work on a history of debt,[5] the idea appears to be that the inability to repay creates an imbalance in the equality between creditor and debtor and may occasion the loss of the status of equals and thus possible subjection to a lesser status. Though Graeber eschews the relationship of debt to other forms of morality, it is possible to see that the downfall of equality he describes may be at the origin of a moral view of debt and, by extension, insolvency as the state of being unable to pay. Taking the conventional economic analysis of relationships through the prism of the market (the exchange of value, etc.) is thus not the correct way to analyse how the role of debt impacts on individuals and society and how it might give rise to a moral viewpoint being taken of the owing of debt. For Graeber, although debt is a 'creature of reciprocity', he admits the inability to honour the obligation causes a loss in the potential of achieving equality between individuals.[6] As such, despite his view that 'there is no such thing as a genuinely unpayable debt',[7] there is also the risk of subjection to a status outside society and the consequent inability to regain status of equals in the debt relationship.

It is, of course, not always possible to pretend to equality. In the religious context, humans can never be the equal of the divine, while, looking to the social context, especially in early societies, the vast majority of individuals could never aspire to equality with the ruler. For Graeber, though, where individuals are notionally capable of achieving equality, while the debt remains unpaid, the 'logic of hierarchy takes hold' and there is a degree of 'unnatural'-ness about the relationship. In that light, a failure to repay is 'so difficult and so painful', because the failure to achieve and/or restore the potential equality through honouring the obligation[8] occasions the ascribing of fault to the individual unable to repay.[9]

5 David Graeber, *Debt: The First 5000 Years* (Melville House 2014).

6 Ibid., 120.

7 Ibid., 120–121.

8 *Pacta sunt servanda* (agreements shall be performed), said to have been first described as a fundamental principle of law in the writings of Henry of Segusio (or Hostiensis) (fl 13th c).

9 Graeber (n 5) 121.

Some credence may be given when considering how language describes the debt environment. The 'debtor' is of course the one who owes (an obligation), while the 'creditor' is the one who believes (that the obligation will be repaid). Addressing the inability to restore equality and the risk of downfall, words such as 'insolvency', meaning the inability to solve or resolve one's debt situation, similar in concept to the French word *déconfiture* (disaggregation, i.e., of property or funds), suggest that achieving balance between the parties is foremost in the nature of the relationship. 'Liquidation' describes the process through which the debtor may try to restore solvency by the encashment of assets. But the idea of status loss and the inability to regain the balance, hence needing a moral viewpoint to be taken ascribing fault, is inherent in many mediaeval words for bankruptcy (itself allegedly coined to describe the process for expelling a defaulter from the market), some of which survive to the present day, such as *faillite* (French) and *fallimento* (Italian), which both contain the same root as 'fall' or 'failure'.

In that light, some questions could be posed to try and understand how perceptions of morality, once entrenched in the insolvency environment, became prevalent and pervasive. So too, questions could be asked as to what morality applies to a commercial relationship, where the taking of risk is a feature of the process, and whether it is different or similar to the way in which personal relations are governed. This is because individuals often view the owing of debts on a commercial basis as very different to those owed on a personal basis. Thus, owing debts to a financial lender is not seen in the same light as debts owed within a family, clan or other close-knit structure, the risk of litigation and enforcement over assets allegedly unlikely to be a feature of personal relationships in the same way as owing debt to a bank would attract consideration of such remedies on the onset and as a consequence of default. This may or may not be true, although it does invite some speculation as to whether there are different moralities to apply to different contexts or to different forms of obligation and their treatment. As an example, Graeber makes the point that debt forgiveness can apply to legal debts, but not always moral ones,[10] a view shared in a traditional Malay *pantun*,[11] which ends: '...*hutang emas boleh dibayar, hutang budi dibawa mati*'.[12]

---

[10] Ibid., 120.

[11] A poetic form, usually of four verses, the first two containing abstract imagery or metaphors, the last two its moral or purpose.

[12] '...a debt of gold can be repaid, [but] a debt of honour is taken to the grave'.

A CHOICE OF CLASSIC PARADIGMS

Set against the background of the history of insolvency in Western Europe and those countries that share the legal heritages from the region, there appear to be two basic paradigms of morality that could apply. There is the Abrahamic belief system, with many, but not all, elements shared by three religious traditions, and there is the Roman framework, to the extent it reflects a unique Roman societal perspective on the owing of debt.[13] In both cases, there is not a single view or perspective that entirely represents either system, a feature that occurs also because these structures have changed over time. Characterisations of 'essential' core elements of each system can only, therefore, be conjectural.

The Abrahamic Tradition

The basic ideas in this tradition are that loans are only ever based on need and are short term in nature. Moreover, a liberal approach to lending and periodic debt forgiveness should be features of the debtor-creditor relationship. In this light, the custom of debt release or forgiveness, which Paulus analyses as a profound limitation on the creditor's ability to recover debt,[14] requires a release at the end of seven years, with exceptions only being permissible for debts owed by foreigners.[15] No further recovery is permissible, as the release is considered to be ordained by divine command.[16] The release appears to be society-wide, as the text continues with the injunction that creditors should not forebear from lending, even though the seventh year is nigh, it being a sin to deny a loan to someone in need.[17] This is especially so, given the acknowledgement in the text of the poor, who always will be present in society and to whom lenders should be open-handed.[18] In the same tradition, perhaps an inheritance from older cultural practices in the region,[19] while debt-bondage was permissible, there were limitations on its duration, service being required for six years and

---

13 For an excellent summation of some historical sources on the debtor-creditor relationship, juxtaposing the two 'diametrically [opposing]' traditions, see Christoph Paulus, 'The Eternal Struggle for Supremacy between Creditor and Debtor' (2022) 31 *Juridica International* 59, 60–62.

14 Ibid., 60.

15 The non-applicability of certain religious injunctions or prohibitions to those outside the community appears to be a feature of the texts. Curiously, *Deuteronomy* 15:6 contemplates lending to those outside the community being permissible, but borrowing not so.

16 *Deuteronomy* 15:1–3.

17 *Deuteronomy* 15:9.

18 *Deuteronomy* 15:11.

19 Paulus (n 13) 60, citing the Hammurabi Codex.

release being given in the seventh (a number of some significance in the tradition).[20] The injunction to be charitable to those leaving such service, whose debt has been consumed by the labour, is also present in the text.[21]

The rationale for the release is said to be the servitude the Israelites experienced in Egypt, from which they were providentially liberated or 'redeemed'. Thus, introducing the idea of forgiveness of others as a corollary of being forgiven or redeemed, the redemption of others is considered to be a commandment.[22] This idea of forgiveness may also be that seen in the daily prayers of Christians, especially that line of the Lord's Prayer that states: '*Et dimitte nobis debita nostra, sicut et nos dimittimus debitoribus nostris.*'[23] Taking the concept of the release further, the tradition mandated a super-release (also called a Jubilee),[24] an ordained ritual of forgiveness every seven 'sabbaths of years'. In this 50th year, liberty would be proclaimed for all inhabitants in the land and the people would be restored to property and to their families.[25] For those who had sold their property through need or poverty, the possibility of redemption by a relative or the debtor him/herself, should circumstances have changed, is made available as an option prior to the Jubilee.[26] Nonetheless, should the property remain in the hands of the buyer until the Jubilee, the text provides for restoration in that year.[27] The powerful appeal of the Jubilee in terms of its redemptory effect is perhaps at the root of its adoption into Christianity through the practice of Jubilee years, first recorded in the mediaeval period, whose purpose is the forgiveness of sins through the undertaking of special pilgrimages and meritorious acts during the Jubilee period.[28] The equation of Jubilee and forgiveness is also said to have been at the root of the Jubilee 2000 campaign[29] and the call by Pope John Paul II for forgiveness of the debts owed by emerging and developing countries.[30]

---

20 *Exodus* 21:2.

21 *Deuteronomy* 15:13–14.

22 *Deuteronomy* 15:15.

23 'And forgive us our trespasses (sins, debts etc.), as we forgive those who trespass against us.'

24 Reputedly from the Hebrew יובל (yobēl), a trumpet made from a ram's horn (now called a shofar), such trumpets being used ceremonially to announce events.

25 *Leviticus* 25:10 and 13.

26 *Leviticus* 25:25-27.

27 *Leviticus* 25:28.

28 Paulus (n 13) 60 (especially the literature cited in footnotes 4 and 10).

29 See: https://www.advocacyinternational.co.uk/featured-project/jubilee-2000 accessed 5 May 2023.

30 Paulus (n 13) 61. See also https://www.vatican.va/content/john-paul-ii/en/messages/pont_messages/1999/documents/hf_jp-ii_mes_19990923_jubilee-2000-debt-campaign.html accessed 5 May 2023.

Within the same tradition, Islamic finance models and structures work subject to the avoidance of '*riba*' (usurious or excessive interest),[31] which, just as in the other Abrahamic faiths, is prohibited.[32] Contracts that contain elements of uncertainty are also prohibited, thus preventing parties entering into gambling and short-selling contracts with higher incidences of risk. There is also a more open and equitable view of the need to share profit and loss between both sides in any transaction. This can be seen in the most common forms of lending for asset acquisition, for example the *musharakah* (joint investment) contract, which sees creditor and debtor pool value into a joint purchase of an asset. In this model, there is a progressive transfer of ownership between debtor and creditor: as the debt is repaid, the debtor acquires more of a share and control of the property. Its counterpart, the *murabaha*, is an agreement as to cost and markup, allowing for the sharing of profits resulting from an investment. Thus, as the value of the underlying asset increases, so there is a progressive distribution of the enhanced value to both debtor and creditor alike. However, a diminution in value would also be similarly distributed. This would be unlikely to lead to creditors needing to take action against the debtors, the risk of loss being a feature of the relationship. Overall, the attitude towards debt-forgiveness can be summed up in the *hadith* (saying) of the Prophet (s.a.w), which states: 'Whoever grants relief to a debtor or absolves his debt, he will be in the shade of the Throne on the Day of Resurrection.'[33] However, equally, the payment of debts by those who can do so is considered an obligation.[34]

The Roman View

The Roman view could not be more different. Rajak suggests a reason when he states that debt was 'a powerful and frequently troublesome factor in ancient society',[35] thus requiring a response from authority. Though he also refers to evidence of a lending culture in Ancient Greece, and to Solon's reforms *circa* 590 BCE, described as a cancellation of debt and prohibition of debt-bondage past and future,[36] it is with the Roman period that more sources can be found

---

[31] The word has the same root as *ārba'a* (four), interpreted to suggest that interest of more than a quarter of capital is usurious.

[32] See also *Exodus* 22:25–27; *Deuteronomy* 23:20–21; *Luke* 6:34–36.

[33] Hadith recounted by Abu Qatadah, collected in Musnad Aḥmad 22023.

[34] Hadith recounted by Abu Hurairah, collected in Ṣaḥīḥ Muslim 1601.

[35] Harry Rajak, 'The Culture of Bankruptcy' in Paul Omar (ed), *International Insolvency Law: Themes and Perspectives* (Ashgate 2008) 8.

[36] Ibid., citing Michel Austin and Pierre Vidal-Naquet, *Economic and Social History of Ancient Greece, An Introduction* (M M Austin tr, 1st edn, University of California Press 1977) 211.

enabling a Roman attitude to debt and debt-forgiveness to be postulated. From the earliest known codification of Roman Law in the XII Tables *circa* 453 BCE, the problem of a debtor who experiences an inability to pay his/her debts is adverted to in the strongest terms.[37] In language that is memorable, the legislation enables debtors to be taken in debt-bondage by the creditor or an associate following default for 30 days. Further default would allow the creditor to cut the debtor to pieces (*in partis secanto*) or to sell the debtor into slavery across the Tiber (*trans Tiberim*), i.e., outside Rome.[38] For Rajak, the harshness of the rules is 'notorious', but helps to quell the 'violence and disturbance' mass indebtedness could give rise to because it is subject to a procedure under supervision,[39] in a way co-opting for the state the power of the creditor to dispense raw justice, howbeit inefficient it might be: a dead debtor does not pay![40] In this context, the link between debt and political and social conflict in the Roman Republic is very interesting.[41] It is perhaps no coincidence that the occasion for Cicero's observation on morals and time, the Catilinian conspiracy, attracted much of its support from followers who were deeply indebted and promised widespread debt relief.[42]

The logic of harshness, in response to the destabilising factor of social unrest, eventually gave way to more nuanced measures. Rajak states that the 'greater commercial sense' was to allow the debtor to work off the debt during debt-bondage, *nexum* (bond or pledge), by which the debtor offered him/herself as collateral for an unpaid loan, and *addictio* (assignment or dedication), which replaced it, both offering this alternative to a more gruesome outcome.[43] Rajak even suggests that, despite the negative connotations, *nexum* or *addictio* could offer the opportunity to raise capital, as the economic advantages of the relationship are 'obvious', perhaps because they create a dependency or network

---

37 Table III of the XII Tables.

38 Rajak (n 35) 9, citing William Buckland, *A Textbook of Roman Law* (3rd edn, Cambridge University Press 1963) 618–620, for 'a clear (and chilling) description of this process (known to the Roman as *manus iniectio*, literally, throwing [the debtor] into the [creditor's] hands.'

39 Ibid.

40 A later variant of this coercive phenomenon, the Debtor's Prison, also suffers from this inefficiency: an imprisoned debtor does not become more likely to pay debt if unable to earn. See Paulus (n 13) 61, for an account of the 19th century literary debate in Germany over Shakespeare's *Merchant of Venice* as an illustration of the desire of creditors to take revenge.

41 Rajak (n 35) 9, citing literature on the phenomenon of debt and social and political unrest, especially Livy's *History of Rome* (on the problems of the 4th century BCE).

42 Ibid., citing Marcus Tullius Cicero, *In L Catilinam Oratio Secunda*.

43 Ibid., citing M Frederikson, 'Caesar, Cicero and the Problem of Debt' (1966) 56 *Journal of Roman Studies* 128, 129.

of mutual obligation. Sometime between the Later Republic and early Empire, Rajak reports the building of a recognisable system of bankruptcy that involves asset forfeiture and sales with a distribution of proceeds, earliest references to which come from the writings of Cicero.[44] However, many questions remain unanswered, for example the status of contingent (or conditional) debts, how the proof of debts process operated, whether action by creditors was individual or collective, etc.[45] Some questions were only resolved much later, such as the protection given to secure and privileged claims, which Rajak suggests offers little insight into how the framework actually evolved.[46] Nonetheless, the development of the bankruptcy framework and rules, such as it was, needs to be understood in the context of the significance of debt and indebtedness in Roman society.

The Roman view of debt can be said to be classist. Senators, for whom a property qualification was required for membership of the institution of state, were supposed to be the aristocracy of Rome. Though men such as Cicero, a *novus homo* (new man), could rise, many senators came from privileged families with inherited wealth. Perhaps because of this, there appeared to be a disdain for wealth gained from commercial activity, subject to limited exceptions, such as the farming of provinces, whose governorships were allocated once a period in a higher magistracy had been served, or receipts from the sale of war tribute, booty or spoils.[47] Of course, there were workarounds: undisclosed partnerships with members of the *equites* (Knights), on whom no such restriction lay, or with freed(wo)men, whose membership of the Senator's *clientela* (clients) enabled funds to be sought or borrowed with little likelihood of adverse publicity or recovery action. On occasion, funds could be obtained from the influencers of the day, Crassus being one such famous figure in the Late Republic, though the parties often went to the pains of concealment, such was the opprobrium of publicity.

In that light, the desire to avoid the risk of the civic penalty for bankruptcy, *infamia* (infamy), can be understood, because of its impact on the indebted individual with no means of avoiding creditor action.[48] Rajak recounts that

---

44 Ibid., citing Marcus Tullius Cicero, *Pro Quinctio* 15.50. See also Paulus (n 13) 61 (especially the literature cited in footnote 17).

45 Ibid., 10.

46 Ibid., citing Gaius, *Institutes* 2.155 and 3.79 (a text dating from the 2nd century CE) and the much later *Digest* (Justinian's 6th century codification) D 42.4.7.1, D 42.5.16.5 and D 42.5.24.2.

47 Curiously similar to the (damning) view in Victorian society of a person being 'in trade'.

48 A debtor with greater social or political connections could well avoid such a risk as long as those connections could be relied upon. The French mediaeval procedure of

a debtor rendered '*infamis*' could be imprisoned for debt and formally banned from the *cursus honorum* (honourable race), meaning prohibition from membership of the Senate, election to the magistracies and inability to plead cases in the law courts. '*Infamia*, in effect, was tantamount to political death', an observation that could also be true of modern bankruptcy laws, which often provide for exclusions from professional and political bodies as a consequence of undischarged indebtedness.[49] Such was the effect of exclusion from civic institutions, which, according to Paulus, only served to thin out those eligible for the magistracies and the Senate, that Augustus is said to have been prompted to act to stem the outflow of those otherwise eligible.[50] The introduction of *cessio bonorum* (transfer of assets), a form of voluntary surrender of property to the creditors as a group, was the result.[51] It served, Rajak says, to avoid the 'taint of *infamia*', but was not available to all, as it was: 'probably [closed] not only to those whose insolvency was due to their own fault, but also to those who had no property worth the mention to hand over to their creditors'.[52] However, there did not seem, in this procedure or any of its earlier predecessors, to be any discharge available (from partly or wholly unpaid debts), a situation that continued to bedevil insolvency frameworks into the present age.[53] Thus, a debtor would continue to be at the mercy of creditors and subject to their voluntary abdication of pursuit, a position that could change depending on the debtor's changing fortunes.

MEDIAEVAL BANKRUPTCY AND THE CHOICE OF INHERITANCES

With these two models to choose from, what shape did mediaeval bankruptcy take? As always, the answer is nuanced. While the origin of the term 'bankruptcy' itself is disputed, some assert that it comes from the Italian *banca rotta*

lettres de répit (letters of respite), which allowed well-connected individuals to obtain a moratorium from the King against creditor enforcement, is illustrative in this regard.

[49] Rajak (n 35) 10. See, e.g., the range of insolvency-related events that give rise to disqualification in the Company Directors' Disqualification Act 1986 (United Kingdom).

[50] Paulus (n 13) 62.

[51] *Cessio bonorum* remained in the French Civil Code procedure of the *cession des biens* (Articles 1265–1270), only being abolished by Law no. 91-650 of 9 July 1990. It still exists on the island of Jersey, where it is partially regulated by the *Loi (1832) sur les décrets*.

[52] Rajak (n 35) 10, citing H Jolowicz, *Historical Introduction to Roman Law* (2nd edn, Cambridge University Press 1952) 226.

[53] Ibid., 11, citing Gaius, *Institutes*, 2.155; Justinian, *Institutes* 4.6.40, *Digest* D 42.3.4, 6 and 7, *Codex Iuris Civilis* 7.72.10.1a.

(broken bench), reputedly referring to the breaking up of the trader's stall in the market.[54] However, the meaning the term otherwise conveys of exclusion from the market through a withdrawal of the privilege to trade is undoubtedly true. If a trader infringed the rules of the market and failed to abide by its essential principle of the honouring of agreements, then the trader was deemed untrustworthy and ejected from the market, resulting in a form of 'commercial death'. Moreover, the shift from administration of commercial justice by market tribunals in some places to the civil courts and the making of rules by the early governments of the Italian city-states did not largely change this emphasis on exclusion. It merely extended the range of penalties that could be imposed, ranging from sumptuary penalties,[55] public shaming[56] and internal exile to harsher penalties, including imprisonment,[57] branding, external exile and, in rare cases, death.[58]

Perhaps because of the continued influence of the *cessio bonorum*, mediaeval laws also failed to confront the possibility of debt-forgiveness, thus accentuating the severity of the penalties to which debtor would be subject. In fact, the language and practices of the criminal law appear to influence the treatment of insolvent debtors, perhaps causing the phenomenon of debtors fleeing these penalties.[59] In that light, the subject matter of early insolvency treaties may not be surprising, given they deal with repatriation of absconding debtors and feloniously taken property,[60] factors that would limit the opportunity of a fresh start for debtors through voluntary exile. Overall, this association with penal laws reinforces the stigma associated with business failure, a feature of insolvency until the present, as a seminal study in 2003 confirmed was still the case.[61] Even the term 'bankruptcy', as inherited in French law, retains the idea

---

[54] *Pro*: Rajak (n 35) 3. *Contra*: Paulus (n 13) 62.

[55] Paulus (n 13) 62, refers to the wearing of distinctive clothing.

[56] Ibid., noting a procedure in Padua that required the debtor to process naked and declare his bankrupt status by beating his body against a pillar in the public square.

[57] Though the imprisonment of debtors at the behest of creditors was prohibited by the Debtors Act 1869 (England and Wales), imprisonment for debt was not fully abolished till 1971.

[58] Paulus (n 13) 62.

[59] Ibid., 63, suggesting that the idea of the 'fugitive' is an insolvency-derived one.

[60] Philip Wood, *Principles of International Insolvency* (Sweet & Maxwell 1995) 291, referring to the Treaties of 1204 (Verona and Trent) and 1306 (Verona and Venice). Rajak (n 35) 12, refers to the purpose of the English Bankruptcy Act 1542, which was to deal with persons who: 'craftily obtaining in their own hands great substance of other men's goods, do suddenly flee to parts unknown…'.

[61] European Commission, Enterprise Directorate-General, *Best Project on Restructuring, Bankruptcy, and a Fresh Start: Final Report of the Expert Group* (2003).

of acts associated with criminality, especially fraud on the creditors.[62] Stigma begets shame and the use of the idea of the Fall (as in the Expulsion of Adam and Eve from the Garden of Eden)[63] creates a potent metaphor of loss of innocence and trust.

Although the foregoing appears to look as if mediaeval bankruptcy took more from its Roman inheritance, it was not true in all cases. Despite the influence of *cessio bonorum*, mediaeval law developed a number of ways to palliate the debtor's predicament, the institution of the *lettres de répit* being one.[64] Although more likely to be accessed by the well-connected, fortunate individuals could obtain the protection of the sovereign (and, later, of the courts)[65] to postpone for a period the claims of creditors, allowing for a suspensory procedure that might improve the debtor's prospects of recovery and creditor repayment. This idea of the stay on creditor claims for a period to enable their discharge through a court-supervised process, is arguably the more proximate ancestor of the moratorium or stay known in most modern insolvency laws.

Another was the *concordato* (settlement), by which means creditors could allow the debtor to recover some assets for the purpose of continuing trading and could even vote to 'cram down' dissenting creditors, with the prospects of the eventual settlement of a goodly proportion of debt that was not otherwise subject to waivers and/or 'haircuts'. While the decision lay mostly in the hands of the creditors, who would need to agree such 'rescues', which could only exist with a high level of trust or the presence of a guarantor as to future conduct and/or liabilities, sanction or support by judicial authority was still required to support such a *concordato*, an indication of the public interest element still present in modern insolvencies.[66] Echoes of a morality requirement can be seen in both these procedures in the requirement for trust and confidence of courts and creditors alike and, with respect to the *concordato*, obtaining guarantees as to future behaviour.

---

[62] '*Banqueroute*' continues to be penalised by Articles L654-1 to 654-7, *Code de Commerce* (France), which provide for five years' imprisonment and a penalty of EUR 75,000. Deprivation of civic rights and disqualification from carrying out professional activities are additional penalties that can be imposed. See Jérôme Sgard, 'Bankruptcy, Fresh Start and Debt Renegotiation in England and France (17th to 18th Century)', in Thomas Safley (ed), *The History of Bankruptcy* (Routledge 2013) 227.

[63] *Genesis* 3 (in extenso).

[64] See (n 48).

[65] For a description of the workings of the French Ordinance of 1673, see Corinne Saint-Alary-Houin, *Droit des Entreprises en Difficulté* (5th edn, Montchrestien 2006) paragraph 11. This procedure also survives in Jersey subject to the terms of the *Loi (1839) sur les remises de biens*.

[66] Sgard (n 62) 224.

Overall, some elements of the Abrahamic dispensation also continued. Paulus refers to the Novellae of Constantine VII Porphyrogenitus (r 913–959), enjoining a more merciful treatment of debtors through the sacrifice of creditors taking Jesus Christ as a model.[67] Moreover, the prohibition of the *pactum commissorium* (advance agreement to forfeiture by the creditor) by the *pactum Marcianum* was earlier maintained by Justinian.[68] While a limited remission of debts, in the form of postponement, was argued for,[69] control over the contract matrix appeared to be limited to the maintenance of the prohibition on lending between Christians at interest and associated usurious practices (i.e., with unfair terms; or providing for foreclosure, etc).[70] Again, such practices were frowned upon as regards lending between members of the same community, which, in England, as elsewhere, resulted in marginalised communities (largely Jews) being coerced into undertaking lending and to suffer the consequences of expropriation, for example through forced debt-purchases and inheritance by the Crown as universal legatee (to the exclusion of family members).

As in the Catilinian conspiracy, the cancellation of debt (at the expense of the Jews) became a manifesto for rebellion, as witnesses the Manifesto of Simon de Montfort in 1264 during the Barons' War with the Crown. Italian banking, which saw a rise in the early Middle Ages, did not place that community in the same position, the Italians being adjudged Christians, though their less than fervent adhesion to the rules on usury enabled avoidance of the strict prohibition on lending at interest.

WHY THE PREFERENCE?

Rajak suggests that the development of merchant trading rules is at the heart of understanding how mediaeval societies conceived of indebtedness and debt recovery law. It is the result of the formation of a Europe-wide body of rules, largely derived from the customary practices of merchants and based principally on the mercantile law of Italy.[71] This 'Law Merchant' was influenced by the law and institutions of Roman Law, perhaps because of the 'rediscovery' of and resurgence of interest in Roman Law through the foundation of the

---

67 Paulus (n 13) 63.

68 *Digest* D.20.1.16.9.

69 Paulus (n 13) 63.

70 See Usury Act 1948 (UK), later repealed and replaced by sections 140A-C, Consumer Credit Act 1974 (UK). An echo of this can be seen in the development of the doctrine of the equity of redemption by the Courts of Equity to allow debtors to recover their equity in the collateral (if any), a position maintained by section 105, Law of Property Act 1925 (England and Wales).

71 Rajak (n 35) 11.

Universities of Northern Italy, a fertile region where many commercial and accounting practices were invented,[72] including banking (referred to earlier).[73] Roman Law is certainly at the heart of the law of contract and property in most European states and, being considered by some a natural or common law, has been mooted as a source of a common European commercial law framework.[74] In that light, it is perhaps not surprising that the bankruptcy regimes in mediaeval Europe owe a lot to the institutions developed in the later Roman Republic.

While some features of the Abrahamic traditions endured, they were largely mitigated by the overwhelming influence of Romanistic legalism. Arguably, this process has been accentuated by the Renaissance and rise of secular thought, but it also owes something to the age of codification in the 19th century, when Napoleon, seeking to emulate Justinian, authorised the codification of French law, beginning with the Civil and Commercial Codes (the latter including insolvency).[75] The paradigms in those codes were reliant not just on mediaeval French law, but on its reinterpretation through the prism of Roman Law. In some cases, appeals to principles of Roman Law (as well as supersession by Roman Law where French law was felt to be deficient) were part of the process. While the reasoning behind codification (and the principles inherent in the process) can be criticised, as Legrand does,[76] the Codes have had a worldwide influence in terms of structure, approach and principles, including moral viewpoints.

INFLUENCES INTO THE PRESENT AND THE WAY FORWARD

In light of the history of insolvency law and the apparent conflict between these two models or approaches, it is possible to see that modern insolvency frameworks continue to owe much to these antecedents and the various viewpoints they represent. This possibly explains lingering antipathy towards insolvency, from the suspicion of fraud to the unwillingness to help in situations of deemed commercial 'irresponsibility', a term which embraces everything from bad bookkeeping to negligent management. In respect of the former, the posi-

---

72 Accounting principles, double-entry book-keeping, promissory notes, etc.

73 The oldest Italian bank still in operation is the Monte dei Paschi di Siena, founded in 1472.

74 Rajak (n 35) 11. Not everyone is convinced by the need for a new *ius commune/droit commun*, for which see Pierre Legrand, 'European Systems are not Converging' (1996) 45(1) *International and Comparative Law Quarterly* 52.

75 Currently in Book VI, *Code de Commerce* (France).

76 Pierre Legrand, 'Against a European Civil Code' (1997) 60(1) *Modern Law Review* 44.

tion in Jersey that once prevailed in relation to accessing the *remise de biens* procedure was described by the commentator, Le Geyt, as being unavailable to persons who had wantonly dissipated their assets by spending their money 'in taverns, on games of chance or with *shameless* [sic] women'.[77]

As an example of 'irresponsibility', there can be cited the case of *Re Citro*,[78] in which two brothers lost their respective family homes, pledged for a business loan, and where the judge observed that the outcome was simply the 'melancholy consequences of debt and improvidence with which every civilised society has been familiar'.[79] The lingering sense of fault, criminality and stigmas, identified in the 2003 EU report previously mentioned,[80] apparently still persists in the idea that there are 'good' and 'bad' debtors as well as 'good' and 'bad' forum shopping that should entitle a court to form a view on whether debtors should have access to insolvency procedures in jurisdictions other than where they are incorporated.[81] There are many other such examples that serve to remind the modern proponent of insolvency law that the views of antiquity continue to inform the attitudes of the present day, including the belated response to the need to legislate for consumer debt forgiveness, perhaps because of the 'selfish' nature of property and debt acquisitions through credit, despite the acknowledgment that consumer debt powers many economies.[82]

This is not to say that there have been no mitigating phenomenon or attempts to palliate some of the harshness of the philosophies of the ancients. The Islamic principles already mentioned continue to be the foundation of Islamic finance frameworks and institutions, not only in countries whose religion and culture is inspired by Islamic models, but in others.[83] Attitudes

---

77 Pierre Le Geyt, *Constitution, Lois et Usages* (Falle 1846) Volume 1, 386. See also Recitals 78–79, Directive (EU) 2019/1023 of the European Parliament and of the Council of 20 June 2019 on preventive restructuring frameworks on discharge of debt and disqualifications, and on measures to increase the efficiency of procedures concerning restructuring, insolvency and discharge of debt, and amending Directive (EU) 2017/1132 [2019] OJ L 172/18 (PRD) on derogations from the principle of debt-discharge for a lack of honesty or good faith.

78 Re Citro [1991] Ch 142.

79 Ibid., 157. See also PRD, Recital 27 on the denial of access to restructuring for those with bad bookkeeping and other accounting infractions to their discredit.

80 See (n 61).

81 See Recitals 5 and 31, Regulation (EU) 2015/848 of the European Parliament and of the Council of 20 May 2015 on insolvency proceedings (recast) OJ L 141/19 (EIR).

82 For a recent assessment of consumer insolvency law in Europe, see Thomas Kadner Graziano, Juris Bojārs and Veronika Sajadova (eds), *A Guide to Consumer Insolvency Proceedings in Europe* (Elgar Publishing 2019).

83 According to a 2021 report, the UK is the leading Western jurisdiction involved in Islamic finance, with UK-based assets totalling USD 7.5 billion (2021 figures) amounting to 85 per cent of total assets held in Europe (Turkey excluded). See:

to insolvency, debt-forgiveness and the honouring of payments continue to be shaped by hallowed tradition.[84] In addition to the calls for debt-forgiveness by Pope John Paul II noted earlier,[85] there have been suggestions that the social and economic doctrines of Catholic Social Thought, deriving from a 19th century encyclical on the dignity and right treatment of employees and the proper valuing of employment (perhaps as a reaction to Marx's observations on the rewarding of labour),[86] could have a role in relation to the functioning of corporate insolvency.[87] Equivalent modern theories on the underpinnings of insolvency, from the creditor bargain theory[88] to the more recent vulnerability theory,[89] attempt to provide a philosophical foundation (often also containing a moral perspective) on how insolvency could be positioned as a means of reforming relationships (contract adjustment becomes contract re-adjustment), especially when talking about a rescue culture and restructuring procedures in general.

CONCLUSION: A FUTURE FOR MORALITY?

The last thought on this subject might be given to Graeber, in whose text appear the words: '…the whole subject of debt [has become] surrounded by a halo of religion'. His view is that the act of paying debt seems the 'very definition of morality', and this because 'so many people fail to do it'.[90] While it is true that the past influences the present, those who do not understand the past are condemned to repeat it.[91] In that light, knowing how the various traditions have played a part in the design and maintenance of insolvency (and now restructuring) frameworks into the present day suggests the possibility that, although morality is not always fathomable in any precise way, it

---

https://www.thecityuk.com/media/1tbbofqr/islamic-finance-global-trends-and-the-uk-market.pdf accessed 5 May 2023.

[84] See the section titled 'Social and religious attitudes to insolvency and debt' in Catherine Bridge, 'Insolvency: A Second Chance' (2013) *Law in Transition* 28, 36–38.

[85] Paulus (n 13) 61. See also https://www.vatican.va/content/john-paul-ii/en/messages/pont_messages/1999/documents/hf_jp-ii_mes_19990923_jubilee-2000-debt-campaign.html accessed 5 May 2023.

[86] Rerum Novarum, Encyclical of Pope Leo XIII (15 May 1891).

[87] Armin Kammel, 'Catholic Social Thought and Corporate Insolvency Law' in Paul Omar (ed), *International Insolvency Law: Reforms and Challenges* (Ashgate 2013) 21.

[88] Thomas Jackson, 'Bankruptcy, Non-Bankruptcy Entitlements, and the Creditor's Bargain' (1982) 91(5) *Yale Law Journal* 857.

[89] Martha Fineman, 'Vulnerability and Inevitable Inequality' (2017) 4(3) *Oslo Law Review* 133.

[90] Graeber (n 5), 377.

[91] Saying attributed to the philosopher George Santayana.

always has the potential to become a point of reference for reform initiatives to come. In that light, quite what type of moral perspective informs the reform process, where there may be different moral perspectives, remains a matter of some contention. While this chapter does not advocate for a particular choice, but for an understanding of what has influenced the choices made thus far, a re-examination of the foundations of insolvency law and policy invites a reassessment of those choices.

3. The liberalisation of bankruptcy law

David Milman

This chapter is divided into four parts. First, the research question is introduced, and key terms defined. A consideration of relevant cultural and religious insights into debt and bankruptcy is then provided. The third part of the chapter tracks the liberalisation of substantive aspects of bankruptcy law in English law in modern times. The critique and conclusions on the processes of liberalisation and future prospects for reform are outlined in the fourth and final part.

INTRODUCTION: DEFINING THE BOUNDARIES OF THE STUDY

The questions posed in this chapter are, first, why the recurrent tendency in the evolution of English bankruptcy law has been a liberal one? Second, has the process of liberalisation of English bankruptcy law run its course, or is more liberalisation on the agenda. In undertaking this study of the process of the liberalisation of the English law of Bankruptcy, one must take account both the theoretical heritage and context in English law. Bankruptcy law has a long history[1] across many legal jurisdictions simply because the phenomenon of a citizen being confronted with unsustainable debt goes back to the beginning of human activity.[2]

One must always remind oneself that there is a close connection between theory, policy, and insolvency practice. This link between theory, policy, and practice is not always clear cut, but it is there all the same.

---

[1] In English law, the first discrete bankruptcy statute appeared in 1542 (34 and 35 Hen VIII c.4). For a brief historical overview see D Milman, *Personal Insolvency Law, Regulation and Policy* (Ashgate 2005) 5–12.

[2] The earliest indication of this can be found in the Code of the Hammurabi (laid down c 1755–1750 BC) where an indebted person could be compelled into slavery. For an excellent modern historical/anthropological survey see D Graeber, *Debt – The First 5000 Years* (Penguin 2011). See also D Skeel, *Debt's Dominion: A History of Bankruptcy Law in America* (Princeton University Press 2001). Note also the concept of *cessio bonorum* in Roman Law, which could, on one level, be seen as liberal in that it protected the debtor's person from seizure at the expense of his assets.

Parliamentary debates on the question of insolvency law reform do, on occasion, illustrate those points of connection.[3] That said, in evaluating this nexus in the bankruptcy context, one is confronted with particular difficulties flowing from the established practice in the English courts in producing their judgments. Judicial attitudes towards theory must be taken into account in a survey of theoretical perspectives. However, there is judicial reluctance in the UK explicitly to invoke theory to support their decisions. Precedent is usually the key influence determining outcome. That said, increasingly, policy documents are cited, most notably the Cork Report.[4] There may, of course, be unconscious judicial resort to theory to support judicial decision-making, but that is difficult to determine from an external viewpoint.

The research question cannot be answered without understanding the institutional context in which bankruptcy operates. Bankruptcy law is an institution which operates within a much larger socio-legal architecture. Until recently, bankruptcy fell very much within the exclusive orbit of the court system. It was only with the introduction in April 2016 of the oddly designated 'adjudication' regime that bankruptcy could be initiated by a debtor without a formal court order.[5] Creditors, however, still have to petition the court to invoke the process to bankrupt a debtor.[6] This change came about with the commencement of section 71 of the Enterprise and Regulatory Reform Act 2013. The policy underpinning this change was designed to economise on public expenditure by saving judicial time.

Moving on to the matter of defining terms, it should be noted that the term 'bankruptcy' as properly understood in English law; it relates to a form of *personal* insolvency. In North America and in other legal systems, it can also cover incidences of corporate insolvency. This linguistic differential can mislead the uninitiated. Personal insolvency law in the English legal system operates on a more basic level than its corporate counterpart. This is because corporate insolvency law builds upon the theory of a company as a separate legal entity and has, at its heart, the security device of the floating charge. These elements are noticeably absent from bankruptcy law. But, in spite of this conceptual simplicity, theory is still important in personal insolvency context.

---

3 See for instance the debates on the Bill that became the Enterprise Act 2002.

4 Insolvency Law and Practice: Report of the Review Committee (Cmnd 8558, 1982). For examples of judicial citation see for instance *Viscount St Davids v Lewis* [2015] EWHC 2826 (Ch) and *Mikki v Duncan* [2017] EWCA Civ 57.

5 For judicial explanation of the process see *Re Budniok* [2017] EWHC 368 (Ch), *Office of the Bankruptcy Adjudicator v Shaw* [2021] EWHC 3140 (Ch).

6 The minimum petition debt claimed by a creditor was increased from £750 to £5K in 2015 to reflect the impact of inflation since 1986.

Theory has always formed part of the essential body of principles constituting bankruptcy law – for instance, the fundamental idea of the *pari passu* principle of rateable distribution amongst unsecured creditors has been globally recognised.[7] What are the origins of this crude model of distributional justice?[8] It has been claimed that its origins lie in the general average in salvage cases in admiralty law. Whatever its genesis, it is effective because it does not require choices to be made between different types of unsecured creditor. It became part of English law through the medium of 1571 Act (13 Eliz I c7). One could also note the concept of collectivism, which still plays a part in modern bankruptcy law.[9]

What is meant, then, by the term 'liberalisation'? In this chapter, it will be used in a non- pejorative sense to reflect a gentler view in the treatment of bankrupts. That designation may also encompass deregulation of procedures designed to deal with debtors and potential bankrupts. It also can be used to reflect a growing awareness of diversity and inclusivity for dealing with distress in a customised way within the broad community of debtors. Fair play between debtors and their creditors and between creditors *inter se* may also be an aspect. It will be established that this liberalisation phenomenon is not new; one can see traces of it with regard to the introduction of the policy of discharge of bankrupts as a result the campaigning work of Daniel Defoe in 18th century.[10]

RELIGIOUS, POLITICAL, AND CULTURAL INFLUENCES

Religious Attitudes Towards Debt

One must never underestimate how religious convictions have impacted upon the development of ideas concerning bankruptcy.

For many religions, failure to pay one's debts is a sin because it involves a breach of promise. That is seen as immoral. Improvidence in lifestyle is also

---

7 The best explanation of this concept is to be found in J Kilpi, *The Ethics of Bankruptcy* (Routledge 1998) 14. Kilpi draws upon the work of J Finnis, *Natural Law and Natural Rights* (Clarendon Press 1980) 190 on distributional justice in insolvency.

8 For discussion see D Milman, 'Priority Rights on Corporate Insolvency' in A Clarke (ed), *Current Issues in Insolvency Law* (Stevens 1991) 57. Note also D Milman, 'Promoting Distributional Justice on Corporate Insolvency in the 21st Century' in J Steele and W van Boom (eds), *Mass Justice: Challenges of Representation and Distribution* (Edward Elgar Publishing 2009) 169.

9 For evidence of the perceived importance of this concept note *Go Capital v Phull* [2020] EWHC 1235 (Ch).

10 See below.

to be condemned. There are traces of this censorious attitude in the *The Holy Bible*, which lies at the heart of the Christian faith. So, for instance, we have a direction to pay our debts found in *2 Kings* Chapter 4 verse 7.

However, a draconian approach towards payment of one's debts was mitigated; there is also the idea of forgiveness to consider. This virtue appears in the Lord's Prayer as a two-sided relationship – 'as we forgive our debtors'– *Matthew* Chapter 6 verse 12. Parables concerning the virtue of debt forgiveness are to be found located in *Matthew* Chapter 18 verses 27–34 and *Luke* Chapter 7 verses 41–46. This liberal approach is further reflected in the concept of the Jubilee[11] and in the seven-year debt release[12] as reflected in *Deuteronomy* Chapter 15 verses 1–2 with the seven-year release of debt. On closer examination these texts refer more to forgiveness rather than to the importance of honouring debt. This is significant when understanding the development of the law in later times.

One must also not forget the virtue of redemption. There is more joy in heaven, so the saying goes.[13] This idea has morphed into modern concepts of the desirability of encouraging rehabilitation of debtors. More of this later.

The Holy Bible has less to say about the practice of usury[14] (lending with interest charged), but for generations, it was seen as an unchristian practice. As a result, such lending became the exclusive province of Jewish traders. This hostile attitude to usury influenced the shape of the law and regrettably fuelled antisemitism. The Christian inspired prohibition on lending for profit was finally[15] abolished in English law in 1854 when all interest charge restrictions based on the idea of usury were finally lifted. Although we live in a predominantly secular society, today, Christian attitudes still influence policymakers and practice, as exemplified by the active role of Christians against poverty in promoting more enlightened attitudes.

The focus in the discussion up to now has been upon the tenets of the Christian faith. However, in today's multi-faith society, attitudes towards the concept of debt in other major religions should also be taken into account. Under Sharia law, many of the same ideas encountered above exist. Thus,

---

11 See *Leviticus* 27:24 in *The Holy Bible*. The Jubilee is an event every 50 years. In modern discourse, this could be termed a 'haircut' for creditors.

12 See also *Nehemiah* 10:31. Note also *Leviticus* 25:10 – 'return each one to his possessions'. Debt relief has been converted into concrete legal action by the Debt Relief (Developing Countries) Act 2010. It is no coincidence that this legislation was sponsored by our former Prime Minister Gordon Brown, a man of deeply religious roots.

13 See *The Holy Bible*, *Luke*, 15:7.

14 But it was condemned in *Leviticus*, 25:36.

15 Many of the usury-related curbs had been removed by legislation in the 16th century in the Tudor period.

The Koran stresses the virtue in offering relief to distressed debtors[16] and the importance of having loans properly recorded as part of a protective strategy for weaker parties is emphasised.[17] *The Koran* emphasises the unacceptable nature of usury.[18] The Jewish approach towards financial distress is reflected in The Old Testament and the idea of forgiveness is to the fore. The Hindu faith adopts a view of debt that focuses upon the debt owed to ancestors. Buddhists take the view that Life itself is a debt that has to be repaid through good work. Individual personal responsibility is stressed as is the benefit for a creditor's wellbeing to forgive. Usury is criticised.

Turning to politics, a capitalist would view personal debt as key component of the market system and thus, deserving of sensitive regulation. At the other end of the political extreme, communists and socialists would view the debt system as just one further aspect of capitalism designed to oppress the masses. Both agree on the importance of debt in society.

Bankruptcy in Literature[19]

Cultural perspectives on bankruptcy go beyond the confines of religion. As history has moved on, these non-religious cultural thoughts have become more influential. It is certainly the case that literary representations may have been influenced by religious insights, but the work of writers is often the way in which religion is conveyed to the wider populace. A pivotal figure in the trend towards liberalisation was the novelist Daniel Defoe (c 1660–1731). He had been bankrupted in 1692 as a result of a business failure. This gave him an acute personal insight into the system, and he was committed to reform.[20] He pushed for the facility of discharge from bankruptcy and was rewarded when this was introduced in the 1705 Act (4 and 5 Anne, c 17). Moving on a century, the work of Charles Dickens (1812–1870) was impactful. The personal experience of the Dickens' family travails looms large in his literature. Those of the older generation will remember the drip feed of Dickens' grim works as a staple part of Sunday television viewing. The messages that were conveyed are hard to forget.

16 Surah 2: Al-Baqarah 280.

17 Surah 2: Al-Baqarah 282.

18 Surah 2: Al-Baqarah 276 and 278.

19 B Weiss, *The Hell of the English: Bankruptcy and the Victorian Novel* (Bucknell University Press 1982) and M Atwood, *Payback: Debt and the Shadow Side of Wealth* (Bloomsbury 2008) Chapter 3.

20 See M Quilter, 'Daniel Defoe: Bankrupt and Bankruptcy Reformer' (2004) 25(1) *Journal of Legal History* 53.

American Insights[21]

There is no doubt that the United States' (US) attitudes towards debt and bankruptcy have influenced recent policy in shaping English bankruptcy law. This is an aspect of what critics might regard as US 'cultural imperialism'. As the world's former pre-eminent imperial power, we are hardly in a position to bridle at that phenomenon. The traditional US approach has been more generous towards debtors.[22] This is reflected in a number of respects. Bankruptcy is viewed not as a punitive regime, but rather, as one that offers a safe harbour and presents an opportunity to make a fresh start.[23] Bankruptcy almost becomes a rite of passage for a capitalist entrepreneur. The 'homestead exception' is but one example of a more generous treatment of bankrupts found in the US.[24]

The US philosophy clearly influenced those behind the enactment of the Enterprise Act 2002 in the United Kingdom (UK). It is well recorded that the influential government minister Peter Mandelson made a fact-finding trip to Silicon Valley in the US in 1998 before the liberal policy reflected by the 2002 Act was set in stone and came back impressed with ideas of how bankruptcy law might be liberalised to enhance enterprise.[25] In particular, the new approach centred on the removal of stigma from bankrupts and the promotion of a fresh start.

Gender Dimensions

Much of the debate on bankruptcy traditionally focuses upon the male perspective. But how does debt and bankruptcy impact upon the female gender? This is important because women have often historically been the collateral damage when a man becomes bankrupt.

Until the Law Reform (Married Women and Tortfeasors) Act 1935, husbands were held liable for the debts of their wives unless those wives operated a separate trade. Married women lost this immunity[26] from being subject to bankruptcy in 1935 and this change reflected a legal recognition of their auton-

---

21 Skeel (n 2).

22 Some of the early population of the State of Georgia consisted of debtors transported from England as part of their punishment.

23 See T H Jackson, 'The Fresh Start Policy in Bankruptcy Law' (1985) 98(7) *Harvard Law Review* 1393.

24 See here US Bankruptcy Code s 522(d) for the federal provision. Many individual states also have their own generous protective rules.

25 This ignored the fact that most insolvents at the time were consumer debtors rather than unsuccessful entrepreneurs!

26 As reflected in *Re Grissell ex parte Jones* (1879) 12 Ch D 484. The immunity from bankruptcy was a mixed blessing because women could still be arrested for debt.

omy. It is now accepted that spouses can be creditors of each other. Personal autonomy between the genders is now respected.

The law has sought to combat the injustice generated by so-called 'sexually transmitted debt'.[27] In a male dominated society, this is debt undertaken by a female person in order to support a male partner. This may take the form of a guarantee or accepting a mortgage commitment over property in which the female holds equity. The problem is that in some instances, the weaker party may have been pressurised into undertaking this commitment. The law has countered this danger by requiring proof that the weaker party acted with the benefit of independent advice. The leading case here now is *RBS v Etridge (No.2)*,[28] which establishes a form of legal choreography as evidence that the interests of the weaker party have been protected.

The phenomenon of the deserted wife's 'equity'[29] posed challenges for bankruptcy law. After disputes at common law, the position remained unsatisfactory until the Family Law Act 1996 backed home occupation rights and the Insolvency Act 1986 (see in particular s 336) dealt with the interface with bankruptcy law. As for the family home generally, the law now permits a one-year period of grace once bankruptcy has commenced. This concession is kept under control and will only be extended in exceptional circumstances (see, e.g., s 335A).[30]

Moving away from the paradigm (and possibly patronising) view of woman caught up in the vortex of male bankruptcy, it should be noted that statistics produced by the Insolvency Service indicate a growing population of female bankrupts. The figures released by the Insolvency Service in the Individual Insolvency Statistics in April 2022 show a continued upsurge in female insol-

---

The Married Women and Property Act 1882 made wives subject to bankruptcy in respect of debts incurred through separate trading.

27 For discussion of this phenomenon see B Fehlberg, *Sexually Transmitted Debt: The Surety Experience in English Law* (Clarendon Press 1997).

28 [2001] UKHL 44, which builds upon *Barclays Bank v O'Brien* [1993] UKHL 6.

29 In *Bendall v McWhirter* [1952] 2 QB 666 the Court of Appeal offered protection to the position of the wife in respect of occupation of the family home against claims made by the trustee in bankruptcy of the now absent bankrupt husband, but this was rejected by the House of Lords in *National Provincial Bank v Ainsworth* [1965] AC 1175. The Matrimonial Homes Act 1967 s 2(5) failed to protect the wife's right of occupation as against the trustee in bankruptcy. The position is now governed by the Family Law Act 1996 and the Insolvency Act 1986, s 335A.

30 This harsh approach is typified by cases such as *Re Citro* [1991] Ch 142, a Court of Appeal ruling criticised by S Cretney 'Women and Children Last' (1991) 107 *Law Quarterly Review* 177 and 'Women and Children Last' (1991) 4 *Insolvency Intelligence* 78. See also J C Hall, 'Insolvency and the Family' (1991) 50(1) *Cambridge Law Journal* 45 and D Brown 'Insolvency and the Matrimonial Home – the Sins of the Fathers' (1992) 55(2) *Modern Law Review* 284.

vents, to the point where they have overtaken men in terms of both Individual Voluntary Arrangement (IVA) and Debt Relief Order (DRO) usage, which are both debt resolution regimes where the initiative lies with the debtor. Men still predominate in the bankruptcy arena, where a person can be forced into a formal insolvency procedure by a creditor. It is important that any future bankruptcy reforms take into account this changing demography.

TRACKING LIBERALISATION THROUGH SUBSTANTIVE CHANGE IN THE LAW

The 19th century in the UK: A Key Formative Period Where Theory Impacted Practice

Moving back to the historical perspective on English bankruptcy law, there is clear evidence of liberalisation in the form of 19th century attitudes towards debtors and bankrupts.[31] This raises questions as to why it occurred and what the underlying influences were?

The enlightened treatment of bankrupts in this period is well evidenced.[32] One finds calls for the removal of the criminal taint attached to debtors – note here the influence exerted by the work of Dickens (*supra*) and Bentham (1748–1832). The end of imprisonment for debt became a reality in 1869. However, one must ask how this liberalisation squares up ethically with the fact that bankrupts have not kept their promise to repay what they owe? *Pacta sunt servanda*, after all, was a dominant philosophy in 19th century England, which saw the rise of notion of freedom of contract. This idea of freedom of contract supports the primacy of secured creditors on debtor insolvency. The answer to this conundrum might lie in the fact that the idea of contract needs to factor in the risk of market failure and therefore, this risk needs to be reduced in order to keep people contracting. The economic policy underpinning capitalism was thus the driving force trumping considerations of personal morality and responsibility.

---

[31] For example, the introduction in 1883 of the 'certificate of misfortune' designed to aid honest bankrupts. See generally V M Lester, *Victorian Insolvency* (Clarendon Press 1995).

[32] Milman (n 1) 7–10.

The Roots of the Liberalisation Trend in English Bankruptcy Law from 1970 Onwards

It is always difficult to pick a precise date when a trend begins to take shape. It has been established in the discussion above that there were definite liberal reforms in the 19th century (particularly through the Bankruptcy Act 1883) and some of these measures became embedded in the consolidating Bankruptcy Act 1914. Things then remained largely quiet for the next 50 years[33] and reforms favouring a more liberal treatment of bankrupts are hard to find in this period. The Blagden Committee[34] recommended some minor changes in the law (e.g., with regard to limited automatic discharge and reduced recourse to public examination) but little was done by way of immediate legal reform in response to this view.

Bankruptcy was still small beer with barely 4,000 debtors joining the bankruptcy ranks in the 1960s. That decade witnessed a general liberalisation in society in the UK across a range of social issues. The arrival of the credit card from the US shores led to an increase in consumer debt. Eventually, this new environment fed through into legal reform and changing attitudes towards the indebted. The Insolvency Act 1976 did change bankruptcy law in that it introduced the idea of automatic discharge from bankruptcy after five years.[35] Discharge is an important feature of liberalisation and a topic that generates much academic discussion.[36] Attempts have been made to justify it via utilitarian reasoning, but the truth of the matter is that it represents forgiveness. But, with this exception, for the most part these were sticking plaster changes. It was however soon recognised by policy influencers[37] and government that fundamental reform was needed to modernise the law of insolvency and so it was left to the Cork Committee on Insolvency Law and Practice (established in 1977)[38] to review matters.

The need to protect consumer debtors was recognised. The final report of the Cork Committee (1982) confirmed that there was now an understanding that debtors fuel the modern consumer/services economy and therefore

---

[33] The Bankruptcy (Amendment) Act 1926 made only minor technical changes.

[34] 1957, Cmnd 221.

[35] This was important because it was estimated that there were some 60,000 undischarged bankrupts in the system at the time.

[36] It plays a central role in Kilpi (n 7).

[37] See Allan Heyman (chair), *Bankruptcy: A Report by Justice* (Justice 1975) para [101] where it was noted that the stable legal regime needed to reflect social change.

[38] It is often forgotten that there was a Cork Report Mark I (1976, Cmnd 6602) that dealt with preliminary background issue. See I Fletcher, 'The Genesis of Modern Insolvency Law – An Odyssey of Law Reform' (1989) *Journal of Business Law* 365.

deserved some protection under the law. Cork's listed goals of Insolvency Law (expressed in para [198] of the Report) included, first and foremost, a desire to protect the casualties of the system of consumer credit. The influence of the Cork Committee in promoting reform was pervasive. So, Cork's idea of rescue led to the advent of the IVA and the consequent decline of bankruptcy.

Many of the ideas promoted by Cork surfaced in the Insolvency Act 1986. So, for instance, the idea of rehabilitation was given voice particularly through the idea of providing effective legal structures to allow debtors to repay their creditors over time. Thus, the IVA was introduced in Part VIII of the 1986 Act to replace the moribund deed of arrangement.[39] A constructive attempt was made to exploit the future income of a bankrupt through the income payments order regime[40] as a way of repaying debt rather than the destructive process of selling up.

Procedures were simplified by removing the archaic idea of 'acts of bankruptcy' and the interim receiving order stage. This may be viewed as a form of liberalisation.

The more lenient approach was reflected by curbs on the feared public examination process (see now Insolvency Act 1986, s 290). This procedure had been criticised by JUSTICE in its 1975 Report.[41] Its grip had then been loosened by the 1976 Act. Post 1986 the use of the public examination of a bankrupt was in future to be the exception rather than the rule. Information could be secured from bankrupts by less oppressive procedures, such as by using a questionnaire or a private examination under section 366 of the Act.

Automatic discharge from bankruptcy was now to occur after the elapse of only three years. This very much reflected a fresh start policy.

With the benefit of hindsight, these changes in the 1986 Act formed but part of a continuum of liberalisation in bankruptcy law. They were also the forerunners of future reform. One should remember that bankruptcy law operates within a broader legal context. Most commentators would agree that the Human Rights Act 1998 reflected a liberal trend in UK society. Bankrupts can take advantage of the rights embodied in this legislation and ultimately in the European Convention on Human Rights and Fundamental Freedoms. But it must always be remembered that rights under the Convention and Act are not absolute. So, the courts have said repeatedly that the institution of bankruptcy does not per se breach human rights protections.[42] Particular aspects

---

[39] Then regulated by the Deeds of Arrangement Act 1914. They became increasingly unpopular and were belatedly abolished by the Deregulation Act 2015.

[40] Insolvency Act 1986, s 310.

[41] See Heyman (n 37) para 54.

[42] See *Nicholls v Lan* [2006] BPIR 1243; *Holtham v Kelmanson* [2006] BPIR 1422; *Foyle v Turner* [2007] BPIR 43; and *Oyesana v Jackson* [2020] EWHC 542 (Ch) as examples.

of the procedure however have had to be modified, for instance the rules on the interception of mail (see s 371).[43] The Welfare Reform and Pensions Act 1999 made a significant change in removing pension benefits from automatic inclusion in the bankruptcy estate.[44]

It should be noted that the Insolvency Act 2000 deregulated the IVA procedure by removing the need for an initial interim order. This technical tweak had profound effects by opening up possibilities for mass-produced IVAs in so-called 'factories'. That has caused difficulties where practices within a particular factory have been found to be deficient.

The Enterprise Act 2002 was a major factor in the ongoing liberalisation policy.[45] Automatic discharge was now to be available after a period no longer than 12 months. A form of homestead exception was introduced by requiring the trustee to take action within three years or lose that opportunity. In particular, it sought to remove some of the stigma associated with bankruptcy by removing certain disqualifications. As a quid pro quo and in an attempt to silence critics who felt that the law was going soft on bankrupts the government introduced the bankruptcy restrictions regime (Bankruptcy Restrictions Order (BRO) and Bankruptcy Restrictions Undertaking (BRU)).

The Enterprise Act 2002 also pursued a policy of decriminalisation, for example, where bankruptcy had been caused by gambling. This form of irresponsible conduct ceased to be a crime in itself but constituted grounds for a bankruptcy restrictions order. But there are still elements of bankruptcy law that interact with the criminal law. For instance, there are criminal offences engaged where a bankrupt seeks to hide assets from creditors. These are no longer capital crimes, but they can attract prison sentences as the tennis player Boris Becker found out to his cost in 2022.[46]

An aspect of the liberalisation philosophy was the growing recognition that not all debtors were cut from the same cloth –[47] this differentiation has led to the labelling of the 'no income, no assets' (NINA) debtor and the emergence of the DRO. This recognition was translated into law via the Tribunals, Court and Enforcement Act 2007, which took effect in 2009. A DRO could be obtained

---

[43] For an explanation of this change, see *Sealy and Milman, Annotated Guide to Insolvency Legislation* (Sweet & Maxwell 2022) 560.

[44] Thereby overturning the decision of Ferris J in *Re Landau* [1998] Ch 223.

[45] For analysis see A Walters, 'Personal Insolvency Law After the Enterprise Act: An Appraisal' (2005) 5(1) *Journal of Corporate Law Studies* 5.

[46] *R v Becker* [2022] BPIR 1609 (Southwark Crown Court).

[47] JUSTICE in its 1994 Report, *Insolvency Law: An Agenda for Reform* (Justice 1994) called at para 4.32 for this differentiation to be applied to bankrupts. This had happened with regard to the advent of summary administration in 1986 but that more liberal elective regime was scrapped by the Enterprise Act 2002 in favour of a general relaxation of bankruptcy law.

by debtors owing modest sums of money in cases where said debtors had few assets and only limited surplus income. Such individuals were unsuited either to the bankruptcy model (no assets) or to the IVA regime (no income to fund the IVA). The arrival on the scene of the DRO in turn has diminished bankruptcy to the extent that the number of DROs now outstrips the statistics for bankruptcy. What about no asset cases?

The 'austerity influence' in managing public expenditure has reared its head but not in the way that one might have expected. This drive to control public expenditure goes back to the Thatcher era[48] and continued in the wake of the Global Financial Crisis through the tenure of the Cameron coalition government (2010–2015). This has resulted in the perceived need for cost effective procedures in bankruptcy. Moral criticism of indebted persons had to give way to economic realism and the cost associated with punishment. This has led to more informal ways of dealing with debtors who would formerly end up as bankrupts. The most obvious manifestation has been the continued support for the DRO procedure, but we also note the adjudication procedure for debtor initiation in bankruptcy was introduced by the Enterprise and Regulatory Reform Act 2013 and came into operation in April 2016. The use of undertakings[49] and agreements[50] in lieu of court orders also reflected this cost saving policy.

A new development came through the Financial Claims and Guidance Act 2018; the debt respite or breathing space mechanism which took effect in May 2021.[51] This policy derived from the Conservative Party Manifesto of 2017. The breathing space idea was intended to facilitate the search for optimum debt solutions by allowing a distressed debtor 60 days' relief against hostile action. The relevant minutiae are to be found in the Debt Respite Scheme (Breathing Space Moratorium and Mental Health Crisis Moratorium) (England and Wales) Regulations 2020.[52] These Regulations are interesting in that they show an awareness of the discrete position of debtors with mental capacity issues and they also remove the need for judicial input thereby reducing cost. Some 63,864 breathing space registrations were made in the first year of operation of the scheme. They continue to be widely used.

---

[48] Most notably when the government floated the idea of withdrawing the official receiver from personal insolvency work (Bankruptcy: A Consultative Document (Cmnd 7967, July 1980)), an idea that was broadly condemned.

[49] Such as the bankruptcy restrictions undertaking (BRU). See Insolvency Act 1986, s 281A.

[50] Such as the income payments agreement (IPA). See Insolvency Act 1986, s 310A.

[51] See I Ramsay, 'Breathing Spaces, Fresh Starts and Personal Insolvency Law' (2021) 64(2) *Canadian Business Law Journal* 123.

[52] SI 2020/1311.

Change in the law can occur through judicial decision, though this is often an incremental process ostensibly tied up with statutory interpretation. For instance, in *Horton v Henry,*[53] the provisions on a bankrupt's pension rights were interpreted by the Court of Appeal in such a way as to protect those rights and to protect them from exploitation by a trustee in bankruptcy.

CONCLUSION: LOOKING FORWARD

History tells us that bankruptcy law is founded upon legislation. It was established via statute and in modern times statute has done much to liberalise it. But bankruptcy as a legal institution is disappearing before our very eyes and that is down to explicit policy changes.[54] It is now very much the junior partner in the triumvirate of legal regimes regulating personal insolvency. Liberalisation of the bankruptcy regime has been motivated by social, religious, and economic theory and that has been embedded in official policy. That liberalisation has been converted into substantive legislative reform. There now exists an operative model for personal insolvency dominated by contract in the form of the IVA – reflecting Henry Maine's view that this transition from status to contract is a common evolution as societies evolve.[55]

Contract is a favoured institution of liberalism.[56] The other widely used regime, the DRO, caters for debtors who are manifestly unsuited to bankruptcy. 'One size fits all' is no longer the favoured policy. The role of bankruptcy is, therefore, to deal with outliers who are not willing to contract with creditors using an IVA and who do not qualify for the DRO. Accordingly, there now exists a multi-faceted legal regime governing personal insolvency. That is commendable for its flexibility, but its diversity is not without cost. Policymakers need to ask whether the current system is now too complex to navigate for a distressed debtor who often has to make a difficult choice under

53 [2016] EWCA Civ 989.

54 Up to 30 years ago this would have been a bizarre comment to make as bankruptcies over the course of the 20th century had grown from a few thousand each year to an annual figure of 40,000 by the turn of the millennium. But the advent of popular alternatives to bankruptcy has since reversed that trend bringing the bankruptcy figures back to the level of 40 years ago.

55 As stated in H J S Maine, *Ancient Law (1861)* (Everyman 1972) 100. The contractual aspect of debt resolution is reinforced by the widespread use of debt management plans, which operate under the radar.

56 But contract needs to be watched. There are suspicions that some debtors are being induced to enter IVAs in circumstances where they have no prospect of meeting their commitments under the arrangement. Regulatory intervention may be on the horizon to stamp out misselling concerns.

pressure?[57] The debt respite scheme introduced in 2021 is in part designed to facilitate informed choice by allowing pause for thought.

The role of bankruptcy law has changed over time. Originally, it was established in order to reassure trade creditors that something was being done by the law to sanction recalcitrant debtors. It then was relaxed somewhat in the 18th century so as to enable trader debtors an easier ride than that offered to personal insolvents. Imprisonment was the norm for the latter group. Changing social attitudes lead to a reappraisal in the 19th century with bankruptcy being made available as a safe harbour to most debtors from 1861 onwards. This has never been cost free: some form of fee payment is required to access bankruptcy whether that access is required by a debtor or creditor. An equilibrium set in place by the 1883 Act was confirmed by the Bankruptcy Act 1914 under which both creditors and debtors were provided for by the same legal institution. Social and economic conditions forced further change in the late 20th century. The transition continues to be towards protecting the interests of bankrupts at the expense of creditors.

It must now be asked whether liberal sentiments will continue to dominate formulation of policy in the years to come? The answer here is in the affirmative. Even in a secular society religious ideas continue to influence policy, particularly where economics underpin a liberal policy. The UK has moved a long way from the idea that most bankrupts are feckless individuals. With the prevalence of divorce, and job insecurity, coupled with the greater incidence of health and education debt, there is a real recognition that debt is not a sign of irresponsibility. Sadly, for many citizens, it is a fact of life. The 'cost of living crisis', highlighted so much in the media these days, will reinforce that point. Stigma has been reduced.[58] A perusal of the Insolvency Service Call for Evidence: Review of the Personal Insolvency Framework issued on 5 July 2022 would indicate that further reform is on the agenda with the emphasis likely to be on liberalisation. Under a separate development, HM Treasury is moving forward with its idea for statutory debt repayment plans.[59] These appear to be a form of state-sponsored IVAs. These are likely to further impinge upon the bankruptcy regime. Implementation of this initiative has been delayed by the ongoing general review of personal insolvency law.

---

57 The solution may be the introduction of a single 'gateway'. See P Walton, 'Individual Insolvency: The Case for a Single Gateway' (2022) 7 *Wolverhampton Law Journal* 1.

58 Ironically this is reflected by the move in the interests of open justice away from the reporting of cases as *Re A Debtor* to a system in which the bankrupt party is almost invariably named in the law report.

59 For details here see the Consultative Document and draft regulations published by HM Treasury on 13 May 2022.

A critic might say that the continued liberalisation of bankruptcy law is simply an example of a repetition of old policies.[60] History repeats itself. There is more than a grain of truth in that observation. The challenge for policymakers is identifying new policies that are both appropriate and cost effective, as opposed to replicating old strategies.

Another issue requires further reflection. How will potential creditors react to further liberalisation of bankruptcy law? Will they stop lending? This was a real fear in the 19th century with the removal of the threat of imprisonment for debtors. This economic reaction never occurred, and one can safely dismiss it today. That said, an overly liberal system favouring borrowers who are in default may have consequences. Interest rates for all borrowers might be affected. Reputable lenders might leave the unsecured finance market, thereby opening up the personal finance market to cowboys. More likely is the fact that creditors will look to other ways to collect unsecured debt[61] or simply to sell it on to debt collectors. So, creditors might turn to the charging order procedure, which has largely escaped the liberalisation trend that has shaped modern bankruptcy law.[62] Third-party debt orders are another option.[63] The HMRC has introduced new procedures[64] to deal with the collection of tax debts by direct deduction and these procedures circumvent the need for bankruptcy. The collective nature of bankruptcy might therefore be supplanted by a system in which individual creditors take the initiative and reap the rewards. That would be a retrograde step and regrettable. Bankruptcy has had (and still has) its faults, but it does prevent the law of partisan self-interest resurfacing to the detriment of social cohesion.

Finally, one must note the need for further research, particularly with regard to the phenomenon of what might loosely be termed 'repeat bankrupts'. If the

---

60 On this see J Tribe's fascinating article 'Nietzsche's "Eternal Recurrence" and the Renaissance of English and Welsh Insolvency Law Reform' (2020) 40(3) *Legal Studies* 441.

61 The courts have repeatedly said that bankruptcy should not be seen as a private debt collection tool (see n 9). But, in reality, that is exactly how it is viewed by creditors. See *Sell Your Car with Us v Sareen* [2019] EWHC 2332 (Ch).

62 See Charging Orders Act 1979. There were, however, some limited liberal reforms introduced in 2013.

63 Note here the potential for individual creditors to avoid inconvenient bankruptcy decisions (which may be viewed as too collective/liberal) and to exploit differentials in the law: *Blight v Brewster* [2012] EWHC 165 (Ch); *Bacci v Green* [2022] EWCA Civ 1393; *Brake v Guy* [2022] EWHC 1746 (Ch); *Lindsay v O'Loughlane* [2022] EWHC 1829 (QB); and *Manolete Partners plc v White* [2023] EWHC 567 (Ch).

64 See Finance (No. 2) Act 2015, s 51 and Sch 8. The state has also protected itself through the reintroduction of preferential status for certain Crown debts via the Finance Act 2020. Crown preferential status had been abolished by the Enterprise Act 2002. This policy of self-preservation sits uneasily in the context of a liberal trend.

fresh start policy is producing the desired and constructive outcomes that were intended, then continued liberalisation is justified. But if that strategy is merely resulting in persons continuing to incur unsustainable debt thereby requiring repeat access to debt resolution models, then further empirical investigation is required, and fresh thought must be given by policymakers to future reform.

4. Insolvency law and the legal feminist movement

Lézelle Jacobs

INTRODUCTION

In 2019 the United Kingdom celebrated 100 years since the Sex Disqualification (Removal) Act of 1919 was passed.[1] The Act paved the way for women to finally practise law in the United Kingdom. Since then, women, across the globe, have made progress in all spheres of life in leaps and bounds.

This progress was, of course, hard won and the struggle continues for women living and thriving in what many would still call 'a man's world'. The struggle persists for a world view that recognises that women should be free to choose where they belong and that no obstacles should exist for actually doing so. Statements like these have, of course, long been the subject of the feminist movement in law and can be seen as a catalyst for the development of feminism in general.[2]

Considering the impact that women and feminism have on the law, questions started to form and an idea developed.[3] How have the feminist movement and ideologies expressed by the movement through its development, influenced that revered area of the law that many call insolvency law? More specifically, how have women influenced the development of the law relating to insolvency? This seemed too broad an issue to consider in a brief piece.

---

1 Sex Disqualification (Removal) Act 1919.

2 H Barnett, *Introduction to Feminist Jurisprudence* (Cavendish Publishing Limited 1998) 3. Barnett explains that the question regarding the appropriate role of women in society dates to the Ancient Greeks, with Plato and Aristotle attempting to answer it.

3 'The range of work generated by feminists, and more specifically by feminist legal scholars, has profoundly challenged the male oriented, male dominant model of the law (and other disciplines and structures) by exposing the valuing of men as a group, the subordination of women as a group, and the invisibility of women': N Dowd, 'Masculinities and Feminist Legal Theory' (2008) 23(2) *Wisconsin Journal of Law, Gender & Society* 201, 201.

A more specific area needed to be considered, one where the theories of knowledge could more easily be evaluated. Consequently, the area of insolvency or bankruptcy theory was chosen to contrast against feminist theories.

Insolvency theory asks the question about in whose interests insolvency law should be formulated. Stated more plainly, it considers who and what should be protected and recognised by insolvency law.

The aim of this chapter is to provide a concise evaluation on whether there is any evidence of feminist ideology to be found in insolvency or bankruptcy theory. To ask whether insolvency theories may also be categorised in relation to ideologies expressed in the legal feminist movement. It aims to adopt a feminist enquiry, to consider a gendered perspective to legal and social arrangements.[4] In other words, recognised and new insolvency theories will be reconsidered and re-evaluated from a new perspective, a legal feminist one.

A WOMAN'S PREROGATIVES AND ITS INFLUENCE ON THE DEVELOPMENT OF THE LEGAL FEMINIST MOVEMENT

In a maiden attempt to write about the feminist movement in law, it became apparent that the adage that 'it is a woman's prerogative to change her mind' also played its part in the development of feminist jurisprudence. Hence, one of the first observations to be made is that this movement is by no means static or axiomatic.[5] Legal feminism has developed and evolved tremendously over the last four centuries[6] and what precisely is meant by the term is not easily pinned down.

It is mainly for this reason that the feminist theoretical project in law is understood as a dynamic process of engagement (a dynamic movement of ideas), rather than a fixed set of principles.[7] This is due to the fact that feminist legal theory engages with a wide range of diverse perspectives and is, therefore, not easily characterised by any essential or fundamental principles.[8] This chapter endeavours to work with this idea and not against it, that is to say, it will make use of all the relevant ideologies expressed at various points in time

---

4 J Conaghan, 'Reassessing the Feminist Theoretical Project in Law' (2000) 27(3) *Journal of Law and Society* 351, 359.

5 Ibid., 356.

6 Barnett (n 2) 3.

7 Conaghan (n 4) 356.

8 Ibid., 358. See also Barnett (n 2) 5: 'Feminist legal scholarship is frequently presented as having differing phases or waves, although none of these is totally distinct or isolated from other phases.'

by the feminist movement and will not only utilise the most recent, generally accepted or popular ideologies of the movement.

'The Other' – Alike but Different and Connected

De Beauvoir's pioneering work highlighted the perception of women being the 'Other'[9] being, something which was also reflected in the law – law was a male construct and the subject of the law was male.[10] Women were for long at worst oppressed by the law, and at best ignored by it.[11] First phase feminism can be characterised by its concern with the male monopoly of law; the quest was for equality before the law.[12]

The quest of the feminist movement means different things to different feminists, but it is all still feminism. The single characteristic shared by all feminist theories can be described as a woman-centred approach to issues.[13] Moreover, many feminist legal theorists do not want to be categorised, as being defined or definition itself is patriarchal.[14] From this, the first ideology can be extrapolated, that is that classification and categorisation can be regarded as 'masculist'.[15] Other feminist scholars fall more easily into traditional categories

---

9 This term was first coined by Simone de Beauvoir in her seminal book *The Second Sex* and forms the core theme of the work. It refers to the idea of women being the 'Other' (sex). By this she means that everything (society, language, thought, religion, family) rests on the assumption that the world is male and that women are excluded from these constructions as women are the 'Other': Barnett (n 2) 4.

10 Barnett, ibid.

11 Ibid.

12 Ibid., 55. See also M Fineman, 'Feminist Theory and Law' (1995) 18(2) *Harvard Journal of Law and Public Policy* 353.

13 C Haddock Seigfried, 'Where Are All the Pragmatist Feminists?' (1991) 6(2) *Hypatia* 1, 7:

> The recovery of a history of feminist writings has also contributed to defining some common features of feminist thought, which is otherwise extremely diverse. These two features are (1) the identification and investigation of the oppressive structures that contribute to women's subordination in order to actively dismantle them and (2) the development of analyses of women's experiences that are not systematically distorted by sexist assumptions.

14 R Silberman, 'Ideas Have Consequences' (1995) 18(2) *Harvard Journal of Law and Public Policy* 409, 409: 'Definition is itself a patriarchal game, played by patriarchal rules, serving patriarchal ends.'

15 This term was adopted by K Lahey and S Salter in their work 'Corporate Law in Legal Theory and Legal Scholarship: From Classicism to Feminism' (1985) 23(4) *Osgoode Hall Law Journal* 543, to refer to work of a non-feminist nature. They state that although this term usually refers to work by men, it could also be used to refer to women who resist feminist analysis. This term will be used in this chapter to denote non-feminist work by male and female scholars as well as a non-feminist approach. The

such as liberal, radical, socialist feminists,[16] postfeminists and post-modern feminists.[17]

Equality feminists wanted the law to stress the similarities and minimise the differences between men and women.[18] According to them, men and women differ in their approach to legal and moral issues.[19] It is here, however, that the sensitivity regarding the multiplicity of women's lives needs to be emphasised. Feminism itself does not purport to represent a unified female voice.[20] Post-modern feminism recognises that there is no 'essential' woman and that women will differ in opinion and belief amongst themselves.[21] However, even if women might differ amongst themselves,[22] their approaches will still differ from those of men.[23]

Woman-centredness is a primary feature of feminist theory, particularly in its engagement with the law.[24] This approach places women's lives and experiences on centre stage and in doing so it (feminism) challenges and displaces our perceived understanding of the world around us: how have women's lives

---

reasoning behind the use of 'masculist' resounds with the reasons Lahey and Salter put forward – 'masculist' can more easily be seen to refer to anyone who resist feminist analysis and remains committed to 'malestream' ideas, including women. They argue that the use of 'masculinist' could too readily be seen as referring only to men.

16 C Grant Bowman, 'Recovering Socialism for Feminist Legal Theory in the 21st Century' (2016) 49(1) *Connecticut Law Review* 117.

17 Silberman (n 14) 409; Conaghan (n 4) 363.

18 Silberman (n 14) 410.

19 Ibid.

20 Conaghan (n 4) 358; Dowd (n 3) 203:

> As feminist theory has developed, it also has been increasingly critical to differentiate among women, particularly so that the experience of a single group of women does not drive and dominate feminist analysis. Intersectionality and anti-essentialism have moved feminists to 'ask the other question,' or questions, of race, class, age, and sexual orientation as those characteristics move singly and in combination to complicate simplistic notions of the operation of gender or to hide hierarchies among women with universal claims of subordination.

21 Barnett (n 2) 158. Essentialism denotes that 'woman' has a particular essence which defines woman as woman. See also Conaghan (n 4) 358; Silberman (n 14) 410. Essentialism also excludes women who '[…] are not part of the white, middle-class, heterosexual, able-bodied group that dominates theory-making': S Williams, 'Feminist Legal Epistemology' (1993) *Berkeley Women's Law Journal* 63, 77.

22 The 'difference/sameness' debate enjoys particular attention in Williams (n 21) 80–82 and J Morgan, 'Feminist Theory as Legal Theory' (1988) 16(4) *Melbourne University Law Review* 743, 744.

23 Silberman (n 14) 410; 412. See also M Fineman 'Feminist Theory in Law: The Difference it Makes' (1992) 2(1) *Columbia Journal of Gender & Law* 1, 17; R Paetzold, 'Feminism and Business Law: The Essential Interconnection' (1994) 31 *American Business Law Journal* 699, 704.

24 Conaghan (n 4) 363.

and experiences influenced their opinions and beliefs?[25] Radical feminists believe that women approach problems from an ethic of care, compassion[26] and connection; men generally by rights and rules.[27] From this a second ideology can be found; an approach to problems that is more inclusive (connectedness – stressing the similarities) and compassionate would be regarded as feminist, one that disregards connection and compassion in favour of rules and rights can be regarded as 'masculist'.

Familiar Feminist Critique of the Corporate Form – from Hierarchy and Fragmentation to Inclusion

'Feminist theory generates challenging new perspectives for analysis of legal phenomena generally, even in the unlikely area of corporate law.'[28] Liberal, socialist and radical feminists have expressed opinions in critique of the patriarchal structure of the corporate form. Liberal feminists' critiques on corporations focus on the constraints and opportunities that organisational structures generate for individuals, especially women.[29] They question the hierarchical structure of the organisation that results in the fragmentation of groups, which in turn generates opposition, competition, blocked opportunities and non-productive behaviour.[30] They advocate instead for decentralised decision-making processes, flattening hierarchies, distributing formal authority more widely, improved communication at all levels, and increased participation by all types of workers.[31] These changes are largely based on the feminist principles of empowerment, which 'stress the importance of increased individual autonomy and discretion within the institution'.[32] More ideologies come to the fore here; hierarchy and fragmentation in the corporation are regarded as 'masculist', while increased participation of all stakeholders is feminist.

Whereas liberal feminism critiques the corporate structure and its effect on women (and men) that work there, the social feminist is more concerned with the effect of the corporate structure on the larger culture, and the role of women

25 Ibid.

26 It is important to note that not all the branches of feminism associate compassion with women. This is in line with the anti-essentialist approach of feminism.

27 Silberman (n 14) 410.

28 Lahey and Salter (n 15) 569.

29 Ibid., 544.

30 Ibid., 548. See also Fineman (n 23) 6.

31 Lahey and Salter (n 15) 548.

32 Ibid.

in that culture.[33] They developed the theory of capitalist patriarchy,[34] and like the liberal feminists also question the hierarchical structure of the corporation. They oppose this fragmentation and hierarchy, as 'the very functions of human existence are split up between the home and the market, and ranked in a hierarchical manner that devalues and oppresses some people along both class and gender lines'.[35] Many feminist legal scholars in the 1970s and early 1980s were influenced by the Marxist 'unclassification'[36] theory and method, especially socialist feminists; who are likewise opposed to hierarchical constructs of corporations.[37] It is interesting then, yet not surprising, to note that the theme of fragmentation runs through all feminist critiques of the corporation.[38] Hence the abovementioned ideologies of increased participation and the flattening of hierarchies can be confirmed as feminist in nature.

Radical feminists focus on the problem of the universal dominance of men over women.[39] They challenge the core structure of society by focusing on its patriarchal ordering.[40] This challenge also extends to the patriarchal structure of the corporate form and how corporate structures oppress women. Radical feminists' views go beyond those expressed by liberal and social feminists; the entire culture of bureaucratic capitalism is questioned; the way in which certain social acts are created and upheld, how certain social objects are valued, how certain languages need to be spoken and how certain behaviours are required.[41] They view this culture as one that displays a distinctly male discourse of power.[42] There is a connection between this 'distinctly male discourse of power' and the corporate form in that organisations operate through discipline and control. The bureaucratic control is dependent on separation, isolation and depersonalisation.[43] The alternative feminist discourse is founded upon women's sense of connection, not through separation and fragmentation,

---

[33] C Grant Bowman 'Socialist Feminist Legal Theory: A Plea' in R West and C Grant Bowman (eds) *Research Handbook on Feminist Jurisprudence* (Edward Elgar Publishing 2019) 91. See also Lahey and Salter (n 15) 549.

[34] Grant Bowman, ibid., 92.

[35] Ibid., 110; Lahey and Salter (n 15) 549.

[36] Not arranged according to characteristics; not assigned to a class.

[37] Conaghan (n 4) 357; Lahey and Salter (n 15) 544. Most interestingly, Marxists ignored women's subordinate status and regarded women merely as support in the struggle for a proletarian revolution; they were not supposed to raise their own issues as this was seen as distractions from the battle. See particularly in this regard Grant Bowman (n 33) 92–93; Grant Bowman (n 16).

[38] Lahey and Salter (n 15) 553.

[39] Barnett (n 2) 163.

[40] Ibid., 164.

[41] Lahey and Salter (n 15) 554.

[42] Ibid.

[43] Ibid.

and women's sense of justice as being achieved through an ethic of responsibility and not through an ethic of rules, rights and entitlements.[44] Herein the recurring feminist ideology of inclusion again raises its head.[45] Feminists wish to provide alternative principles for organisation based on the ethics of care, responsibility, connection and sharing.[46]

A Woman-centred Epistemology

Conaghan states that having a woman-centred epistemology means to engage in a manner that displaces and destabilises 'dominant understandings of social and legal phenomena'.[47] Feminist scholarship in law tends to be fuelled by the idea that things ought not to be as they currently are and that feminist theory can play a part in envisioning how things might be.[48] Feminism is, therefore, concerned not only with interpreting legal concepts in a woman-centred way, but also with changing them and effecting transformation.[49] This transformation is to be informed, amongst other things by social justice.[50] Social justice is of course much broader in scope and concern than merely the plight of women in society. The *Oxford Dictionary* defines social justice as: justice in terms of the distribution of wealth, opportunities and privileges within a society.[51] This

---

44 Ibid., 556.

45 It is a fair conclusion to reach that most feminist theories can be described as inclusive in nature. However, the liberal feminist movement was criticised for not being inclusive based on race. In this regard see L Hilal, 'What is Critical Race Feminism?' (1998) 4 *Buffalo Human Rights Law Review* 367, 368:

> The international rights of women are modeled on the norm of nondiscrimination and manifest similar dilemmas highlighted by critical race feminists. As their writings reveal, conventional nondiscrimination ideology forces women into narrow, rigid categories in order to realize rights that neither embrace the totality of their experience nor the discrimination they face. This leads to bifurcated identities and injuries, lower or irrelevant legal protections, and fragmented political movements. Critical race feminist scholarship effectively illustrates these conditions and negative outcomes. Critical race feminism is an informative legal discussion on race and gender that advances critique of liberal paradigms pertinent at both the national and international levels [...]

See also Williams (n 21) 77.

46 Lahey and Salter (n 15) 556.

47 Conaghan (n 4) 364.

48 Ibid., 375.

49 Ibid.

50 Ibid. Transformation ought also to be informed by sexual equality and individual self-development. See also Fineman (n 12) 358.

51 *Oxford Dictionary Online*, https://www.lexico.com/en/definition/social_justice accessed 6 May 2023.

would mean that to some extent feminism is also concerned with transforming society for everyone.[52]

With the anti-essentialism view that post-modernist feminists advocate in mind,[53] it is an interesting notion to consider that women have a privileged vantage point on patriarchy and 'masculist' views.[54] This is due to the fact that women's lives are structurally different from men and are privileged, because their perspective is that of the oppressed group.[55] Because of this it is argued that women have different, perhaps 'unique'[56] views and experiences that relate to the issues and circumstances regulated and controlled by law.[57] The argument is that women tend to understand the plight of the oppressed and vulnerable better than most, as they have suffered oppression and vulnerability themselves. This argument also clarifies some of the ideologies identified, such as inclusion, care and compassion.

INSOLVENCY THEORY[58]

The insolvency theories can broadly be divided into two categories; firstly, theories that are centred around the creditors and secondly, theories that place an emphasis on the inclusivity of other stakeholders such as shareholders, employees, suppliers and even the community. Having already identified certain 'masculist' and feminist ideologies (general and with specific reference to the corporation), an attempt will now be made to determine whether they are

---

52 Paetzold (n 23) 704: '[...] the more global aspect of how *all* law (which would include all aspects of business law) is a feminist concern – i.e., of how our entire legal system is gendered, and what kinds of changes would be required to remove this gendering from legal doctrine and procedure'.

53 Barnett (n 2) 158. Essentialism denotes that 'woman' has a particular essence which defines woman as woman; anti-essentialists view women as unique individuals who cannot be pinned down as being a specific type of being with similar views and ideas. See also Conaghan (n 4) 358; Silberman (n 14) 410.

54 Conaghan (n 4) 379.

55 Ibid.

56 'Unique' is often regarded with disdain by feminists as it suggests that the women's view is again the 'other' with the men's view being the standard or norm. Uniqueness in this context is, however, meant to refer to a point of view that only women can have due to their shared history of oppression and is thus true to its meaning – unique.

57 Fineman (n 23) 11.

58 This brief discussion does not do any real justice to the vast amount of literature on theories and the intricacy with which they have been articulated and argued but it does provide a sufficient overview that warrants consideration in the discussion to follow.

present in the main insolvency theories and to categorise insolvency theories as either 'masculist' or feminist.

'Masculist' Theories on Insolvency Law?

The main ideologies the feminist movement associate with a 'masculist' view or approach can be summarised as follows: 'masculist' views often promote fragmentation, classification and hierarchy that isolate individuals, depersonalise them and place them in competition often resulting in oppression. 'Masculist' approaches to organisational issues rely on rules, rights, and entitlements, often turning a blind eye to compassion.

The first insolvency theory that displays some of these approaches is a contractarian theory. This theory is generally based on wealth maximisation and the idea that the law should maximise the collective return to creditors to the exclusion of other stakeholders.[59] This theory, therefore, fixates on fragmenting the stakeholders in insolvency, classifying them and placing creditors in a position of priority – at the top of the hierarchy. The theory is also in line with the Proceduralist Approach to insolvency, which contends that insolvency law should address issues that only arise out of insolvency and believe that non-insolvency claims and entitlements should not be protected by insolvency law unless this would result in a greater return for creditors.[60] Here, the heavy reliance on what should happen based on the contractual entitlements of the stakeholders is indicative of a 'masculist' approach. The lack of inclusivity of the interests of other stakeholders (apart from the creditors) in these theories is also indicative of the lack of compassion, or sympathy for the misfortune of the lower ranked stakeholders, for example, employees. Compassion and inclusion as feminist ideologies are thus clearly ignored by these insolvency theories.

A recognised branch of contractarianism in insolvency theory is the Creditors' Bargain Theory (CBT).[61] The CBT is based on the premise that

---

[59] P Walton, 'When is Pre-packaged Administration Appropriate? – A Theoretical Consideration' (2011) 20(1) *Nottingham Law Journal* 1, 3-4.

[60] D Baird, 'Loss Distribution, Forum Shopping, and Bankruptcy: A Reply to Warren' (1987) 54(3) *University of Chicago Law Review* 815; H Nsubuga, 'Corporate Insolvency and Employment Protection: A Theoretical Perspective' (2016) 4(1) *Nottingham Insolvency and Business Law e-Journal* 4, para 2; J Wood, 'Corporate Rescue: A Critical Analysis of its Fundamentals and Existence' (PhD thesis, University of Leeds 2013): 'Contrary to proceduralists, traditionalists believe that insolvency law is not a tool solely reserved for the creditors in which they can pursue their own interests.'

[61] The CBT was developed by Jackson in the early 1980s. Walton (n 59) 4; Nsubuga (n 60) para 58.

creditors enter into a bargain with the debtor company during negotiations for credit and thereby establish their position and possible remedies upon default by the company, such as on insolvency.[62] Upon the debtor company's insolvency the creditors with an interest will try to recover their debt and will enter into a frenzied race with other creditors to enforce their private contractual agreements with the company. This could cause depreciation in value of the business assets creating uncertainty of returns for all creditors. The CBT proposes to solve this problem by replacing individual enforcement rights of creditors with a collective right to share in the proceeds of the insolvency proceeding, giving rise to the collectivist approach.[63] This insolvency theory is therefore premised on the creditors' entitlement and rights in insolvency based on what they negotiated for, to the exclusion of the other stakeholders.

It is evident that the CBT exhibits a 'masculist' approach to solving the problem of insolvency by consulting 'rights and entitlements', instead of turning to the feminist ideals of connection and compassion. The CBT does not support redistribution to other stakeholders in insolvency.[64] Rather, it argues that the main role and objective of insolvency law should be to maximise the collective return to creditors, and it is not (and should not be) concerned with the interests of the debtor or the interests of the community.[65] All of the ideologies associated with a 'masculist' approach are present in the contractarian theories described in this section; a hierarchy of stakeholders with the creditors at the top, fragmentation and classification of parties involved with only those with priority entitled to protection and the resulting oppression of the others.

---

[62] Nsubuga (n 60) para 58. Walton is of the opinion that one of the shortcomings of the CBT is the fact that it only considers 'hypothetical contract creditors': Walton (n 59) 5.

[63] E Warren, 'Bankruptcy Policy' (1987) 54(3) *University of Chicago Law Review* 775, 797–799. The Collectivists believe the single justification for bankruptcy to be the enhancement of the collective return to the creditors. See also Nsubuga (n 60) para 61; Walton (n 59) 5.

[64] L LoPucki, 'A Team Production Theory of Bankruptcy Reorganization' (2004) 57(3) *Vanderbilt Law Review* 741, 748: '[...] the Creditors' Bargain was essentially a bargain that in the event of bankruptcy, the creditors would get everything.'

[65] J Jackson and R Scott, 'On the Nature of Bankruptcy: An Essay on Bankruptcy Sharing and the Creditors' Bargain' (1989) 75(2) *Virginia Law Review* 155, 160; Wood (n 60) 91.

Insolvency Theories with a Woman's Touch?

The main ideologies identified that can be associated with the feminist movement[66] include: an approach of inclusion and connectedness, not isolation and fragmentation – stressing similarities; sharing; compassion; a feminist approach to corporation advocates for increased participation by all stakeholders; flattening of hierarchies; and some feminist views promotes wider social justice.

Many insolvency theories incorporate some of these ideals. The first of these can be found in the Team Production Theory (TPT) of Corporate Law (this theory is also contractarian in nature).[67] The TPT is based on a social contract and is much more inclusive in nature than the wealth maximisation ideals of the CBT. The TPT of Insolvency Law developed by LoPucki builds on the ideology that shareholders are not the only parties that contribute to the production process of a company during solvency; other parties such as trade suppliers and the workforce all contribute in order to produce the end product.[68] By the same reasoning, creditors are not the only parties that stand to lose something should the company then fail. The TPT, therefore, promotes the inclusivity of all team members during insolvency proceedings and supports the idea of redistribution of some of the interest of one stakeholder (team member) to another.[69] This idea of redistribution on insolvency reflects the ideology of sharing present in some of the feminist theories. TPT further reflects the feminist ideology that similarities should be stressed, that is, that

---

[66] The reader should be reminded that a feminist approach to insolvency does not necessitate the involvement of women only.

[67] The Team Production Theory of Corporate Law was originally developed by Blair and Stout: M Blair and L Stout, 'A Team Production Theory of Corporate Law' (1999) 85(2) *Virginia Law Review* 247; LoPucki (n 64) 744; Nsubuga (n 60) para. 72.

[68] LoPucki (n 64) 749: 'The team members include all who make firm-specific investments but are unable to protect those investments by direct contracting, personal trust or reputation. Team members may include stockholders, creditors, executives, other employees, suppliers, customers, local governments, regulatory agencies, and others'; Nsubuga (n 60) para 73; Blair and Stout (n 67) 250: 'Executives, rank-and-file employees, and even creditors or the local community may also make essential contributions and have an interest in as enterprise's success.'

[69] Nsubuga (n 60) para 77: 'The TPT being an inclusive theory, advocates honouring all team members' interests on the insolvency of the company, whether in terms of financial gain or losses.' The problem with the TPT might be that it is too wide and includes too many team members who cannot realistically nor economically always benefit from the insolvency proceeding. LoPucki contends that TPT in insolvency entitlements are entitlements to 'rents and surpluses' and it goes without saying much that there will not be a lot of surplus in the case of insolvency. This theory closely resembles some of the Traditionalist theories on insolvency.

all members in the team contribute to the success of the company and all stand to lose something should the company enter insolvency proceedings. It also incorporates the feminist ideology of increased participation by all stakeholders and a flattening of hierarchies in that it does not place the creditors at the top with all other stakeholders oppressed. The traditional theorists agree with the TPT and are against the idea that insolvency law should exist only to serve creditors' interests and are, consequently, also inclusive in nature.[70]

Communitarianism looks to balance the interests of a wide range of different stakeholders in the insolvency of the debtor and even to consider the welfare of the community at large.[71] An element of social justice and connectedness as feminist ideals can be seen here. It 'considers limiting the rights of high ranking creditors to give way to some extent to others including the community at large'.[72] It also subscribes to the notion of redistribution, that is, to redistribute the consequences of the debtor's default.[73] Communitarian theorists seek to focus on the fact that those involved in, and dealing with, companies are humans and corporate law should not be depersonalised.[74] Approaches that rely on depersonalisation and isolation form part of the feminist movement's critique against the corporate form and can therefore be regarded as 'masculist' in nature. Due to its advocacy against depersonalisation, this theory is displaying feministic ideology. Moreover, the Communitarian theory reflects the feminist principles of empowerment, which 'stress the importance of increased individual autonomy and discretion within the institution'.[75] This approach (of limiting creditors' rights) also flattens hierarchical structures as stakeholders are placed on a more equal footing in the insolvency of a company.

---

70 Wood (n 60) 88: 'Contrary to proceduralists, traditionalists believe that insolvency law is not a tool solely reserved for the creditors in which they can pursue their own interests.' Nsubuga (n 60) para 3.

71 Walton (n 59) 7; D Millon, 'New Directions in Corporate Law Communitarians, Contractarians, and the Crisis in Corporate Law' (1993) 50(4) *Washington and Lee Law Review* 1373, 1379: 'Communitarians also differ from contractarians in emphasizing the broad social effects of corporate activity.'

72 Walton (n 59) 7.

73 Warren (n 63) 777.

74 A Keay, 'Tackling the Issue of the Corporate Objective: an Analysis of the United Kingdom's "Enlightened Shareholder Value Approach"' (2007) 29(4) *Sydney Law Review* 577, 586. The Cork Report also seemed to validate at least some aspects of the communitarian theory. Cork Report on Insolvency Law and Practice Cmnd 8558 [1982] para 204: 'The chain reaction consequent upon any given failure can potentially be so disastrous to creditors, employees and the community that it must not be overlooked.' The criticism levelled against this theory relates to the difficulty of defining the community and determining how far it may stretch is cumbersome. See in this regard, Walton (n 59) 7; Millon (n 71) 1388.

75 Lahey and Salter (n 15) 548.

The Communitarian theory has a lot in common with Warren's Multi Value Approach or Eclectic Approach.[76] In a corporate insolvency context this approach requires recognition of those who are not directly 'creditors'.[77] A clear correlation with this approach and the ideology of inclusion (not isolation) and social justice of the feminist movement can be made. Warren refers to the notion that it was intended that insolvency law address concerns that are broader than just the debtor's immediate problems and that of its creditors.[78] It should involve considering other internal or external stakeholders such as employees, suppliers or tax authorities and in some instances to 'protect interests that have no other protection'.[79] Here, a sense of the feminists' compassion can be seen.

The feminist ideals of inclusion, connectedness, social justice and the flattening of hierarchies are to a greater or lesser extent visible in all the insolvency theories that tend to focus on more than just the interests of creditors.

The Enlightened Creditor Value Approach

As part of this author's research into the beneficiaries of insolvency practitioners' fiduciary duties, she developed her own insolvency theory – the Enlightened Creditor Value Approach (ECV). Like its counterpart in solvency, the Enlightened Shareholder Value Approach, the ECV sets out to strike a balance between the competing interests of the different stakeholders to benefit creditors ultimately. It can be seen as a compromise between the creditor focused theories and stakeholder theories.

The ECV theory encourages an approach to insolvency that would achieve the best outcome for creditors by taking into account all the relevant considerations for that purpose; this involves the taking of a proper balanced view of the short and long term – the interests of the shareholders and employees, customers, suppliers, financiers and others – as well as to consider the impact of the company's possible demise on the community. The basic position is that insolvency practitioners are required to treat creditors' interests as paramount, that is, 'creditors first', not 'creditors only'. The interests of employees or other

---

76 Walton (n 59) 10.

77 Ibid; Warren (n 63).

78 Warren (n 63) 788.

79 Ibid; Walton (n 59) 10–11. It is, however, criticised as 'too widely expressed to be much specific assistance in developing a policy'. It also does not provide enough guidance as to the weight that has to be afforded to each of the interests and priorities that come into play in an insolvency context. 'It is not clear which principles are to be seen as core and which are of peripheral relevance.'

stakeholders should be considered in performing these duties – but only where this would be in the creditors' interest.

It is clear the ECV displays ideals that can be viewed as both feminist and 'masculist' in nature. Whilst it distinguishes and fragments stakeholders by focusing on creditors' interests first, it does not lose sight of the interests of other stakeholders and attempts to minimise the competing interests that invariably arise in insolvency scenarios.

ANALYSIS AND CONCLUDING REMARKS

In this chapter the concept of insolvency theory (that informs our traditional understanding of insolvency law) was re-thought and re-evaluated through a feminist and women-centred lens.[80] There is some clear, preliminary evidence of feminist ideology (and lack thereof) to be found in recognised insolvency theory.

It was interesting to note that the insolvency theories that are focused on the creditors' interests in insolvency display ideologies that the feminist movement have identified as being non-feminist or 'masculist' in nature. These theories divide, exclude and create hierarchies amongst stakeholders in insolvency, leading to oppression of certain stakeholders who are left without much power in the insolvency proceedings due to their classification. In contrast, the theories of insolvency that follow a more inclusive approach to stakeholder interests seem to be more feminist in nature by displaying some feminist ideological characteristics. These theories tend to flatten hierarchies and attempt to level the proverbial playing field by being more inclusive of all stakeholders. They also tend to display elements of compassion and social justice, which have at times been associated as ideologies of the feminist movement.

It seems based on this initial enquiry that it may in fact be possible to categorise insolvency theories as either feminist or 'masculist' in nature. This contribution would, however, be meaningless if nothing is to be gleaned from it.

Should insolvency systems and the theories underpinning them be influenced by a categorisation of being feminist or 'masculist'? Arguably not, but it can be argued that insolvency systems should be influenced by certain ideologies – ideologies that better reflect a balanced and equitable process in line with the progress towards greater social justice occurring throughout the world today, perhaps with a few glaring aberrations in 2023.

During the recent Coronavirus Global Pandemic many jurisdictions moved to minimise the consequent fallout on individuals and companies. What most of the measures had in common was that they reflect a more inclusive

---

80 Paetzold (n 23)705.

and communitarian approach to insolvency than the usual creditor-focused approach. The plight of debtors, their management and their employees were given priority, whilst creditors and especially financial creditors were required to be patient and cooperate with the efforts of ensuring the survival of companies. It is as though the Pandemic provided some perspective and a heightened realisation that insolvency matters affect more than just the creditors.

At the risk of sounding too idealistic, perhaps insolvency systems ought to have more of a 'woman's touch' and reflect more care, compassion and inclusion.

5. A Dworkinian approach to insolvency law

Catherine Brown and Colin Anderson

INTRODUCTION[1]

A fundamental issue to be resolved under insolvency – or bankruptcy – law in any jurisdiction is the question of what each of the legitimate claimants to the insolvent estate are entitled to from available funds. There are many factors that influence how each jurisdiction's insolvency regime deals with this question. Whilst most jurisdictions probably start from a principle of equality to some extent, it can also be widely observed that one of the key issues in relation to corporate insolvency is whether, and to what extent, there should be a priority for the collection of taxation revenue.

The priority position of taxation authorities will inevitably be determined by reference to competing, and often conflicting, policy objectives. In the context of corporate insolvency law, policy objectives must address the basis on which the distribution of scarce assets is to be determined. Determining the priority for the payment of an insolvent entity's taxation debts requires specific consideration in the development of insolvency law theory as these debts are likely to be present in most corporate insolvencies.[2] Further, it may be the case that the taxation authority is the most significant creditor when a corporation becomes insolvent and, as such, has the capacity to overshadow the rights of other creditors. This is particularly so where a jurisdiction's tax legislation provides the taxation authority with significant debt collection powers.[3]

1 This chapter has been extracted from C Brown, 'Revisiting the Priority of Taxation in Corporate Insolvency: An Application of Dworkin's Rights Thesis and Equality Theories' (Doctoral thesis, Queensland University of Technology 2019) https://eprints.qut.edu.au/134140/ accessed 6 May 2023.

2 See, e.g., Frances Hill, 'Toward a Theory of Bankruptcy Tax: A Statutory Coordination Approach' (1996–97) 50(1) *Tax Lawyer* 103, 103.

3 In, e.g., Australia, s 260-5 of Schedule 1 to the Taxation Administration Act 1953 (Cth).

The approaches taken by various nations in determining whether the collection of taxation revenue should be afforded a priority in insolvency range from a *pari passu* approach to a statutory priority, with most showing a combination of these for different parts of the taxation system.[4] This chapter challenges traditional theoretical approaches to priority disputes by applying Ronald Dworkin's rights thesis and equality theories to the intersection of corporate insolvency and taxation law. In doing so, this chapter considers and justifies the *pari passu* principle to the resolution of priority disputes between taxation authorities and other creditors in insolvency.

A key issue, particularly in common law jurisdictions, is whether, and to what extent, there exist inconsistent or incoherent legal rules in relation to the priority of taxation in corporate insolvency. This chapter, therefore, considers Dworkin's seamless web theory and argues that *pari passu* is the principle of 'best fit' in resolving 'hard cases' on priority disputes. The more challenging issue for jurisdictions to resolve is determining the policy basis on which priority position of taxation authorities should be based, particularly where the taxation debts of an insolvent corporation are significant. Should the policy approach to insolvency laws and taxation debts be underpinned by a strict *pari passu* approach? If not, should policy makers be more persuaded by an approach which focusses on maximising the collection of taxation revenue? This chapter argues that Dworkin's equality theories provide a cohesive and unifying approach to developing policy and future law reform, particularly in relation to laws that either directly, or indirectly, impact the priority of taxation debts in corporate insolvency. Specifically, this chapter contends Dworkin's equality theories align the *pari passu* principle, which underpins the development of insolvency law, with the various tenets of equality, simplicity and certainty that typically underpin the imposition of taxation.

THE CONFLICTING POSITION OF TAXATION AUTHORITIES

The taxation system in any jurisdiction will inevitably sit within a complex matrix of social, economic, and political factors. Moreover, the taxation system will likely intersect with the corporate insolvency regime at various junctures in this matrix.[5] At this intersection, an important issue must be resolved, that of how to deal with taxation claims.

---

4 Barbara Morgan (Day) 'Should the Sovereign be Paid First? A Comparative International Analysis' (2000) 74 *American Bankruptcy Law Journal* 461.

5 Ibid., 462.

The taxation authorities of each jurisdiction are, arguably, placed in a position of conflict as a creditor in insolvency.[6] This is because taxation authorities are generally accountable for the collection of taxation revenue and ensuring the social costs of non-collection are minimised.[7] Indeed, it can be argued that the resentment often felt by other creditors to any taxation authority priority,[8] and the arguments for and against providing such priority,[9] is a clear example of the way in which competing theory and policy objectives impact the development of taxation and insolvency law.

Taxation authorities are also often instrumental in developing policy approaches and laws aimed at both the imposition and collection of taxation revenue.[10] Thus, it is the consideration of establishing the strongest possible collection arrangements in favour of the taxing authority which often guides the development of taxation law and policy. In Australia, for example, the Australian Taxation Office (ATO) plays a significant role in the development of sound tax policy.[11] However, in reviewing the documents associated with the development of taxation law in Australia, it is rare to find consideration of what may happen if an entity becomes insolvent and there is virtually no con-

---

6 For an explanation of some of the special features of taxation authorities as a creditor see, Shu-Yi Oei, 'Who Wins when Uncle Sam Loses? Social Insurance and the Forgiveness of Tax Debts' (2012) 46(1) *University of California, Davis Law Review* 421, 428–429.

7 Gerard McCormack, 'Priorities and Fairness in Restructuring and Insolvency Law' (INSOL International 2021) 9–10 https://insol.azureedge.net/cmsstorage/insol/media/document-library/other%20publications/insol-scholar-paper-priorities-and-fairness-in-restructuring-and-insolvency-law-9-nov-2021.pdf accessed 19 May 2023.

8 Morris G Shanker, 'The Worthier Creditors (and a Cheer for the King)' (1976) 1(3) *Canadian Business Law Journal* 340, 342.

9 See, e.g., the Australian position summarised in the Harmer Report: Australian Law Reform Commission, *General Insolvency Inquiry* (Report No 45, 1988) paras 734–743; Christopher F Symes, 'Reminiscing the Taxation Priorities in Insolvency' (2005) 1(2) *Journal of the Australasian Tax Teachers Association* 435, discussing the Australian position. For discussion of the priority of taxation in the UK, see, Joshua Kieran Glennon, 'First among Equals: The Revenue Commissioners as Preferential Creditors in Corporate Insolvency' (2021) 20(1) *Hibernian Law Journal* 1.

10 In Australia, e.g., the Australian Taxation Office has a significant role in developing laws relevant to the use of illegal phoenix arrangements to avoid liability for taxation. See, PricewaterhouseCoopers (PwC), *The Economic Impacts of Potential Illegal Phoenix Activity* (Report Commissioned by the Australian Taxation Office, Australian Securities and Investments Commission and the Fair Work Ombudsman, July 2018) https://www.ato.gov.au/uploadedFiles/Content/ITX/downloads/The_economic_impacts_of_potential_illegal_Phoenix_activity.pdf accessed 6 May 2023.

11 Catherine Brown, 'The Tax Priority in Australian Corporate Insolvency: A Dworkinian Approach' in INSOL International (ed), *A Collection of Short Papers by INSOL Early Research Academics* (INSOL ERA), (INSOL International 2021) 10.

sideration given as to how a particular measure may impact on any insolvency administration.[12]

The need to ensure that rigorous collection mechanisms exist might overwhelm the development of taxation legislation and policies that apply in respect of taxation debts in insolvency. However, whether a specific priority for the collection of taxation debts in insolvency results in an overall increase in total taxation revenue is unclear.[13]

THE TAXATION PRIORITY JUSTIFIED

There is a substantial amount of literature that specifically addresses the manner in which scarce assets should be dealt with on insolvency and inevitably the question as to whether some creditors are entitled to a priority arises. Wood notes that the priority of certain creditors is generally justified on the argument that public interest is greater than the private interests of other creditors in insolvency, although he acknowledges that there is significant international dispute about acceptance of this argument.[14] It is, therefore, instructive to consider what type of creditor a taxation authority is in the context of insolvency, and what public interest arguments might prevail in terms of granting a specific priority for taxation claims.

First, there is the argument that a taxation authority is an involuntary creditor and, therefore, cannot diversify the risk of non-payment of debts in the event of insolvency. Related to this is the notion that a taxation authority is a statutory creditor, rather than a contractual one. Shuchman argues that any priority payment in insolvency should be justified on a moral basis and that, '[f]rom the standpoint of most moralities, the debt obligation not freely assumed should not be judged in the same manner as one voluntarily undertaken'.[15]

While a taxation authority is an involuntary creditor, it often has legislative powers that put it in a different position to that of other involuntary creditors

---

[12] See, the case of *Deputy Commissioner of Taxation v PM Developments Pty Ltd* [2008] FCA 1886 as well as the discussion in Colin Anderson and David Morrison 'GST and Insolvency Practitioner Liability: Who Are You?' (2001) 11 *Revenue Law Journal* 23 and Catherine Brown, Colin Anderson, and David Morrison 'The Certainty of Tax in Insolvency: Where Does the ATO Fit?' (2011) 19(2) *Insolvency Law Journal* 108.

[13] See, e.g., the Harmer Report (n 9) para 737 where it was considered that 'there is no indication that abolition of the priority would endanger the revenue'.

[14] Philip R Wood, *Principles of International Insolvency* (Sweet & Maxwell 1995) 23.

[15] Philip Shuchman, 'An Attempt at a "Philosophy of Bankruptcy"' (1973–1974) 21(2) *UCLA Law Review* 403, 432.

such as, for example, torts claimants.[16] These powers are often considered necessary for the collection of taxation revenue in a cost-efficient manner and are not available to other unsecured creditors. On this basis, it has been argued that there is no justification for affording the taxation authority a priority in insolvency, despite being an involuntary creditor.[17]

Second is the general argument that community interests should prevail as a matter of public policy. Reviews of insolvency law generally suggest that this view is not widely supported in Australia.[18] In the context of the United States of America (USA), Arner noted that one of the justifications for retaining priority of taxation claims was the particular operation of the USA tax collection mechanisms at that time.[19] However, as Arner pointed out, the US government was of the view a departure from *pari passu* for the prioritisation of taxation debts was not justified.[20] Furthermore, the revenue foregone in insolvency claims was comparatively small when compared to gross tax revenue and, therefore, should not be at the expense of other creditors.[21] By contrast, Shanker disputes the government's ability to better absorb losses in insolvency through the redistribution of those losses among other tax payers, arguing that there must be a more formative approach.[22] He argues that the removal of the taxation priority must be based on factors other than 'the fact that business creditors do not much like it.'[23] More recently, the UK government enacted legislation to re-introduce a priority in favour of the UK HM Revenue & Customs (HMRC) for the collection of certain taxes in insolvency.[24]

---

[16] Stephanie Ben-Ishai, 'Technically the King Can Do Wrong in Reorganizing Insolvent Corporations: Evidence from Canada' (2004) 13(2) *International Insolvency Review* 115, 126. In Australia, see s 260-5 of sch 1 to the Taxation Administration Act 1953 (Cth) which to collect amounts of unpaid tax from third parties on issuing of a written notice.

[17] Morgan (n 4) 482–483, discussing the New Zealand, *Priority Debts in the Distribution of Insolvent Estates*, noting that the government had made a conscious choice to have the debtor act as tax collector, and noting that there are other involuntary creditors, such as tort claimants, who are not entitled to priority.

[18] See, e.g., John Duns and John Glover, 'The Taxation Priority in Insolvency: An Australian Perspective' (2005) 14(3) *International Insolvency Review* 171, 173, who drew an analogy between taxation debts and fines, which are not afforded a priority in insolvency.

[19] Michael Reed Arner, 'The Worthier Creditors (And a Cheer for the King) – Revisited' (1979) 53 *American Bankruptcy Law Journal* 389, 392.

[20] Ibid., 392.

[21] Ibid., 393.

[22] Shanker (n 8).

[23] Ibid., 342.

[24] Finance Act 2020 ss 98 and 99 amending s 386 of the UK Insolvency Act 1986, s 129(2) of Bankruptcy (Scotland) Act 2016 and art 346 of the Insolvency (Northern

The policy basis for the priority was stated as 'taxes paid in good faith by its employees and customers and temporarily held by the business go to fund public services rather than being distributed to other creditors'.[25]

Third is the argument that the taxation authority is merely acting as agent of the company, as is the case in Australia for withholding tax and employee obligations. As Morgan states, the priority of taxation claims 'operates to prevent a windfall to general unsecured creditors who have no fair claim to the collected funds'.[26]

What appears to be the most relevant justification for the removal of the tax priority is the argument that it is lacks the necessary fairness and equity elements that decisions on the priority of distribution in insolvency require.[27] As stated in the UK Report of the Review Committee on Insolvency Law and Practice (Cork Report) published in 1982:

> Since the existence of any preferential debt militates against the principle of *pari passu* distribution and operates to the detriment ordinary unsecured creditors, this can be justified by reference to principles of fairness and equity which would be likely to command general public acceptance.[28]

In Australia, the importance of equity was also a major determining factor in the Harmer Reports recommendation that the Commissioner's priority be abolished, specifically that it ensures 'the general body of taxpayers are not called upon unnecessarily to shoulder the added burden of having to bear tax that was not remitted by defaulting taxpayers'.[29]

Ireland) Order 1989 to establish HMRC as a preferential debt, specifically for those tax debts collected and held by businesses in relation to other taxpayers (e.g., employee withholding taxes and Value Added Tax).

25 Explanatory notes to the Finance Bill 2020 para 13 https://assets.publishing.service.gov.uk/government/uploads/system/uploads/attachment_data/file/873637/Finance_Bill_2020_Explanatory_Notes.pdf accessed 6 May 2023.

26 Morgan (n 4) 464.

27 As Symes notes, 'Australia has a longstanding principle of equal sharing between creditors.' See, Christopher F Symes, 'Do Not Dismiss the Employee as a Statutory Priority Creditor in Corporate Insolvency' (1998) 26(6) *Australian Business Law Review* 450, 462.

28 Insolvency Law and Practice Committee (United Kingdom), Report of the Review Committee on Insolvency Law and Practice Cmnd 8558 para 1396.

29 Harmer Report (n 9) para 734.

COMPETING MAXIMS AND NOTIONS OF EQUALITY

In many jurisdictions, there are certain canons of taxation which are well recognised and underpin the implementation of taxation reform.[30] Typically, these include principles such as equality, simplicity, and certainty. While there is divergence as to the importance placed on these various canons of taxation, generally, the application of those principles relates largely to the *burden* of taxation, rather than the *collection* of taxation debts. In the normal course of events, there may not be separation between the imposition and collection of taxation, but in the case of an insolvent company, the fact that there is a legitimate debt owing to a taxation authority does not assist in answering whether or how much of that debt should be paid in preference to other legitimate claimants.

Accordingly, the general cannons of taxation, without specific consideration of the principles on which the insolvency law are based, are likely to be of little assistance to informing the debate on the priority for the collection of taxation revenue in corporate insolvency. Nevertheless, one of the common underlying objectives of both taxation and insolvency law is the notion of equality. In the context of taxation reform, the equality theme generally refers to the requirement that the implementation of taxation reform should consider the extent to which the burden of taxation is imposed on taxpayers in proportion to their respective circumstances. So, for example, taxpayers in similar economic circumstances should share the burden of taxation equally, whereas those taxpayers whose economic resources are greater than others should be subject to higher rates.[31] The equality principle in taxation law also suggests that there should be some form of social justice in determining tax policy, leading to a more equal distribution of economic wealth.

The principle of equality applied to insolvency law is derived from the Latin phrase '*pari passu*', meaning equal footing. In the absence of some alternative justification, *pari passu* in its simplest form means that all unsecured creditors receive an equal share of available assets which are available for distribution on insolvency.[32]

---

[30] Adam Smith, *The Wealth of Nations: An Inquiry into the Nature and Causes of the Wealth of Nations* (first published 1776, Dent 1910) 307–308.

[31] Helen Hodgson, 'Theories of Distributive Justice: Frameworks for Equity' (2010) 5(1) *Journal of the Australasian Tax Teachers Association* 86, 88.

[32] See, generally Vanessa Finch, *Corporate Insolvency Law: Perspectives and Principles* (3rd edn, Cambridge University Press 2018); Rizwaan Jameel Mokal, *Corporate Insolvency Law: Theory and Application* (Oxford University Press 2005).

The *pari passu* principle is not without criticism.[33] Mokal argues that there is no such 'normal rule' under which all creditors are treated equally due to the fact that the *pari passu* principle will not apply to secured creditors and preferential claims.[34] Mokal further contends that the *pari passu* principle does not accurately explain the law regarding decisions about the distribution of assets on insolvency as '[i]t neither imposes a requirement which insolvency must fill, nor does it shape that law in any way'.[35] Thus, while traditional approaches to determining the priority of creditors in insolvency are often based on some form of the *pari passu* principle, these approaches do not assist in determining whether an exception should be applied to *pari passu* for the payment of taxation debts.

Finch posits that there exists a strong and weak form of *pari passu*, arguing that the weak form provides for a system where creditors are ranked by class and afforded differential treatment, such is the case that frequently applies to preferential employees.[36] Similarly, Mokal proposes that the underlying objective of the equality principle in insolvency law should be aimed at achieving some level of *substantive* equality, rather than formal equality, which would dictate that the same distribution rules apply to all creditors in insolvency.[37]

Aligning the concept of substantive equality to the development of both taxation and insolvency law requires consideration of an overarching framework that addresses both the resolution of laws that are inconsistent and a policy approach to the reform or development of the law itself. It is suggested in this chapter that Dworkin's rights thesis and equality theories provides such a framework. It is argued that Dworkin's rights thesis supports the adoption of *pari passu* in the resolution of conflicting laws, referred to as 'hard cases'. Furthermore, it is contended that *pari passu* should be incorporated in the development of taxation laws that impact insolvency and, on the basis of Dworkin's equality theories, the view of taxation authorities on whether a departure from *pari passu* can be justified should be excluded as an 'external preference'.

---

33 See, e.g., Rizwaan Jameel Mokal, 'Priority as Pathology: The *Pari Passu* Myth' (2001) 60(3) *Cambridge Law Journal* 581.

34 Mokal (n 32) 96.

35 Mokal (n 33) 584.

36 Finch (n 32) 599.

37 Ibid., 606–607.

INTERESTING INSOLVENCY AND TAX LAW: DWORKIN'S RIGHTS THESIS

It is often the case that the rules relevant to insolvency and taxation laws are found in statute and, in the event of conflicting rules, some form of interpretation as to the prevailing authority is required. Hill argues that there is in implicit assumption that the resolution of issues related to the priority of the taxation authorities in insolvency can be resolved by the interpretation of a singular piece of legislation.[38] Yet, despite the importance of tax claims in insolvency, Hill contends that insolvency and taxation laws are not 'systematically coordinated', thus neither insolvency nor taxation theory provide a framework for this statutory coordination.[39] Accordingly, in the absence of clearly articulated statutory 'tie-breaker' rules, it is impossible to determine what approach should be taken to resolve any conflict between distribution on insolvency and the collection of taxation revenue.

Dworkin sees the law as a 'seamless web' comprising rules and other standards, which together provide one 'right' answer. For example, according to Dworkin insolvency and taxation law are not two distinct areas of law, separated by some form of dividing line; rather, they are an interconnected set of rules and standards. As Dworkin states, '[t]he law may not be a seamless web; but the plaintiff is entitled to ask [the courts] to treat it as if it were'.[40] A 'hard case' is essentially one which cannot be resolved by the application of existing legal rules, either because the existing legal rules are indeterminate and incoherent, or they are conflicting. It may be there are no existing statutory provisions that are applicable to the case, or that the applicable provisions have some degree of uncertainty or incoherence.[41] Alternatively, it may be that there are conflicting legal rules that are equally applicable to the case, requiring that the courts look beyond those rules to determine the 'right' answer. An example may be seen in the Australian context with the imposition of a value added tax (known as the Goods and Services Tax) which, on introduction, resulted in uncertainty due to the drafting of the Australian legislation as to whether the ultimate tax debt was incurred by the company or the liquidator in the event of a company being wound up in insolvency.[42]

---

38 Hill (n 2) 103.

39 Ibid., 105.

40 Ronald Dworkin, 'Hard Cases' (1975) 88(6) *Harvard Law Review* 1057, 1092.

41 Ronald Dworkin, *A Matter of Principle* (Harvard University Press 1985); Dworkin (n 40) 1057.

42 See, the case of *Deputy Commissioner of Taxation v PM Developments Pty Ltd* [2008] FCA 1886 as well as the discussion in Anderson and Morrison (n 12) and Brown, Anderson and Morrison (n 12).

Dworkin goes on to argue that '[i]n most hard cases there are right answers to be hunted by reason and imagination'.[43] To Dworkin, right answers are determined by reference to legal rules and other standards.[44] Dworkin uses the term 'standards' to describe both principles and policies, but importantly contrasts the term 'principle' which he uses in both a general sense with a standard that is more akin to a legal rule. He states:

> [t]he distinction can be collapsed by construing a principle [in the general sense] as stating a social goal… or by construing a policy as stating a principle…or by adopting the utilitarian thesis that principles of justice are disguised statements of goals (securing the greatest happiness of the greatest number).[45]

For this reason, Dworkin contrasts between *legal* rules and principles, and then contrasts principles and policy, defining the term 'policy' as 'that kind of standard that sets out a goal to be reached, generally an improvement in some economic, political, or social feature of the community'.[46] Legal rules, being those that must either be accepted or rejected when argued, would typically consist of statutory provisions and doctrinal precedent. Accordingly, if one statutory provision is in conflict with another, one might prevail over the other because it has constitutional validity,[47] or because the legislation contains some form of conflict provision,[48] or by virtue of case law precedent. By contrast, standards, or what can be referred to as legal principles, are those which do not function as legal rules, but which are nevertheless observed because concepts of justice, fairness or morality require them to be followed, as opposed to economic, political or social objectives.[49]

A legal principle in this sense might be understood more clearly as the basis on which statutory provision might be interpreted. Unlike legal rules, legal principles are afforded validity because they are considered appropriate by society and the courts. The distinction between rules and principles is not always clear, and it may be that the distinction 'is almost a matter of form alone'.[50] However, central to the understanding of Dworkin's rules/principles

---

[43] Ronald Dworkin, *Law's Empire* (Belknap Press 1986) viii–ix.

[44] Ronald Dworkin, *Taking Rights Seriously* (Duckworth 1978).

[45] Ronald Dworkin, *Taking Rights Seriously* (revised edn, Bloomsbury Publishing 2013) 39.

[46] Dworkin (n 44) 22.

[47] For example, where a Commonwealth Act is in conflict with a State Act, the Commonwealth Act will prevail: Australia Constituion, s 109.

[48] For example, one statute or legislative provision is made 'subject to' another statute or legislative provision.

[49] Dworkin (n 45) 39.

[50] Ibid., 44.

distinction, and the application of rules and principles to the resolution of 'hard cases', is the extent to which judges can exercise discretion.[51] Dworkin argues that the resolution of a hard case is more than a mere process of bridging gaps in statute and precedent through the exercise of judicial discretion. He contends that discretion is a relative concept which 'like a hole in a doughnut, does not exist except as an area left open by a surrounding belt of restriction'.[52] Discretion in adjudication is distinguished by Dworkin in a strong and weak sense. A strong form of discretion exists where a person is not bound by any particular form of standard or rule set by some higher level of authority.[53] In contrast, the weak form of discretion exists where the standards to be applied cannot be applied mechanically or are open to some form of review.[54] Dworkin states: 'if a lawyer thinks of law as a system of rules, and yet recognize, as he must, that judges change old rules and introduce new ones, he will come naturally to the theory of judicial discretion in the strong sense'.[55]

Importantly, Dworkin argues that is it not the judge's role to exercise a strong form of discretion to resolve inconsistent legal rules. Discretion, in that sense, has a policy dimension that should, rightly, rest with the legislature.[56] While the resolution of hard cases may be achieved by application of standards,[57] which might be either based in policy or by reference to a legal principle, the distinction between the two is important when determining the role of the courts.[58] Specifically, judicial decisions should be based on legal principles alone, and it is not open to judges to exercise their discretion by applying policy.[59] Accordingly, the resolution of hard cases is achieved by the application of legal principles.

The 'Best Fit' Principle

In addition to the argument that legal principles provide a standard which can be applied in resolving hard cases, Dworkin also contends that it is the role of the courts to determine the principle of 'best fit'. Unlike legal rules, where there will be one clear rule that must be adhered to, Dworkin contends that

---

51 Dworkin (n 41) 120.
52 Dworkin (n 45) 48.
53 Ibid., 49.
54 Ibid.
55 Ibid., 56.
56 Ibid.
57 Ibid., 38.
58 Dworkin (n 44) 84.
59 Freeman summarises this as 'Judges are to decide according to principle litigants' entitlements, not what serves the community best. 'See, Michael D Freeman, *Lloyd's Introduction to Jurisprudence* (9th edn, Sweet & Maxwell 2014) 594.

there may be numerous principles which might apply to the resolution of hard cases, and these competing principles can be resolved by reference to their relative weight or importance.[60]

Dworkin asserts that in most hard cases, principles already exist but must be discovered. It is, therefore, the duty of the judge (in Dworkin's case, an ideal judge called Hercules) to find the principle that best explains and justifies the settled law and decide on those areas that remain incoherent. Dworkin asserts that when interpreting hard cases, each judge is deciding on what represents the 'better' reading of a 'chain' of decisions prior to the case before him or her.[61] It is this chain of decisions that enable Dworkin's Hercules judge to determine the 'right' answer. However, when determining the right answer, judges are constrained by the notion of 'integrity and coherence of law as an institution.'[62] As Kress notes: 'In Dworkin's scheme, argument by analogy, coherence, or institutional fit (that the soundest theory of law must explain the settled law) competes with moral appeal (that the soundest theory of law must justify the settled law) in the account of legal reasoning.'[63]

When deciding between competing constructions of law, Dworkin asserts that judges should justify their decisions by constructing a 'scheme of abstract and concrete principles' which shows the law 'in its best light'.[64] The scheme of principles and rules should be tested in terms of fit and substance. 'Fit' refers to what is considered accepted law, whereas 'substance' refers to morality. For example, Dworkin argues that the principle of best fit applied by the Court in *Riggs v Palmer* was one based in morality, being that 'no man may profit from his own wrong'.[65] If the legal principle that should be applied by the courts to resolving a hard case is the principle of 'best fit', being the principle that has the dimension of greatest weight relevant to the case being determined, the question is what principle should be applied in relation to resolving disputes regarding the priority for taxation debts in insolvency? This requires consideration of *pari passu* as a principle in a Dworkin sense, and not just as a basis for determining insolvency law policy.

---

60 Dworkin (n 45) 55.

61 Ronald Dworkin, 'Law as Interpretation' (1982) 60(3) *Texas Law Review* 527, 542–543.

62 Dworkin (n 41) 161.

63 Kenneth J Kress, 'Legal Reasoning and Coherence Theories: Dworkin's Rights Thesis, Retroactivity and the Linear Order of Decisions' (1984) 72(3) *California Law Review* 369, 383.

64 *Riggs v Palmer* 115 NY 506 (1889) [511]–[512]; Dworkin (n 40) 1094.

65 *Riggs v Palmer*.

Pari Passu as the 'Best Fit' Principle

It is argued here that the *pari passu* principle is both a legal rule and a legal principle on which hard cases can be resolved. In relation to insolvency law, the *pari passu* principle may be a legal rule in the sense that it is enshrined in legislation. So, for example, in Australia section 555 of the *Corporations Act 2001* (Cth) provides: 'Except as otherwise provided by this Act, all debts and claims proved in a winding up rank equally and, if the property of the company is insufficient to meet them in full, they must be paid proportionately.'

The explicit exception to the *pari passu* rule, however, will only apply in the context of other provisions of the Corporations Act 2001 and does not apply to other legislation, such as taxation law which is determined under separate legislation. Therefore, in Australia, the legal rules relevant to taxation law that operate inconsistently with those enshrined in section 555 cannot be resolved by reference to section 555 of the Corporations Act 2001. Consequently, the provisions of taxation law which are either inconsistent with the Corporations Act 2001, or are incoherent in their application, will need to be resolved by the courts on the basis of legal principles.

If Dworkin's theory is applied in the context of the priority of taxation in insolvency, it must first be determined which principles can be applied to reconcile insolvency and taxation law, and then which is the principle of 'best fit.' While *pari passu* is generally referred to as a 'principle', whether it necessarily constitutes a legal principle in a Dworkin sense needs to be established. Furthermore, it must be established that *pari passu* is the principle that has the 'dimension of greatest weight' relevant to the case being determined.

There are arguably two competing principles that could be applied in resolving issues related to the Commissioner's priority in insolvency; the first being the *pari passu* principle and the second being a public policy argument that relates to revenue retention and moral obligations to pay taxes. Whereas *pari passu* can be supported on the basis that it is a requirement of justice or fairness, the public policy argument is better understood as a policy on the basis that it relates to improvement in economic, political, or social features of the community.[66] In Australia, support for this view can be found in court decisions in Australia, such as in *Ackers (as joint foreign representative) v Saad Investments Company Limited; In the matter of Saad Investments Company Limited (in official liquidation)* where the *pari passu* principle was applied to determining whether the provision of a tax debt could be made.[67] In that case, the Federal Court considered the context in which Australia had abolished the

---

66 Dworkin (n 45) 58.
67 [2013] FCA 738.

Commissioner's priority in insolvency the Court, acknowledging the competing taxation and insolvency 'principles'. The Court stated:

> The taxation legislation relied on by the Commissioner here evinces an indubitable public policy that taxation and civil penalties, first, be paid and, secondly, be recoverable in insolvencies, pari passu with debts owed to other unsecured creditors.
> It is fundamental to any society that its government be able to require its citizens and others who operate a business or reside within that society, to pay taxation so as to maintain the State.[68]

The obligation to pay taxation, while fundamental, is nevertheless one which arises *ex ante* insolvency and does not determine what priority that debt should be paid *ex post* insolvency. Consequently, it is argued that *pari passu* is a legal principle that has been applied, at least by Australian courts, to the resolution of inconsistencies in insolvency and taxation laws in relation to statutory priority rules. Furthermore, *pari passu* is the principle that 'best fits' disputes relating to the taxation priority in insolvency. The alternative argument, being that there is a moral obligation to ensure taxation is paid, is a policy decision that should be that of the legislature.

MATTERS OF POLICY

Many of the inquiries into insolvency law recognise the *pari passu* principle as, at least, a starting point in designing the rules set out in legislation. For example, in Australia, the recommendation of the Harmer Report was that the *pari passu* principle be retained as the policy which should underpin insolvency law. That recommendation was subject to certain qualifications, most notably that: '[a]ny departure from this approach should only be countenanced by reference to clearly defined principles or policies which enjoy general community support'.[69]

The key policy themes that impact the priority of a jurisdiction's taxation authority should theoretically be based on the notion of equitable treatment that is similar to the maxims of taxation law. In an insolvency context, horizontal equality is achieved by treating all members of a similar class in the same manner. In that regard, horizontal equality can be likened to Jackson's creditors bargain, being that creditors will notionally agree *ex ante* to what

[68] *Ackers (as joint foreign representative) v Saad Investments Company Limited; In the matter of Saad Investments Company Limited (in official liquidation)* [2013] FCA 738 [44]–[45].

[69] Harmer Report (n 9) para 713.

is a fair and equal unless some specific form of priority should prevail.[70] It is this notion of equality that forms the basis of the *pari passu* principle. For example, in recommending that the claims in insolvency should be ranked on a *pari passu* basis, the United Nations Commission on International Trade Law (UNCITRAL) Legislative Guide on Insolvency Law stated:

> The objective of equitable treatment is based on the notion that, in collective proceedings, creditors with similar legal rights should be treated fairly, receiving a distribution on their claim in accordance with their relative ranking and interests. This key objective recognizes that all creditors do not need to be treated identically, but in a manner that reflects the different bargains they have struck with the debtor. This is less relevant as a defining factor where there is no specific debt contract with the debtor, such as in the case of damage claimants (e.g. for environmental damage) and tax authorities. Even though the principle of equitable treatment may be modified by social policy on priorities and give way to the prerogatives pertaining to holders of claims or interests that arise, for example, by operation of law, it retains its significance by ensuring that the priority accorded to the claims of a similar class affects all members of the class in the same manner.[71]

What is less clear is the manner in which vertical, or substantive, equality is achieved. Specifically, the question is what policy approach should be applied to the justification of an exception to the *pari passu* principle, and in what context should taxation authorities be afforded such a priority. In fact, it is arguable that one of the main causes of inconsistencies between insolvency and taxation laws regarding the priority for taxation debts in insolvency has been the general lack of policy in relation to the exceptions to *pari passu*.

In the context of both insolvency and taxation law, it would appear that achieving some level of equality which factors in the economic and social differences within the broader community is an important policy objective. Articulating a theoretical approach aimed at achieving substantive equality in the context of priority of taxation debts in insolvency is more challenging.

As Keay notes, '[t]he concern for *pari passu* distribution or equality among creditors has meant that the maxim "equity is equality" is the main theme of liquidation administration'.[72] Dworkin criticises this notion of equality, arguing that the various concepts of equality be differentiated in order to deter-

---

70 Thomas H Jackson, 'Bankruptcy, Non-Bankruptcy Entitlements, and the Creditors' Bargain' (1982) 91(5) *The Yale Law Journal* 857.

71 United Nations Commission on International Trade Law (UNCITRAL), *UNCITRAL Legislative Guide on Insolvency Law* (UNCITRAL 2005) 11–12 https://uncitral.un.org/sites/uncitral.un.org/files/media-documents/uncitral/en/05-80722_ebook.pdf accessed 6 May 2023.

72 Andrew Keay, 'An Exposition and Assessment of Unfair Preferences' (1994) 19(3) *Melbourne University Law Review* 545, 545.

mine the ideal that is most politically attractive.[73] According to Dworkin, the 'equity is equality' argument only works in an egalitarian society, that is, one in which people, particularly in terms of politics, economic and social life, are equal.[74] Dworkin views the rights of the individual as a safeguard that prevents the corruption of the egalitarian ideal.[75] In this context, Dworkin distinguishes between the personal preferences of an individual in terms of a given policy approach and external preferences, being what might be expressed on behalf of others as ideal, is fundamental to achieving equality. He argues: 'If external preferences tip the balance, then the fact that a policy makes the community better off in a utilitarian sense would not provide justification compatible with the right of those it disadvantages to be treated as equals.'[76]

Dworkin contends external preferences should be excluded in determining the basis for equality, any policy supported by the need to retain tax revenue for the better good of society must also be excluded. Furthermore, any policy decision not grounded in the rights of the individual, such as the creditors in insolvency, but rather expressed as being for the greater good of the community, being the justification put forward by most taxation authorities, is one based on external preferences. Support for the view that *pari passu* should form the underlying policy is found in the international standards which 'represent the international consensus on best practices for evaluating and strengthening national insolvency and creditor rights systems'.[77] The World Bank's *Principles for Effective Insolvency and Creditor/Debt or Regimes* state:

> Following distributions to secured creditors from their collateral and the payment of claims related to the costs and expenses of administration, proceeds available for distribution should be distributed *pari passu* to the remaining general unsecured creditors, unless there are compelling reasons to justify giving priority status to a particular class of claims. Public interests generally should not be given precedence over private rights. The number of priority classes should be kept to a minimum.[78]

Accordingly, Dworkin's theory of equality supports the view that the priority for taxation debts in insolvency should be grounded in *pari passu*, and any

---

[73] Ronald Dworkin, 'What is Equality? Part 1: Equality of Welfare' (1981) 10(3) *Philosophy and Public Affairs* 185, 185.

[74] Dworkin (n 45).

[75] Ibid., 282.

[76] Ibid.

[77] The World Bank, *Principles for Effective Insolvency and Creditor/Debtor Regimes* (World Bank 19 November 2016) https://www.worldbank.org/en/topic/financialsector/brief/the-world-bank-principles-for-effective-insolvency-and-creditor-rights accessed 6 May 2023.

[78] Ibid., 25, Principle C12.2.

argument given by taxation authorities that the retention of tax revenue is paramount cannot be considered a justification for any taxation or insolvency law that provides a direct, or indirect, exception to the *pari passu* principle.

CONCLUSION

This chapter has considered the challenges facing many jurisdictions in resolving the inherent conflict between the jurisdiction's taxation authority and other creditors in insolvency. It is argued that the application of Dworkin's rights thesis and equality theories assist in developing a framework for determining the priority that should be afforded to taxation authorities in insolvency. First, when resolving incoherent or inconsistent laws, it is argued that Dworkin's principle of 'best fit' is prima facie *pari passu,* being that all unsecured creditors receive a rateable or proportionate distribution in the settling of claims in insolvency. Second, in drafting taxation legislation that is likely to impact the taxation authority's priority in insolvency, *pari passu* should form the theoretical and policy basis for drafting and interpreting those provisions. This approach achieves formal equality as a starting point in any policy debate.

In circumstances where a departure from *pari passu* is considered appropriate by government, due weight must be afforded to the personal preferences of the participants in the insolvency process. This approach achieves substantive equality in a Dworkin sense. Any policy justification for a departure from *pari passu* that is premised on the external preferences of the relevant taxation authority, namely that the collection of taxation revenue must be prioritised for the benefit of society as a whole, should be disregarded. Furthermore, any policy approach to laws which impact the priority in insolvency, being based on *pari passu* or a clearly articulated basis on which an exception should apply, should be stated explicitly as one of the purposes for which the legislation has been drafted. This will enable a statutory interpretation approach which incorporates the objectives of both insolvency and taxation laws.

6. A Nietzchean approach to debt and human thought

John Tribe[1]

INTRODUCTION

The work of Friedrich Nietzsche (1844–1900) provides a fascinating lens through which to examine insolvency issues[2] and the law more generally.[3] But what of the underlying debtor-creditor relationship, which has the potential to lead to technical insolvency?[4] Does Nietzsche offer any assistance in the analysis of this fundamental relationship – an association which provides the very bedrock of commercial activity? In fact, he offers much more. He has argued that the debtor and creditor relationship has had a formative influence on the very make-up of the human mind and emotions. This is Nietzsche's crucial insight and the subject of the novel critical examination in this chapter.

[1] I would like to thank the editors of this collection, Dr Stephen Baister, and Dr Karen Atkinson, for their helpful and constructive feedback on earlier drafts of this chapter. This chapter is better for all their efforts. Any errors or omissions are the sole responsibility of the author.

[2] See further J Tribe, 'Nietzsche's Eternal Recurrence and the Renaissance of English and Welsh Insolvency Law Reform' (2020) 40(3) *Legal Studies* 419. See also J Tribe, 'Big Bankruptcies: Evidencing "Insolvency" Eternal Recurrence, Bankruptcy Tourism and the Failure of Limited Liability' (2021) 14 *Corporate Rescue and Insolvency* 3; J Tribe, 'The Cost of Living in 2022 through the Lens of Eternal Recurrence: Drivers, Effects, and Personal Insolvency Responses', presented at InsolvencyLive!2022, organised by the Insolvency Service (July 2022).

[3] See e.g.: T A Cowan, 'Nietzsche' (1960) 14 *Vanderbilt Law Review* 151; *Nietzsche und das Recht. Vortrage der Tagung der Schweizer Sekton der Internationalen Vereinigung fur Rechts und Sozialphilosophie, 9–12 April 1999 in Basel* (Franz Steiner Verlag 2001). See also P Goodrich and M Valverde (eds), *Nietzsche and Legal Theory – Half-Written Laws* (Routledge 2005).

[4] In the cash flow and balance sheet sense, e.g., Insolvency Act 1986 s 123.

In Nietzsche's 1887 book *On the Genealogy of Morality*,[5] there is an examination of 'nothing less than the evolution of the human mind and how its basic ways of thinking have come into being'.[6] As part of this exposition, Nietzsche discussed the debtor-creditor relationship and its formative impact on the human mind. In this context Nietzsche's exposition includes a discussion of, inter alia, the genesis of guilt, the equivalence between injury and pain, and pleasure as compensation. This is all against the backdrop of the debtor-creditor relationship, so Nietzsche also dwells on the actions of debtors and creditors, punishment of the debtor, and suffering as compensation for debts. Ultimately, Nietzsche paints the creditor God or 'ultimate creditor'[7] and the debtor humans suffering from eternal indebtedness. It is these debtor-and-creditor-derived ingredients which make up the contents of a work that became 'one of the key texts of European intellectual modernity'.[8]

This chapter has two objectives. First Nietzsche's analysis of the debtor-creditor relationship and the themes which spring from it, including guilt are examined.[9] The second is an examination of Nietzsche's use of legal history, including Roman law, and the possible legal influences on Nietzsche. To reflect this treatment, the chapter is divided into two sections. Section A introduces Nietzsche and his philosophy. Section B examines the constituent elements of Nietzsche's conceptualisation of the debtor and creditor relationship in *On the Genealogy of Morality*. The underlying influence[10] of legal writers – such as Josef Kohler, professor of law at the University of Berlin – on Nietzsche is examined against the backdrop of Nietzsche's use of other writers, such as Kant and Spinoza, both of whom Nietzsche mentions directly in his examination of the debtor-creditor relationship.[11] Finally, Nietzsche's use of the debtor-creditor relationship as the genesis of guilt is examined.

This chapter offers two novel insights. The first relates to the creditor and debtor relationship by bringing the critical tools to bear which Nietzsche

---

[5] F Nietzsche, 'On the Genealogy of Morality' in K Ansell-Pearson, *Cambridge Texts in the History of Philosophy* (Cambridge University Press 2017) 40. See further R Schacht (ed), *Nietzsche, Genealogy, Morality: Essays on Nietzsche's On the Genealogy of Morals* (University of California Press 1994).

[6] Nietzsche (n 5) xviii.

[7] Ibid., xxiv.

[8] Ibid., ix.

[9] On this strand, see further: A Snelson, 'Nietzsche on the Origin of Conscience and Obligation' (2019) 50(2) *Journal of Nietzsche Studies* 310; B Reginster, 'What is the Structure of Genealogy of Morality II?' (2018) 61(1) *Inquiry* 1.

[10] Nietzsche's ideas were in turn influential on later legal writers. See e.g.: P Vinogradoff, *Introduction to Historical Jurisprudence* (Oxford University Press 1920) 43–46.

[11] Nietzsche (n 5) 43.

highlighted in his 1887 work. The second is the link between Nietzsche and the history of law. The chapter answers Brobjer, who in 1997 noted that '[...] many important topics such as Nietzsche's relation to the history of law ... also have not been explored'.[12]

This chapter exerts a novel influence on the academic field, enabling future scholars to re-assess the relationship between Nietzsche, legal sources, and his use of legal writers and their work. In insolvency theory terms this chapter, for the first time, provides a foundation for the consideration of the debtor-creditor relationship in private law.

SECTION A: BACKGROUND

Friedrich Nietzsche and his Philosophy[13]

From Nietzsche's colossal output,[14] we are able to draw some principal Nietzschean philosophical ideas. These are: self-overcoming (*Selbstüberwindung*) in the context of the 'over man' (*Übermensch* – 'great individual' or 'higher man'). This type of human can embrace and overcome the vicissitudes of life, becoming 'who we [humans] really are' by mastering the internal chaos of himself. According to Nietzsche, mediocrity and conformity are the path for the individual who does not go through this struggle and transition.[15]

To achieve this goal, humans need to undertake a number of steps. First, an individual must own up to envy. They are then able to use envy as a guide. This guide will identify what they really want. In this way the individual is able to identify their principal desires, and perhaps most importantly, progress down a route that will achieve those desires.

Secondly, Christianity must be totally rejected ('the most awful moral catastrophe in history'[16]). In Nietzsche's view, Christianity serves to protect

---

[12] T H Brobjer, 'Nietzsche's Reading and Private Library, 1885–1889' (1997) 58(4) *Journal of the History of Ideas* 663.

[13] On Nietzsche's philosophy, see C Cate, *Friedrich Nietzsche* (Hutchinson 2002). See also R Hayman, *Nietzsche: A Critical Life* (Weidenfeld and Nicolson, Oxford University Press 1980); F J Mootz and P Goodrich (eds), *Nietzsche and Law – Philosophers and Law* (Routledge 2008).

[14] On Nietzsche's life see R J Hollingdale, *Nietzsche: The Man and his Philosophy* (Cambridge University Press 1999).

[15] It is these elements of Nietzsche's philosophy that were misused by his sister following Nietzsche's decline into insanity and following his death. On this use of the work, see R H Thomas, *Nietzsche in German Politics and Society, 1890–1918* (Manchester University Press 1983).

[16] Cowan (n 3) 151.

people ('the herd') from envy. Christianity seeks to make a virtue of this cowardice. This is the 'herd morality' or as Nietzsche called it *Sklavenmoral*, i.e., slave morality.

Thirdly, Nietzsche encouraged abstention from alcohol. For Nietzsche, alcohol performed a similar function to Christianity. Alcohol was for him a ruinous narcotic. Nietzsche argued that achieving that which mattered was painful and difficult. Alcohol served to reduce the ability to achieve these aims and to progress towards improvement.

Fourthly, Nietzsche built on his end-of-faith view through the idea that God is dead. He insisted instead that the artificial construct of religion, and the focus on an afterlife which it encouraged, should be replaced with culture. This life-promoting approach to existence would emulate that of the Ancient Greeks. By focusing on culture, humans would stave off despair because if life had no meaning, purpose or goal, nihilism would follow.

Fifthly, Nietzsche argued that suffering has created the greatest enhancements of man to date. It is the self-hate in not being as good as the *Übermensch*, and the desire and motivation to grow and overcome so that she is more like the *Übermensch*, that drives the individual. They might not attain this goal in totality, Nietzsche thought she might in rapturous moments.

Sixthly, and finally, the individual would need to affirm life. If they progressed down this path, she would come to have *amor fati*, a love of fate. She would completely affirm life even in the presence of ugliness. She would have the potential for growth and self-overcoming. If she had reached that stage in development and could accept the *Eternal Recurrence*,[17] i.e., that she was bound to repeat the exact same life again and again without limit in an eternal cycle or recurrence, including the struggle, she would become the *Übermensch* and not be satisfied with the peace of non-existence. Instead, she would say 'Was *that* life? Well then! One more time!'[18]

It is against this philosophical backdrop that Nietzsche came to consider the nature of the debtor-creditor relationship and how it kindled the emotion of guilt.

---

[17] See further Tribe, 'Nietzsche's Eternal Recurrence and the Renaissance of English and Welsh Insolvency Law Reform' (2020) 40(3) *Legal Studies* 419.

[18] F Nietzsche, *Thus Spoke Zarathustra* (Cambridge University Press 2006) 125. Nietzsche's italicised emphasis.

Influences

It is an axiom that Nietzsche was influenced by the work of Arthur Schopenhauer.[19] Whilst an undergraduate at the University of Leipzig, Nietzsche stumbled across Schopenhauer's work in a bookshop sometime between October 1865 and August 1867.[20] This was four to six years after Maine's *Ancient Law* was published and sold across Europe. Nietzsche was open and direct about the influence of Schopenhauer. He penned an essay discussing the "physiological influence" of Schopenhauer on him.[21] It has been observed that:

> [f]ull of the ardour of discipleship, he [Nietzsche] had read his own ideas in to the other's [Schopenhauer's] words, and even while making use of the Schopenhaurian form had filled them with a different content.[22]

Nietzsche's university tutors, including Friedrich Albert Lange,[23] also exercised an influence. Richard Wagner and Burkhardt, whose lectures Nietzsche attended in Basel, were also influences.

Nietzsche's writings also make frequent references to Berkeley, Descartes, Hume, Kant, Locke, Plato, and Spinoza. Jensen also cites other influences including 'Brobjer, Campioni, Cancik, D'Iorio, Orsucci, Porter, Reibnitz, Small and Stack, Spir, Boscovich, Gerber, Rée'.[24] In terms of historians of civilisation, Nietzsche also makes reference in section four of the first essay in *On the Genealogy of Morality* to the Englishman Thomas Henry Buckle (1821–1869), albeit to criticise Buckle's 'lack of a real historical sense'.[25]

On occasion, Nietzsche's writings take extensively from the work of others, as Palmeri noted when he stated, 'Nietzsche borrowed extensively from Bagehot's *Physics and Politics.* In *Human, All Too Human* (1878-80)

---

[19] A Schopenhauer, *The World as Will and Representation I* (1818). See further Nietzsche's notes on Schopenhauer (October 1867 to April 1868) in F Nietzsche, *Writings from the Early Notebooks* (Cambridge University Press 2018) 1; G N Dolson, 'The Influence of Schopenhauer upon Friedrich Nietzsche' (1901) 10(3) *Philosophical Review* 241.

[20] E Forster-Nietzsche, *Das Leben Friedrich Nietzsche's Vol I* (Forgotten Books 2018) 231.

[21] F Nietsche, *Unzeitgemasse Betrachtungen Vol 3: Schopenhauer als Erzieher* (E W Fritsch 1893) 402–403.

[22] Dolson (n 19) 242.

[23] F A Lange, *History of Materialism and Critique of its Present Significance* (1866).

[24] A K Jensen, 'Friedrich Nietzsche: Writings from the Early Notebooks' (2010) 18(3) *British Journal for the History of Philosophy* 531, 534.

[25] Nietzsche (n 5) XV.

and *Daybreak* (1881), he argues in terms very close to Bagehot's for custom constituting morality, and for morality of custom.'[26]

The key function of this chapter is to consider whether Nietzsche engaged in similar activity in relation to legal writers. It is to that question that we can now turn.

Legal Influences[27]

We have some clear indication of Nietzsche's political thought[28] and impact on science,[29] but what of his approaches to law and legal issues? Vinogradoff has observed that Sir Henry Maine, sometime Corpus Professor of Jurisprudence in the University of Oxford was influenced by a small group of German scholars of the historical school of jurists,[30] including Savigny (1779–1861),[31] Puchta (1798–1846), and Eichhorn (1781–1854).[32] Was Nietzsche also reading these scholars in his native language? What law and legal authors was Nietzsche reading?

Nietzsche library has been preserved. It contains a number of law books.[33] Brobjer has noted:

> *On the Genealogy of Morals* (1887) is to a large extent a response to Nietzsche's reading of, and about, 'English psychologists,' especially including Paul Rée, anthropology, cultural history, and the history of law. (His library contains ten books within the field of law, and the majority of these he annotated.)[34]

---

[26] F Palmeri, *State of Nature, Stages of Society – Enlightenment Conjectural History and Modern Social Discourse* (Columbia University Press 2016) 165; 178.

[27] For a discussion of Nietzsche's influence on legal philosophy, see J Kohler, *'Nietzsche und die Rechtsphilosophie'* (1907/1908) Vol 1, No 3 (1907/1908) 355–360.

[28] See e.g., K Ansell-Pearson, *Introduction to Nietzsche as Political Thinker* (Cambridge University Press 1994).

[29] See further B E Babich, *Nietzsche's Philosophy of Science: Reflecting Science on the Ground of Art and Life* (State University of New York Press 1994).

[30] H U Kantorowicz, 'Savigny and the Historical School of Law' (1937) 53(3) *Law Quarterly Review* 326.

[31] J Ruckert, 'Friedrich Carl von Savigny, the Legal Method, and the Modernity of Law' (2006) *Juridicia International* XI/2006 55; H Klenner, 'Savigny's Research Program of the Historical School of Law and Its Intellectual Impact in 19th Century Berlin' (1989) 37(1) *American Journal of Comparative Law* 67.

[32] P Vinogradoff, 'The Teaching of Sir Henry Maine' (1904) 20(2) *Law Quarterly Review* 119, 125.

[33] G Campioni et al (eds) *Nietzsches persönliche Bibliothek* (De Gruyter 2003); T H Brobjer, 'Nietzsche's Reading and Private Library, 1885–1889' (1997) 58(4) *Journal of the History of Ideas* 663.

[34] T H Brobjer, *Nietzsche's Philosophical Context: An Intellectual Biography* (University of Illinois Press 2008) 18.

Josef Kohler

Kohler (1849–1919) was a well-known German jurist whose main contributions were on German copyright and patent law as well as the philosophy of law and the comparative history of law. A graduate of the Universities of Heidelberg and Freiberg, Kohler became a doctor of laws in 1873. In 1889, he was appointed to a chair in law at the University of Berlin after a period as a judge in Mannheim and as a law professor at Wurzburg. Kohler was then a contemporary of Nietzsche.[35] They were both publishing in Germany during the same time period.

Brobjer tantalisingly notes that Nietzsche's personal library contained, 'books about comparative law and the history of law, especially Kohler's three books which probably influenced Nietzsche's writing in *Zur Genealogie der Moral*'.[36] Unfortunately, Brobjer does not elaborate. Included in this collection are three law books in Nietzsche's library that contain his own annotations. These are three works by Kohler. They are: (1) *Das Recht als Kulturerscheinung: Einleitung in die vergleichende Rechtswis- senschaft* (Wurzburg, 1885); (2) *Zur Lehre von der Blutrache* (Wurzburg, 1885); and (3) *Das chinesische Strafrecht: Ein Beitrag zur Universalgeschichte des Strafrechts* (Wurzburg, 1886).

In the 25 pages of *Das Recht als Kulturerscheinung: Einleitung in die vergleichende Rechtswis- senschaft* (Wurzburg, 1885), Kohler discusses "schuldenrecht" [law of contract], an important theme in *On the Genealogy of Morality*.

Kohler's *On the Doctrine of Blood Revenge* was published in 1885, some two years before the 1887 publication of *On the Genealogy of Morality*. It seems likely that Kohler's work of 1885 influenced Nietzsche's 1887 publication. But there is an earlier work that might have also been influential.

The most important work in terms of potential inspiration for Nietzsche's *On the Genealogy of Morality* is Kohler's 1883 *Nachwort zu Shakespeare vor dem Forum der Jurisprudenz*.[37] Here Kohler examines law in the work of Shakespeare in its historical context.[38] Kohler focuses on the *Merchant of*

[35] On contemporary views of Nietzsche, see S L Gilman (ed), *Conversations with Nietzsche: A Life in the Words of his Contemporaries* (Oxford University Press 1987).

[36] Brobjer (n 12) 679.

[37] J Kohler, *Nachwort zu Shakespeare vor dem Forum der Jurisprudenz* (Wurzburg 1883).

[38] On which see further O Hood Phillips, *Shakespeare and the Lawyers* (Methuen & Co Ltd 1972); P Raffield and G Watt (eds), *Shakespeare and the Law* (Hart Publishing 2008).

Venice and the law of debt[39] and the activities of Shylock. It is this treatment of Shakespeare by Kohler that seems to have served as an influence on Nietzsche when he came to write *On the Genealogy of Morality*.

In his 1921 book *Philosophy of Law*,[40] published 21 years after Nietzsche's death, Kohler again mulls on the debtor-creditor relationship. He also mulled on how Nietzsche used his work. Writing in 1908, he observed:

> Remarkable is that what Nietzche has to say often accords with the ideas I have expressed since my Shakespeare in the Forum of Jurisprudence. **It has now been established that Nietzsche was familiar with some of these writings of mine, such** as Blood feuds and Chinese Criminal Law; and it is with some satisfaction that I can say that his sister has told me that as long ago as 1885 he spoke of my writings at a time when others were meeting them with blank refutation.[41]

This gives pause for thought on the originality of this element of Nietzsche's writing. It certainly goes some way to counterbalance what Figgis referred to in 1916 as Nietzsche's characteristic claim to be original.[42] This 'similarity of ideas' point is not unique to Nietzsche. Cocks has demonstrated how Maine's work itself bears close resemblance to earlier authors, e.g., James Caulfield Heron.[43]

---

39 As well as *Measure for Measure* (pardon) and *Hamlet* (blood feuds).

40 J Kohler, *Philosophy of Law* (The Macmillan Company, 1921), 150; 160.

41 See J Kohler, *Nietzsche und die Rechtsphilosphie [Nietzsche and legal philosophy]* (1907/1908) 1(3) Wirtschaftsphilosophie 355, 366–360. I am grateful to Dr Stephen Baister who translated this passage from the original German. Chapter author's bold emphasis.

42 J Figgis, *The Will to Freedom: Or, The Gospel of Nietzsche and the Gospel of Christ - Being the Bross Lectures* (1916) lxix

43 R C J Cocks, *Sir Henry Maine: A Study in Victorian Jurisprudence* (Cambridge University Press 1988) 15 citing J C Heron, *Introduction to the History of Jurisprudence* (J W Parker 1860).

Sir Henry Maine[44]

Was Nietzsche influenced by English jurists? Sir Henry Maine (1822–1888)[45] and his pathbreaking 1861 book *Ancient Law*[46] and his *Early Law and Custom*[47] are sources that Nietzsche may have been able to use despite his critique of the English 'psychology school' of Hume, Buckle, etc. In the preface to *Ancient Law*, Sir Henry Maine, sometime Whewell Professor of International Law at the University of Cambridge, observed that the purpose of the book was 'to indicate some of the earliest ideas of mankind, as they are reflected in ancient law, and to point out the relation of those ideas to modern thought'.[48] This is exactly what Nietzsche sought to do some 26 years later in 1887 with the publication of *On the Genealogy of Morality*.

To what extent was Nietzsche influenced, if at all, by the work of Sir Henry Maine?[49] We know that *Ancient Law* was 'probably the best-selling English law book of the nineteenth century: it sold around the world, sometimes in translation'.[50] It is not inconceivable that Nietzsche had sight of the work. We also know that Sir Henry Maine was interested in Eastern and Western thought and comparisons between the same as a result of his membership of the governor-general's council in India.[51] This interest in Eastern thought was shared by Nietzsche. Nietzsche's *Eternal Recurrence* has a profound Eastern influence.[52]

---

44 Cocks, ibid. See also A Diamond (ed), *The Victorian Achievement of Sir Henry Maine: A Centennial Reappraisal* (Cambridge University Press 2006); K Kumar, 'Maine and the Theory of Progress', in: *The Victorian Achievement of Sir Henry Maine: A Centennial Reappraisal* (Cambridge University Press 1991) 79, where it is observed, 'I would put Maine closer not so much to the nervous liberalism of Weber or Durkheim as to the radical despair of a Burckhardt or Nietzsche.' See also J Figgis, *The Will to Freedom: Or, The Gospel of Nietzsche and the Gospel of Christ - Being the Bross.* Lectures Delivered in Lake Forest College, Illinois (reprinted by Forgotten Books 2017) where Maine and Nietzsche's shared disillusioned viewed is briefly mentioned.

45 R C J Cocks, 'Maine, Sir Henry James Sumner' in *Oxford Dictionary of National Biography* (Oxford University Press 2004).

46 H Maine, *Ancient Law: Its Connection with the Early History of Society, and Its Relation to Modern Ideas* (John Murray 1861).

47 H Maine, *Dissertations on Early Law and Custom: Chiefly Selected from Lectures Delivered at Oxford* (John Murray 1883).

48 Maine (n 46) ix.

49 Both men were appointed to chairs at an early age. Henry Maine was 25 in 1847 when he was appointed Regius Professor of Civil Law in the University of Cambridge.

50 Cocks (n 43).

51 Ibid.

52 See further Tribe (n 17).

Both men also shared a deep interest in philology. Whilst Nietzsche's first university chair was in philology, Maine's very thought processes were dominated by the subject according to Cocks, and Burrows before him.[53]

It is also acknowledged that Maine was a 'force in European thought',[54] having influenced theorists such as Ferdinand Tönnies and Émile Durkheim, who as 'continental theorists [...] respected Maine'.[55] As Maine's biographer notes, he was, '[t]he least parochial of English jurists, after the publication of *Ancient Law*, his ideas became a part of continental thought'.[56] Was Nietzsche one of those who was influenced by Sir Henry Maine?

Maine's work is not, however, helpful to Nietzsche's creditor and debtor as the genesis of guilt thesis. Maine observed that, 'inferences [...] about societies earlier than the foundational texts on Roman law are speculative and baseless'.[57] This of course undermines Nietzsche's speculative use of the debtor-creditor relationship (see below). However, Maine himself engaged in conjecture despite his 'methodological strictures'.[58]

Maine's work does not appear in the published catalogue of Nietzsche's library.[59] Nor does any mention of the influence of Maine on Nietzsche appear in major work on Maine.[60] Maine's 1883 *Early Law and Custom* did however make frequent references to the Roman law of the Twelve Tables,[61] and other legal areas mentioned by Nietzsche in his 1887 book or with which he was familiar, e.g., the Laws of Manu.[62] Maine, much like Kohler would do in his own work, also made reference to Shakespeare in *Early Law and Custom*.[63]

---

53 Cocks (n 43) 20, citing J W Burrow, *Evolution and Society. A Study in Victorian Social Theory* (Cambridge University Press 1966) 149–153.

54 Vinogradoff (n 32).

55 Cocks (n 43).

56 Ibid.

57 Palmeri (n 26) 215.

58 Ibid.

59 There is no Maine reference between Mainländer (P Mainländer, *Die Philosophie der Erlösung* (Grieben 1876) and Maistre (F-X de Maistre, *Oeuvres choisies du Comte. Xavier de Maistre contenant: La jeune Siberienne, le Lepreux de la cite d'Aoste, et Quelques jour du voyage autour de ma chambre. Suivies d'une HarmoniePoetique au comte Xavier de Maistre par Lamartine* (E Hallberger 1868).

60 P Stein, *Legal Evolution: The Story of an Idea* (Cambridge University Press 1980); F E Dowrick, 'Legal Evolution: The Story of an Idea by Peter Stein' (1982) 41(1) *Cambridge Law Journal* 182, who mentions Savigny and Ihering in Germany and elsewhere individuals whom Maine influenced, including Vinogradoff and Weber. Nietzsche is not mentioned.

61 See e.g., Maine (n 47) 3; 6; 66; 75; 115; 337; 367; 369; 388.

62 Ibid., 30; 40; 41; 64; 70; 83; 94.

63 Ibid., 143–144.

Other important 19th century work on law is also absent from Nietzsche's library and writing.[64] This does not necessarily mean that he did not read it and was not influenced by it.

Nietzsche's Notebooks – References to Maine, Kohler, etc.

The second port of call for legal influences on Nietzsche are the notebooks that Nietzsche's carried around with him to jot down thoughts and ideas. The fruit of these notebooks are most famously, and controversially, represented by *The Will to Power*, a published collection of these notebooks. These were problematically drawn together by Nietzsche's sister, Elisabeth Förster-Nietzsche,[65] following his decline into insanity. This volume has been described as textually inaccurate and substantively misleading.[66]

The notebooks that date from the period when Nietzsche was writing *On the Genealogy of Morality* are particularly noteworthy. At least one of these notebooks survives.[67] In his 1904 inaugural lecture as the Corpus Professor of Jurisprudence at the University of Oxford, Sir Paul Vinogradoff was able to say, 'I can claim Maine as one of my most influential teachers.'[68] Do Nietzsche's published notebooks contain any such influence in terms of any influence on him of Sir Henry Maine or other legal scholars such as Josef Kohler? The short answer is that there is nothing of substance in the early notebooks which covers Nietzsche's legal influences. However, there is

---

64 E.g. H Broom, *The Philosophy of Law* (1876). See also S Amos, *The Science of Law* (D Appleton 1874); *A Systematic View of the Science of Jurisprudence* (Longmans Green 1872).

65 See further C Diethe, *Nietzsche's Sister and the Will to Power – A Biography of Elisabeth Förster-Nietzsche* (University of Illinois Press 2007).

66 F Nietzsche, *Writings from the Late Notebooks* (edited by R Bittner and translated by K Sturge) (Cambridge University Press 2003).

67 Octavo jotter (10.8 × 17.2) bound in a brown and yellow speckled cover, comprising 188 lined pages, written on throughout. The sheet forming pages 144/145 has been torn out. The jotter contains studies from the period when Nietzsche was planning to write a work called *The Transvaluation of All Values*. These studies were partly used for *Beyond Good and Evil* and for *On the Genealogy of Morals*. They include drafts, fragments, plans and preliminary notes, along with an index (on pages 131–121). Besides these, the jotter also contains various casual jottings and drafts of letters. The preliminary notes were set to paper between April and June 1885; the drafts of letters date from between 16th of April 1885 and the beginning of June 1885 http://www.nietzschesource.org/DFGA/N-VII-3 accessed 25 May 2023.

68 Vinogradoff (n 32) 119.

a major caveat for at least one published version of these notebooks, as Jensen has observed:

> There is a third problem with the selection [...] A considerable portion of Nietzsche's note-writing is permeated with the influences of the authors he was then reading. As is typical for any reader, Nietzsche would jot ideas, themes, criticisms and sometimes even direct phrasings from what he was reading into his notebooks, often without providing citation. A vast amount of scholarly effort has been spent tracing those all-important references within the notes, revealing Nietzsche to be in constant dialogue with the authors alongside or against whom he posited his views. Yet here no mention is made of Spir, Boscovich, Gerber, Rée or a host of other authors who had a vast and pervasive influence on Nietzsche during this time of writing.[69]

These omissions could also include legal writers who influenced Nietzsche. These omissions could include Kohler and Maine.

The late notebooks are also interesting.[70] At this stage in his life Nietzsche had resigned his university chair (1879) and had moved to the Engadine region of Switzerland to engage in a sustained period of writing. This productive ten-year period would last until 1889, when Nietzsche had the mental collapse from which he would never recover. His notebooks for this period, leading up to the 1887 publication of *On the Genealogy of Morality*, are the main source for potential clues on legal writers and their influence on Nietzsche's thoughts – both leading up to the publication of the book and in relation to the long cogitation on ideas that would eventually be expounded upon in the book when it was published in 1887.

The notebooks indicate that at some point between April and June 1885, Nietzsche jotted down the following: 'Our age feeds off, lives off the morality of previous ages.'[71] Was Nietzsche reading Kohler at the time he made this observation, and in particular Kohler's various passages on ancient law? Was Kohler's work present when Nietzsche was assimilating his thoughts on early society, and the law of debt and credit, and guilt and morality?

Nietzsche's late notebooks also contain a number of references to law and Rome. The references to law are, however, to a broader conception of natural law, whilst in relation to Rome, Nietzsche observes, 'Greek and Roman antiquity had need of a tyrannical and exaggerating anti-nature morality [...].'[72]

---

69 A K Jensen, 'Friedrich Nietzsche: Writings from the Early Notebooks' (2010) 18(3) *British Journal for the History of Philosophy* 531.

70 Nietzsche (n 66).

71 Ibid., 34[11], 1.

72 Ibid., 44[7], 53.

Again, did this thought permeate his feelings during the production stage of *On the Genealogy of Morality* leading up to 1887?

Interestingly, Nietzsche appears to contradict his published views on debt and punishment coalescing, at least in terms of how Rome's *Law of the Twelve Tables* might be conceptualised. At some point in the autumn of 1887, Nietzsche noted: '[l]ikewise, punishment should not be taken as penance; or as clearing a debt, as if there were a relation of barter between guilt and punishment – punishment does not purify, for crime does not pollute'.[73] However, as is demonstrated below, punishment was at least provided for as a *quid pro quo* of debt repayment failure. Indeed, it is this very relationship that Nietzsche himself harnesses in his quest to define the genesis of the emotion of guilt.[74]

The only substantial reference that is made to law comes in the spring of 1888 in notebook 14. Here Nietzsche notes: '[t]he lex talionis *may* be dictated by the spirit of retaliation (i.e., by a kind of moderation of the instinct for revenge); but in the case of Manu, for example, it's the need to have an equivalent, so as to expiate, to be 'free' again in a religious sense'.[75]

Nietzsche was therefore familiar with Manu, the author of a Sanskrit legal code,[76] and the principle of *lex talionis*, i.e., that punishment should reflect the injuries that have been caused through a criminal act. The Laws of Manu contained provisions for dealing with debt.[77] An edition of the Laws of Manu had been published at Oxford in 1886, a year before *On the Genealogy of Morality*, edited by a German.[78]

There is certainly evidence that Nietzsche was using Roman history in the same way that Maine, Spence[79] and Savigny had done. Nietzsche was using Roman law for 'the purpose of illustration[s] in the course of explaining human progress'.[80]

Nietzsche's correspondence provides another source of information on potential legal influences. The correspondence reveals that Nietzsche taught

---

73 Ibid., 10[50], 183.

74 Ibid., 10[2], 172; 10[7], 174.

75 Ibid., 14[193], 266.

76 Nietzsche's emphasis on 'may'.

77 A Kocourek and J H Wigmore, *Sources of Ancient and Primitive Law. Evolution of Law: Select Readings on the Origin and Development of Legal Institutions Vol 1* (Little, Brown and Company 1915) 469; P Haldar, 'The Sublime Codes of Manu: Law and Eighteenth Century Orientalism – A Special Issue on India' (2008) 9(3) *German Law Journal* 285.

78 G Buhler, *Seven Commentaries* (Clarendon Press 1886).

79 G Spence, *Inquiry into the Origin of the Laws and Political Institutions of Modern Europe, Particularly those of England* (John Murray 1826).

80 Cocks (n 43) 28.

lawyers[81] during his time as a lecturer in rhetoric and he also had friends in the legal profession.[82]

Nietzsche's correspondence also sheds light on his view of credit and debt in the period of his life after he left Bassel. He noted: '[t]he Sorrento manuscript has gone to the devil; my move and the eventual departure from Bassel have done away completely with several things – a blessing for me, for such old manuscripts eye me like creditors'.[83]

It is almost certain that Nietzsche was influenced by the work of Jospeh Kohler; the main piece of evidence being Kohler recounting his conversation with Nietzsche's sister.

SECTION B: NIETZSCHE'S USE OF LEGAL HISTORY

In this part of the chapter, Nietzsche's use of legal history in *On the Genealogy of Morality* is examined. This includes Nietzsche's use of Roman law.[84] Following this treatment, Nietzsche's guilt genesis thesis is examined. It has been observed that 'Nietzsche takes almost no notice of the civil law'.[85] What follows proves this contention to be wrong, whichever way civil law is defined. Nietzsche was familiar with both private law and Roman law.

Nietzsche had a number of reasons to mull on the debtor-creditor relationship and insolvency. He was from a relatively poor family. On his youthful appointment at the University of Basel in 1869, Nietzsche received his first salary, a factor which played no small part in his deciding to take up the philology post, even though his heart had already turned to philosophy. This newfound wealth enabled Nietzsche to seriously indulge his love of clothes (in addition to cakes). He would always be immaculate, bordering on dandyish.

Nietzsche's books didn't sell well, particularly during his sane lifetime. Indeed, he wrote and published *On the Genealogy of Morality* specifically to improve the sales of his earlier books.[86] Great fame and an associated increase in the sale of those books came after his decline into insanity and subsequent death.

---

81 Basel, November 7th, 1872 from Nietzsche to Malwida von Meysenbug, in C Middleton (ed), *Selected Letters of Friedrich Nietzsche* (Hackett Publishing Company 1996) 107.

82 Basel, mid-March [1873] to Erwin Rodhe, in Middleton (n 81) 117.

83 Middleton (n 81) 117.

84 For a discussion of Nietzsche use of Greek history see H Heit and A K Jensen (eds), *Nietzsche as a Scholar of Antiquity* (Bloomsbury 2015).

85 Cowan (n 3)152.

86 See Letter to Peter Gast, 18 July 1887, in Middleton (n 81) 269.

On the Genealogy of Morality contains Nietzsche vision of the pre-history of the human animal. For him, this period is the most important historical period in human history. It is in this time period that he says the constituent characteristics of man were forged. In the second essay, Nietzsche observes: '[...] every injury has its *equivalent* and can be paid in compensation, if only through the *pain* of the person who injures'.[87]

Nietzsche continues:

> and where did this primeval, deeply-rooted and perhaps now ineradicable idea gain its power, this idea of an equivalence between injury and pain? ...*in the contractual relationship between creditor and debtor,* ***which is as old as the very conception of a 'legal subject'*** *and itself refers back to the basic forms of buying, selling, bartering, trade and traffic.*[88]

Is Nietzsche correct in terms of his view that the law of debtor and creditor made up some of our earliest approaches to law? Establishing this is important, as this view provides the foundation upon which Nietzsche builds his subsequent view of the genesis of guilt.

It is not clear whether Nietzsche read Maine. As noted above, Nietzsche's notebooks do not contain reference to the Corpus Professor of Jurisprudence. Sir Henry Maine's main book on early history was published in 1861, some 26 years before the publication of *On the Genealogy of Morality* in 1887. As Vinogradoff observes, Maine's work included 'an extensive criticism of Rosseau's speculations on primitive man'.[89] Maine was actively engaged in writing about early society and the activity of early man.

Early Credit Use

Early society was based on barter; the simple exchange of goods between citizens.[90] Credit did not exist, as we now know it.[91] As Levinthal has observed, '[c]edit is an institution that lives by virtue of man's confidence in

---

[87] Ibid., 41.

[88] Ibid., chapter author's italicised and bold emphasis.

[89] Vinogradoff (n 32) 122.

[90] For a discussion of this stage of human development see: P Vinogradoff, *Outlines of Historical Jurisprudence. Vol 1 – Introduction & Tribal Law* (Oxford University Press 1920) 163. Vinogradoff briefly engages with Nietzsche's work. After quoting various extracts he notes, 'It is something of an anti-climax to survey the pale statements of popular utilitarians after having caught a glimpse of the fierce glare of Nietzsche's invectives.' (45).

[91] For a discussion of the growth of credit (and its absence in early societies) see: I Fletcher, *The Law of Insolvency* (Sweet & Maxwell 2014) 3–4.

his fellow-man's good faith'.[92] Good faith is therefore a key ingredient in the credit relationship and because, as Maine has observed, early society and good faith were strangers,[93] we find little evidence of credit and systems to deal with its casualties. It has been observed that commercial credit was not in use at the time of *Magna Carta*,[94] or before; '[p]rivate credit, that bane of society, did not at that period exist, nor even some time after the conquest, exist in this country'.[95] As Freedman observed, '[l]ife then [1269] was primitive, trade undeveloped, and confidence was extended within the narrow compass of close intimacy and kinship'.[96] Consequently, with this undeveloped market in credit, very early responses to debt default were largely non-existent until the 19th Century. Saxon laws,[97] we are told, had no mechanisms for dealing with debtors because contracts for credit were non-existent.[98]

So is Nietzsche correct to argue that debt and credit relations existed *prior* to the advent of society? Nietzsche is engaging in conjecture; speculation about a time period when there is no evidence to support his claims. As Palmeri has observed, in relation to *On the Genealogy of Morality*, Nietzsche provides, 'a history of the origins of morality in times and manners for which there is little if any direct evidence, describing a process by conjecture and speculation'.[99] This is a conjectural history of 'an unknowable past'.[100]

The Debtor's Body as Security

Nietzsche makes a number of interesting observations regarding the body of the debtor whilst he explores ingredients in the cauldron of early human devel-

[92] L E Levinthal, 'The Early History of Bankruptcy Law' (1918) 66 *University of Pennsylvania Law Review* 223, 228.

[93] Maine (n 46) 303.

[94] June 15, 1215. See: *TO. An Inquiry Into the Practice of Imprisonment for Debt and A Refutation of Mr James Stephen's Doctrine. To which is added a Hint for Relief of both Creditor and Debtor. London, Printed for J. Towers in Fore-Street. M.DCC. LXXIII,* at preface and 7.

[95] Ibid., 7. Caution has to be exercised with this text as an 18th century text is not good evidence for the situation in 1215.

[96] A L Freedman, 'Imprisonment for Debt' (1928) 2(4) *Temple Law Quarterly* 330, 331.

[97] For a discussion of law in this period see J Hudson, *The Oxford History of the Laws of England Volume II – 871–1216* (Oxford University Press 2012).

[98] Ibid., 8.

[99] Palmeri (n 26) 179.

[100] Ibid.

opment. These comments touch on the law of Ancient Egypt and Roman law. For example, Nietzsche notes:

> The debtor, in order to inspire confidence that the promise of repayment will be honoured, in order to give a guarantee of the solemnity and sanctity of his promise, and in order to etch the duty and obligation of repayment into his conscience, pawns something to the creditor by means of the contract in case he does not pay, something that he still 'possesses' and controls, for example, his body, or his wife, or his freedom, or his life (or in certain religious circumstances, even his after-life, the salvation of his soul, finally, even his peace in the grave: as in Egypt, where the corpse of a debtor found no peace from the creditor even in the grave – and this peace meant a pot precisely to the Egyptians).[101]

He continues:

> the creditor could inflict all kinds of dishonour and torture on the body of the debtor, for example, cutting as much flesh off as seemed appropriate for the debt: – from this standpoint there were everywhere, early on, estimates that went into horrifyingly minute and fastidious detail, legally drawn up estimates for individual limbs and parts of the body.[102]

His editor, Ansell-Pearson summarises this as:

> at the same time the creditor is entitled to inflict all kinds of dishonour and torture on the body of the debtor; for example, 'cutting off as much flesh as seemed appropriate for the debt'. Pleasure is taken in the cruelty inflicted on the debtor, and this is part of the compensation and enjoyment of the right to exercise power.[103]

Ansell-Pearson continues: '[t]his particular and curious experience of pleasure also becomes a spectacle for the community or society and gives it a festive aspect'.[104]

How accurate is this use of history by both Nietzsche and his editor? To what extent have we seen this sort of behaviour in insolvency treatment over time?

Imprisonment for debt and hanging were of course not the only treatments that were known to early insolvents.[105] Numerous other methods of punishment were used right up to the early modern period.

---

101 Nietzsche (n 5) xxx.
102 Ibid.
103 Ibid., xxi.
104 Ibid.
105 J Tribe, 'The Imprisonment for Debt Jurisdiction' (2018) 31 *Insolvency Intelligence* 92; 'Bankruptcy and Capital Punishment in the 18th and 19th Centuries' (2019) 22 *Insolvency Intelligence* 44.

An Act for the better relief of the creditors against such as shall become bankrupts[106] stipulated that if a bankrupt refused to provide information on examination by the bankruptcy commissioners as to the whereabouts of his possessions, once lawfully convicted he would be made to, 'stand upon the pillory in some public place by the space of two hours, and have one of his ears nailed to the pillory and cut off'.[107] Being placed in the pillory often resulted in death for the unfortunate incumbent.[108]

Whipping[109] was used by the bankruptcy commissioners to obtain information from debtors who did not freely speak of the whereabouts of their property. In one early bankruptcy bill introduced by Sir Francis Crane, a suggestion was made that some bankrupts should be whipped to death. Punishment could also include transportation for life and imprisonment with hard labour.

One of the least callous treatments forced upon debtors was the wearing of conspicuous apparel or, as Ford has observed, 'distinguishing garb'.[110] The garments ensured that debtors were singled out from ordinary individuals. This led to stigmatisation[111] which one commentator has called a 'happy expedient'.[112] In Scotland, insolvents were forced to wear an outfit consisting of a yellow and brown bonnet and tights whilst sitting in the public square between 10 and 12

---

[106] James I 1604 c15.

[107] James I 1604 c15. This practice was not restricted to the English courts. Shaiman has suggested that as late as 1785 the American 'Bankruptcy Act 1785 [...] section XVII [...] provided that upon conviction for fraud the bankrupt shall be set upon the pillory for two hours and have one of his ears nailed to the pillory and cut off.' This statute had jurisdictional effect in the State of Pennsylvania, see S L Shaiman, 'The History of Imprisonment for Debt and Insolvency Laws in Pennsylvania as They Evolved from the Common Law' (1960) 4(3) *American Journal of Legal History* 204, 216.

[108] W Andrews, *Bygone Punishments* (William Andrews & Co 1899)156.

[109] Ibid., 209. See also C Hill, *The Century of Revolution: 1603–1714* (Routledge 1980) 25, where he observes that 'whipping home' was a prescribed penalty for unlicensed beggars. As Hill further observes at page 45, this treatment would not be extended to the gentry, who 'were exempt from the servile punishment of flogging'.

[110] 'Many debtors who escaped imprisonment were compelled to wear a distinguishing garb' (R Ford, 'Imprisonment for Debt' (1926) 25(1) *Michigan Law Review* 24, 26).

[111] For a relatively modern example of stigmatising activities, see B Egan, *The Debt Merchants* Focus, vol.3, no.10, 14 October 1968, which describes debt default registers and their use to shame debtors into paying. The wearing of clothes as a tool of punishment has a long history. Male Greek deserters were forced to wear female apparel and then made to appear in public (Heinrich Oppenheimer, *The Rationale of Punishment* (University of London Press 1913) 127).

[112] '[...] it seems a happy expedient to stigmatise and make public certain kinds of willful misconduct', Westminster Review, *Review of the Law of Bankruptcy*, Volume 52 (1849) 452.

o'clock after adjudication of their bankruptcy.[113] In France, insolvents were forced to wear a green hat.[114] In Rotterdam and Leyden, debtors were not forced to wear distinguishing garments; indeed, the opposite was true. They were forced to undertake public penance in their 'undermost garments'. The debtor would undertake this before the Town House for a proscribed period of days for one hour a day from half past eleven until half past twelve.[115] In Spain, insolvents were made to wear an iron collar 'one finger thick'.[116]

Satisfaction could also be made to the creditor through debtor servitude. This was certainly a feature of Roman insolvency law. It is to Nietzsche's observations on that topic that we can now turn.

Nietzsche and Roman Law[117]

Nietzsche used the famous Twelve Tables in his discussion of the origin and development of human qualities. He noted:

> I regard it as definite progress and proof of a freer, more open-handed calculation, of a more Roman and pricing of justice, when Rome's code of the Twelve Tables decreed that it did not matter how much or how little a creditor cut off in such a circumstance, 'si plus minusve secuerunt, ne fraude esto'.[118]

---

[113] S A Riesenfeld, 'The Evolution of Modern Bankruptcy Law: A Comparison of the Recent Bankruptcy Acts of Italy and the United States' (1947) 31 *Minnesota Law Review* 401, 441, citing Acts of Sederunt, February 26th 1665, January 23rd, 1673, July 18th, 1688, 1 Acts of Sederunt, 58, 78, 161. Oppenheimer (n 111) reminds us (at page 127) that a Spartan treatment for cowardice would involve similar stigmatising approaches. A Spartan coward would be forced to clothe themselves in rags, remain unshaven and be thrashed.

[114] Ibid., citing J Wessels, *History of Roman-Dutch Law* (African Book Company 1908) 665.

[115] Riesenfeld (n 113), citing Ordinance of July 30th, 1501; Leyden; 1519, Rotterdam, cited by S Van Leeuwen, *Comm. On Roman Dutch Law* (transl. by Kotze 1923) 334.

[116] Riesenfeld (n 113), citing Law of 1490, *Nueva Recopilacio,* Book 5, Title 15, Law 6. Drinker-Bowen observes that during a whipping of a miscreant, 'the Spanish fashion [was to] let hot bacon be dripped on him with every lash!' (See C Drinker Bowen. *The Lion and the Throne: The Life and Times of Sir Edward Coke (1552–1634)* (Little Brown and Company 1985) 442).

[117] For a discussion of Roman approaches to insolvency see R W Lee, *The Elements of Roman Law* (Sweet & Maxwell 1952) 441–445.

[118] Nietzsche (n 5).

Is this an accurate reflection of the operation of the Roman law of debt? How were debtors treated in the classical period?[119] It has been noted that 'debt was a powerful and frequently troublesome factor in ancient society'.[120] One commentator has observed, '[i]n ancient systems of law, insolvency *per se* was looked upon as something irregular and fraudulent, whether the debtor was actually honest or dishonest'.[121] There were consequentially responses to breakdown in these debt relationships. The Greeks took an approach to insolvency that was based very much on the idea that a creditor would be justifiably damaged if they had been so careless as to lend to a debtor who could not pay back the sum owed.[122] This 'serves you right' approach was deemed advantageous in that in caused creditors to be more cautious about future lending decisions. This approach is perhaps best exemplified by a mid-19th century commentator, who observed, '[...] he who gives credit deserves any loss which may arise therefrom [...]'.[123]

It has long been recognised that Roman law contained some of the seed elements of regulation that subsequently dealt with what we would now call insolvency issues.[124] Indeed, Roman law approaches to insolvent estate management have even been highlighted as possibly influencing the Tudor legislature when they introduced the 1542 Act.[125] The systems that Roman law[126] formulated to deal with credit breakdown were to some extent typified by a harshness that is perhaps best enunciated by Portia's vivid depiction of the fate of a non-paying merchant in Shakespeare's *The Merchant of Venice*,

---

119 On this treatment see further H Rajak, 'The Culture of Bankruptcy' in P Omar, (ed). *International Insolvency Law: Themes and Perspectives* (Ashgate, 2008) 8–11; Levinthal (n 112), 230–231, for a brief exposition of the Code of Hammurabi, Hebrew debt provisions, the approach of the Pharaohs and the law of Rome.

120 Rajak (n 119).

121 Levinthal (n 92) 237.

122 M Gagarin, *Early Greek Law* (University of California Press 1986).

123 Editorial in *Bankruptcy Law Reform.* Bankers Magazine and Journal of the Money Market (1849) 9, 322-326, 324. The commentator notes that such a view is 'fallacious'.

124 See e.g., T H Jackson, *The Logic and Limits of Bankruptcy Law* (Harvard University Press 1986) 1. Jackson's historical treatment is rather brief and mixes the classical and medieval treatment of debtors in a little under two sentences. He fails to discuss the alternative derivation of the term bankruptcy and relies perhaps too heavily on Treiman.

125 R H Helmholz, *Canon Law and the Law of England* (Hambledon Press 1987) 305.

126 For one 19th century critique of Roman law's approach to debt see G J Bell, *Commentaries on the Laws of Scotland, and on the Principles of Merchantile Jurisprudence, Considered in Relation to Bankruptcy; Competitions of Creditors; and Imprisonment for Debt* (William Blackwood 1826) 3.

arguably the most famous literary illustration of what might happen to a fictional Venetian debtor who did not pay their creditor. Portia darkly observes:

> this bond is forfeit,
> And lawfully by this the Jew may claim
> A pound of flesh, to be by him cut off[127]

The 'terrible law of the Twelve Tables'[128] advocated a cruel choice for the debtor. They faced banishment beyond the Tiber or having their body divided amongst their creditors in proportionate pieces to their respective claims,[129] which has a curious echo in later English insolvency law. The debtor and his family could also imprisoned, chained and pressed into hard labour.[130] Perpetual banishment into foreign slavery beyond the Tiber could also befall a debtor and his family.[131] Servitude, as one commentator has noted, was a feature of many early societies.[132] Forcing a debtor to work to make repayment to his creditor was seen as both a recovery mechanism and a prohibitive measure against irresponsible credit use.[133] This rather strict approach to debtor treatment by the Romans has a forerunner in the ancients. As Maine observes, in the context of early contract law, 'I mean the extraordinary and uniform severity of very ancient systems of law to debtors, and the extravagant powers which they lodge with creditors.'[134] Nietzsche may have been familiar with this piece of writing from Maine.

There were other treatments at Roman law that were particularly forward-looking. Treatment was not wholly restricted to what we might consider severe. Roman law[135] also provided for a number of remedies that have echoes in modern approaches to insolvent estate management. *Cession*

---

[127] W Shakespeare, *The Merchant of Venice*, Act Four, Scene One (1600).

[128] W Blackstone, *Commentaries on the Laws of England, Book the Second. Volume II* (Clarendon Press 1829) 472.

[129] Ibid. Blackstone notes that this interpretation of '*de debitore in partes secando*' is potentially problematic and that some esteemed commentators have commented to this effect.

[130] Ibid.

[131] Ibid.

[132] W R Cornish and G N Clark, *Law and Society in England 1750–1950* (Sweet & Maxwell 1989) 228.

[133] On roman debtor treatment, see further M W Frederikson, 'Caesar, Cicero and the Problem of Debt' (1966) 56 *Journal of Roman Studies* 128.

[134] H S Maine, *Ancient Law: its Connection with the Early History of Society and its Relation to Modern Ideas* (14th edn, John Murray 1891) 267.

[135] W W Buckland, *A Textbook of Roman Law from Augustus to Justinian* (Cambridge University Press 1921); *A Textbook of Roman Law from Augustus to Justinian* (3rd edn, Cambridge University Press 1966).

allowed a debtor to place all of his property into the hands of his creditors. In exchange he would not be imprisoned by his creditors. *Cessio bonorum*[136] also permitted debtors to compromise with their creditors. The Romans also recognised a species of moratorium within a voluntary arrangement.[137]

Relief or apportionment for the debtor was also provided at Roman law. The *beneficium competemtiae* allowed the debtor to keep some of his property.[138]

Rajak has highlighted that both *nexum* and *addicto* existed at Roman law as a method of termly repayment whereby the debtor worked off his indebtedness to his creditors.[139] Radin has also shown that Roman law developed mechanisms to deal with fraudulent conveyances.[140]

SECTION 3: NIETZSCHE AND GUILT

The Consciousness of Guilt[141]

This takes us to Nietzsche and his discussion of the debtor-creditor relationship.

Nietzsche published *On the Genealogy of Morality*[142] in 1887. In the second essay in the book, Nietzsche states that 'the main moral concept "Schull" ("guilt") descends from the very material concept of "Schulden" ("debts")'.[143] It is with this observation that Nietzsche introduces a link between guilt and credit obligations. It is also with this observation that Nietzsche first discusses his view of the debtor-creditor relationship.

As Sturge has noted, Nietzsche engaged in 'extraordinary punning exploitation of the etymological relationships between German words'.[144] In relation to 'schuld' ('guilt') and 'schulden' ('debts'), this give rise to pause for thought in relation to translation issues but also to etymological issues with the two terms.

---

136 On *cessio bonorum* and related subjects see: G J Bell, *Commentaries on the Recent Statutes Relative to Diligence or Execution against the Moveable Estate, Imprisonment, Cessio Bonorum, and Sequestration in Mercantile Bankruptcy, with the Relative Acts of Parliament.* 4to Edinburgh, 1840.

137 D Graham, *Tudor Insolvencies* (1997) June(23) *Phoenix* 13.

138 W W Buckland, *Main Institutions of Roman Law* (Cambridge University Press 1931) 395.

139 Rajak (n 119) 9.

140 M Radin, 'Fraudulent Conveyances at Roman Law' (1931) 18(2) *Virginia Law Review* 109.

141 For a discussion of Nietzsche and guilt from a criminal law perspective see M Valverde, 'Pain Memory, and the Creation of the Liberal Legal Subject: Nietzsche on Criminal Law' in P Goodrich and M. Valverde (eds), *Nietzsche and Legal Theory: Half-written Laws* (Routledge 2005) 67.

142 Nietzsche (n 5) 40–43.

143 Ibid., 40.

144 Nietzsche (n 66) xlii.

Here, then, we see Nietzsche commencing his explanation of the evolution of guilt. Indebtedness provides the genesis of guilt. Obligation is seen as debt, debt in turn manifests itself as guilt.

Nietzsche's editor notes that 'in the earliest societies a person is answerable for their deeds and there is an obligation to honouring debts'.[145] This was the 'original economic relationship'[146] which emphasises 'the importance of understanding the economic basis of human life'.[147]

The editor continues '[f]or Nietzsche this [...] establishes the basic relationship between the community and the individual, that of creditor and debtor'.[148]

As has been shown, debt has a long and interesting history.[149]

Guilt and Barter?

If Nietzsche is right that the debtor-creditor relationship is the foundation of guilt as a human emotion, was it possible to have guilt before that relationship? Did humans in societies based on barter have guilt as a consequence of barter relationships? Indeed, this is if humans did live in groups prior to the advent of the debtor-creditor relationship.

Did individuals reflect after the barter has been done, that they individually profited by bartering a less valuable item? Do they then feel guilt regarding that imbalance? Or does the simple act of barter, mutual exchange, mean just that, namely, that in engaging in barter they recognise that the goods are of equal value and no subsequent guilt can arise from the exchange. So, any barter exchange is intrinsically a fair exchange of goods.

CONCLUSION

Writing in 1960, Cowan asked: '[w]hy should we crowd into the dilapidated, overpopulated and understaffed mansions we call our minds so unruly a tenant as Nietzsche? I answer that we should let him in because he is both absolutely honest and also highly talented'.[150]

The analysis in this chapter has shown that Nietzsche is certainly worth letting in to help us think about private law issues and the debtor-creditor relationship in particular. However, the chapter has shown that the honest use of ideas and sources is not necessarily a cardinal aspect of Nietzsche's work.

---

145 Nietzsche (n 5).
146 Ibid., xx.
147 Ibid., xxi.
148 Ibid., xxii.
149 See further D Graeber, *Debt: The First 5,000 Years* (Melville House 2011).
150 Cowan (n 3) 166.

In the realm of insolvency law, the application of Nietzsche reminds us of the deep undercurrents which subsist beneath the surface of the subject of insolvency. For Nietzsche, the human condition springs from the debtor and creditor relationship. This contextualises the consequences for those suffering in debt, in terms of anxiety, stress and the relief that comes from discharge. As with Schopenhauer, who shows us that the will to life elicits powerful feelings in love, Nietzsche offers some consolation to those struggling with debt and its consequences.

7. A Rawlsian approach to preventive restructuring

Stathis Potamitis and Xenophon Paparrigopoulos

INTRODUCTION

The philosophical underpinnings of insolvency law, especially as concerns the extension of collective proceedings to situations preceding formal insolvency (thus extending to debtors who are facing only a likelihood of insolvency) have not been sufficiently developed. In this chapter, we explore the application of Rawls' two principles of justice to justify the workings of a restructuring proceeding, for example with the features introduced into the laws of the European Union by the 2019 Restructuring Directive. We conclude that the Rawlsian perspective seems eminently appropriate to illuminate and guide the Directive's implementation.

SOME INTRODUCTORY COMMENTS ON RAWLS' THEORY OF JUSTICE

Rawls' theory of justice is intended to apply to society's 'basic structure'.[1] It is about how the fundamental constitutional arrangements of a society must be fashioned for a society to be just and 'well ordered'.[2] Predictably, these fundamental principles, as concretised in Rawls' two principles of justice,

---

1 J Rawls, *A Theory of Justice* (Belknap 1999) 6.

2 Rawls defines a society as 'well-ordered' if it is 'designed to advance the good of its members and effectively regulated by a public conception of justice [...] it is a society in which everyone accepts and knows that the others accept the same principles of justice, and the basic social institutions satisfy and are known to satisfy these principles': Rawls (n 1) 397. Rawls notes elsewhere, that in a well-ordered society, 'while men may put forth excessive demands on one another, they nevertheless acknowledge a common point of view for which their claims may be adjudicated': Rawls (n 1) 4.

provide for the absolute and equal protection of fundamental rights, but also for the principles which should govern the distribution of economic and other social benefits.

As restated in the second edition of *A Theory of Justice*,[3] Rawls' two principles of justice read as follows:

> First: each person is to have an equal right to the most extensive scheme of equal basic liberties compatible with a similar scheme of liberties for others. Second: social and economic inequalities are to be arranged so that they are both (a) reasonably expected to be to everyone's advantage, and (b) attached to positions and offices open to all.

As further elaborated, the second principle of justice, known as the 'difference principle', states that: 'Social and economic inequalities are to be arranged so that they are both (a) to the greatest expected benefit of the least advantaged and (b) attached to offices and positions open to all under conditions of fair equality of opportunity.'[4]

Notice already, that, within Rawls' theory, property rights, traditionally included in the 'classic catalogue' of fundamental rights, are dealt with within the context of the second principle of justice. They are not absolute.

The guiding idea behind the two principles of justice is that the principles of justice for the basic structure of society are the object of an 'original agreement' reached among 'rational persons concerned to further their own interest' and accepted 'in an initial position or equality'.[5] Among the essential features of the original position is that: '[N]o one knows his place in society, his class position or social status, nor does anyone know his fortune in the distribution of natural assets and abilities, his intelligence, strength, and the like.'

In other words, the principles of justice are chosen behind what Rawls calls 'a veil of ignorance'.[6]

According to Rawls, the principles of justice chosen under the conditions ensured by the veil of ignorance guarantee that these principles will be fair; and thus, Rawls calls his concept of justice, 'justice as fairness'.[7]

The device of the original position seems to be placing Rawls in the tradition of social contract theories. However, it is to be noted that, ultimately, the justification and the normative force of the two principles of justice does not depend or ensue from an agreement, properly speaking, but, rather, from the

---

3 Ibid., 53.
4 Ibid., 72.
5 Ibid., 10–11.
6 Ibid.
7 Ibid., 3.

fairness of the conditions which apply to the original position and lead, in fact, to an unanimous consent, or, better, to conclusions which no reasonable and fairly-minded person can negate.[8] Indeed, as Rawls himself notes, the original position, rather than being the justificatory foundation of the normative validity of the two principles of justice, is more of a 'device of representation'.[9]

Rawls describes the imaginary process of deliberation which takes place behind the veil of ignorance as a process of discussing and choosing among various possible candidate-theories of social justice.[10] Utilitarianism is one of them and readily rejected by the parties at the original position.[11] Wealth (or utility, or preferences) maximisation is not an appealing principle from the standpoint of the original position. As the veil of ignorance hides from participants the knowledge of their actual social and economic status, their natural endowments or handicaps, but also of their particular beliefs, inclinations, religious affiliation, etc., the participants at the original position have no reasonable incentive to opt for a social structure and a constitution which, by outcome, favours majority preferences and disfavours minorities.

Notice, however, that a quasi-utilitarian element subsides in the difference principle: even from the standpoint of the original position participants have no incentive to ban entirely all social and economic inequalities which may favour wealth maximisation, provided, however, that permitted, relatively minor inequalities, work for the 'greatest benefit of the least advantaged.' Rawls hopes that by allowing such differences, his theory of justice will still be consistent with the demands of efficiency.[12]

When a society's basic structure is just, i.e., fair and in conformity with the two principles of justice, people are entitled to form 'legitimate expectations' on the basis of the rights and duties accorded by positive law. These 'legitimate expectations' are to be honoured irrespective of the fact that they may lead occasionally to outcomes which may not always seems as morally satisfactory. For example, the market may end up allocating certain benefits to people who would not be generally seen as 'deserving' them in the moral sense; and, indeed, Rawls notes that this is frequently the case.[13] However, honouring

---

8 As commentators have observed, hypothetical agreements cannot be binding as such: Nagel succinctly noted: 'it is not the agreement that justifies what has been agreed to, but rather whatever justifies the agreement itself', T Nagel, 'Rawls on Justice' in N Daniels (ed.), *Reading Rawls – Critical Studies of A Theory of Justice* (Blackwell 1975) 5.

9 J Rawls, *Political Liberalism* (Columbia University Press 1993) 25.

10 Rawls (n 1) 105.

11 Indeed, Rawls' theory is meant to provide an alternative to the dominant utilitarian tradition in moral and political theory.

12 Rawls (n 1) 73.

13 Ibid., 273.

legitimate expectations is just, provided, of course, that the fundamental constitutional principles of the society are just in a Rawlsian sense, and that positive law respects such constitutional principles.

Assuming that society's basic structure satisfies the two principles of justice, the Rawlsian approach may seem *prima facie* unsuitable when it comes to assessing secondary, so to speak, legal expectations which have arisen within the context of an existing system of positive law. However, Rawls' theory contains some fundamental insights which may be useful in assessing the fairness of the distribution of rights and duties whenever a situation of conflicting interests may potentially arise. It may therefore possibly be fruitfully applied when, e.g., the interests of creditors, shareholders and other stakeholders of a distressed company are in conflict, and a solution through restructuring is on the table.

WHY LEGISLATE A PREVENTIVE RESTRUCTURING PROCEEDING?

The terms of a potential restructuring of an enterprise could, in principle, have been the subject of an *ex ante* agreement – i.e., when parties became stakeholders in the enterprise (employees, shareholders, creditors, suppliers, etc.) they could have been asked to agree to the terms of an agreement that would spell out the fate of their respective claims in the event that the enterprise got into such difficulties as to require a preventive restructuring to avoid insolvency. In that case we would have a level of confidence that the distribution of rights and benefits (as well as sacrifices, such as write-offs) provided by that *ex ante* agreement should be seen as fair (the Rawlsian idea of the 'original position').

Such an original agreement would reflect the bargain struck among the stakeholders at the time when they had no knowledge of how their respective investment in the enterprise would perform, (the Rawlsian idea of the 'veil of ignorance'). One can also presume that it would reflect the parties' respective appetite for risk, and the position in which they would accept to find themselves in the case of failure, so as to reveal what would be acceptable as the outcome for the least advantaged of the group of the stakeholders.

However, such an agreement is impossible in practice; instead, different jurisdictions have introduced rules to permit a *post facto* agreement among stakeholders for the restructuring of a troubled entity. The attempt in this chapter is to examine whether Rawls' principles of justice help in devising and assessing the fairness of a legislated restructuring framework.

Since such frameworks (such as the one introduced by the Directive[14] that we shall use as our test case in this chapter) allow for an agreement to be contracted by majority, even against the opposition of a significant minority of creditors, Rawls' idea that a fair agreement should not be the outcome of a utilitarian calculus that would maximise overall utility but which would inevitably leave minority stakeholders worse off would render the treatment of those dissenting minorities of critical significance in terms of the fairness of the scheme.

One might also consider in assessing such a scheme from the point of view of whether it adopts a disinterested and intersubjective point of view when considering possible outcomes for the different stakeholders, whether it reflects a balancing of the interests not only of creditors (and of each of those classes) but also of employees, shareholders, customers, suppliers, and the broader economic environment that may be impacted by the failure of an enterprise. If those criteria were to be satisfied one could possibly accept the legislative rules as an acceptable substitute of the unanimous assent of all stakeholders at the original stage.

As already noted in our introductory comments, Rawls' second principle of justice – the so-called 'difference principle' – also furnishes a possibly valuable substantive insight: namely, that a just distribution of benefits (economic and moral advantages) *does not* preclude a (reasonably) unequal distribution of such advantages, *provided*, however, that this unequal distribution works also for the benefit of the stakeholders who turn out to be worse off.

The idea is that even when a particular distribution is assessed from an *ex ante* point of view, the fair outcome that would be unanimously chosen by all potentially affected parties would not necessarily consist in a (pro-rata) absolutely equal distribution of benefits, but would leave room for a potentially unequal (albeit not completely lop-sided) distribution, if this inequality would lead to a greater share in the resulting benefits of the worse-off stakeholder.

The intuitive idea is simple: worse-off stakeholders would be willing to forego certain of their rights and allow other stakeholders to end up in a relatively better position than a mathematically equal distribution would warrant, if this relative advantage would work in the former's relative benefit. The intervention by means of legislation of a restructuring proceeding is intended to allow this intuition to be translated into concrete practical outcomes.

---

[14] Directive (EU) 2019/1023 of the European Parliament and of the Council of 20 June 2019 on preventive restructuring frameworks, on discharge of debt and disqualifications, and on measures to increase the efficiency of procedures concerning restructuring, insolvency and discharge of debt, and amending Directive (EU) 2017/1132 (Directive on restructuring and insolvency [2017] OJ L 172/18.

It bears emphasising that apart from the issues of fairness and efficiency as directly concern the stakeholders of the business in question, there is the issue of the interests of the wider community to which they belong and in which they transact. For example, preserving the absolute priority of certain secured creditors (e.g., creditors secured with financial collateral, per the collateral directive (2002/47)), may be neither efficient nor fair from the point of view of the stakeholders of the business in distress, in particular as it may deprive it from the most liquid assets at a time when liquidity is needed the most. However, as the businesses that are not in distress are normally many more than those in distress and allowing them to grant effective security increases the overall economic efficiency, the preferential treatment can be justified. Issues of fairness and efficiency that concern the stakeholders of the business in distress cannot be insulated from considerations of the impact of policy choices on the wider community.[15]

This approach is fully compatible with a number of principles of restructuring: to restructuring as such, as an alternative to letting the distressed entity go bankrupt to the detriment of workers, suppliers, possibly non-secured creditors and, certainly, the society at large; also, with the 'best-interest-of-creditors' test and the prerogatives accorded to majority stakeholders who, presumably, have a greater interest in securing the viability of the distressed business in the long-run.

Insolvency law focuses on the maximum possible preservation of value in the event of a failure; to the extent that the focus is on business failures, insolvency law serves the maximum possible preservation of the value of that business. Traditionally, the value of a business would reside primarily in its tangible assets, fixed assets such as real estate, machinery, and production lines, as well as raw materials, inventory and claims from its customers. This may explain why the main focus of traditional business insolvency proceedings is on the orderly liquidation of such fixed assets. However, recent economic developments mean that, at least in developed economies, business value resides less in tangible assets and increasingly more in intangible assets.[16]

---

[15] We would like to thank our partner Alexandros Metallinos for this insight.

[16] 'Over the last two decades, intangible assets have grown in importance in many OECD economies and the growth rate of intangible investment has often surpassed that of tangible investment (Carol A Corrado and Charles R Hulten, 'How Do You Measure a "Technological Revolution?"' (2010) 100(2) *American Economic Review* 99). There has been growing recognition that besides R&D activities, new software, database, copyrights, designs, trademarks, organisation and distribution networks are increasingly important for productivity growth. Overall, intangible assets have become a key component of the production function for many firms, a driver for innovation and growth. The unprecedented development of new technologies is increasingly perceived as the source of future growth and potentially a new engine to reverse the productivity slow-

However, intangible assets are tied, to a significant extent, to a business maintaining its going concern. This may explain why liquidation valuations of troubled debtors are limited to the expected recovery from the sale of assets, excluding most intangible assets. Accordingly, in economies where a significant part of the value of a business resides in its intangible assets, a process by which going-concern value could be preserved in the case of a failing business would seem to offer improved recovery prospects for the creditors of that business. This is what preventive restructuring purports to do, by keeping the business or at least its viable part alive, and may be seen on that basis to be better suited to debtors with greater investment in intangibles and to the economies in which they are active.

THE EU PREVENTIVE RESTRUCTURING DIRECTIVE AND SOME ETHICAL CHALLENGES

European legislators only recently began to focus on preventive restructuring as an option. European insolvency law, drawing on their Roman origins, focused on creditor rights, creditor control and creditor satisfaction.[17] However, it has become apparent that this emphasis on punishment of the debtor and distribution of its assets for the benefit of the creditors did not promote sustainable growth and prosperity.[18] Accordingly, the European Commission called for the abandonment of the historical punitive approach to business failure and the adoption of a new approach that would help sound businesses survive and provide entrepreneurs with a second chance.[19] Consistently with this approach, the EU adopted, in 2019, the Directive (EU) 2019/1023 of the European Parliament and of the Council of 20 June 2019 on preventive restructuring frameworks, on discharge of debt and disqualifications, and on measures to increase the efficiency of procedures concerning restructuring, insolvency and

down observed in many OECD economies (Dan Andrews, Giuseppe Nicoletti, and Christina Timiliotis, 'Going Digital: What Determines Technology Diffusion among Firms?' (Background Paper) (Ottowa Global Forum on Productivity 2018) https://www.oecd.org/global-forum-productivity/events/Background-paper-Going-digital-What-determines-technology-diffusion-among-firms-Ottawa-2018.pdf accessed 8 May 2023).' L Demmou et al, 'Productivity Growth and Finance: The Role of Intangible Assets – a Sector Level Analysis' (2019) OECD Economics Department, Working Paper No. 1547 www.oecd.org/eco/workingpapers accessed 8 May 2023.

17 J Kilburn, 'The Personal Side of Harmonizing European Insolvency Law' (2016) 25 *Journal of Bankruptcy Law & Practice* 581.

18 Ibid.

19 See COM(2012) 742 final Communication from the Commission to the European Parliament, the Council, and the European Economic and Social Committee A New European Approach to Business Failure and Insolvency [2012].

discharge of debt, and amending Directive (EU) 2017/1132 (the 'Directive'). Our discussion of restructuring proceedings from a Rawlsian perspective relies on some of the main provisions of the Directive and considers whether they may be justified in terms of their contributions to a fair outcome.

The Rawlsian perspective seems to justify the preventive approach adopted by restructuring as opposed to the traditional corporate insolvency perspective. Indeed, the latter places emphasis almost exclusively upon the maximisation of creditors' wealth and the strict enforcement of pre-existing property rights and contractual entitlements. It disregards the interest of stakeholders who are not creditors such as entities on the failing entity's supply line, customers and including possibly the interests of the society at large.

Specific aspects of the restructuring process reflect concern for the fairness of both the procedure and the outcome of the restructuring process: the preference for unanimous or quasi unanimous consent of all stakeholders, the care for minority or dissenting stakeholders as expressed in the principle of the 'best-interest-of-creditors', etc. What is more, by preserving wealth and value in the long run, restructuring seems to be consonant with the main idea behind the Rawlsian difference principle, i.e., the idea that the distribution of advantages should not only respect short-term efficiency criteria, but should work to the advantage of worse-off or weaker stakeholders in the long run.

As insolvency practitioners know from experience, a debtor facing likely illiquidity finds itself in a situation of great stress and uncertainty. The same may be said for its different stakeholders, not only creditors but also employees and suppliers. The risk of economic loss creates incentives for unilateral action to enforce claims and limit exposure to the distressed enterprise. All of that is likely to be perfectly legal (excluding the provisions of insolvency law but, e.g., consistent with provisions for the enforcement of claims and security interests) and in line with the contractual rights and arrangements of the parties. However, if unchecked, it is likely to produce a suboptimal outcome. As has been noted:

> Market imperfections, such as coordination problems, incomplete contracts and information asymmetries, call for insolvency procedures that facilitate the exit of failing firms in an orderly fashion. For instance, when a debtor is suspected of being insolvent, creditors have an incentive to engage in a 'rush to the exit', rapidly enforcing their individual claims, even if it results in a reduction in the total value of recoverable assets.[20]

[20] M Adalet McGowan and D Andrews, 'Design of Insolvency Regimes Across Countries' (2018) OECD Economics Department, Working Paper No. 1504, section 2.1 www.oecd.org/eco/workingpapers accessed 11 May 2023.

The assessment of the outcome is not only based on the overall utility (e.g., harm to the overall economy) but primarily because in the absence of a collective proceeding (such as the preventive restructuring framework introduced into European Union legislation by the Directive), some stakeholders may extract maximum benefits at the expense of all others.

This may provide us with an explanation of why it would make sense to introduce a collective proceeding, i.e., a proceeding that interferes with individual enforcement at a stage prior to the traditional point of cessation of payments, or other test used by the various national legislations to define insolvency.[21] Indeed the Directive (Art. 4 para. 1) provides that a restructuring proceeding should be available where there is a likelihood of insolvency of the debtor.[22] Recital 24 of the same enactment specifies that access to the restructuring proceeding must be available 'at an early stage' prior to actual insolvency. As Recital 28 further clarifies, the circumstances that trigger the likelihood of insolvency need not be financial problems, provided that they may lead to financial distress and illiquidity. A likelihood of insolvency is obviously an estimate – not a specific event and the estimation of different stakeholders as to its likelihood may reasonably differ. However, what is important is that if a sufficient number of the stakeholders consider insolvency a likely outcome of current difficulties, they may be moved to act to protect their interests in a way that will endanger the survival of the debtor and the interests of all other stakeholders.

It would follow that a stakeholder contemplating outcomes behind the 'veil of ignorance' as to its actual standing at the time of future possible turbulence, would not consider it fair to allow the debtor to actually end up in general and permanent inability to meet its financial obligations as they fall due,[23] where, action taken at an earlier stage could have prevented its insolvency and ensured its viability. As that action concerns the avoidance of a collective proceeding and, even more importantly, impacts the totality of the debtor's stakeholders, it makes sense that the restructuring also be pursued within a collective proceeding.

---

[21] Garcimartin provides a detailed analysis of the likelihood of insolvency test: see F Garcimartin, 'Article 4' in C Paulus and R Dammann (eds), *European Preventive Restructuring: Article-by-article Commentary* (Hart 2021) 85, 91.

[22] As the recitals to the Directive make clear, the difficulties that may justify commencement of restructuring proceedings may be non-financial.

[23] This is the Greek definition of cessation of payments, which is the factual trigger for an insolvency proceeding. See law 4738/2020 Art. 77. As has been noted, even within the EU, there are different definitions of insolvency: see J M Garrido et al, 'Restructuring and Insolvency in Europe: Policy Options in the Implementation of the EU Directive' (IMF eLibrary 2021) https://www.elibrary.imf.org/view/journals/001/2021/152/article-A001-en.xml accessed 11 May 2023.

For the same reason of providing the same kind of publicity, transparency and procedural fairness, at least at the same level as the insolvency proceeding that restructuring seems to avoid, it makes sense that the proceeding be under the supervision of a judicial or administrative body with appropriate competence and authority.[24]

It is therefore reasonable to expect that when an enterprise enters a rough patch it may encounter such difficulties that some of its stakeholders, possibly those that are in the strongest enforcement position, may decide to move swiftly to enforce on collateral or discontinue the provision of supplies or take other steps in self-protection that may finish of the troubled business. An effective restructuring regime must provide a means to avoid that outcome.

The remedy provided by the Directive is multifaceted and would appear wholly justified from a Rawlsian perspective. In the remainder or this chapter, we look at a few specific rules of the restructuring framework and consider whether they are compatible with the Rawlsian principles. In particular we will examine in some greater detail ways in which the Directive seeks to create negotiating conditions similar to a putative *ex ante* bargain and sets the conditions for an efficient response to the insolvency threat while also maximising outcomes for the least privileged stakeholders.

ENSURING THAT RESTRUCTURING AGREEMENTS THAT AFFECT DISSENTERS ARE ONES TO WHICH STAKEHOLDERS WOULD BE EXPECTED TO CONSENT BEHIND THE VEIL OF IGNORANCE

Perhaps the most critical condition imposed by the Directive is that they may bind dissenting parties only if ratified by a competent administrative or judicial authority: 'Confirmation of a restructuring plan by a judicial or administrative authority is necessary to ensure that the reduction of the rights of creditors or interests of equity holders is proportionate to the benefits of the restructuring and that they have access to an effective remedy.'[25]

Parties, especially those in a strong bargaining position are allowed full freedom to exploit that advantage, as a court or administrative authority, as each member state is free to elect, must be persuaded that sacrifices by the weaker parties are proportionate to the benefit they derive from the restructuring plan. In other words, the task of the ratifying agency is to ensure that the

---

24 Directive 2019/1023 (n 14) Art. 10, para 1, in conjunction with Art. 25, which requires that members of such bodies receive 'suitable procedures training and have the necessary expertise for their responsibilities'.

25 Ibid., Recital 48.

agreement actually reached is one to which all affected parties would reasonably have agreed behind the veil of ignorance.

The possibility envisaged by the Directive of the appointment of an insolvency practitioner evidences the same concern with establishing a fair balancing of interests, this time as between the debtor on the one hand and its creditors on the other. The importance of the appointment of a practitioner is highlighted by the fact that the same article specifies that at all stages of a restructuring proceeding the debtor remains in possession of the business (unlike the standard insolvency provision that the insolvency estate passes under the control of an administrator) and, therefore, some extra scrutiny and oversight on the debtor's conduct and decisions may be warranted.

Article 5 of the Directive provides that the judicial or administrative authority that has competence to deal with a potential restructuring (as ratifying authority) may appoint an expert (the Directive speaks of 'a practitioner in the field of restructuring', normally an insolvency practitioner).[26] The expert would be entrusted to safeguard the interests of the parties, particularly where there is a stay of enforcement proceedings or where it is expected that certain classes of creditors will not agree to the proposed restructuring plan.

The appointment of the insolvency practitioner may be seen as the type of safeguard in the event of a restructuring effort that would appear as reasonable and fair in the event of an *ex ante* bargain among the stakeholders of the enterprise.

DEALING WITH RESISTANCE TO NEGOTIATE AND TO HOLDING-OUT

While the provisions previously discussed try to preserve the fairness of an agreement to which the requisite consent has already been recured, i.e., protect minorities from the abuse by majorities, a fair agreement may be thwarted by minorities unfairly exploiting their legal rights. This phenomenon is known in economic theory as 'holding-out' and there are several aspects of the Directive that seem geared to address it. We will discuss the provision of stays of enforcement, approvals by majority vote, as well as the possibility of a cross-class cram-down.

---

[26] Ibid., Art. 28 and European Commission, Directorate-General for Justice and Consumers, J Dahlgreen, S Brown, A Keay et al, 'Study on a New Approach to Business failure and Insolvency: Comparative Legal Analysis of the Member States: Relevant Provisions and Practices' (European Commission, Directorate-General for Justice and Consumers, Publications Office 2016) para. 6.4 https://data.europa.eu/doi/10.2838/8751 accessed 8 May 2023.

The avoidance of illiquidity is directly tied to the preservation of the business as a going concern. One of the most critical threats that the business would face would be, as already noted, the enforcement of individual claims and security rights. It is extremely common for distressed businesses to have a significant debt burden and to have encumbered their most valuable assets, usually their core business assets.

For that reason, the operation and effectiveness of preventive restructuring schemes requires the availability of stays at the time when the restructuring attempt is being made. Article 6 of the Directive, in recognition of this need, provides a general requirement for the availability of stays, regardless of the nature of the claim, including secured claims and claims that enjoy any type of privilege.[27] While stays are usually limited to four months, the authority, whether administrative or judicial, that is entrusted with the supervision of the proceeding can provide an extension so that the stay may have an aggregate duration of up to 12 months.[28] It follows that the drafters of the Directive have a clear understanding of the need to provide protection from individual enforcement that may extend up to a whole year, so as to permit parties to agree to a restructuring agreement, secure the necessary buy-ins as well as the required confirmation to give it effect over the objections of dissenting parties (in most cases, those dissenters would include stayed creditors).[29]

Stays serve to ensure that parties that can extract a full or high recovery of their claims at the expense of the recovery of others are prevented from exploiting their advantageous position.[30] However, stays are disruptive of existing contractual and, in some cases, legislative arrangements. Accordingly, stays should be tailored to address the specific needs of a debtor to preserve its going concern and not interfere with claims' whose enforcement would not

---

[27] Directive 2019/1023, ibid., Art. 6, para. 2. However, this general requirement does not include employee claims, unless guarantees for their satisfaction have been provided.

[28] Ibid., Art. 6, paras 6 and 7.

[29] As Tomas Richter comments in his commentary on Art. 6 of the Directive, the obligation to enact a stay is tied to the need to 'support the negotiations of a restructuring plan in a preventive restructuring framework'. However, as Richter rightly points out, the same need to preserve the going concern also exists between the filing of a plan and its confirmation – and, therefore, the provision should be interpreter broadly to cover that period, too: see T Richter, 'Article 6' in C Paulus and R Dammann (eds), *European Preventive Restructuring: Article-by-article Commentary* (Hart 2021) 103, 105.

[30] This addresses an externality to collective bargaining that has been identified as 'rush to the courthouse' or 'grab race'. See N Roubini, 'Do We Need a New Bankruptcy Regime?' https://www.brookings.edu/wp-content/uploads/2002/01/2002a_bpea_roubini.pdf accessed 11 May 2023.

represent a threat to the continuation of the business,[31] as it would not seem to adversely affect other stakeholders whose recovery prospects depend primarily on the preservation of the business as a going concern. This is reflected in paragraph 4 of Article 6 of the Directive, which directs member states to exempt certain claims or categories of claims for the stay if their enforcement would not be expected to undermine the restructuring of the debtor's business. The same paragraph also acknowledges that for some claimants the disruption caused by a stay may be very prejudicial; for that reason, member states are directed to permit exceptions for stays where the prejudice would be unfair to the respective creditors.[32]

The intent of limiting the disruption caused by a stay is also reflected in the discretion provided to authorities of member states to lift stays when it becomes apparent that the dissenting creditors are in a position to block a restructuring agreement or where the stay could cause a creditor to become insolvent. The moral underpinning of the approach seems to be that individual claims should not trump a solution that would be objectively optimal, but they should otherwise be honoured and protected.

One may observe that at a very high level of abstraction, the rules for the stay reflect an effort to balance efficiency (the preservation of the value of a business for the benefit of all, including society at large) with fairness (limit interference with individual rights to the minimum necessary for the purposes of the restructuring effort). However, the balancing in this case (as with the application of most if not all legal rules) requires the consideration of the facts of each case and the respective merits. Courts or administrative authorities that have the competence to impose stays and decide on exceptions are called up to consider what in each particular case would contribute to the preservation of the viable business without unduly interfering with individual rights.[33]

---

[31] As Richter (n 29), 110, notes:

> Viewed as a *common-pool problem* in which individual rationality may lead to a collective disaster, situations in which a debtor is sliding into a general default require rules that prevent individually rational asset grabs that could destroy the *value of the debtor's assets* as an entirety, while not unduly trampling of the *value of the individual rights.*

[32] It is possible that the exception of employee claims noted above may also fit in the general category of claims that would be unfairly prejudiced by a stay, given that employees constitute a vulnerable category of claimants that may be deserving of special consideration.

[33] Richter (n 29), 110, comments on the similar problem of difficulties of transposition into national laws:

> The proposition of a Pareto efficient stay is as trivially true when stated in conceptual terms as it may be quite difficult to implement into actual legal rules that will operate tolerably well on the ground in the reality of collective civil

From a Rawlsian perspective acceptance of a stay on enforcement would also be consistent with the insight that property rights (which include the enforcement rights) are not absolute; where stays are necessary to preserve value for the benefit of all, including those that are in the least privileged position, they can be shown to be fair for all stakeholders (in that they would reasonably form part of an *ex parte* agreement among all of them).

The Directive is clear that it would be preferable for a restructuring agreement to receive the consent of all classes of creditors that are affected by the plan. Classes of creditors are formed under the Directive on the basis of community of interests predicated upon verifiable criteria. Accordingly, the Directive sets as the preferred route to confirmation of a restructuring plan the unanimous consent of all classes (the consent of each class being provided by a majority vote for which the threshold is to be set by national law.[34]

However, the Directive anticipates the possibility that one or more classes may not consent to the proposed restructuring plan by the required majority and also allows for the confirmation of the plan on the basis of 'cross-class cram-down', provided that it is supported by a majority of voting classes or affected parties, at least one of which is senior to the ordinary unsecured creditors.[35]

The Directive is clear that the consent of all classes should not be required.[36] On this point, as also happens in respect of the treatment of shareholders of the distressed debtor, the emphasis seems on the avoidance of holding-out. This again may be totally in line with the Rawlsian approach. The *ex ante* agreement in Rawls is based on the disinterestedness and objectivity of the contracting parties, as none of them has knowledge of the position it will find itself in the future allocation of benefits (and burdens, in the case of restructuring). By contrast, an agreement negotiation *ex post facto* is negotiated among parties that are fully subjective and fully apprised of their bargaining position, as well as those of their counterparties. This gives rise to the impetus to hold-out, i.e., for creditors to refuse to consent to an otherwise reasonable restructuring plan.

The hold-out problem has received considerable consideration in restructuring literature, especially relating to sovereign insolvencies.[37] It is an example

---

proceedings conducted in real time by the real-life institutions available to any particular jurisdiction.

34 Directive 2019/1023 (n 14) Art. 9.

35 Ibid., Art. 11.

36 Ibid., Recital 54.

37 'The third externality is the 'free rider' problem (also called the 'hold-out' or 'rogue creditor' problem). In situations where initiatives to restructure debt require unanimity among the creditors, minority hold-out creditors may scuttle a restructuring even though it is advantageous to the majority. Although exchange offers may sidestep

of the prisoner's dilemma, where an individual creditor seeks to obtain a better outcome for itself at the expense of a collectively better outcome through the successful negotiation of a restructuring plan.[38] Both the majority rule as to the consent by each class, as well as the cross-class cram-down provision may be seen as ways to minimise the incentive for individual creditors to seek to enhance benefits for themselves at the expense of the interests of the stakeholders as a group. Indeed, the same may be said for the introduction of the possibility for the negotiation and enforcement of plans to be protected via a stay of enforcement, thereby blocking individual creditors from seeking to frustrate the restructuring through the enforcement of their individual claims.

However, in line with the need to combine efficiency with fairness, a cross-class cram-down should not lead to the unfair prejudice of dissenting classes. As the recitals to the Directive clearly state:

> In the case of a cross-class cram-down, Member States should ensure that dissenting classes of affected creditors are not unfairly prejudiced under the proposed plan and Member States should provide sufficient protection for such dissenting classes. Member States should be able to protect a dissenting class of affected creditors by ensuring that it is treated at least as favourably as any other class of the same rank and more favourably than any more junior class. Alternatively, Member States could protect a dissenting class of affected creditors by ensuring that such dissenting class is paid in full if a more junior class receives any distribution or keeps any interest under the restructuring plan (the 'absolute priority rule'). Member States should have discretion in implementing the concept of 'payment in full', including in relation to the timing of the payment, as long as the principal of the claim and, in the case of secured creditors, the value of the collateral are protected. Member States should also be able to decide on the choice of the equivalent means by which the original claim could be satisfied in full.[39]

It is therefore evident that the Directive seeks to enable majorities to overcome minority creditor holding-out without creating the conditions for the oppression of those minorities by the majority creditors.

---

the unanimity problem, the hold-out problem may remain serious. If a hold-out creditor can choose not to accept the offer and then, through later litigation, receive the full amount of its claim while those who accepted the offer receive less, a strong incentive arises for creditors to hold out. If this creditor coordination problem cannot be solved, a disorderly workout will result, even if a cooperative solution would be in the interest of all creditors. Thus, making a restructuring plan approved by a majority of creditors binding on all creditors (through a 'cram-down' or majority enforcement provision) would solve this externality.' Roubini (n 30) 323.

[38] J M Garrido, 'Out-of-Court Debt Restructuring' (World Bank Study 2012) https://documents1.worldbank.org/curated/en/417551468159322109/pdf/662320PUB0EPI00turing09780821389836.pdf accessed 11 May 2023.

[39] Directive 2019/1023 (n 14) Recital 54.

A similar collective action problem would arise if the shareholders, in the event that they are not recognised as a separate creditor class (as is the case with the laws of a number of EU member states), would have the ability on the basis of company law provisions to scuttle a restructuring agreement. This problem would arise in cases where particular provisions of a restructuring agreement would require shareholder approval. One such example would be the conversion of debt into equity for the purpose of lessening the debt load of the troubled entity as a measure of ensuring its viability. The conversion of debt into equity is a type of capital increase and the EU company rules require that such changes to a company's capital structure secure the approval of shareholders.[40]

The position of the Directive is clear:

> The effectiveness of the process of adoption and implementation of the restructuring plan should not be jeopardised by company law. Therefore, Member States should be able to derogate from the requirements laid down in Directive (EU) 2017/1132 of the European Parliament and of the Council concerning the obligations to convene a general meeting and to offer on a pre-emptive basis shares to existing shareholders, to the extent and for the period necessary to ensure that shareholders do not frustrate restructuring efforts by abusing their rights under that Directive [...] Such derogations should be limited in time to the extent that Member States consider such derogations necessary for the establishment of a preventive restructuring framework. Member States should not be obliged to derogate from company law, wholly or partially, for an indefinite or for a limited period of time, if they ensure that their company law requirements do not jeopardise the effectiveness of the restructuring process or if Member States have other, equally effective tools in place to ensure that shareholders do not unreasonably prevent the adoption or implementation of a restructuring plan which would restore the viability of the business.[41]

Dealing with shareholder hold-out is critical for the success of restructuring efforts as in most cases the value of equity in distressed entities may be very small especially by comparison to the value of third-party claims, and therefore the incentive for abuse maybe the strongest of any stakeholder class. It is therefore highly significant that the EU Directive provides for the possibility of derogation from basic rules of EU company law in order to avoid such abuse conduct.

---

40 Directive (EU) 2017/1132 of the European Parliament and of the Council of 14 June 2017 relating to certain aspects of company law, as amended and in effect [2017] OJ L 169/46, Art. 68.

41 Directive 2019/1023 (n 14) Recital 96.

CONCLUDING REMARKS

Without losing sight of efficiency, the Directive certainly seems to be inspired by Rawlsian sensitivities.

This is clearly reflected in the Directive's recitals, which repeatedly refer to the need for restructuring frameworks to protect the rights 'of all parties involved [...] in a balanced manner' (Recital 3), to base restructuring 'on a dialogue with the stakeholders' (Recital 10), to the need to 'minimise loses for all stakeholders including not only contractually secured creditors, but also of creditors further down in the supply chain, but also to preserve know-how and skills and the interests of the wider economy' (Recital 16). It is certainly reflected in the Directive's guiding principle of safeguarding the 'best-interest-of-creditors' as announced in Recital 52 and clearly defined in Article 2§1(6) of the Directive.

Indeed, fairness and equal treatment of all classes of creditors, inclusive negotiations, the preference towards unanimously approved plans, and the protective treatment of weaker stakeholders permeate the entire Directive. Not only in a declaratory manner, but in a very concrete and detailed manner, as can be seen in many key provisions of the Directive.

Consider, for example the conditions which the Directive sets for the approval of the restructuring plan: Restructuring plans are preferably reached by unanimity of all interested classes of stakeholders. According to Article 9§6 of the Directive:

> [a] restructuring plan shall be adopted by affected parties, provided that a majority in the amounts of their claims or interests is obtained in each class. Member States may, in addition, require that a majority in the number of affected parties is obtained in each class.

Class formation is to respect 'commonality of interests' (Art. 9§4), while workers' claims are to be treated in a separate class of their own (Art. 9§4). Additionally, class formation must be done 'with a particular view to protecting vulnerable creditors such as small suppliers' (Art. 9§4). Thus, as a principle, the restructuring plan must ensue as the outcome of an agreement, reached unanimously by all stakeholders concerned, with particular concern for vulnerable stakeholders which are not left out nor can they be summarily excluded by the majority of stronger stakeholders who may wish to maximise gains by insisting on the full enforcement of privileged property rights. The latter's bargaining power is, so to speak, neutralised by the device of class-formation and the requirement of cross-class agreement, which operates in this case in a manner reminiscent of the Rawlsian veil of ignorance.

Certainly, within classes, majoritarian principles do operate (Art. 9§6). However, one can reasonably say that, since each class is characterised by a sufficient commonality of interests, the majoritarian decision-making process within a class does not undermine the fundamental principle of equal treatment of all stakeholders, as every class in fact stands as the collective representative of one and the same stakeholder interest. Majoritarian decision-making within a class can therefore more appropriately be analogised to a deliberative process similar to the process by which Rawlsian deliberators arrive to a point of 'reflective equilibrium' after weighting a variety of aspects and 'considered judgments'.[42]

Does the possibility of cross-class-cram-down, envisaged in Article 11 of the Directive, mean that the restructuring process set up by the Directive, bows, after all, to an ultimate principle of efficiency and utility maximisation, which does not fit comfortably with the Rawlsian principles of justice? It seems to us that a closer look at the matter does not support this conclusion. Indeed, cross-class-cram-down is permitted provided that it satisfies certain stringent requirements of fairness as set out in Article 11 of the Directive, including, notably, that 'dissenting voting classes of affected creditors are treated at least as favourably as any other class of the same rank' (Art. 11§1(c)) and that 'no class of affected parties can, under the restructuring plan, receive or keep more than the full amount of its claims or interests'.

Thus, even cross-class-cram-down seems to respect the Rawlsian principles of justice and, more specifically, the Rawlsian difference principle. Indeed, given the constraints that Article 11 places on the adoption of a cross-class crammed-down restructuring plan, it appears that such a plan is envisaged by the Directive only when a unanimously approved plan has become impossible, because of the unreasonable (unfairly biased) disagreement of some of the affected classes. This outcome is, again, reminiscent of the Rawlsian notion that the binding force of an agreement lies not with the agreement as such, but, rather, with the substantive fairness of the agreement itself. It also fits with the Rawlsian insight that fairness requires that the deliberating parties are not seeking to hold-out on privileges which they may turn-out to enjoy in fact but should deliberate behind a veil of ignorance which temporarily hides from their horizon the existence of such privileges.

Refusal to adhere to a plan which is substantively fair and just, is thus unfair and cannot vitiate the plan's claim to be binding on all considered stakeholders. Unreasonable disagreement is not fair disagreement, and disagreement to

---

[42] On Rawls' concept of reflective equilibrium see: Rawls (n 1) 18–19; 42–45. On the concept of considered judgments see Rawls (n 1) 42; 17–19.

a plan that would satisfy the conditions of Article 11 would precisely appear to be unreasonable in the Rawlsian sense.[43]

There is no doubt that the Directive's principal aim is to find an efficient solution to the problem of distressed commercial entities who risk failing at great societal detriment. However, it seems equally clear that the Directive is also inspired by principles of fairness and equal treatment which go well beyond the requirements of efficiency. Thus, it appears that the Directive may be better understood and interpreted if seen to reflect these principles, and the Rawlsian perspective seems eminently appropriate to illuminate and guide the Directive's implementation.

[43] The concept of 'reasonableness' as distinguished from the concept of 'rationality' does indeed appear in Rawls' later work on *Political Liberalism* (n 9), 48–50:

> Persons are reasonable in one basic aspect when, among equals say, they are ready to propose principles and standards as fair terms of cooperation and to abide by them willingly, given the assurance that other will likewise do so […] The reasonable is an element of the idea of society as a system of fair cooperation and that its fair terms be reasonable for all to accept is part of its idea of reciprocity.

PART II

An inward-looking study of insolvency law

8. Decision theory and insolvency law

John M. Wood[1]

INTRODUCTION

Set within the inward approach section of this book, this chapter examines how the pursuit of a rescue objective is encouraged by the design and interpretation of the insolvency text that governs corporate rescue procedures. The selected procedures have been chosen on the basis that they allow different agents within the process to be examined;[2] namely, directors and their input in the new standalone moratorium, the court-focused new restructuring plan, and the insolvency practitioner (IP) led administration process with the role of creditors also considered.[3]

To address how decisions are made, the classic approach, otherwise known as the rational model, will be referred to, which strives to account for how decisions should be made to achieve a desired outcome. Under this approach, decisions are rationalised to arrive at the most advantageous decisions given an uncertain environment or situation. While decision theory brings together psychology, statistics, philosophy, and mathematics to analyse the decision-making process, it is ultimately concerned with behaviour and human

1 I am grateful to the SLS annual conference 2022 for the comments received during the presentation of an earlier draft of this work.

2 Note that 'agents' refers to an entity, usually an individual person, that is capable of deliberation and action.

3 Other rescue procedures include scheme of arrangement, company voluntary arrangements, the 'light touch' administration process and pre-packaged administration. For further reading on these procedures, see A Keay, P Walton and J Curl, *Corporate Governance and Insolvency: Accountability and Transparency* (Edward Elgar Publishing Ltd 2022) Ch 5.

judgement.[4] Yet, what often informs behaviour are the end results.[5] The role of the law is not concerned with the enforcement of an existing utilitarian morality that tells people what to do; instead it strives to provide a mechanism that generates normative guidelines where they do not exist.[6]

It is these guidelines that define the level of input that different agents can have in the respective insolvency regimes. Yet, decisions based on human judgment may also lead to preferences where a choice exists.[7] These could for example reflect the desires of the directors when submitting a moratorium, or reflect the practitioners' own choices, or that of the firm when undertaking insolvency work.[8] Despite the potential for conflicts between competing interests, the negotiation of payoffs between the likes of directors, IPs, and creditors, is often avoided due to the wording of insolvency text or case law as this will often dictate that the focus of the processes remains firmly on the secured creditors of the company who are likely to have their interests protected.[9]

However, the broader rescue objective covers an array of interests that go beyond merely the creditors. From a utilitarian perspective, good social norms that benefit stakeholders should be applied within a particular 'community', [10] not universally,[11] to avoid the objective of rescue being diluted to the point that it does not well serve any interest. This does not mean that only the secured creditors matter. Instead, it is better understood to favour the interests of those that allow the insolvent company to benefit from a rescue attempt. How these interests are determined is largely described in insolvency text, but this does

---

4 Human judgement and the influences that may impact such decisions in an insolvency context are examined in J Wood, 'Assessing the Effectiveness of the UK's Insolvency Regulatory Framework at Deterring Insolvency Practitioners' Opportunistic Behaviour' (2019) 19(2) *Journal of Corporate Law Studies* 333.

5 J Bentham, *Introduction to the Principles of Morals and Legislation* (J H Burns and H L A Hart (eds), Oxford University Press 1996) 34, 38; J Bentham, *Constitutional Code Rationale. In First Principles Preparatory to Constitutional Code* (P Schofield (ed) Clarendon Press 1989) 232.

6 D Priel, 'Bentham's Public Utilitarianism and Its Jurisprudential Significance' (2021) 34(4) *Ration Juris* 415, 415.

7 This may also involve psychological biases, see Chapter 16 of this book.

8 The recent consultation by the Insolvency Service, *The Future of Insolvency Regulation* (21 March 2022) highlights the tension between the commercial interests of the firm and the statutory responsibilities of the practitioner, see Part B.

9 The protection of creditors' interests is well noted, see *Liquidator v West Mercia Safetywear Ltd v Dodd* (1988) 4 BCC 30, [1988] BCLC 250. More recently, this 'creditor duty' was confirmed in *BTI 2014 LLC v Sequana SA* [2022] UKSC 25.

10 J Bentham, *The Works of Jeremy Bentham* (J Bowring (ed) William Tait 1841) 2:537–538; J R Dinwiddy, *Radicalism and Reform in Britain, 1780–1850* (Hambledon Press 1992) 317–138, 335–337.

11 Priel (n 6) 431.

not, in itself, provide reasons for how a rescue outcome could be improved; something which can be the result of empirical investigation, but not hindsight since this does not evaluate commercial decisions in context with the information known at the time.[12]

Thus, what emerges is the measurement of how effective legislation is, and whether a superior outcome is feasible at the time of assessment. It does not follow that there is an ideal outcome to imitate, but rather, that there is a process of improvement. How 'improvement' occurs and to whom should this benefit is left to the discretion of the certain agents, who will have to justify such decisions. From this, it is understood that a desired rescue outcome is reliant on the application of the rational model to provide the means for this to be realised. Given that insolvency outcomes can be uncertain, whether a rational outcome has been achieved is sometimes difficult to determine. The decision as to whether rescue is appropriate, or the type of rescue being pursued, will achieve the best outcome provides for an intrigued discussion on how failure and optimum rescue outcomes are assessed. It is further subject to how these rescue proposals, depending on the rescue procedure, are interpreted by the company directors, IPs, and the courts.

This poses two questions that need to be addressed. First, how the theories of choice under conditions of certainty, risk and uncertainty have influenced the decision-making to rescue a distressed company? Second, whether because there is a desirability to achieve certain outcomes, this has led to the relaxation of rationality so that rescue objectives can emerge? It is responses to the latter question that require a closer examination of how decisions are made in relation to the insolvency text, and whether any noticeable divergence from this tend to results in irrational rescue decisions.[13] In response to these questions, this chapter considers whether the rescue objective can be rationalised to a greater degree with reference to the decision theory to produce a new model that can achieve certain outcomes despite the occurrence of what may be perceived as irrational decisions made in pursuit of the rescue objective. The examination of these questions is crucial since they ensure the continued re-examination of insolvency law and theory from a modern perspective. To appreciate the elasticity of the current law, and to better understand how it could be improved so that it remains relevant in an ever-changing environment, it is necessary to expand the discussion into established divergent critical theories and apply more novel concepts. In this regard, decision theory, which includes elements

---

[12] See *Re T&D Industries plc* [2000] 1 WLR 646, 657. See also, *Re Consumer & Industrial Press Ltd (No.2)* (1988) 4 BCC 72 [74]; J Wood, 'Insolvency Office-holder Discretion and Judicial Control' (2020) 6 *Journal of Business Law* 451, 466.

[13] This term will refer to decisions which result in outcomes that either go beyond the scope of the insolvency text or provide for decisions which contradict the text.

of applied probability theory and analytical philosophy, offers an opportunity to examine insolvency law from a new perspective; an imperative undertaking that ensures the continued development of sound policy considerations in this significant area of commercial law.

THE RELEVANCE OF DECISION THEORY TO INSOLVENCY PROCESSES

The number of problems that require attention within an insolvent company are in abundance. A key question is whether a company can be rescued, and if so, what form this should take. It is a question that requires both the value of corporate failure and its potential rescue value to be determined as legible outcomes.[14] It is only when these values are ascertained that the decision of what to do can be reached.

Decision theory principally consist of two categories. First, there is the descriptive decision theory that attempts to provide explanations for, and predictions of, the choices that are made by individuals and groups facing choices such as those evident within an insolvent company. Second, the normative decision theory, which addresses the questions of what decisions agents should make and how they should make them. This includes, how the agents should evaluate the alternatives before them, what criteria they should employ, and what procedures they should follow. This chapter will focus on the latter theory,[15] albeit from a more philosophical and less mathematical approach than other writers.[16]

Applied to insolvency, the theory does have some shortcomings as agents within the insolvency process are afforded wide discretion to make commercial decisions, which can lead to systematic deviations from the normative models. These are otherwise known as biases – reasons why certain decisions are preferred. If biases are not found, it should be attempted to explain why not

---

[14] See J Wood, *The Interpretation and Value of Corporate Rescue* (Edward Elgar Publishing 2022); and J Wood, 'Creative Destruction and the Post COVID-19 Economy: A Critique of the (Un)creative Rescue Value Contained within the Permanent CIGA 2020 Reforms' (2023) 3 *Journal of Business Law* 197.

[15] See D E Bell and H Raiffa, 'Marginal Value and Intrinsic Risk Aversion' in D E Bell, H Raiffa and A Tversky (eds), *Decision Making: Descriptive, Normative, and Prescriptive Interactions* (Cambridge University Press 1988) 384–397; D Hausman and M McPherson, *Economic Analysis, Moral Philosophy and Public Policy* (Cambridge University Press 2006); M Malecka. 'The Normative Theory in Economics: A Philosophy of Science Perspective: The Case of the Expected Utility Theory' (2020) 27(10 *Journal of Economic Methodology* 36.

[16] See, e.g., A Wald, 'Contributions to the Theory of Statistical Estimation and Testing Hypotheses' (1939) 10(4) *Annals of Mathematical Statistics* 299.

since human judgement is influenced by behaviour. If biases are found, there should be an attempt to understand, and explain them by making descriptive modules or legal theories. These responses offer a way to correct the biases, that in turn could improve the judgements to the normative standards. If this can be provided, this could assist better rescue outcomes as the decisions made throughout the process are justified not only on commercial grounds, but also the issues that influenced those decisions are well accounted for since they are aligned against an identifiable legal approach.

Yet, while this could bring a level of certainty to creditors, the term 'better' is problematic since it implies that the normative model defines what better means. As a concept 'better' or 'betterment' is a challenge as it is rarely given the attention it requires; something which this chapter aims to address. There are also questions as to who the betterment should benefit, a matter which is examined towards the end of this chapter. Should no betterment be identified then the position which fulfils the administrative objective of whatever insolvency procedure is undertaken must be pursued.

A further consideration is the 'sunk cost effect' as it generally encourages people to continue an endeavour, or continue consuming or pushing an option, if they have invested time or money or some resource into it.[17] This is likely to dictate some insolvency processes, such as the UK Company Voluntary Arrangement (CVAs), restructuring plans, and administration since the processes can be complex and are driven towards a set purpose in which the company may be rescued.[18] Yet, caution must be applied as sunk cost refers to costs that have already been incurred and cannot be recovered. As such, sunk costs are excluded from future decisions because the costs will be the same regardless of the outcome. Instead, models that address biases may instruct to do whatever results in the best outcomes for the future.[19] In that respect, the insolvency process that can deliver the best rescue outcome within the circumstances can be rationalised, even if it may appear to be based on irrational decision making by the agent in question. Since the circumstances may be generic to the extent that it provides an extensive scope for pursuing preferences unimpeded, what is required is how three key agents, namely the directors of the insolvent company, the IPs, and the courts approach their decision-making.

---

17 Although the effect of monetary sunk costs on decision-making has been widely discussed, research is still fragmented, and results are sometimes controversial, see S Roth, T Robbert and L Straus, 'On the Sunk-cost Effect in Economic Decision-making: a Meta-analytic Review' (2014) 8 *Business Research* 99.

18 Insolvency Act 1986 (IA 1986) Sch B1, para 11.

19 A matter which has been deemed to be effective, see generally R P Larrick, J N Morgan, and R E Nisbett, 'Teaching the Use of Cost-benefit Reasoning in Everyday Life' (1990) 1(6) *Psychological Science* 362.

INSOLVENCY REGIMES

Directors' Decision-making in the New Free-standing Statutory Moratorium

The UK's free-standing moratorium for distressed but viable companies was introduced by the Corporate Insolvency and Governance Act 2020 (CIGA 2020) which is primarily intended to be used to support a rescue of a company as a going concern (as opposed to the rescue of only the company's business).[20] The moratorium provides companies with a period of protection from creditor action, which is designed to support restructures and significantly control the costs of the process. The moratorium also provides a window whereby greater opportunities may be explored for company survival to determine which option would benefit the company the greatest.

The moratorium is director led which leaves directors in management to trade the company while the IP acts as a 'monitor' to oversee the company's affairs.[21] Although in control, directors are subject to certain controls where permission may be required from the court or consent needed from the monitor.[22] That said, the CIGA measures have made the UK insolvency market more debtor-friendly; an intended move that will increase the focus on decisions that lead to the implementation of rescue measures.

The monitor plays a crucial role to ensure that rescue remains the only objective.[23] Accordingly, the monitor must use their professional discretion to determine whether rescue as a going concern is feasible in cases where a moratorium is sought.[24] What amounts to going concern in such cases will be interpreted in a similar manner as to that of the primary objective of administration, but it should be noted that recent case law indicates that a return to solvency rather than the restoration of the company as a going concern is sufficient to satisfy the test.[25] In this respect, the case law promotes a broader rescue outcome than the one originally dictated in the moratorium text.

---

20 See IA 1986, Part A1.

21 The role of the monitor and their duties is contained within CIGA 2020, Part A1, Chapter 5.

22 The monitor is required to be a licensed insolvency practitioner.

23 See CIGA, Part A1, A6(1)(e). The same criteria also apply to extensions, see e.g., CIGA 2020, Part A1, A10(1)(d). See also, 'A Guide for Monitors', which was published on 26 June 2020 by the Insolvency Service.

24 There must be a real prospect of rescue, see *Re Harris Simons Construction Ltd* [1989] 1 WLR 368.

25 Although both *Davey v Money* [2018] EWHC 766 (Ch), [2018] Bus L R 1903 and *Re Zinc Hotels (Holdings) Ltd* [2018] EWHC 1936 (Ch) suggest that the primary objective of administration under para. 3(1)(a) of Sch B1 of the Act requires restoration

While the rescue outcome may be broad, the IP must still establish what rescue should entail and what outcomes are considered reasonable in the circumstances. To this end, the scope to which the discretion is applied can vary, which will mean that the moratorium threshold that justifies rescue will also vary; a factor that could cause confusion amongst creditors who have little knowledge of how the insolvency industry operates in practice. Should rescue not be considered possible then the moratorium must be terminated. The discretion of the monitor in this instance will again be broad but as an officer of the court the monitor will be expected to conduct themselves in line with the fiduciary duties.[26] In addition, the consent of the monitor will be required should directors wish to undertake certain transactions, otherwise the day-to-day management of the business remains with the directors, thus making the moratorium a debtor-in-possession process. Yet, this does not prevent directors from being able to challenge the decisions made by the monitor, where actions, decisions, or failure to act on the grounds of (actual or perceived) unfair can cause harm to the applicate. Crucially, as the directors remain in their positions, a monitor can also challenge those decisions on the same basis,[27] which potentially opens the possibility for an increase in disputes and litigation.

In a post-COVID-19 environment and in an effort to encourage an element of integrity in the viability process, a new offence was introduced in the UK by CIGA 2020: that of fraud committed during, or in anticipation of a moratorium, and false representation to obtain a moratorium, to deter directors from leading on investors or the monitor to believe the company is viable and can be rescued.[28] This is a countermeasure to what is perceived to be wide discretion afforded to those involved with the moratorium process, and acts as a check-and-balance tool to ensure the pursuit of rescue is authentic. This is crucial for accurate decisions to be made since preferences, which may be informed by bias as noted above, may be altered in accordance with information that compels alternative measures to be considered.

Since the rescue of the company must be possible, it is imperative that this term is fully understood. Rescue in this respect means that the company can continue to trade and pay certain debts, which includes new debt, payment for new supplies, rent in respect of the moratorium period, certain payments to

---

of the company as a going concern, *Lehman Brothers International (Europe) (in admin)* [2020] EWHC 1932 (Ch) suggests a return to solvency without being a going concern will be sufficient.

26 For an overview of the insolvency practitioner, see Wood (n 4).

27 There is also a right for a subsequently appointed administrator or liquidator to challenge the monitor's remuneration as excessive.

28 CIGA 2020, Chapter 7.

employees, and debts under financial contracts. Should these debts not be satisfied then the moratorium will cease, which makes the support from lenders crucial to the success of the moratorium. As such, it is apparent that the value of rescue is firmly in the hands of the banks or key creditors who will determine whether the support needed for the moratorium is justified with what they can expect in return. Even in instances where the monitor may consider that a company could be rescued, this will be dependent on the availability of finances needed to see the rescue through, as well as the effect of the moratorium on insolvency proceedings and the enforcement of rights.[29]

Despite the limited use of moratoriums so far,[30] the recent case of *Minor Hotel Group MEA DMCC v Dymant*,[31] provides some useful legal commentary on how a moratorium may operate. In this decision, the meaning of 'to pay' and 'is unable'[32] were subject to much discussion, since a monitor was obliged to keep under review whether it would remain likely that the moratorium would result in the rescue of the company as a going concern, and the moratorium had to be brought to an end if the monitor 'thinks that the company is unable to pay'[33] a pre-moratorium finance debt.[34] In brief, the joint monitors concluded that it was likely that the company would be rescued as a going concern and that it was likely that the loan would be paid in full in the near future, and so they declined to terminate the moratorium. The creditor in this case wished to terminate the moratorium so that they could appoint administrators and made an application to the court to state that the moratoria would unfairly harm its interests. The court decided that if the moratorium continued, then the subsidiaries of the parent company were likely to be rescued as going concerns.[35] To

---

[29] While the moratorium may be new to practitioners, there are concerns about whether it will be applied consistently without pre-existing case law guidance. See, the Insolvency Service report, *Corporate Insolvency and Governance Act 2020 – Interim Report March 2022* (21 June 2022) section 4.1.

[30] Between 26 June 2020 and 28 February 2022, 33 moratoriums were obtained. See monthly Insolvency Statistics February 2022 on GOV.UK https://www.gov.uk/government/statistics/monthly-insolvency-statistics-february-2022/commentary-monthly-insolvency-statistics-february-2022 accessed 15 March 2022. It should also be noted that the low figures can be linked to the overlap between the CIGA permanent measures and COVID-19 temporary measures.

[31] *Minor Hotel Group MEA DMCC v Dymant* [2022] EWHC 340 (Ch).

[32] Ibid. These terms are examined in greater detail at paras [26], [30], [33].

[33] This is not the same question as whether the company is 'unable to pay debts as they fall due' for the purposes of the cash-flow insolvency test in s 123 of the IA 1986. What is important is can the finance obligation be paid immediately; this is a matter of commercial judgment for the monitor to determine. See *Minor Hotel* (n 31) [30] and [33].

[34] IA 1986, s A38(1).

[35] The court has discretion to act under IA 1986, s A42(5).

that end, the harm suffered as a result of the moratorium was less significant than the potential harm the companies would suffer if the creditor was permitted to commence insolvency proceedings against them.[36] On that basis the moratorium was permitted to continue until lapse.[37] The decision is likely to place an emphasis on the value of what is being rescued and the impact that the moratorium has on the creditor and debtor. It will also place much of these decisions on the monitor since this is classed as commercial judgements and one that the courts are unlikely to challenge.

Court Sanctioned Restructuring Plans

The UK's Part 26A restructuring plans are designed for companies in financial difficulties that are or will affect its ability to carry on business as a going concern.[38] The plan is facilitated by the court, a factor that will provide flexibility and find favour with companies that are keen to bind stakeholders to a rescue plan and avoid well-structured restructuring proposals being derailed by certain creditors.[39] The court's oversight and approval are like that seen in schemes of arrangements in that there are two hearings.[40] The first hearing considers class composition, jurisdictional issues and what information is provided to creditors.[41] Of interest, is the cross-class cram-down feature which will have implications for how rescues are implemented and perhaps the type of rescues that could occur.[42] If the cross-class cram-down rules are met this would permit a restructuring plan to be approved and imposed on a dissenting class of creditors.[43] The rules dictate that the plan can be applied provided that at least one class of creditors 'who would receive a payment, or have a genuine economic interest in the company, in the event of the relevant alternative'

---

[36] *Minor Hotel* (n 31) [41].

[37] Ibid., [38], [41].

[38] See new CA 2006, Part 26A, s 901A(2).

[39] The flexibility also applies to the size of the company, since it includes small-to-medium enterprises, see *Re Houst Ltd* [2022] EWHC 1941.

[40] See Companies Act 2006, Part 26.

[41] There is precent for the court to allow plan creditors to raise issues of class composition and jurisdiction at any sanction hearing, see *Re Hong Kong Airlines Limited* [2022] EWHC 3210 (Ch).

[42] Further issues are likely to arise as to what amounts to 'fair' or 'just and equitable' in such circumstances with the court careful not to apply its own views, but rather apply the rationality test, see Snowden J in *Virgin Active, Holdings Ltd* [2021] EWHC 814 (Ch), [221] onwards.

[43] A focus on compromise is evident in the new Part 26A, s 901F(1), yet the costs of challenging such plans are seen as excessive which hinders the policy of protecting dissenting creditors. See, the Insolvency Service Report (n 29) 4.2.

voted in favour of the restructuring plan.[44] This is dependent on the second requirement that dissenting creditors would not be any worse off under the plan than they would have been upon the court deciding what to do with the company should the restructuring plan be rejected.[45]

The new restructuring process was first used in the financial restructuring of *Virgin Atlantic Airways*,[46] which also highlighted the input of creditors and shareholders in the valuation process. The restructuring plan generally permits a compromise of both the debt and equity claims of creditors and/or shareholders which the court is satisfied have no 'genuine' economic interest in the company.[47] A crucial consideration here, which differs, for example, from the scheme of arrangement, is that while every creditor or member of the company whose rights are affected by the compromise must be permitted to participate in a meeting, this does not apply if these persons have no genuine economic interest in the company.[48] The additional requirement of economic interest could lead to valuation arguments as to whether a creditor is in line to receive money, which if not could render them without a genuine economic interest and as such ineligible to vote on the restructuring plan. Future case law on this front will be useful to determine what valuation evidence would suffice, and what instances would show whether a creditor is 'out of the money' in terms of economic interest; a matter that will be complex when multiple classes of creditors are evident.

There is also a requirement that the court would have to sanction the restructuring plan, a matter that would inevitably involve a review of the creditor interests to determine fairness.[49] In this respect, fairness would include non-creditor interests and the impact that failure would have on them. It is, however, important to be mindful that not all interests are equal, nor can all

---

44 CA 2006, Part 26A, s 901G(5). What constitutes a meeting of dissenting creditors includes a meeting attended by a sole creditor, or indeed where no-one attended, see *Re Listrac Midco Ltd and others* [2023] EWHC 460 (Ch).

45 Although the same general principles of class composition applied to Part 26A plans as applied to Part 26 schemes, a rigid application of those principles might not always be appropriate in the different context of a Part 26A plan, *Re Virgin Atlantic Airways Ltd* [2020] RWHC 2191 (Ch); *Re Gategroup Guarantees Ltd* [2021] EWHC 304 (Ch); *Re Virgin Active* (n 42).

46 [2020] EWHC 2191 (Ch).

47 CA 2006, s 901C(4).

48 *Virgin Atlantic* (n 45) [44].

49 In regard to a Part 26 scheme the court would not at the convening hearing consider the merits of fairness of the proposed scheme, see *Virgin Atlantic* (n 45) [35]. If the scheme was approved by the statutory majority, then fairness would be considered, see *Re Telewest Communication Plc (No1)* [2004] BCC 342, [14]. However, in *Virgin Atlantic*, it was held that para 6d of the Practice Statement should be adopted at the convening hearing for a Part 26A restructuring plan.

interests be defined within an insolvency context. The approach of the court is to assesses the fairness of the result,[50] and should the court be satisfied with its findings, then the restructuring plan will be confirmed at the second hearing, which will mean that the plan would become binding on affected creditors and shareholders.[51]

Since restructuring plans are driven by the applicant, which is usually the debtor company, the court will not usually intervene. Yet, while the plan is most likely to be initiated by the financially distressed company,[52] it is possible for creditors and shareholders to make an application to court to commence the procedure.[53] While this could prove to be useful, the significant task to undertake a viable and realistic restructure plan would mean it is unlikely that the stakeholders would account for many applications; a factor that likely leaves such plans in the hands of the company. That said, the court has demonstrated that it will refuse to sanction a restructuring plan should it be required.[54] The decisions made within this context are, however, likely to reflect those of the distressed company and as such the decisions of the courts are unlikely to divert or produce regular different outcomes to those desired by the applicant.

Insolvency Practitioner and the Controlled Administration Procedure

The overriding objective of paragraph 3, Schedule B1 of the UK Insolvency Act 1986 is that it strongly implies a causal relationship between the use of the IPs functions and the achievement of the objective of rescuing the company as a going concern.[55] Yet, it is noted that the objective of rescue must be read in context of the legislation as a whole to determine how the administrator should perform their functions. An administration order can only be provided if it is

---

50 *Telewest* (n 49) [41].

51 Guidance on the explanatory statement was given in *Re Sunbird Business Ltd* [2020] EWHC 2493 (Ch).

52 The financial difficulties entry threshold should be construed broadly, which includes a loss-making company, a company in a terminal state of financial difficulties, and a solvent wind-down of a company, see *DeepOcean* [2021] EWHC 138 (Ch).

53 CA 2006, s 901A(3). It is also important to note that the court requires the company (by its directors or shareholders, or where the company is in an insolvent regime, by the relevant office holder) to consent to and agree to enter into the relevant scheme of arrangement and/or compromise, see *Re NGI Systems & Solutions Ltd v The Good Box Co Labs Ltd* [2023] EWHC 274 (Ch).

54 *Re Hurricane Energy plc* [2021] EWHC 1759 (Ch). The plan was rejected that it failed to satisfy the criteria set out in s 901G, namely, that for cross-class cram-down, no members of the dissenting class are worse off under the plan when compared with the relevant alternative.

55 *Lehman* (n 25) [38].

reasonably likely to achieve the 'purpose of administration'.[56] This provides the administrator with options, and as such, if he or she assumes office with the thought to achieve one objective of administration, but on review finds that the circumstances compel them to alter the plans and seek to achieve it another way, then this is permissible and the correct interpretation of the objectives.[57] To that end, if a company rescue is considered possible (meaning that the prospects of success is more than mere hope), then the administrator must make a statement of proposals to achieve that end,[58] which under paragraph 49(2)(b) includes an explanation as to why the administrator thinks that the objective in paragraph 3(1)(a) or (b) cannot be achieved.[59]

If it is not reasonably practical to pursue this objective, and it is established that a better result can be achieved for the creditors as a whole then the prime objective of rescue can be disregarded. At the heart of the subsections is the need to consider the interests of the creditors as a whole;[60] a marked contrast to administrative receivership where the receivers only obligation is primarily to the secured creditor who has appointed them.[61] Yet, it should be noted that the court has an express, unfettered discretion to authorise implementation if an administrator's proposals notwithstanding opposition from a majority of creditors.[62]

Given the complexities, interests and various outcomes that must be negotiated, commercial decisions tend to be pragmatic in nature.[63] Pragmatism, therefore, provides the scope for what could be perceived as irrational decisions since it is not expected that administrators link every step taken to the

---

[56] IA 1986, Sch B1, para 11(b).

[57] See IA 1986, para 11(b) of Sch B1. See also, *Key2 Law (Surrey) LLP v De'Antiquis* [2011] EWCA Civ 1567; [2012] BCC 375, [98]; the approach was applied by the Court of Appeal in *R (on the application of Monarch Airlines Ltd (in admin) v Airport Coordination Ltd* [2017] EWCA Civ 1892, [56].

[58] IA 1986, Sch B1, [49].

[59] See, *Re Fortuna Fix Ltd (In Administration)* [2020] EWHC 2369 (Ch); [2020] 9 WLUK 30, [113]–[114].

[60] This contrasts with the position under receivership, which was altered under EA 2002, subject to certain specific exceptions, see IA 1986, s 72A. For a detailed examination, see Sealy and Milman, *Annotated Guide to the Insolvency Legislation*, (25th edn, Sweet & Maxwell 2022) 689.

[61] Subject to the statutory rights of the company's preferential creditors, and obligations in respect to the prescribed part under IA 1986, s176A. However, note the changes implemented by the EA 2002.

[62] See *Re Structures & Computers Ltd* [1998] BCC 348. [1997] 9 WLUK 153; *DKLL Solicitors v Revenue and Customs Commissioners* [2007] EWHC 2067 (Ch), [2007] BCC 908.

[63] See *Denny v Yeldon* [1995] Pens LR 37; see also, Wood (n 12) 455.

pursuit of the rescue objective stated in paragraph 3.[64] Instead, paragraph 3 provides for a more general approach to the implementation of the functions since they are not defined in statutory terms, and propose an overall goal as opposed to be explicit aim. The broadness of this direction should not be misunderstood or misconstrued to produce outcomes that are inconsistent with the relevant statutory purpose, but this is not to imply that 'every exercise of every power must be capable of being shown specifically to advance the statutory objective in a definable way. Such a requirement would be unworkable'.[65] The scrutiny of the decisions taken should therefore not be expected to provide an entirely causal narrative to the rationality of how this would achieve the statutory objective.[66] Rather, the functions of the administrator should not be constructed narrowly and instead the administrators have the scope to perform their functions in line with pursuing the desired objective.[67]

This approach inevitably provides a level of discretion that has been broadly conceived to permit rescue, where feasible, to occur. In consideration of this point, a final issue that should also be noted is the low level of administrations that occur each year and the impact of professional fees on the choices that are made. Around 10 per cent of companies that move into insolvency enter administration, which provides an indication of how slim such work is within the insolvency industry.[68] While the aim is to secure the entirety of the fees for the work undertaken by the IP, often it is the case that large sums are written off at a loss.[69] Operating in such circumstances can influence choices that can sometimes have a bearing on the rationality of the decisions made.[70] There is

---

64 *Denny*, ibid., [40] where Jacobs J said: 'To ask me to suppose that the draftsman had a coherent plan running throughout each provision is to ask too much.'

65 *Lehman* (n 25) [41].

66 In *Re One Blackfriars Ltd* [2021] EWHC 684 (Ch) [211]–[222], it was held, *inter alia* that, unlike receivers, administrators do not owe an *absolute* duty to obtain the best reasonably obtainable price (a non-delegable duty in strict liability) for an asset. Instead, as an aspect of the overall duty to take reasonable care and skill, an administrator is only required to take reasonable care to obtain the best price that the circumstances permit as they reasonably perceive them to be. The decision follows that by Snowden J in *Davey* (n 25) [388], which approved *Re Charnley Davies Ltd (No.2)* [1990] BCC 605, 618B-C.

67 *Lehman* (n 25) [42]; *Denny* (n 63), [17]. See also, S Ellina, 'Administration and CVA in Corporate Insolvency Law: Pursuing the Optimum Outcome' (2019) 30(3) ICCLR 180

68 In October 2022, administrations accounted for 5 per cent of registered company insolvencies. See Insolvency Service monthly insolvency statistics October 2022.

69 See R3, *Insolvency Fees and the Cost of Regulation* (2022) 13–20.

70 Wood (n 4).

nothing unethical about this approach, merely commercial pragmatism, and it should be noted that insolvency fees are highly regulated.[71]

THE PERSPECTIVES OF BENEFIT IN DECISION THEORY

Central to decision theory is the premise that some options are more rational than others when an agent is faced with certain features within a particular environment. Yet, the economic setting is not the only feature that matters, since another significant factor also concerns who is affected by the actions, and the location where this occurs.[72] While these are important variables, they should be contrasted with perspectives on benefit, which provide a standpoint from which a judgement is made. Different judgements may be legitimately reached because two people have different standpoints: this may mean different evidential and reasoning skills, different interests and biases that lead to different viewpoints to be formed. Thus, divergent outcomes based on different rationale is not in itself reason to question the logic of the decisions made.

Yet, the nature of decisions implies that a preference is evident, which also suggests that an agent prefers one option over another; the agent has accordingly considered an option more desirable or choice-worthy which makes preference a comparative attitude.[73] To that end, a preference would indicate a preference ordering, this being the ordering of the options preferred by the decision-maker. To what extent must these options offer 'completeness' before a choice can be made is debated?[74] Should these preferences merely represent choice behaviour, otherwise referred to as 'revealed preference theory' amongst economists,[75] then completeness is automatically satisfied on the assumption that a choice must inevitably be made. Choice, in this respect, does not equate to the best outcome, nor does it mean that a better available outcome must always be selected, only that its viability satisfies what can be justified by the decision-maker. Alternatively, if decisions are made based on optimum

---

[71] See generally Insolvency Act 1986, Insolvency (England and Wales) Rules 2016, SIP 9.

[72] The term 'locations' refers to the variables that may influence a decision. For a general discussion, see J Broome, *Weighing Goods* (Basil Blackwell 1991).

[73] See generally, ibid.

[74] For example, if completeness relies on choice behaviour, then it is automatically satisfied, see A Sen, 'Behaviour and the Concept of Preference' (1973) 40 *Economica* 241. If it concerns judgement about the best option then there are doubts about whether completeness should be satisfied, see M Mandler, 'A Difficult Choice in Preference Theory: Rationality Implies Completeness or Transitivity but Not Both' in Elijah Millgram (ed), *Varieties of Practical Reasoning* (MIT Press 2001) 373.

[75] Sen (n 74).

outcome to creditors ('payoffs'), then issues that concern completeness are addressed.[76] It is this interpretation of preference that dominates decision theory and explains choice behaviour as seen in insolvency decision-making.[77]

In respect to rationality, while most decision theorists tend to argue that it requires preferences to be *coherently extendible*,[78] other conditions such as transitivity, which governs preference, are also crucial.[79] Nonetheless, what is imperative to different interpretation of preference is the comparison of options. Specifically, how preferences are responsive to conditions attached to the insolvent company. For example, if on comparison a company can be rescued in two ways, namely AA and BB, and the distinction between the two provides for going concern outcomes that makes BB no worse than AA, the prominent features when comparing rescue objective BB and CC are: (i) the return for creditors; and (ii) that CC is no worse than BB in this regard. Further, if on comparison between AA and CC, the prominent feature of distinction is longevity, but the difference is slight, then it could be argued that transitivity is irrelevant to the preferences concerning AA, BB, and CC.[80] However, some commentators argue that transitivity is non-negotiable since it is core to the objective comparative desirability, which forms the rationality for how preferences may be chosen based on their betterment.[81] In this respect, the desirability of a decision should not vary when compared to other options since this would indicate that context affects how the decision-maker perceives the options. In this regard, the type and scope of rescue that is undertaken could be unduly influenced by bias that is not based on sound information. As such, rational decisions would be improbable, which would lead to irrational decisions to be made.

---

76 Mandler (n 74) 373–402.

77 D M Hausman, 'Mistakes about Preferences in the Social Sciences' (2001) 41(1) *Philosophy* of the Social Sciences 3–25; also, *Preference, Value, Choice, and Welfare*, (Cambridge University Press 2011); R Bradley and H Orri Stefánsson, 'Counterfactual Desirability' (2017) 68(2) *British Journal for the Philosophy of Science* 485.

78 This means that even if your preferences are not complete, it should be possible to complete them without violating any of the conditions that are rationally required, see R Jeffrey, 'Bayesianism with a Human Face' in John Earman (ed), *Testing Scientific Theories* (University of Minnesota Press 1983) 133.

79 For a detailed discussion, see M Regenwetter, J Dana, and C Davis-Stober, 'Transitivity of Preferences', (2011) 118(1) *Psychological Review* 42.

80 L Temkin, *Rethinking the Good: Moral Ideals and the Nature of Practical Reasoning* (Oxford University Press 2012) 162–193.

81 Broome (n 72) 100–103.

CONCLUSION

Commercial decisions are often complex, and highly susceptible to variables that are unknown until the exact moment that they must be made. They are subject to the effectiveness of legislation to deal with emerging trends and changes to the commercial environment. In turn, decisions are frequently influenced by different stakeholders who have an array of interests, all of which may not be in common. While to some degree the directors, IPs and the courts have an input into certain decisions, these are often in those marginal cases where commercial discretion must be exercised. These types of decisions may not always be well received, but nonetheless they are permitted within insolvency and indeed wider commercial legislation. Given that these decisions are made on commercial grounds the courts will rarely question or permit challenges brought by disgruntled creditors since the court does not second-guess such decisions, nor does it permit decisions to be reviewed in hindsight. While this discretion could lead to deviations from the legislation, it is recognised that a level of latitude is required for insolvency law to operate. As such, there may be variances in outcomes reached in similar cases, but that is justified on the grounds that different choices emerge in each company. Therefore, what is rational in one case, may not be in another, which means that rationality must be relaxed so that desired outcomes can be reached. In other words, irrational decisions may nevertheless lead to rational outcomes.

The secured creditors continue to retain a large influence in all the insolvency regimes since they have their interests protected or are given opportunities to make decisions within the process that concerns their interests. In that respect, they are largely removed from the decision-making process since the decisions that must be taken regarding their interests is for most part pre-determined in pre-existing rights prior to the point of insolvency. In the new measures introduced by CIGA 2020, the standalone moratorium provides that the directors must ensure that they can prove to the IP that rescue is a viable option; if so, the IP will give their consent for the moratorium to be pursued. Notwithstanding the focus on the rescue objective, rescue outcomes are broad, and it is inevitable that case law will be required to build a clearer picture what amounts to reasonable rescue outcomes in the circumstances. As it stands, the decisions made by IPs in this context are likely to be broader than the real prospect test like that seen in administration, to include instances where a return to solvency can be achieved.

In the restructuring plans, the courts' role is clear – ensure all the plans are fair; a process that requires objectivity to determine whether the plan is viable. While the court initiates the two hearings that are required to approve the plan, creditors must still play their role in the cross-class cram-down decision. Early case law has indicated that creditors and shareholders will play a role in the valuation process whereby the plan permits a compromise of both debt and equity claims. Yet it remains to be seen what valuation evidence would be considered sufficient to prove whether a creditor has a genuine economic interest; decisions on this issue are likely to be complex where there are multiple classes of creditors.

Finally, the administration process led by an IP is obliged to first consider whether the company can be rescued as a going concern. It does not specify how this should be undertaken, which provides scope for choices to be made. The IP could show a preference for a certain approach, and this could be one option of many alternatives that exist. Each could lead to the same outcome, but bias could inform the decision-making process. If only one approach is evident, then biases could still exist as to how the process will be undertaken.

Upon reflection, rational choices may appear irrational at the time, but they can still produce rational outcomes. The form that decisions and choices can take provide the means for outcomes to be reached. Given the nature of insolvency law and corporate rescue, the relaxation of rationality permits the pursuit of rescue, but this is on the condition that it continues to do so with reference to an identifiable and effective insolvency framework.

9. The competing goals theory and insolvency law

Jason Harris

INTRODUCTION

Theory is important to a complete understanding of insolvency law. Insolvency law is a complex body of rules, duties, obligations and liabilities that operate directly through a formal insolvency procedure, and indirectly by framing the scope of legal rights that are gained or bargained for prior to a debtor's formal insolvency. Understanding how legal rights may be affected by insolvency processes shapes the ex-ante negotiation of those legal rights through voluntary dealings. A central feature of corporate insolvency law in Australia is the modification or suspension of the exercise by creditors of pre-insolvency enforcement rights against the debtor during an insolvency procedure in favour of participating in a collective insolvency process.[1] This raises the question of what the ultimate goal (or goals) of insolvency law are? Are insolvency laws purely to benefit creditors or do they serve broader public interest goals?

Insolvency law may be described as an extension of the private law of debtors and creditors, which is primarily based on the exercise and enforcement of private contractual rights and obligations against the debtor. There are many features of insolvency law that are aimed at protecting and promoting the private interests of creditors, particularly their interests in obtaining repayment of their debts and claims. Insolvency practitioners are considered to act in a fiduciary capacity to the creditors as a whole.[2] Only creditors have the right to vote in meetings of the insolvent debtor.[3] Indeed, in a standard insolvency case, non-creditor groups usually have limited or no rights to participate as they are not creditors and do not have the rights that creditors have.[4]

---

1 Corporations Act 2001 (Cth) ss 440D, 471B, 500.

2 *ASIC v Edge* [2007] VSC 170; *Macks v Viscariello* [2017] SASCFC 172.

3 Insolvency Practice Rules (Corporations) 2016 (Cth), ss 75–85.

4 For example, in Part 5.3A voluntary administration, the purpose of the procedure is to provide a better return for creditors and members, but members don't have a voting

Insolvency law may therefore be seen as coming within the sphere of private law because it is concerned with the exercise and adjustment of rights between debtors and creditors.

Insolvency law cannot be said to be solely concerned with the private rights of creditors and there are many features that are characteristics of public law. These include the appointment of a government sanctioned and controlled external administrator, who may act as an officer of the court and in a quasi-judicial capacity.[5] External administrators are required to undertake extensive investigations and reporting activities, even in circumstances where such activities in fact exhaust the remaining pool of funds available to creditors. As will be discussed below, in the vast majority of insolvency cases in Australia, unsecured creditors receive no financial return. Insolvency practitioners are not required to auction off the debtor's assets for only the highest price offered,[6] and the courts will take into account concepts of the public interest and commercial morality when deciding on whether to make orders affecting the insolvency matter.[7] Insolvency practitioners may therefore be said to owe duties to act in the public interest, not merely to serve the private interests of creditors.

Insolvency law involves a constant balance, and in many cases a trade-off, between the private and public interests that arise from the debtor's state of insolvency. This chapter builds upon an existing theoretical debate concerning the primacy that should be given to creditors in modern corporate insolvency law. It considers the value of the creditors' bargain model as a theoretical lens through which to understand how and why Australian corporate insolvency law works the way that it does. It is argued that there has always had a strong public interest and public law dimension and so the creditors' bargain model is, at best, an incomplete explanation of the operation, structure and ultimate justification for Australian corporate insolvency law.

---

right: s 435A. See also ss 563A; 600H (shareholders claiming creditor status are postponed to other creditors).

5 *Re Biposo* (1995) 13 ACLC 1, 271.

6 *Robit Nominees Pty Ltd v Oceanlinx Ltd (in liq) (recs and mgrs apptd)* [2016] FCA 225.

7 *Adelaide Brighton Cement Ltd v Concrete Supply Pty Ltd (Subject to DOCA) (No 2)* [2018] FCA 1003.

THE CREDITORS' BARGAIN MODEL (CBM)

Overview

The CBM is the predominant analytical tool used in insolvency theory in the common law world,[8] although it is subject to extensive criticism.[9] The CBM relies on ex-ante reasoning from a law and economics approach, which favours the protection of individual rights and private ordering.[10] This may be contrasted with more socially progressive theories that use ex-post reasoning and advocates the use of insolvency laws to pursue social goals beyond the mere private benefits to those with contractual claims against the company, which are discussed below.

The Original CBM

Thomas Jackson argued in a series of articles starting in the early 1980s,[11] and then culminating in a widely cited book,[12] that insolvency law can be justified as a system that creditors would agree to once they recognised the common pool problem that insolvent firms present.

The common pool problem posed by insolvency is that creditors all have claims against the company, whose assets are insufficient to satisfy all the claims. If one or more creditors is active in monitoring and takes enforcement action against the debtor, then this will diminish the remaining resources for all other creditors.[13] In such a case, the creditors could rationally agree that

---

[8] H Anderson, 'Theory and Reality in Insolvency Law: Some Contradictions in Australia' (2009) 27(8) *Company and Securities Law Journal* 506, 509; A Levitin, 'Bankrupt Politics and the Politics of Bankruptcy' (2012) 97(6) *Cornell Law Review* 1399.

[9] See, in particular, the work of Professor (now Senator) Elizabeth Warren and Professor David Carlson, discussed further below.

[10] M Trebilcock, 'Law and Economics' (1993) 16(2) *Dalhousie Law Journal* 360, 304.

[11] T H Jackson, 'Bankruptcy, Non-Bankruptcy Entitlements, and the Creditors' Bargain' (1982) 91(5) *Yale Law Journal* 857; T H Jackson, 'Of Liquidation, Continuation, and Delay: An Analysis of Bankruptcy Policy and Non-bankruptcy Rules' (1986) 60(4) *American Bankruptcy Law Journal* 399; T H Jackson and Robert Scott, 'On the Nature of Bankruptcy Sharing and the Creditors' Bargain' (1989) 75(2) *Virginia Law Review* 155.

[12] T H Jackson, *The Logic and Limits of Bankruptcy Law* (Harvard University Press 1986). See also D Baird, 'A World Without Bankruptcy' (1987) 50(2) *Law and Contemporary Problems* 173.

[13] This is an example of the 'tragedy of the commons' concept used in economics: see G Hardin, 'The Tragedy of the Commons' (1968) 162(3859) *Science* 1243, 1244; S

a better process would be to prevent enforcement action and distribute the debtor's assets in some fair way between the creditors. A collective process is preferable and, crucially for the justification proffered of the CBM, would be preferred by creditors if they were asked prior to dealing with the debtor.[14]

The CBM argues that the role of insolvency law is to ensure that the debtor's assets are distributed to creditors as quickly and as cheaply as possible, so as to maximise returns to creditors. The *raison d'être* of insolvency law is therefore to provide a more efficient system compared with allowing individual creditor enforcement when the company becomes insolvent. Essentially, this view sees the goal of insolvency law to supplement the non-insolvency law of debtor and creditors.[15] Jackson argues that this is the *only* appropriate role for insolvency law.[16]

The CBM argues that creditors would agree that allowing individual enforcement during the firm's insolvency would make most, if not all of the creditors, worse off and hence they would agree to the mandatory collective system with a stay in order to maximise returns to all creditors. One central element of the CBM is the respect that insolvency law should give to pre-insolvency rights and priorities.[17] The CBM argues that the role of insolvency law in providing an efficient collection and distribution process is not to redistribute wealth among various claimants.[18] Jackson and Baird argue that the question of how to distribute the proceeds of the insolvency estate to creditors should be separate from the question of how much each creditor should receive, with only the first question relevant to insolvency law. Insolvency law should uphold pre-insolvency rights and priorities as much as possible.[19] After all, each layer in the debtor's capital structure receives a payment according to the risk that they agreed to assume, and this should be respected by bankruptcy law. Secured creditors charge a lower interest than unsecured creditors, and equity holders receive an open-ended claim against future profits (i.e., a higher

Gordon, 'The Economic Theory of a Common-Property Resource: The Fishery' (1954) 62(2) *Journal of Political Economy* 124.

14 Jackson 1982 (n 11) 860; Jackson (n 12) Chapter 1.

15 Jackson (n 12) 3 ('bankruptcy law, at its core, is debt-collection law'); Jackson 1986 (n 11) 401.

16 Jackson (n 12) 209.

17 Jackson and Scott (n 11), 155.

18 Jackson (n 12) Chapter 2; D Baird, 'The Reorganisation of Closely Held Firms and the Opt Out Problem' (1994) 72(3) *Washington University Law Quarterly* 913.

19 Jackson and Scott (n 11) 160. For an economic critique of this assumption see R Rasmussen, 'Behavioral Economics, the Economic Analysis of Bankruptcy Law and the Pricing of Credit' (1998) 51(6) *Vanderbilt Law Review* 1679, who argues based on the Coase Theorem that debtors and creditors would bargain with each other to achieve the lowest cost credit regime regardless of the pre-existing state law collection rights.

interest on their investment) because they assume the most risk, as they are at the bottom of the capital structure and are paid last.[20]

The CBM argues that each tranche in the capital structure understands this priority ranking and bargains accordingly.[21] To disturb this priority ranking by redistribution of wealth in insolvency proceedings would cause increased risk through uncertainty and lead to higher corporate borrowing costs, leading inexorably to lower economic returns for society as a whole.[22] This, of course, is referring to creditors as a whole, rather than the credit pricing/risk evaluation undertaken by individual creditors. The CBM contends that secured creditors would support the mandatory collective regime because it protects their pre-insolvency rights.[23] Put simply, the question of how much each creditor should receive should be answered by non-insolvency law.[24] In preserving pre-insolvency priorities, the law will put the onus of monitoring the debtor on those creditors with the highest risk of default, who (being paid last) therefore will have the right incentive to monitor the insolvency case.[25] A failure to protect pre-insolvency rights could lead to attempts to game the system to take advantage of rights in insolvency that would not otherwise be available outside of insolvency and thereby extract economic rents that would impose a cost on the whole system, as other both creditors and debtors increase monitoring and hence transaction costs to limit rent seeking.

Analysing the rationale and benefits of formal insolvency processes from the ex-ante position is a central feature of the CBM, which provides the presumed consent that legitimates the CBM. Jackson describes this by relying upon the Rawlsian veil of ignorance.[26] The creditor's autonomy to regulate their own dealings with the debtor, i.e., their presumed consent to a collective insolvency process, should be respected and upheld. The CBM adopts a form of the original position Rawlsian veil to place creditors in a position where they are unaware of what may happen in the absence of insolvency law,

---

[20] F Easterbrook and D Fischel, 'Voting in Corporate Law' (1983) 26(2) *Journal of Law & Economics* 395.

[21] Rasmussen (n 19).

[22] R Rasmussen, 'An Essay on Optimal Bankruptcy Rules and Social Justice' (1994) *University of Illinois Law Review* 1.

[23] D Baird and T H Jackson, 'Corporate Reorganizations and the Treatment of Diverse Ownership Interests' (1984) 51(1) *University of Chicago Law Review* 97.

[24] T H Jackson, 'Translating Assets and Liabilities to the Bankruptcy Forum' (1985) 14(1) *Journal of Legal Studies* 73, 87.

[25] T H Jackson and A Kronman, 'Secured Financing and Priorities Among Creditors' (1979) 88(6) *Yale Law Journal* 1143.

[26] Jackson (n 12) 25. For a critique of Jackson's approach on this issue, see R Mokal, *Corporate Insolvency Law: Theory and Application* (Oxford University Press 2005).

although they would be aware of their role (e.g., secured or unsecured status) and their position under pre-insolvency law.[27] Hence, creditors would agree to maintain their pre-insolvency position and priorities and to allow these priorities to be processed through a collective, rather than an individual, insolvency system because to do so is likely to give them a better return than allowing for individual enforcement.[28]

The primary focus of the CBM is therefore on voluntary contractual creditors. As the name suggests, the justification of the CBM is that ex ante, the creditors would agree to the insolvency system. Not every company has involuntary creditors, such as tort claimants and victims of environmental harm, but every trading company has contractual creditors, from suppliers of goods, leasing companies and finance providers. According to the CBM, if stakeholders such as employees or tort claimants (as non-consensual creditors) lose out in priority contests to secured creditors, then this is what all of the contractual creditors would have agreed to prior to insolvency, with knowledge that non-insolvency law will be responsible for dealing with their claims. Put simply, social concerns are not part of insolvency law and should be dealt with by non-insolvency laws, such as social security laws and product liability laws. Insolvency law should only be used for distributing returns to creditors. This is justified by the CBM on the basis that wealth redistribution goals, if valid and necessary, should be implemented not merely in insolvency law, but across non-insolvency law.[29] If employees need protection, why should their special insolvency priority not be replicated outside insolvency law?

The CBM has received extensive criticism, in part based on the narrow focus of the theory through the exclusion of involuntary creditors from the deemed consent model. Jackson and Scott subsequently added to the CBM a recognition that some involuntary creditors, such as employees and tort claimants could be considered to be part of a common disaster that would be likely to affect all creditors, in which case the creditors may agree to a limited amount of risk sharing by justifying their inclusion in bankruptcy procedure.[30]

The Varied CBM

Jackson and Scott varied the original CBM due to persistent evidence of the redistributive effect of insolvency law in the United States (US). The varied CBM sought to examine the redistributive efforts in insolvency to determine

---

27 Jackson 1982 (n 11) 869.

28 Jackson and Scott (n 11) 160–161.

29 Jackson (n 12) Chapter 9; D Baird, 'The Uneasy Case for Corporate Reorganizations' (1986) 15(1) *Journal of Legal Studies* 127.

30 Jackson and Scott (n 11).

whether these were consistent with the ex-ante wishes of creditors. Jackson and Scott added several new elements to the CBM including (i) consensual sharing of the common risks of business failure among creditors;[31] (ii) discouraging self-interested 'eve of bankruptcy' decisions that are not in the interests of the creditors as a group;[32] (iii) recognition of non-monetary values in firms where there are idiosyncratic values attributed to the owner-managers (i.e., equity) where this would provide a better opportunity for rehabilitation.[33]

Jackson and Scott argued that risk sharing in insolvency is not the same as redistributing wealth to non-consensual creditors.[34] They treated the need for such sharing as being similar to a common disaster fund, where voluntary creditors would anticipate the need to share distributions with involuntary creditors such as tort claimants.[35] This can be justified on the basis that involuntary creditors had no choice or ability to obtain further protection for their position before becoming a creditor.[36] Differences in the payment priorities of a company's capital structure are also inherently concerned with risk sharing between creditors.[37] This is still part of core insolvency law because insolvency law is inherently concerned with managing competing claims against the debtor in insolvency,[38] and the focus is not on how any particular creditor does in insolvency cases but on the collective welfare of all creditors.[39]

The CBM and Corporate Rescue Laws

Jackson's view of corporate rescue laws is encapsulated in this statement: 'the problems of business failure are not bankruptcy problems. The resolution of them should not be thought of as bankruptcy specific'.[40]

The CBM seeks to limit the role of rescue to situations where the common pool problem exists.[41] Rescuing businesses in financial distress, so as to minimise losses to employees and related communities, is not solely aimed at maximising returns to creditors as efficiently as possible and therefore should not be the role of insolvency law. The CBM thus rejects the justification of

---

31 Ibid., 164.
32 Ibid., 169.
33 Ibid., 196.
34 Ibid., 156.
35 Ibid., 157.
36 Ibid., 177.
37 Ibid., 165.
38 Ibid., 158; D Baird, 'The Bankruptcy Exchange' (2009) 4(1) *Brookings Journal of Corporate, Financial and Commercial Law* 23.
39 Jackson and Scott (n 11) 160.
40 Jackson (n 12) 209.
41 Ibid.

rescue laws as giving firms in financial distress time to assess workout options in order to save jobs.[42] One reason for this, as noted above, is that a goal of keeping businesses operating so as to benefit employees and other stakeholders should be implemented across the law, not only in insolvency law. If the law does not stop business owners shutting down and laying off workers prior to insolvency, then why should insolvency be any different?

Jackson also argues against rescue as a legal goal because of the difficulties of valuing a business on an ongoing basis as opposed to simply putting the business and its assets up for public auction to let the market determine the value of the assets.[43] Valuation disputes are usually determined in court, which further increases costs. In Australia, while the courts do not have a similar role to US bankruptcy courts in a chapter 11 case, the courts can be called on to determine valuation issues, although this has tended to be determined by letting the creditors vote on competing proposals for a deed of company arrangement (DOCA).[44]

There is also a concern with loss sharing between levels in the capital structure. The costs of continuing to trade, and the cost of delayed repayment should not be shared equally between claimants on the debtor, but rather should borne by the lowest tranche in the capital structure.[45] In short, the CBM argues that rescue laws such as chapter 11 of the US Bankruptcy Code are only justified in the limited circumstances where it can be proven that they provide a greater return to creditors than liquidation, which CBM adherents usually argue, is rare[46] due to inherent problems in valuing businesses and projecting future cash flows.

In recent years, the rise in judicial sales through chapter 11 cases, rather than pursuing a restructuring plan to voting by creditors has led some scholars to question whether formal corporate rescue laws are still relevant given that many large cases are resolved by a quick sale rather than negotiating a restructuring plan.[47] Further arguments point to the rise in debt trading as a destructive

---

42 Ibid., 210.

43 Ibid., 211–212; Baird (n 29) 136–139.

44 See e.g., *Re TEN Network Holdings Ltd (Admins Apptd) (Recs and Mgrs Apptd)* [2017] NSWSC 124. See generally J Harris and T Ng, 'Valuation Issues in Restructuring: An Overview of Common Valuation Methodologies and How They Have Been Handled by the Courts' (2019) 31(1) *Australian Restructuring Insolvency & Turnaround Association Journal* 20.

45 Baird (n 29) 134–135.

46 Ibid.

47 D Baird and R Rasmussen, 'The End of Bankruptcy' (2002) 55(3) *Stanford Law Review* 751.

force that produces an anti-commons problem rather than a common pool problem that insolvency law is designed to solve.[48]

Conclusion

The CBM, whether in its original form or its varied form, offers a narrow view for insolvency law that is founded squarely on promoting the interests of creditors. The CBM sees insolvency as squarely within private law, as an extension of debtor-creditor law that has value in maximising financial returns for creditors by preserving and enhancing the debtor's divisible assets for the collective benefit of creditors.

THE TRADITIONALIST CRITIQUE OF THE CBM

One advantage that the CBM has as a theory of insolvency law is that, like many variations of theoretical law and economics, it is a relatively simple argument: creditors as a whole would be worse off without insolvency law, and so they would therefore agree to an insolvency law that is likely to make them better off as a collective group. Several scholars have pointed out the inherent circularity with the CBM, given its Rawlsian veil of ignorance and narrow focus. The CBM justifies insolvency law by asking contractual creditors if they would prefer to maintain their pre-insolvency priority position if the company became insolvent, and enter a mandatory collective regime that would ensure that their pre-insolvency rights are protected, provided that doing so maximises the total pool of assets available to creditors. Anyone hurt by their regime would need to be compensated by some other law. The theory assumes the answer to the question it poses to hypothetical creditors.[49]

The CBM presumes creditor consent based on an assumption that creditors would want to respect pre-insolvency rights, particularly the priority of secured debt. Professor Finch has described the ex-ante consent model of the CBM as 'the equality of Animal Farm' and assuming a level of common interest among creditors that is unrealistic.[50] Why would creditors necessarily

---

48 D Baird and R Rasmussen, 'Antibankruptcy' (2009) 119(4) *Yale Law Journal* 648.

49 D Carlson, 'Philosophy in Bankruptcy' (1987) 85(5/6) *Michigan Law Review* 1341; D Korobkin, 'Rehabilitating Values: A Jurisprudence of Bankruptcy' (1991) 91(4) *Columbia Law Review* 717, 737.

50 V Finch, 'The Measures of Insolvency Law' (1997) 17(2) *Oxford Journal of Legal Studies* 227, 233. See also V Finch, 'Corporate Rescue in a World of Debt' (2008) 8 *Journal of Business Law* 756, for a discussion of differences between credi-

want to exclude or minimise consideration of stakeholders, particularly if the business will continue following a corporate rescue attempt?

The group of scholars who critique the CBM on the basis that it ignores the traditional role of insolvency law in addressing inequalities based on the ex-post adverse effects on stakeholders in insolvency are referred to as 'traditionalists'.[51] A central feature of traditionalist arguments is that insolvency law is too complex to be accurately or usefully described by one overarching theory.[52] Insolvency law reform is often the product of a compromise between a range of commercial, social, political and legal factors.[53] The influences on insolvency law reform are not necessarily, and indeed rarely, made up of consistent and coherent policies that fit wholly within the boundaries of any single theory of insolvency law, let alone a theory that only considers contractual creditors.

The CBM builds on contractarian corporate law analysis to argue that creditors should be the focus of insolvency law because they are the residual risk bearers.[54] Traditionalists question whether consensual creditors really are the residual risk bearers, particularly once the focus broadens from direct economic loss and includes consequential loss and non-economic values. Traditionalists argue that insolvency does recognise, and always has recognised, a broader range of stakeholders than merely consensual creditors, with employees typically treated as non-consensual creditors given the firm specific nature of their labour and the general difficulty in diversifying their risk between multiple employers.[55]

A major counter argument to the CBM's disfavour for corporate rescue is founded on the notion that insolvency law is, and always has been, concerned with inequalities that arise during times of financial distress rather than on reinforcing existing private rights. The theme underpinning traditionalist theories is that bankruptcy policy must ensure both that relief from the most

---

tors during a restructuring; H Anderson, 'Theory and Reality in Insolvency Law: Some Contradictions in Australia' (2009) 27(8) *Company & Securities Law Journal* 506, 510.

[51] D Baird, 'Bankruptcy's Uncontested Axioms' (1998) 108(3) *Yale Law Journal* 573.

[52] Carlson (n 49); E Warren, 'Bankruptcy Policy' (1987) 54(3) *University of Chicago Law Review* 775; K Gross, *Failure and Forgiveness: Rebalancing the Bankruptcy System* (Yale University Press 1997).

[53] Warren, ibid.; Gross, ibid.; Anderson (n 50).

[54] See M Jensen and W Meckling, 'Theory of the Firm: Managerial Behaviour, Agency Costs and Ownership Structure' (1976) 3(4) *Journal of Financial Economics* 305; F Easterbrook and D Fischel, *The Economic Structure of Corporate Law* (Harvard University Press 1991).

[55] E Warren, 'The Untenable Case for Repeal of Chapter 11' (1992) 102(2) *Yale Law Journal* 437.

devastating effects of financial failure is given to those in need and that the cost of this relief is not borne by those least able to pay.[56]

Adopting a positivist approach, evidence of this can be seen in the long-standing system of priority given to certain creditors who would otherwise be general unsecured creditors, such as employees, creditors owed injury compensation and holders of insurance policies.[57] Insolvency law (as with most individual statute laws) is a policy compromise between various political, economic and commercial interests that are brought together in the context of failing and failed businesses. With insufficient assets to meet all claims, hard choices need to be made about who is to be paid and how much. While a rational, dispassionate, economic actor might choose a collective process aimed at stabilising the estate for efficient collection, the reality is that insolvency processes are interconnected with (and between) individual stakeholders and their circumstances.[58]

Traditionalist scholars also criticise many of the underlying assumptions of the CBM. As Professor Warren has said, contractual models (such as the CBM) are more focused on theoretical simplicity rather than reality.[59] One foundational feature of traditional law and economics analysis is the assumption that individuals are rational utility maximisers. That is, individuals will act in their own best interests. But this ignores the problems of information asymmetries and bargaining inequality that pervade actual dealings between debtors and creditors.[60] Furthermore, developments in behavioural economics, building on the principle of bounded rationality,[61] suggest that in the real world people do not always act rationally or in ways that pursue their own self-interest.[62] The basic idea that creditors would ordinarily pursue repayment

---

56 Gross (n 52); C Frost, 'Bankruptcy Redistributive Policies and the Limits of the Judicial Process' (1995) 74(1) *North Carolina Law Review* 75, 80–81.

57 Corporations Act 2001 (Cth), ss 556(e)–(h), 562. See further C Symes, *Statutory Priorities in Corporate Insolvency Law: An Analysis of Preferred Creditor Status* (Ashgate 2008).

58 Warren (n 52) 811, this includes their own states of bounded rationality that carry with them behavioural biases as decision-making heuristics.

59 E Warren and J Westbrook, 'Searching for Reorganization Realities' (1994) 72(3) *Washington University Law Quarterly* 1257, 1260.

60 C Tabb, 'Of Contractarians and Bankruptcy Reform: A Skeptical View' (2004) 12(1) *American Bankruptcy Institute Law Review* 259. See also Gross (n 52), who argues that creditors should be treated according to equality of outcome.

61 H Simon, 'A Behavioral Model of Rational Choice' (1955) 69(1) *Quarterly Journal of Economics* 99; O Williamson, *The Economic Institutions of Capitalism* (The Free Press 1985).

62 See also Gross (n 52), who argues that human nature supports broader ideals of support and community rather than single minded self-interest.

at some point is not seriously contested though.[63] Furthermore, the nature and operation of market efficiency have come into question with developments in behavioural economics.[64]

The most prominent traditionalist theorist is Elizabeth Warren (now Senator Warren), who rejects the single over-arching creditor wealth maximisation goal that underpins the CBM, which she describes as a 'neat solution', in contrast to the model she offers 'a dirty, complex, elastic, interconnected view of bankruptcy from which I can neither predict outcomes nor even necessarily fully articulate all the factors relevant to a policy decision'.[65]

The CBM's approach is said to be too simplistic, offering a narrow, myopic view that cannot properly explain insolvency law, which is far too complex, and subject to too many influences, to be justified on the grounds of a single goal. This is certainly consistent with major reviews of insolvency law in both Australia and in the United Kingdom (UK).[66]

Warren argues that the history of insolvency law shows that it has always been concerned with redistributive goals,[67] thereby rejecting the CBM's central focus on respecting pre-insolvency rights. Warren argues that this process is inevitably one of redistribution, which, together with further examples of redistribution, such as the *pari passu* rule and its exceptions, supports her view that insolvency law's role is inevitably to redistribute wealth.[68] Insolvency law is not, and has never been, a sub-category of non-insolvency debt collection law, because while non-insolvency collection law is based on single defaults by debtors, insolvency law is concerned with multiple (collective) defaults.[69] Insolvency law is therefore something different from debtor creditor law, and this special role includes recognition of, and respect for, those affected by financial distress.

Warren supports rescue as a legal policy goal, on the basis that the legislative purpose of chapter 11 is to maximise enterprise value and thereby help

---

63 Rasmussen (n 19) 1682–1683. Rasmussen argues that behavioural biases within credit intermediaries could drive lower lending costs if private auctions were conducted in favour of formal reorganisation under chapter 11 bankruptcy.

64 See D Dick, 'The Chapter 11 Efficiency Fallacy' (2013) *Brigham Young University Law Review* 759.

65 Warren (n 52) 811.

66 Law Reform Commission, *General Insolvency Inquiry* (Report No 45, 1988) para 33; United Kingdom Insolvency Law Review Committee, Report on Insolvency Law and Practice, Cmnd 8558 (1982) para 198; Finch (n 50).

67 Warren (n 52) 785; E Warren, 'Bankruptcy Policymaking in an Imperfect World' (1993) 92(2) *Michigan Law Review* 336, 353.

68 Warren (n 52); Warren, ibid., 353.

69 Warren (n 52) 784.

to save jobs and further the public interest.[70] Maintaining a rescue goal gives the opportunity at least to extract greater value for stakeholders by trading on the business, rather than selling the assets through liquidation.[71] Facilitating continued trading can help employees deal with financial distress, while shifting the economic burden onto commercial creditors who may be better able to manage this risk through diversification.[72] While this may involve further costs, and potentially lower returns to creditors in particular cases, these costs must be balanced against the public interest in saving business.[73]

The Traditionalist critique of the CBM reveals clear limitations in the model. The narrow singular focus of the model on creditors' interests means that it has limited explanatory power for actual insolvency law. The next section demonstrates that the goals of actual insolvency law are much broader than simply maximising returns to creditors.

THE GOALS OF INSOLVENCY LAW

The precise shape of specific insolvency laws is influenced by numerous policy objectives pertaining to a variety of goals, rights and interests.[74] The nature of domestic insolvency laws is often described across a spectrum between pro-debtor and pro-creditor.[75] Jurisdictions such as Australia that provide rights for secured creditor enforcement, a system of external administration rather than debtor-in-possession and general creditor control over the appointment of the insolvency practitioner are classified as pro-creditor. Jurisdictions such as the US, with a flexible debtor-in-possession restructuring model and strong constraints on enforcement by secured creditors are classified as pro-debtor.

---

70 Ibid., 788; Warren (n 67) 344. For a similar argument applied to the Canadian corporate rescue law, see J Sarra, *Creditor Rights and the Public Interest* (University of Toronto Press 2003).

71 Warren (n 52) 350.

72 Warren (n 67) 358.

73 Warren (n 52) 798.

74 World Bank, *Principles and Guidelines for Effective Insolvency and Creditor Rights Systems* (2001) para 74.

75 See P Wood, *Principles of International Insolvency* (Thomson Reuters 2019); P Wood, *International Insolvency: Jurisdictions of the World* (Thomson Reuters 2019).

The goals of insolvency law include both public and private interests. The International Monetary Fund has noted two overarching goals of insolvency law:[76]

1. That the allocation of risk among participants in a market economy in a predictable, equitable, and transparent manner.
2. To protect and maximise value for the benefit of all interested parties and the economy in general.

Both of these goals include public and private interests, benefiting the debtor and the creditors (interested parties) as well as the broader economy. The Australian Law Reform Commission's *General Insolvency Inquiry* (the 'Harmer Report') listed several aims of insolvency law that include providing efficient and expeditious administrations that provide a convenient means of recovering property for payment of the debts and liabilities of the insolvent. The Harmer Report also lists supporting the commercial and economic processes of the community and trying to harmonise insolvency and the general law as goals, which are not solely concerned with creditor returns.[77] The recognition of non-creditor interests is even stronger in the list of goals provided by the Cork Report in the UK, which includes protecting the credit system, investigating conduct of the debtor that may warrant punishment and promoting international respect for English insolvency processes.[78] Both the Harmer and Cork Reports stress the important role that insolvency law has in supporting the economy, that is, beyond merely the private interests of creditors.

PUBLIC AND PRIVATE INTERESTS IN INSOLVENCY LAW

The distinction between public and private law has produced a long-standing debate between legal scholars.[79] Public law may be described as encompassing the framework of government organisation and decision making[80] and the reg-

[76] International Monetary Fund, *Orderly & Effective Insolvency Procedures* (1999) Chapter 2.

[77] Australian Law Reform Commission, *General Insolvency Inquiry*, Report No 45 (AGPS 1988) para 33.

[78] UK Insolvency Law Review Committee (n 66), para. 198.

[79] R Pound, 'Public Law and Private Law' (1939) 24(4) *Cornell Law Quarterly* 469; C Harlow, 'Public and Private Law: Definition without Distinction' (1980) 43(3) *Modern Law Review* 241.

[80] M Loughlin, *The Idea of Public Law* (Oxford University Press 2004) Chapter 2.

ulation of the interactions between individuals and the state.[81] Private law on the other hand is concerned with interactions between individual private actors (such as enforcing property and contractual rights).[82] It has been pointed out that public institutions are increasingly taking on roles as commercial actors through contracting with private parties.[83] While a lawsuit involving sovereign immunity or executive discretion will fit comfortably within the realm of public law, a lawsuit for breach of contract between a government-owned commercial corporation and another private actor will fit within the realm of private law despite involving a government enterprise.[84]

The distinction between public and private law has been extensively criticised and is, at best, a blurred line rather than a clear division, or indeed a series of blurred lines given their multiple differences.[85] The distinction is however useful when examining the utility of the CBM for understanding the design and operation of insolvency law. If insolvency law is concerned with upholding the private rights of private actors as creditors against the debtor, and the CBM suggests that this is the only proper role for insolvency law to have, then insolvency law should be seen as falling within the sphere of private law. On the other hand, if insolvency law is validly concerned with public interests that are not solely tied to maximising returns to creditors, and instead is concerned with broader public interests and the role and powers of public officials (insolvency practitioners as officers of the court), then it may be said that insolvency law sits within the realm of public law.

A preferrable characterisation is that insolvency law involves an overlap between both public law and private law. Some of the elements of insolvency law involve public law interests and other aspects of insolvency law will involve private law interests.

Insolvency law involves various private law interests, particularly the interests of creditors in obtaining some form of repayment. Creditors also have a private interest in identifying what has happened to the debtor and understanding why it has become insolvent, although this is also clearly in the public interest.[86] Insolvency affects the private rights of creditors by imposing a stay

---

81 M Elliott and D Feldman, 'Introduction' in M Elliott and D Feldman (eds), *The Cambridge Companion to Public Law* (Cambridge University Press 2015) 1.

82 W Lucy and A Williams, 'Public and Private: Neither Deep nor Meaningful?' in K Barker and D Jensen (eds), *Private Law: Key Encounters with Public Law* (Cambridge University Press 2013) Chapter 2.

83 J McLean, 'For a Law of Public Contract Per Se: An Intervention from Liberal Contract Theory' (2019) 39(4) *Oxford Journal of Legal Studies* 856.

84 See however McLean ibid, who argues to the contrary.

85 Lucy and Williams (n 82).

86 Note, e.g., that examinations of the debtor and related persons are undertaken in open court: Corporations Act 2001 (Cth), s 597.

on their private enforcement rights against the debtor during the insolvency proceedings. Creditors' private law enforcement rights are converted into rights to participate in a collective insolvency process. Creditors have private rights to receive information from the liquidator and may participate in votes conducted during the insolvency. Creditors can also participate on a creditors' committee[87] to advise and oversee the course of the liquidation.[88]

Insolvency practitioners[89] are fiduciaries[90] and are required to act in the best interests of the creditors as a whole;[91] they are also required to gather in and protect the debtor company's assets and to investigate the company's financial position, including determining what the provable debts and claims are. Voluntary administrators are required to convene two creditor meetings and liquidators may convene a meeting of creditors, but are not generally bound to do so. Insolvency practitioners will often convene a creditors' meeting to approve certain contracts and to approve their remuneration.[92] Insolvency practitioners may work closely with a committee of inspection if one has been appointed by the creditors. Each of these tasks are clearly promoting the private interests of the creditors.

Insolvency practitioners also have extensive reporting and investigation obligations. Many of the matters to be reported on involve information that is not directly in the interests of the creditors, such as whether there have been any offences committed by officers of the debtor. It is likely that such activities will be paid for from the debtor company's assets that are otherwise available to creditors and in some cases, where the asset levels are very low, this may mean that the insolvency practitioner's fees and expenses exhaust the funds that would otherwise be available for distribution to creditors.

One pervasive problem with insolvency cases is the lack of assets and funds available to pay for the work that is required to be done by the insolvency practitioner. Most debtors enter insolvency proceedings with little or no assets. This creates a situation where there may be no insolvency practi-

---

[87] This is called a committee of inspection in Australia: Insolvency Practice Schedule (Corporations) Div 80.

[88] This may include nominating who the liquidator will be (Corporations Act 2001 (Cth), s 496(5)) and replacing the liquidator at a subsequent creditor meeting: Insolvency Practice Schedule (Corporations), s 90-35.

[89] For the purpose of this discussion, insolvency practitioners refer to liquidators and voluntary administrators. Receivers are also registered company liquidators but generally act only in the best interests of the secured creditor who appointed them: *Expo Ptd Ltd (in liq) v Chant* (1979) 4 ACLR 679.

[90] *ASIC v Edge* [2007] VSC 170; *Macks v Viscariello* [2017] SASCFC 172.

[91] *Macks v Viscariello*, ibid.

[92] The court is also able to approve remuneration: Insolvency Practice Schedule (Corporations), s 60-10(1)(c).

tioner willing to accept the appointment, at least without an indemnity from creditors for their fees. In such a case, the debtor's management may simply abandon the company and it may not be subject to insolvency proceedings. In circumstances where the insolvency practitioner's administration of the debtor's estate exhausts the remaining funds it must be said that the work of the insolvency practitioner is not primarily in the interests of creditors, at least not in the economic interests of the creditors, but rather in the public interests.

Australia does have the Assetless Administration Fund, which is administered by ASIC and provides small funding for insolvency practitioners where there are insufficient assets in the company to fund basic investigations and examinations. However, ASIC's guidance on the AAF shows that applications are geared at identifying criminal offences and are not concerned with returns to creditors.

In many jurisdictions, the problem of low or no asset debtors and insolvency proceedings is addressed by having a government office that can perform the role of a default liquidator. This operates in the UK, with the Official Receiver (OR), who takes on the role of default liquidator on the making of a winding up order by the court.[93] The OR may then be replaced by a vote of the creditors.[94] In the UK, the OR position was established in the 1883, initially for personal bankruptcy and then subsequently for the compulsory liquidation of companies.[95] The OR's office has had an important role in insolvency matters where there are significant public interest considerations but insufficient assets available in the debtor's estate,[96] or where the risk of personal liability (e.g., where there are extensive environmental clean-up costs) for a liquidator is too great for a private practitioner.[97] The OR also has an important investigation function.[98] An OR office has a similar role under Hong Kong Law,[99] under Singaporean Law,[100] and under New Zealand law (where it is called the Official Assignee).[101] Maintaining a government liquidator role demonstrates that much of the work that insolvency practitioners do is in the public interest. Where there is a low asset or no asset insolvency, creditors might naturally refuse to fund a liquidator and government intervention may be needed. In

93 UK Insolvency Act 1986, s 136.
94 Ibid., s 139.
95 M Lester, *Victorian Insolvency* (Clarendon Press 1995) Chapter 1.
96 For example, Carillion and Thomas Cook.
97 For example, British Steel.
98 UK Insolvency Act 1986, s 132.
99 Hong Kong Companies (Winding Up and Miscellaneous Provisions) Ordinance, Cap 32, s 194.
100 Singapore Insolvency, Restructuring and Dissolution Act 2018, s 134.
101 New Zealand Companies Act 1993, s 241.

such cases, there is unlikely to be a return for creditors and the work is carried out primarily in the public interest.

Australian law adopted an OR-style position for personal insolvency in the form of the Official Trustee in Bankruptcy,[102] however a similar role was not adopted for corporate debtors. Corporate insolvency practitioners in Australia are all private practitioners, registered and regulated by the Australian Securities and Investments Commission.[103] While there is no longer any compulsion to accept an appointment over an insolvent company (e.g., on the basis that there are insufficient funds to conduct the liquidation) due to the repeal of the position of 'Official Liquidator' in 2016,[104] and the need for a liquidator to consent to the appointment,[105] many liquidators undertake unpaid or underpaid work due to the financial position of the company when it enters liquidation.[106]

The vast majority of companies that enter insolvency proceedings in Australia have little or no assets. Almost 18 per cent of company liquidations in Australia involve no remuneration for liquidators and a further 67 per cent involve remuneration from $1 to $50,000, which could involve some matters that are underfunded;[107] 37 per cent of all companies that enter external administration each year in Australia have no assets and only 20 per cent of companies have more than $50,000 in assets;[108] 92 per cent of companies that enter external administration involve no payment to unsecured creditors, and a further 4 per cent involve returns of 10 per cent or less for unsecured creditors.[109] While liquidators are not obliged to incur expenses for a liquidation if there are inadequate funds to do so,[110] basic reporting and investigations must still be carried out despite there being no prospect of returns for creditors nor payment for the liquidator. Liquidators are also charged fees by ASIC for lodging documents, searching ASIC's registers to obtain required information and an additional annual industry funding levy even if they accept not appointments in a given financial year.

---

[102] Bankruptcy Act 1966 (Cth), s18. The Official Receiver in bankruptcy performs a regulatory function in issuing notices and receiving documents: see for example ss 54A; 139ZQ.

[103] Insolvency Practice Schedule Corporations (Cth) Div 20, 40.

[104] Insolvency Law Reform Act 2016 (Cth).

[105] Corporations Act 2001 (Cth), s 532(9).

[106] ARITA, 'The End of the Role of Official Liquidators' (27 July 2016); A Coneyworth (nee Phillips), 'An Analysis of Official Liquidations in Australia' (2013). Both are available from www.arita.com.au accessed 29 May 2023.

[107] ASIC, Insolvency Statistics Series 3 2018-2019, Table 3.3.13 (last available due to pending revision of this report).

[108] Ibid., Table 3.3.7.

[109] Ibid., Table 3.3.13.

[110] Corporations Act 2001 (Cth), s 545(1).

Liquidators may commence proceedings for voidable transactions to increase the pool of funds available for distribution to creditors, but many of these actions do not involve any meaningful return to unsecured creditors. Liquidators will have first priority over the recovered funds to satisfy their costs and remuneration.[111] The courts have held that it is not an abuse of process for a liquidator to undertake litigation where there are low prospects of a return to creditors.[112] Liquidators are seen both by the courts and by ASIC, the corporate law and corporate insolvency regulator, to be gatekeepers who act in the public interest, not merely in the economic interests of creditors.[113]

Furthermore, if creditors were the central focus of insolvency law in Australia, then we might expect creditors to have direct rights to control the work of insolvency practitioners, or at least to hold them accountable for their actions. While creditors may be able to refuse to approve of the insolvency practitioners fees,[114] they have no role in approving or disapproving of their expenses and other disbursements.[115] While creditors may issue directions to insolvency practitioners, either through a resolution of creditors or through a committee of inspection, these are not binding on insolvency practitioners.[116] Insolvency practitioners can also bypass creditors and seek approval of their remuneration from the courts.[117] Creditors also have considerable difficulty in bringing litigation against insolvency practitioners, with the courts generally respecting their commercial decision making.[118] Insolvency practitioners may be fiduciaries and required to act in the best interests of creditors as a whole, but this does not involve a duty owed directly to creditors or one that is enforceable by creditors.[119] The most that the creditors may do is remove the insolvency practitioner or seek a review of their conduct either by the court or by a reviewing liquidator.[120]

CONCLUSION

The CBM has been influential in debates about the scope and purpose of insolvency laws all over the common law world. There is no doubt that its focus on

---

111 Corporations Act 2001 (Cth), s 556(1).
112 *Hall v Poolman* [2009] NSWCA 64.
113 *ASIC v Edge* [2007] VSC 170; *Macks v Viscariello* [2017] SASCFC 172.
114 Insolvency Practice Schedule (Corporations) (Cth), s 60-10.
115 *Onefone Australia Pty Ltd v One.Tel Ltd* [2010] NSWSC 1120.
116 Insolvency Practice Schedule (Corporations) (Cth), s 80-35, Div 85.
117 Ibid., ss 60-10; 60-11.
118 *Macks v Viscariello* [2017] SASCFC 172. See further J Wood, 'Insolvency Office-holder Discretion and Judicial Control' (2020) 6 *Journal of Business Law* 451.
119 Ibid.
120 Insolvency Practice Schedule (Corporations) (Cth), ss 90-10; 90-15; 90-35.

the position of creditors, and their rights in insolvency, tells an important story about why insolvency works in the way that it does, at least some of the time.

The discussion above raises the question of whether corporate insolvency in Australia is primarily focused on maximising returns to creditors. While insolvency practitioners are required to act as fiduciaries in the interests of creditors as a whole, and are responsible for paying creditor debts and claims, the reality is that creditors receive little or no payment in over 90 per cent of corporate insolvencies and in large numbers of matters insolvency practitioners are either not paid or underpaid. The insolvency system requires insolvency practitioners to conduct extensive investigations and reporting, but much of the information is in the public interest rather than in the direct interest of creditors. This suggests that the CBM is not an accurate or helpful explanation of what Australian corporate insolvency law is, or why it operates the way that it does. There are aspects of the CBM that are consistent with Australian insolvency law, such as the automatic stay, liquidator recovery powers and the requirement to preserve, protect and realise the debtor company's assets at least notionally for the interests of the creditors. However, in most cases there are little or no assets and any reporting and investigation of the debtor company is largely for the public interest rather than for the benefit of creditors.

Insolvency law is formed through a combination of social, economic, political and legal choices about how insolvent debtor companies should be dealt with. In practice, many of them are simply abandoned because there are no assets available to pay for a private insolvency practitioner to administer them. Even for those companies that are placed into formal insolvency proceedings, most of the companies have insufficient assets to pay for the work required of the insolvency practitioner by insolvency law. Any work that is undertaken cannot solely be for maximising returns to creditors as set out by the CBM, because there are almost never any returns to creditors. The work undertaken by insolvency practitioners is better characterised as fitting within the public interest, and certainly not solely within the private interests of the creditors.

This situation could be characterised as market failure for the provision of corporate insolvency services in Australia, because the system does not contain sufficient funds and assets to pay for its own maintenance. Such a position calls out for a publicly funded liquidator, similar to the OR or the Official Assignee found in other common law jurisdictions.[121] A system such as this is clearly not fully explained by the CBM, which offers only a partial explanation of some aspects of insolvency law and practice.

---

[121] For further discussion of this point see M Murray and J Harris, 'Rebuilding the Structure of the Australian Insolvency System' (2022) 22(1&2) *Insolvency Law Bulletin* 14.

10. Successor liability theory and insolvency law

Laura N. Coordes

INTRODUCTION

Under the doctrine of successor liability, an asset purchaser that becomes a successor entity to a company can be held liable for the asset seller/predecessor's own liabilities or tortious conduct. The various theories of successor liability law seek to balance the need for finality in business transactions with the policy of allowing injured parties to seek a remedy.

Successor liability is in tension with many of the policies behind United States (US) bankruptcy law, and consequently when a company restructures or is sold in bankruptcy one often hears that bankruptcy law pre-empts successor liability law. Although the US Bankruptcy Code does not explicitly protect buyers from potential successor liability in sales that occur in the absence of a Chapter 11 plan of reorganisation,[1] many courts are inclined to extend this protection to buyers in the asset sale context out of concern that a prospective buyer will walk away if it cannot be certain that successor liability will not be a problem.[2]

Successor liability also implicates the bankruptcy policy of equality of distribution to creditors.[3] If successor liability claims can survive a bankruptcy, known creditors, whose claims are discharged in the bankruptcy process, may be disadvantaged when compared with similarly situated but unknown creditors, who may be able to bring successor liability suits against the purchaser after the bankruptcy.[4]

---

1 M B Jacoby, 'Shocking Business Bankruptcy Law' (2021) 131 *Yale Law Journal Forum* 409, 418.

2 Ibid.

3 J M Tucker, 'The Clash of Successor Liability Principles, Reorganization Law, and the Just Demand that Relief be Afforded Unknown and Unknowable Claimants' (1995) 12(1) *Bankruptcy Developments Journal* 1, 7.

4 Ibid.: 'If the principle of equality is paramount in bankruptcy, federal law must preempt any contrary state law that frustrates that principle.' R P Corcoran, 'Why

Although the Bankruptcy Code does not explicitly pre-empt successor liability in the context of an asset sale, many courts have declined to allow successor liability suits in this context, and their reasoning is supported by scholarly commentary. However, large Chapter 11 practice in the US is undergoing a significant transformation. Many of the largest Chapter 11 cases filed in recent years have the goal of shedding mass tort liability. Companies such as Johnson & Johnson and 3M have used Texas divisional merger law to create liability filled subsidiaries, which then file for bankruptcy while the rest of the company continues life outside the bankruptcy court. In light of these recent events,[5] this chapter argues that it is time to rethink the role of successor liability theories in US bankruptcy law. As bankruptcy becomes an increasingly popular arena in which to address mass tort liability, bankruptcy law's pre-emption of successor liability, both real and perceived, threatens to deprive tort victims of a remedy that they may otherwise be able to receive under applicable non-bankruptcy law. This chapter will consider various scholarly recommendations to rectify this problem before concluding that challenging the theory and reasoning behind bankruptcy law's pre-emption of successor liability is a critical piece of a larger project: rethinking bankruptcy's place in the broader US legal system.

The chapter proceeds as follows. The first section describes the successor liability doctrine and the various theories of successor liability. The following section explains the tension between successor liability and US bankruptcy law and how this tension is frequently resolved by the assertion that the Bankruptcy Code pre-empts successor liability. Using a discussion of the General Motors bankruptcy, the chapter goes on to explain why scholars have questioned pre-emption in the context of bankruptcy asset sales and evaluates some scholarly recommendations for rethinking successor liability in bankruptcy. The chapter concludes by explaining that the need to rethink successor liability is increasingly urgent in light of current trends in large Chapter 11 practice and by situating the need to rethink successor liability as part of a larger project of rethinking the changing role of bankruptcy in the US legal system.

Successor Liability Claims Are Not "Interests in Property" Under Section 363(f)' (2010) 18(2) *American Bankruptcy Institute Law Review* 697, 699:

> There is no Congressional history to support the view that [successor liability] claims should be treated differently by bankruptcy law than how other general unsecured claims are treated. To hold otherwise would run counter to the priority rules of the Bankruptcy Code and the bankruptcy goal of equality of the treatment to similarly situated creditors.

5 L A Friedman, Reforming Corporate Bankruptcies to Stop the Mass Tort Shakedown (Bloomberg Law 25 April 2022 https://news.bloomberglaw.com/bankruptcy-law/reforming-corporate-bankruptcies-to-stop-the-mass-tort-shakedown-16 accessed 12 May 2023.

THE SUCCESSOR LIABILITY DOCTRINE

In the US, successor liability is primarily a creature of state law.[6] The doctrine refers to the concept that a purchaser of a company (or the bulk of its assets)—the 'successor'—can be held liable for pre-existing or future claims against the seller. Successor liability arises out of the actions of the purchaser rather than from the property sold.[7] Successor liability is actually an exception to the general rule: in general, a purchaser of a company does *not* assume the seller's liability.[8]

The possibility of successor liability is a concern whenever a company is being sold, because the amount of the purchaser's offer will be influenced by whether successor liability will be present after the sale.[9] If the risk of successor liability is sufficiently unclear, a prospective buyer may lower its offer or refrain from making one entirely.[10]

There are four 'traditional' theories of state law successor liability and two 'newer' theories. Under the first traditional theory, if the purchaser assumes successor liability, then the doctrine will apply.[11] A purchaser may explicitly assume successor liability by stating as much in an asset purchase agreement, or a court may hold that the purchaser has implicitly assumed successor liability through its conduct. For example, courts have found implicit assumptions of successor liability even in the presence of an explicit disclaimer of liability in a purchase agreement when the purchaser takes actions that contradict the language in the agreement.[12]

Under the second traditional theory, successor liability can be found when the purchase is found to be a de facto merger.[13] Like the assumption theory,

---

6 'Buyer Beware: The Federal Common Law of Successor Liability Can Create Unexpected Liability' (Dechert LLP 18 October 2021) https://www.dechert.com/knowledge/onpoint/2021/10/buyer-beware---the-federal-common-law-of-successor-liability-can.html accessed 12 May 2023. Several circuits have also recognised a federal common law of successor liability stemming from various federal statutes: Friedman (n 5).

7 T W Swett III, '"Free and Clear" Bankruptcy Sale Orders and State Law Successor Liability Claims: The Overlooked Question of Preemption' (2017) 25(2) *American Bankruptcy Institute Law Review* 275, 281.

8 Hon J N Feeney et al, *Bankruptcy Law Manual* (Thomson Reuters 2021) §15:14: 'The general rule under state laws is that a purchaser will not assume the liabilities of a seller.'

9 Ibid.

10 Ibid.

11 M W Kavanaugh and R B Soref, *Business Workouts Manual* (Thomson Reuters 2020) §37:36.

12 Ibid.

13 Ibid.

even if the language of the purchase agreement disclaims successor liability, courts have found successor liability if, under a multi-factor analysis, they determine that the parties have in fact merged, instead of acting as buyer and seller.

The third traditional theory is described either as 'mere continuation' or as 'substantial continuity'.[14] Under this theory successor liability is permitted when the successor and the predecessor corporations share stock, shareholders, and directors such that the successor is in actuality merely a continuation of the predecessor.

The fourth and final traditional theory is fraud.[15] Successor liability can be found if the sale transaction itself is found to be fraudulent, or done with the intent to hinder, delay or defraud creditors.

These four traditional theories are widely recognised by courts. The two newer theories to be discussed have not been as widely adopted and are instead recognised in a 'substantial minority' of states.[16]

The first of these 'minority' theories is the product line exception,[17] developed by the California Supreme Court in *Ray v Alad Corp*.[18] Under this theory successor liability can be found when the purchaser continues to manufacture the same product line as the seller, under the same trade name, with no disclosure of change of ownership, and when the seller has been dissolved such that parties cannot recover against it.[19] Put differently, when a purchaser benefits from the goodwill associated with the seller's product, and the seller itself no longer exists, successor liability will hold the purchaser responsible for harms caused by that product.[20]

The second of the less-widely adopted theories is continuation of the enterprise.[21] This is really a variation on the mere continuation theory and asks whether the purchaser is perpetuating the seller's business by, for example, retaining the same employees, facilities and name; producing the same products; and holding itself out to the public as a continuation of the seller.[22]

Some of the four traditional theories of successor liability are rooted in corporate or contract law. All share the common goal of curbing sharp dealing and enforcing the priority of creditors over shareholders of an insolvent

14 Ibid.
15 Ibid.
16 Swett (n 7) 279.
17 Kavanaugh and Soref (n 11).
18 *Ray v Alad Corp*, 560 P2d 3, 11 (Cal 1977).
19 Swett (n 7) 279.
20 Kavanaugh and Soref (n 11).
21 Swett (n 7) 279.
22 Ibid.

company. The two newer theories of successor liability, however, differ in that their roots lie in tort and product liability law. These theories aim to distribute the cost of accidents and to force businesses to internalise the impact of their product-related torts.[23] In addition, as successor liability doctrine is rooted in state law, its exact application varies from state to state, and courts may have various other rationales for finding – or declining to find – successor liability in particular cases.[24]

Although successor liability is most frequently viewed as a state law doctrine, courts have found successor liability in connection with federal statutes, such as the Employee Retirement Income Security Act (ERISA).[25] These doctrines comprise a body of federal law distinct from that described above.[26] Because the majority of successor liability-related issues in a bankruptcy case involve state law successor liability doctrine, however, this chapter's focus will be on state law successor liability.

THE TENSION BETWEEN SUCCESSOR LIABILITY AND US BANKRUPTCY LAW

As mentioned in the introduction, successor liability is in tension with many of the goals and policies underlying US bankruptcy law. For example, applying successor liability against purchasers who made their purchase pursuant to a Chapter 11 plan can frustrate the bankruptcy solution to the common pool problem by discouraging purchasers from making offers to purchase the business as a 'going concern'.[27] Consequently, the US Bankruptcy Code provides that a Chapter 11 plan can be confirmed 'free and clear of all claims and interests of creditors', including claims of successor liability.[28] Bankruptcy is thus sometimes characterised as 'the exception to the exceptions' of successor liability because the Code's pre-emption of successor liability claims means that the general rule that successors are not liable for their purchaser's liabilities holds in most cases.[29]

---

23 Ibid., 280.

24 V S J Buccola and J C Macey, 'Claim Durability and Bankruptcy's Tort Problem' (2021) 38(4) *Yale Journal on Regulation* 766, 792: '[S]uccessor liability is an uncertain doctrine. It might not be applied by a subsequent state court or by a court in a different state.'

25 Swett (n 7) 281.

26 Ibid., 281–82; see also 'Buyer Beware' (n 6).

27 Tucker (n 3) 3–4.

28 11 USC §1141(c) (2010).

29 R L Nichols, 'Exploring Whether §363(f) Permits Asset Sales Free and Clear of Unsecured Successor Products Liability Claims' (2013) 22 *Journal of Bankruptcy Law and Practice* 3.

However, many courts have gone a step further, holding that a debtor in bankruptcy can sell its assets free and clear of successor liability via §363 of the Bankruptcy Code and without going through a plan confirmation process.[30] The enforceability of a court order allowing a §363 sale of assets free and clear of successor liability is the subject of some debate.

Both §1141(c), the provision addressing Chapter 11 plan confirmation, and §363(f), the provision addressing bankruptcy asset sales, expressly permit 'free and clear' sales.[31] Notably however, the text of §363 differs somewhat from the language found in §1141. Instead of saying that property can be sold 'free and clear of *all claims and* interests of creditors',[32] §363 provides only that property can be sold 'free and clear of any interest in such property'.[33] Despite this difference, bankruptcy policies, such as maximisation of sale value and equality of treatment of similarly situated creditors, could indicate that a sale should be free and clear of successor liability claims as well.[34]

Ultimately, whether an asset can be sold free and clear of successor liability using §363 of the Bankruptcy Code depends on whether the sale is free and clear of an 'interest', which is not defined anywhere in the Bankruptcy Code. Some courts interpret the word 'interest' narrowly so as to include only *in rem* interests in the sold property itself. Because successor liability stems from the purchaser's actions, a sale order that narrowly interprets the word 'interest' would not provide for the property to be sold free and clear of successor liability. Other courts have taken a broader approach, interpreting 'interest' to include obligations that flow from property ownership, including claims of successor liability.[35] In recent years, it appears that courts are increasingly willing to absolve buyers from successor liability via a §363 sale process, particularly with respect to currently existing claims, as long as due process requirements are met.[36]

---

30 Feeney et al (n 8).

31 Nichols (n 29).

32 Emphasis added.

33 11 USC § 363(f) (2019).

34 Feeney et al (n 8).

35 Ibid.; see also G W Kuney, 'Misinterpreting Bankruptcy Code Section 363(f) and Undermining the Chapter 11 Process' (2002) 76 *American Bankruptcy Law Journal* 235, 236 arguing that bankruptcy courts disregard §363(f)'s plain meaning and interpret the words 'any interest' to in fact mean 'any claim or interest', thereby stripping off liens, claims, and other interests during the §363 sale process.

36 Feeney et al (n 8): 'In more recent decisions, most courts now agree that a purchaser has no successor liability for existing claims as a result of a §363 sale as long as existing claimants received notice of the sale and its terms'; see also B Rochelle, 'Assets Sold Free and Clear of a Multi-Employer Pension Plan's Withdrawal Liability' (*Rochelle's Daily Wire* 20 July 2022) https://www.abi.org/newsroom/daily-wire/assets

More disagreement exists over whether a bankruptcy court can prohibit successor liability for future claims, those that have not arisen at the time of the bankruptcy case but that may arise at some point in the future.[37] The Second Circuit, home to a popular venue for bankruptcy cases, has held that successor liability claims cannot survive §363 sales; however, other courts have disagreed.[38]

What is the rationale for cutting off successor liability in the §363 sale context when the text of the Bankruptcy Code seems to suggest otherwise? One basic Chapter 11 policy is to provide purchasers the opportunity to receive the 'going concern' or 'enterprise' value of the debtor's assets.[39] The 'free and clear' language of the Code is designed to facilitate creditors receiving the maximum profits possible in a sale.[40] If a purchaser is vulnerable to successor liability, the price the purchaser will offer for the assets is likely to be lower than if this vulnerability did not exist.[41] This disadvantages present creditors of the debtor when compared with future creditors who can sue the purchaser later on a successor liability theory.[42] Specifically, allowing successor liability claims to persist after the sale raises the possibility that some unsecured claims will turn into 'super-priority' claims that can be collected in full after the bankruptcy is over.[43] As one of the significant tenets of bankruptcy law is equality of treatment among similarly situated creditors, courts reason that bankruptcy law should pre-empt any contrary state law, such as successor liability, that frustrates that goal.[44] This reason underlies pre-emption of successor liability in the plan confirmation context,[45] but has also been held to support pre-emption in the sale context as well.

Despite this policy rationale, many scholars have been critical of the court-approved sale of assets free and clear of successor liability in the §363 sale context. While recognising that most courts interpret the phrase 'interest in such property' to include successor liability claims, they point out that such

-sold-free-and-clear-of-a-multi-employer-pension-plan%E2%80%99s-withdrawal accessed 12 May 2023, describing a decision by an Illinois bankruptcy judge that a sale under §363(f) removed liability from assets sold for withdrawal from a pension fund.

37 Feeney et al (n 8).

38 Ibid.

39 Tucker (n 3) 7.

40 Nichols (n 29).

41 Tucker (n 3) 7: 'If certain creditors are free to sue and recover from purchasers of assets in bankruptcy, however, the prices obtained for the assets in bankruptcy will likely fall to their "scrap" value.'

42 Ibid.

43 Nichols (n 29).

44 Tucker (n 3) 7.

45 Ibid.

a broad interpretation creates legal and practical problems.[46] First, having a successor liability *claim* arguably does not, by itself, grant a claimant an 'interest in property'.[47] Indeed, if a claim somehow did constitute an 'interest in property', that claimholder would be entitled to all of the same rights as those with interests in property, including the right to adequate protection of that property interest pursuant to §363(e).[48] This right to adequate protection, scholars have argued, may in turn provide successor liability claimants better treatment than similarly situated unsecured creditors, which in itself frustrates the principle of equality of treatment.[49] In addition, others have pointed out that the Bankruptcy Code's clear text evinces no intent to pre-empt successor liability in §363 sales.[50]

IN RE MOTORS LIQUIDATION CO AND SCHOLARLY QUESTIONING OF BANKRUPTCY PRE-EMPTION OF SUCCESSOR LIABILITY

A case stemming from the bankruptcy of General Motors, the largest automaker in the US, provides fertile ground for thinking about the relationship between bankruptcy and successor liability. In *Elliott v General Motors, LLC (In re Motors Liquidation Co.)*,[51] the Second Circuit Court of Appeals held that the sale of General Motors (GM)'s assets in bankruptcy was not 'free and clear' of claims belonging to parties prejudiced by GM's failure to provide sufficient notice of the sale, in addition to 'future claimants' – 'parties whose claims did not amount to rights to payment arising before the filing of the bankruptcy petition'.[52] Although this may seem like a radical departure from

---

46 Corcoran (n 4) 698.

47 Ibid: 'As the Code itself is silent as to what constitutes an 'interest in property,' both practitioners and courts across the country have struggled to determine what constitutes an 'interest in such property' for purposes of subsection (f)'s free and clear treatment.'; '[N]either state law nor federal common law doctrines of successor liability grant successor liability claimants 'interests in property' by virtue of their claims.' (Ibid., 699)

48 Ibid 699; 11 USC §363(e) (2019).

49 Corcoran (n 4), 699.

50 B Warner, 'Reconciling Bankruptcy Law and Corporate Law Principles: Imposing Successor Liability on GM and Similar "Sleight-of-Hand" 363 Sales' (2016) 32(2) *Emory Bankruptcy Developments Journal* 537, 563.

51 Case No 15-2844 (2d Cir July 13, 2016).

52 A G Lizotte, 'Buyer Beware: Ruling Saddles 'New' GM with Successor Liability' (Murphy & King 29 August 2016) https://www.murphyking.com/buyer-beware-ruling-saddles-new-gm-with-successor-liability/ accessed 12 May 2023.

the standard treatment of successor liability claims in bankruptcy, the *Motors Liquidation* case had very unusual facts.[53]

After GM filed for bankruptcy, the federal government became involved in the case out of concern for the impact on the US economy. Specifically, the government loaned GM over $13 billion so that it could exit bankruptcy. To effectuate its bankruptcy strategy, GM created a new entity (New GM) that would purchase the assets of the bankrupt company (Old GM). Although they had different names, New GM was nothing but a 'legal fiction': notably, the company continued to manufacture the same products. With the government's money, New GM purchased the assets of Old GM pursuant to §363 of the Bankruptcy Code. The bankruptcy court's sale order took a broad view of the word 'interests' and provided that the assets were sold 'free and clear' of successor liability.[54]

In 2013, it was revealed that many of GM's vehicles had an ignition switch defect, which caused the vehicles to shut down unexpectedly while in motion. It was subsequently revealed that GM had known of this defect for over a decade and had been actively concealing it. Nevertheless, when the defect came to light, New GM attempted to disclaim liability for that defect on the basis of the bankruptcy court's free and clear sale order.[55]

When the case reached the Second Circuit, the court first considered claims from those affected by the defect who had not received notice of GM's asset sale. The US Constitution's Fifth Amendment contains a due process clause, which requires 'notice, reasonably calculated, under all the circumstances' to interested parties in situations such as the asset sale.[56] The court found that Old GM knew, or reasonably should have known, about these claims and therefore that it should have provided actual notice of the asset sale, prior to the sale hearing, to these claimants.[57] Instead, the claimants merely received 'constructive notice' by newspaper publication, which the court found to be insufficient to satisfy the due process clause's notice requirement. The court thus held that the bankruptcy court's free and clear sale order could not apply to claims from 'claimants who could have benefitted from constitutionally adequate notice that wasn't provided'.[58]

The court then turned to an analysis of future claims. Here, the court reasoned that the power to sell assets 'free and clear' pursuant to the §363 sale process could not exceed the power to release 'claims'. Unlike the word

---

53 Ibid.
54 Ibid.
55 Ibid.
56 Ibid.; U.S.Constitution, Amendment V.
57 Lizotte (n 52).
58 Ibid.

'interest', the word 'claim' is defined in the Bankruptcy Code as, among other things, a 'right to payment'.[59] The court reasoned that if a 'right to payment depends on the occurrence of future events, it must result from pre-bankruptcy conduct' that fairly gives rise to that claim.[60] The court held that the bankruptcy court's sale order could not be interpreted to authorise the sale of assets 'free and clear' of rights belonging to a claimant that had no contact or relationship with the debtor at the time of filing, or arising from a non-debtor's acts or omissions, such as those of New GM because, in either of these cases, 'the debtor could not have identified the claimant'.[61] Thus, Old GM could not sell its assets free and clear of claims of purchasers who had bought used GM cars after the sale had closed, and who had no knowledge of the ignition switch defect, since these purchasers had no relationship with Old GM prior to its bankruptcy. The court further held that Old GM could not sell its assets free and clear of claims based on the conduct of New GM, thus opening the door for purchasers of newer GM vehicles to sue New GM as well.[62]

At first blush, the Second Circuit's disposition of the case seems like a win for successor liability claimants. After all, those harmed by GM's defective vehicles were given a chance to use successor liability doctrine to obtain a remedy.[63] Yet, it is equally important to recognise what the Second Circuit did *not* do: notably, it did not interpret the word 'interests' in §363 narrowly. Thus, the Second Circuit continues to recognise that assets sold pursuant to §363 could be sold 'free and clear' of successor liability, even while acknowledging that, in this particular case, they could not.

In re Motors Liquidation Co is only one of a growing number of bankruptcy cases that somehow involve mass tort liability. If bankruptcy is to become the new forum for resolution of mass torts, the role of successor liability should be re-examined. In particular, as bankruptcy has increasingly become a forum for resolving mass tort litigation, there is a growing concern that bankruptcy's pre-emption of successor liability can harm mass tort claimants by prohibiting them from holding companies liable for the harms they have perpetuated.[64] Others have criticised successor liability doctrine on a different ground: coher-

---

[59] Ibid.; 11 USC §101(5) (2022).

[60] Lizotte (n 52).

[61] Ibid.

[62] Ibid.

[63] See Warner (n 50) 561: '[S]uccessor liability should be imposed on the company exiting bankruptcy so that the costs are equitably distributed between the corporation and those harmed by its vehicles.'

[64] N L Jones, 'A Catastrophic Collision: Due Process and Section 363 Free and Clear Asset Sales Meet Head-On in the GM Bankruptcy' (2017) Article 1 (citing the GM case).

ence. Vincent Buccola and Joshua Macey have remarked that '[t]he doctrine's vague predicates are a case study in the indeterminacy of transcendental nonsense'.[65] Evidence from their work, however, shows that judges 'disproportionately' find successor liability when a failure to do so would provide less than full recovery for involuntary creditors, including tort claimants. The availability of successor liability is particularly important for tort claimants, providing them with a pool of assets for them to satisfy their claims.[66]

Despite Buccola and Macey's evidence that judges will sometimes allow successor liability in bankruptcy, even they acknowledge that modern Chapter 11 practice often cuts off successor liability.[67] They therefore suggest that 'bankruptcy judges embrace successor liability by preserving or even strengthening the norm that tort claims follow a business'.[68] In doing so, they argue, the threat of successor liability, far from stifling dealmaking, may actually facilitate it.[69] Buccola and Macey thus suggest a revival and restrengthening of successor liability, in contrast to modern bankruptcy practice in the US.[70]

Other scholars have argued for victims to be able to access successor liability in the §363 sale context because there is no concern about granting the corporate debtor a 'fresh start' in the context of an asset sale - or even in the context of Chapter 11 more broadly.[71] If the debtor is selling all of its assets to a new entity, in theory there is no debtor anymore with a fresh start to protect.

Bankruptcy's growing place in the mass torts arena has special implications for those newer successor liability theories that are grounded in tort. Trevor Swett has contended that the rationales for interpreting §363 sale orders as extinguishing state law successor liability claims are particularly weak when dealing with these new forms of successor liability.[72]

George Kuney has emerged as one of the most vocal critics of court interpretations of §363. He argues that courts' overly broad interpretations of the word 'interests' shield purchasers and insiders in ways that are otherwise

---

65 Buccola and Macey (n 24) 785.

66 Ibid., 785 n77: 'Successor liability ensures that *some* pool of resources exists toward which tort claimants can look for satisfaction.' (emphasis in original).

67 Ibid., 787–88.

68 Ibid., 789.

69 Ibid., 810: 'There is also every reason to think that tort claimants would bargain with other stakeholders to relinquish durability when debt overhang would otherwise threaten their joint return.'

70 Ibid., 816: 'This Article has shown that a durability norm is in many respects theoretically equivalent to the super-priority rule for which scholars have long advocated.'

71 Warner (n 50) 548: 'The "fresh start" policy goal therefore differs remarkably for a corporate debtor in chapter 11, as a discharge of debt is not a prerequisite for a successful rehabilitation of the corporate debtor.'

72 Swett (n 7) 278.

unavailable under non-bankruptcy law.[73] This broad interpretation, combined with relatively weak mechanisms for appellate review in US bankruptcy law, separates bankruptcy practice from congressional intent and makes the bankruptcy courts an unduly attractive forum for businesses that want to sell assets, regardless of whether those businesses are experiencing financial distress. Further, Kuney argues that if parties can get the same 'free and clear' benefits from a §363 sale as they can obtain through a Chapter 11 plan, they will almost always choose a §363 sale, as it is less intrusive, faster and cheaper than the process of getting a plan confirmed.[74]

Although Kuney argues that the problems he identifies can be resolved merely by reverting back to the plain meaning of the text of §363, he acknowledges that courts are unlikely to reverse course on their own.[75] He therefore suggests that legislative reform is important to ultimately change courts' interpretation of §363.[76]

Although Kuney and others seek legislative change, arguably the most radical reform comes from Buccola and Macey, who argue that tort claims should follow a debtor's assets out of bankruptcy unless a deal is reached for a different arrangement.[77] Buccola and Macey's 'super-durability norm'[78] would effectively reverse the pre-emption of successor liability in all bankruptcy cases, as opposed to only cases involving §363 sales.

CONCLUSION: IS IT TIME TO RETHINK SUCCESSOR LIABILITY'S ROLE IN BANKRUPTCY?

US bankruptcy law is increasingly displacing civil litigation as an option for companies dealing with mass tort liabilities. As bankruptcy becomes an increasingly fertile ground for resolution of mass tort liability, the presence or absence of successor liability becomes correspondingly more important. This

---

73 Kuney (n 35) 235.

74 Ibid., 273: 'Some counsel already generally advise purchasers of those businesses that the preferred method of acquisition is through a quick Chapter 11 case featuring a pre-negotiated asset purchase agreement and a preplan §363(f) sale free and clear. Indeed, it may already be malpractice not to at least advise clients of the potential benefits of this process in many circumstances.'

75 Ibid., 237.

76 Ibid., 287: '[U]nless Congress or the courts act to either enforce the plain language of the statute or modify the statute to provide for preplan sales that close due process gaps and successor liability loopholes that Congress did not intend.'; see also Jones (n 79) also arguing for legislative reform.

77 Buccola and Macey (n 24) 783.

78 Ibid.

is particularly the case for those newer successor liability doctrines that are grounded in tort law.

Recently, companies such as 3M and Johnson & Johnson have sought to place only their tort liabilities in bankruptcy, while continuing to do business outside the bankruptcy process. These companies are not themselves experiencing significant financial distress; instead, they spin off their tort liabilities into subsidiary companies, fund those subsidiaries with a set amount, and allow these liability-filled subsidiaries to navigate the bankruptcy process. The propriety of this strategy is still being tested; however, several courts thus far have been inclined to let these cases proceed.[79] In light of strategic moves such as these, successor liability's place in bankruptcy should be re-examined, paying particular attention to the newer successor liability theories grounded in tort law because of the shift in companies using bankruptcy law to address mass tort liability.

Rethinking successor liability's role in bankruptcy is one facet of a much larger project: rethinking bankruptcy's place in the US legal system. If the bankruptcy process is becoming a forum for resolving litigation traditionally addressed outside the bankruptcy court, how unique should bankruptcy relief be if the 'debtors' using this system increasingly show little resemblance to the debtors US legislators were anticipating would use the system when it was created? To put it bluntly, a liability filled subsidiary of Johnson & Johnson or 3M is a different type of debtor even than companies that have sought to discharge mass tort liabilities via bankruptcy in the past.[80]

Bankruptcy law does not exist in a vacuum; rather, it interacts with and is impacted by many other areas of law and policy. Rethinking the role of successor liability is one piece of a larger, more complex puzzle about how to situate bankruptcy law's changing role within the broader US legal system.

---

[79] See, e.g., S Church, 'J&J's Controversial Bankruptcy Strategy Upheld By Judge' (*Bloomberg* 25 February 2022) https://www.bloomberg.com/news/articles/2022-02-25/j-j-s-controversial-bankruptcy-strategy-upheld-by-federal-judge accessed 12 May 2023, describing how a bankruptcy judge refused to dismiss a chapter 11 case filed by Johnson & Johnson's subsidiary; D Levine and M Spector, 'How a Bankruptcy "Innovation" Halted Thousands of Lawsuits From Sick Plaintiffs' (*Reuters* 23 June 2022) https://www.reuters.com/investigates/special-report/bankruptcy-tactics-two-step/> accessed 12 May 2023, describing how companies 'have used the "Texas two-step" to divert tens of thousands of lawsuits into bankruptcy court – without filing for Chapter 11 themselves'.

[80] M A Francus, 'Texas Two-Stepping Out of Bankruptcy' (2022) *Michigan Law Review Online* https://michiganlawreview.org/texas-two-stepping-out-of-bankruptcy/#:~:text=Unlike%20the%20businesses%20that%20pioneered,laden%20business%20file%20for%20bankruptcy accessed 12 May 2023, arguing that 'the Texas Two-Step offers debtors something new'.

11. Vulnerability theory and insolvency law

Jennifer L. L. Gant

INTRODUCTION

The purpose of insolvency law is underpinned by an approach to fairness among 'stakeholders'[1] which generally takes into account pre-insolvency (or restructuring) legal or contractual entitlements. There are a number of internal mechanisms that seek to introduce this fairness into collective procedures, particularly for stakeholders who have less power in the process, such as employees. Typically, such less powerful stakeholders that are given advantages in a company's insolvency or restructuring process can still establish a contractual connection to the company in financial distress as some direct species of creditor. However, there are a number of other entities and individuals that may have a vested interest in a company's continuation or liquidation that may not be connected by choice or may have less of a capability to adjust themselves to the circumstances of a company's financial distress. They may not have 'pre-insolvency entitlements' *per se*. Such stakeholders may include tort creditors, environmental claims, certain parties to executory contracts, non-employee workers, and the wider communities within which the company operates.

The idea of considering the interests of all stakeholders in corporate law and insolvency law is certainly not new. Stakeholder theory as a business ethics proposition has been around in some form or fashion for half a century. These ideas have crept into the realm of insolvency theory in the communitarian and contractarian visions and even into some of the more nuanced approaches to the creditors' bargain. However, there, the identification and assessment of stakeholders and their relative positions in an insolvency as well as the social

[1] See the following section for an extensive discussion on the definitions of stakeholder and stakeholder theory, providing a basis upon which a new approach to fairness in collective procedures based in measures of vulnerability and resilience can be situated.

and moral obligations that these may entail have usually been a separate philosophical question based on a 'values network' (shared purposes and values in the company) that has tended to conflict with the strategic 'value chain', which is more squarely focused on financial value.[2]

The following chapter will introduce a new way of considering stakeholders in a collective procedure (insolvency or restructuring) that seeks to internalise the 'values network' by considering the vulnerability and resilience of the various stakeholders insofar as it affects their power within such procedures. This approach offers a much-needed adjustment to the theoretical underpinning of global insolvency systems to place the human at the centre of the matter and challenges the traditional views of corporate financial distress and the categorical and fragmented approach traditional processes tend to take for its resolution. Vulnerability stands as a challenge to the traditional law and economics approaches to resolving corporate financial distress and builds upon the communitarian and traditionalist approaches promoted by academics such as Elizabeth Warren and Donald Korobkin with a view to creating measurable tests that will recalibrate fairness towards all stakeholders from a basis of equity.

This chapter will reach beyond entities possessing pre-contractual entitlements to provide a perspective on the fair treatment of a broader array of stakeholders, embracing both a contractarian and communitarian style of vision while advancing a combination of the two towards a more measurable test of fairness that can be applied to create bespoke priorities for the *dramatis personae* of stakeholders in a particular collective procedure. The end result builds upon the early conceptualisation of stakeholder theory and recognises how it has been used within theoretical discussions about insolvency and restructuring (intentionally or otherwise) in the works of Jackson, Baird, Dworkin, Korobkin, Warren, Westbrook and others. It then advances and builds on these approaches by applying Martha Fineman's vulnerability theory to create a new framework within which fairness toward a variety of stakeholders can be tested and achieved in treatment, priorities, and distribution from within collective processes.

STAKEHOLDER THEORY

There is a close relationship between corporate theory, business ethics, and insolvency theory. The conclusions of this chapter build upon some of the historical discussions in both these theoretical realms to establish a new the-

---

2 R E Freeman, Robert Phillips and Rajendra Sisodia, 'Tensions in Stakeholder Theory' (2018) 59(2) *Business & Society* 213, 217.

oretical paradigm that extends and deepens the application of established and legitimate theories that have been accepted and applied in corporate and insolvency law scholarship as well as in policy approaches to drafting and reforming related legislation. Stakeholder theory is one of the earliest approaches to considering company strategy that began to divert from the pure stockholder focus that had underpinned the concept of the limited company since the financial revolutions of the seventeenth and eighteenth centuries.

Stakeholder Approach to Strategic Management

In 1984, R Edward Freeman published a book[3] that would become the bible for stakeholder theory for decades, with both the concomitant dogmatic criticisms from scholars who otherwise perceived the corporate entity and at times evangelical defences from purists. Freeman himself was merely writing a textbook for business policy strategy courses,[4] so there was no intention to create an entire movement that would guide, confuse, and consternate scholars for decades to come. In fact, he was 'amused and somewhat horrified' at being called the 'father of stakeholder theory'.[5] Rather, he credited serendipity and other writers for the broad appeal of the theory.[6]

Stakeholder theory has mostly been connected to business strategy and was initially developed as a way of organising information which, in modern business vehicles, has become increasingly important to strategic planning.[7] The concept of stakeholders is implied in works published in Sweden as early as 1965 by Eric Rhenman and Bengt Styme[8] and enjoyed early applications by Russell L Ackoff[9] to assist a Mexican brewer in 'understanding the importance of government in their business model'.[10] However, it was Freeman who first presented what was perceived by scholars, if not himself, as a legitimate theoretical framework for the corporation with stakeholders at the centre.[11] Simply

---

[3] R E Freeman, *Strategic Management: A Stakeholder Approach* (Pitman 1984).

[4] Freeman, Phillips and Sisodia (n 2) 215.

[5] R E Freeman, 'The Development of Stakeholder Theory: An Idiosyncratic Approach' in K G Smith and M A Hitt (eds), *Great Minds in Management: The Process of Theory and Development* (Oxford University Press 2005) 417, 433.

[6] A O Laplume et al, 'Stakeholder Theory: Reviewing a Theory that Moves Us' (2008) 34(6*) Journal of Management* 1152, 1152–1153.

[7] Freeman, Phillips and Sisodia (n 2) 214.

[8] E Rhenman and B Styme, *Företagsledning I en foäränderlig värld* (Aldus/Bonniers 1965).

[9] R L Ackhoff, *Redesigning the Future* (John Wile, 1974) and *Creating the Corporate Future* (John Wiley 1981).

[10] Freeman, Phillips and Sisodia (n 2) 214–215.

[11] Laplume et al (n 6) 1157.

put, he argued that 'exiting management theories were not equipped to address the "quantity and kinds of change which are occurring in the business environment"'.[12] This he placed at the feet of shifts in the corporate environment among both internal and external stakeholders and cautioned that managers should 'take into account all of those groups and individuals that can affect, or are affected by, the accomplishment of the business enterprise'.[13] This simple view would become the foundation for scholarly arguments and repartee for decades to come.

Defining Stakeholders

The invention of the term 'stakeholder' has been viewed as deriving from 'stockholder' 'to signify that there are other parties having a "stake" in the decision-making' of the company in addition to shareholders.[14] Stakeholders, as defined by Freeman, include 'any group or individual who can affect or is affected by the achievement of the organization's objectives'.[15] One might think that this could extend to any individual or entity touched by the company's activities; however, in reality the early view of the individuals who is 'affected by' the organisation is actually taken from the perspective of how those particular individuals might come to affect the company in the future, should their interests not be considered in decision-making. This approach is further explained by Freeman:

> Groups which 20 years ago had no effect on the actions of the firm, can affect it today, largely because of the actions of the firm which ignored the effects on these groups. Thus, by calling those affected groups 'stakeholders', the ensuing strategic management model will be sensitive to future change.[16]

The view of Kenneth Goodpaster on this approach asserts that such a strategic stakeholder approach does not actually introduce an ethical parameter into managerial decision making nor is it immoral; rather, he describes it as 'nonmoral'. The strategic reasoning based on this model is concerned with the consequences of one's actions insofar as those consequences could affect the best outcomes of the company on a future date rather than adopting a genuine moral concern for avoiding injury or unfairness of those affected by the

---

12 Freeman (n 3), p. 5.

13 Ibid., 25.

14 K E Goodpaster, 'Business Ethics and Stakeholder Analysis' (1991) 1(1) *Business Ethics Quarterly* 53, 54.

15 Freeman (n 3) 46.

16 Ibid.

actions of the company, regardless of the retaliatory potential of any aggrieved parties.[17] While it would seem that such an approach might capture most stakeholders, Goodpaster asserts that absent a pre-established linkage between a company's success and ethical success, some stakeholders will sometimes be affected quite a lot, but will not be able to affect the company in any major way to bring them within the 'affected by' definition enough for a company to justify a legitimate consideration of their interests that will also be in the future interests of the company in this paradigm.[18] The stakeholder approach, from this limited perspective in which importance is placed on effective business strategy rather than genuine ethical concerns for those affected by the activities of a business, is not, at its core, therefore, an enlightened approach that shifts focus from profit to the inherent social obligations of business as a social construct in the service of humankind.

Combining Business Strategy and Business Ethics

Freeman responds to Goodpaster's interpretation of his stakeholder theory suggesting that separating the ethical from the business does not help the progress of a more enlightened approach to fairness in a corporate setting that also serves the interests of the company. Freeman acknowledges that this separation is ingrained in business school pedagogy, describing it as a Separation Thesis that makes it possible to hold certain business concepts up to ethical ideals and glorifying or condemning business as a practice. Freeman sarcastically notes that as long as the two discourses remain separate, business ethicists will need to continue to make it up as they go along by holding pieces of business activity or ideals up to the light of reason. Keeping ethics to the side, business theorists remain free to make up 'supposedly morally neutral theories such as agency theory, which can be used to justify a great deal of harm'.[19] Freeman asserts that instead, the whole point of adopting a stakeholder approach is to get rid of the whole Separation Thesis idea and reject what he calls the 'Principle of Who and What Really Counts' and to set aside the 'Principal of Making it up as You Go along'.[20] Rather, ethics should form a part of business theory, and by extension those theories underpinning collective procedures.

Freeman goes a step further in defining a collective of normative cores upon which a legitimate stakeholder theory might be based. He adopts contractarian, communitarian and, interestingly, ecological cores around which a stakeholder

---

17 Goodpaster (n 14) 60.

18 Ibid., 61.

19 R E Freeman, 'The Politics of Stakeholder Theory: Some Future Directions' (1994) 4(4) *Business Ethics Quarterly* 409, 412.

20 Ibid.

theory could be designed. Whereas the contractarian approach largely echoes traditional approaches to corporate stakeholder interests, the communitarian version adopts a feminist standpoint that rethinks how 'value creating activity' could be structured according to principles of caring and connection.[21] The ecological approach would mean a corporation would be run 'in accordance with the principle of caring for the earth'.[22] It has been argued that environmental issues are completely left out of a stakeholder theory that considers operations with the firm at its core.[23] However, the approach suggested at the end of this chapter shifts the focus from a firm-centred approach to that of fairness measured against vulnerability and resilience of stakeholders, redefined to include any impact of a company that could be compensated in an insolvency or rescue process, whether that is to entities, individuals or in relation to *chose* in action, such as environmental claims.

If one considers these issues from a social contract perspective, in which it is not only economic connections that defines relationships and obligations, there are other values that can also be considered in the stakeholder approach. Stakeholder theory should include the human actors in the corporate processes beyond situations in which they add economic value to include the 'alignment of values, norms and ethics as mechanisms for efficient and effective flourishing within and among organizations'.[24] This embraces the concept of the social contract within the stakeholder context. As recognised by Friedman and Miles, social realists:

> [...] recognize that society depends on human activities and that both society and people are changeable and affected by each other. Social realists also accept that, in the context of social interaction, actions are taken and ideas formed in relation to a perceived (socially constructed) reality, thereby changing the social reality.[25]

Companies and corporate structures are essentially a construct of our society that has been framed within law and principle. In reality, they would not exist without the permission of the human beings who such institutions should serve. Thus, it is sensible to consider the wider implications of the corporate form, beyond the economic and financial value that can be ascribed to the

---

21 See e.g., A Wicks, D Gilbert and R E Freeman, 'A Feminist Reinterpretation of the Stakeholder Concept' (1994) 4(4) *Business Ethics Quarterly* 475; R E Freeman and J Liedtka, 'Corporate Social Responsibility: A Critical Approach' (1991) 34(4) *Business Horizons* 92.

22 Freeman (n 19).

23 A L Friedman and S Miles, 'Developing Stakeholder Theory' (2002) 39(1) *Journal of Management Studies* 1, 3.

24 Freeman, Phillips and Sisodia (n 2), 219.

25 Friedman and Miles (n 23) 4.

traditional emphasis on shareholder value. As further noted by Friedman and Miles from a Law and Economics perspective:

> [...] social structures and systems of ideas endow different sections of society with different vested interests and opportunity costs associated with different responses to those structures and systems. These do not force actions, rather they put prices and premiums on different interpretations of situations as well as associated activities.[26]

In short, if one considers the corporation with the inherent aim to serve humanity, then it is only logical to consider a wider view of the impact of the corporation and its financial viability. The consideration of such wider impacts satisfies the obligations of those implicit contracts derived from social duty and moral obligation. Further, it 'reflets a coherent worldview of business that reflects a broader awareness about its role, purpose, and full range if immediate and long-term impacts on society'.[27] Taking this perspective limits the idea that the only relevant stakeholders 'affected by' the company should be those who may eventually affect the company without that consideration because it flips the obligation from a tacitly self-interested consideration to a direct obligation based in the broader obligations of the social contract.[28] Rather, '[i]t is rooted in a more humanistic conception of the business as a vehicle for human cooperation to realise outcomes not otherwise attainable'.[29] With all that being said, without a purpose that embraces these social obligations derived from the original social contract, as it were, the natural default of businesses will return to profit maximisation. In addition, without a coordinated purpose based in shared values, even stakeholders will eventually operate at cross-purposes to pursue their own interests.[30] As such, measures need to be incorporated into the fabric of business principles and, by extension, insolvency and restructuring principles, to achieve these higher aims.

INSOLVENCY THEORY AND THE SOCIOLOGY OF LAW

Fundamentally, the end recommendation of this chapter will be to adopt a specific socio-legal approach based on Martha Fineman's vulnerability theory to an assessment of fairness in insolvency and restructuring frameworks. Such an approach eschews the positivist and isolated conception of law as an institution

---

26 Ibid.
27 Freeman, Phillips and Sisodia (n 2) 219.
28 Friedman and Miles (n 23) 7.
29 Freeman, Phillips and Sisodia (n 2) 219.
30 Ibid., 220.

whose concern is technical and prescriptive and integrates the explanatory and descriptive characteristics of sociology. Although such an approach may render the clear lines of the law a bit fuzzier, it also introduces a reality to the consideration of law and legal reform that admits to the social relationships that the law administers. Legal relations are clearly not solely economic nor are they all explicable in purely economic terms,[31] as Law and Economics scholars often claim, and which tends to underpin traditional approaches to insolvency theory. However, the social aspects of insolvency and restructuring are not unheard-of considerations among insolvency law theorists, either.

Given the multi-layered and highly complex web of relationships in the global economy, there is value to considering the wider impact of a collective corporate process in terms of the fairness of these processes for non-adjusting and involuntary creditors. This is in addition to employees, who have long been recognised as being in a weaker bargaining position and unique as not only being a creditor, but also a key stakeholder, for a company in financial distress.[32]

Vanessa Finch provided an in-depth survey of the most commonly debated theoretical approaches to insolvency law in a prescient article in 1997. In it, she considered the viability of the current (at the time) measures of insolvency law, including the classical creditors' bargain theory;[33] the oft-cited broad-based contractarian approach;[34] a communitarian vision that has often been referred to as a traditionalist approach;[35] a forum vision;[36] an ethical vision; and a mul-

---

[31] R Cotterrell, *The Sociololgy of Law: An Introduction* (Butterworths 1992) 5.

[32] Jennifer L L Gant, 'Reconsidering Fairness for Vulnerable and Involuntary Stakeholders in Insolvency and Restructuring' in E Vaccari and E Ghio (eds), *Insolvency Law: Back to the Future* (INSOL Europe 2022) 55.

[33] First introduced in T H Jackson, *The Logic and Limits of Bankruptcy Law* (Harvard University Press 1986).

[34] See D R Korobkin, 'Contractarianism and the Normative Foundations of Bankruptcy Law' (1993) 71(3) *Texas Law Review* 541 and 'Rehabilitating Values: A Jurisprudence of Bankruptcy' (1991) 91(4) *Columbia Law Review* 717.

[35] See E Warren, 'Bankruptcy Policy' (1987) 54(3) *University of Chicago Law Review* 775 and 'Bankruptcy Policymaking in an Imperfect World' (1993) 92(2) *Michigan Law Review* 336; K Gross, 'Taking Community Interests into Account in Bankruptcy' (1994) 72(3) *Washington University Law Quarterly* 1031; B Adler, 'A World without Debt' (1994) 72(3) *Washington University Law Quarterly* 811.

[36] See A Flessner, 'Philosophies of Business Bankruptcy Law: An International Overview' in J S Zeigel (ed), *Current Developments in International and Comparative Corporate Insolvency Law* (Clarendon Press 1994) 13; P Miller, 'Calculating Corporate Failure' in Y Dezalay and D Sugarman (eds), *Professional Competition and Professional Power: Lawyers, Accountants and the Social Construction of Markets* (Routledge 1995) 51; R B Stewart, 'The Reformation of American Administrative Law' (1975) 99(8) *Harvard Law Review* 1667.

tiple values/eclectic vision.[37] For the purpose of this chapter and its focus on updating the stakeholder approach to introduce measures that can be used to test and apply fairness criterion to collective processes, the following section will focus on those that are relevant as building blocks to the new socio-legal paradigm suggested herein. What is clear is that despite the wealth of theoretical debate and discussion, a complete view of the appropriate measure of insolvency law still fails to emerge.[38] Although many of these theories do consider the social impact of insolvency and rescue, they tend to continue to start from an economic standpoint and deviate from that along fairly predictable lines.[39]

Recalling the Creditors' Bargain

The best-known approach to fairness in insolvency law focuses on contractual creditors who, behind a Rawlsian veil of ignorance, bargain to create a collective process that ensures fairness among creditors vying for repayment of their debts from a financially distressed debtor based on a pro-rata distribution according to pre-insolvency entitlements.[40] The aim of this creditors' bargain is to maximise the collective return to creditors by avoiding the free-for-all of enforcement during times of corporate crisis that would otherwise dissipate assets to the detriment of the overall collective of creditors and, of course, the ultimate survival of the debtor (if possible). These approaches focus on this 'common pool' problem that is created when creditors assert their rights

---

[37] See P Schuman, 'An Attempt at a "Philosophy of Bankruptcy"' (1973) 21(2) *UCLA Law Review* 403.

[38] V Finch, 'The Measures of Insolvency Law' (1997) 17(2) *Oxford Journal of Legal Studies* 227, 242.

[39] Gant (n 32).

[40] See Jackson (n 33) chapters 1 and 2. See also D Baird and T Jackson, 'Corporate Reorganizations and the Treatment of Diverse Ownership Interests: A Comment on Adequate Protection of Secured Creditors in Bankruptcy' (1984) 51(1) *University of Chicago Law Review* 97; D G Baird, 'The Uneasy Case for Corporate Reorganizations' (1986) 15(1) *Journal of Legal Studies* 127; D G Baird, 'A World without Bankruptcy' (1987) 50(2) *Law and Contemporary Problems* 173; T H Jackson and R E Scott, 'On the Nature of Bankruptcy: An Essay of Bankruptcy Sharing and the Creditors' Bargain' (1989) 75(2) *Virginia Law Review* 155; B E Adler, 'A World without Debt' (1994) 72(3) *Washington University Law Quarterly* 811; B E Adler, 'A Theory of Corporate Insolvency' (1997) 72(2) *New York University Law Review* 343; D G Baird and R K Rasmussen, 'The End of Bankruptcy' (2002) 55(3) *Stanford Law Review* 751; B E Adler, 'The Creditors' Bargain Revisited' (2018) 166(7) *University of Pennsylvania Law Review* 1853; and T H Jackson, 'A Retrospective Look at Bankruptcy's New Frontiers' (2018) 166(7) *University of Pennsylvania Law Review* 1867.

against the common pool of the debtors' assets.[41] The 'creditors' bargain' based insolvency framework justifies:

> the compulsory, collectivist regime of insolvency law on the grounds that were the company creditors free to agree to collectivist forms of enforcement of their claims on insolvency, they would agree to collectivist arrangements rather than procedures of individual action or partial collectivism.[42]

There are many pragmatic arguments that naturally favour an approach that protects creditors' rights in the circumstances of a debtor's financial distress; however, it is arguable as well that such an approach makes more sense in the more straightforward insolvency solutions that lead to the sale of corporate assets and dissolution of a company through liquidation as there are fewer choices of resolution available. Once other victims of corporate decline are thrown into the mix and the aim becomes the rescue of a viable corporate entity or business, the bargain becomes fraught with conflict due to the significantly different interests that stakeholders such as employees will have. Jackson and other creditors' bargain theorists get around this by arguing that the protection of non-creditor interests such as employees, managers, and members of the community, and indeed the aim of keeping firms in operation at all, is not and should not be one of the goals of insolvency law.[43]

It is perhaps not surprising, therefore, that the strict creditors' bargain approach has been subject to significant criticism. Concerns have focused on the principle that an insolvency process should be strictly a debt-collection process for the benefit of contractual creditors. However, it has been said that such a view fails to recognise the legitimate interests of many others who do not fall into the category of contractual creditors.[44] Whereas an end-of-life corporate situation may be suited to a strict creditors' bargain approach, modern solutions to financial distress are not necessarily suited to this narrow view, particularly given the focus today on the rescue of viable companies and businesses.

In the last few decades, however, and in particular since the turn of the millennium, there has been a steady shift from an acceptance of liquidation as an inevitable outcome of corporate insolvency for most companies, to a policy and regulatory emphasis on a desire to rescue viable companies where

---

41 Jackson (n 33) 17.

42 Finch (n 38) 231.

43 Ibid.

44 See e.g., the works of E Warren and K Gross, 'Taking Community Interests into Account in Bankruptcy: An Essay' (1994) 72(3) *Washington University Law Quarterly* 1031.

possible. Justifying this shift has been discussed by many eminent academics, usually with a focus on not only the financial benefit of preserving value, but also the social benefits often associated with the preservation of corporate life. Given the overall approach is geared towards the broad economic and social benefits of the preservation of viable corporate entities, it is also surely appropriate to consider these as stakeholder deserving of consideration in any collective process that might be undertaken to rescue that entity or its business.

Broad-based Contractarianism

Broad-based contractarianism was introduced by Donald Korobkin within a Rawlsian paradigm, somewhat similar to the creditors' bargain theory.[45] Although the 'contractarian' aspect would seem to closely reflect the Jacksonian approach, Korobkin takes the concept of the contract beyond that of the purely legal connection aimed to maximise the returns to contractual creditors into a broader approach under the more philosophical social contract principles.[46] Although both Jackson and Korobkin produce their insolvency law paradigms from behind a Rawlsian veil of ignorance, Korobkin includes not only the contractual creditors, but representatives of all the stakeholders who might potentially be affected by a company's decline. Such stakeholders include employees, managers, owners, tort claimants, and members of the community.[47] One commonality that most of these stakeholders share is that they do not 'assume the risk' of a debtor's default or financial distress.[48]

In typical Rawlsian fashion, Korobkin justifies insolvency frameworks by introducing a veil of ignorance behind which the included stakeholders would agree to how they should be treated within the process resolving a debtor company's financial distress. Principles are chosen without knowledge of individual legal status, position within the company or other characteristics that might lead them to prefer personal interests over those of the collective. Parties behind the veil, Korobkin argues, would first introduce a 'principle of inclusion' which would make all affected parties eligible to press their demands. The second would be a principle of 'rational planning' that would determine whether 'and to what extent persons would be able to enforce legal rights and exert leverage'.[49] These principles would lead to a 'maximisation

45 J Rawls, *A Theory of Justice* (Oxford University Press 1972).

46 D Korobkin, 'Contractarianism and the Normative Foundations of Bankruptcy Law' (1993) 71(3) *Texas Law Review* 541, 575–589.

47 Finch (n 38) 234.

48 D Korobkin, 'Employee Interests in Bankruptcy' (1996) 4(1) *American Bankruptcy Institute Law Review* 4, 6.

49 Korobkin (n 46) 575–589.

of aims' rather than a maximisation of wealth, which would be sought by the application of creditors' bargain principles. The maximisation of aims would inherently include formulating the most rational long-term plan to realise the best interests of the business enterprise and all affected stakeholders, a goal that is specifically excluded in most creditors' bargain approaches.

Korobkin's approach also provides a basis for accounting for the vulnerabilities of stakeholders bargaining behind the veil of ignorance. Applying Rawls' 'difference principle', there would also be a mandate that those stakeholders in the worst off or most vulnerable/least resilient position, such as non-adjusting and involuntary creditors, should be protected over those who are in more powerful positions with the resilience to adjust to the debtor's financial distress and the processes that may occur to resolve that distress. Stakeholders in such worse off positions 'would be those relatively powerless to promote their aims, yet with the most to lose on the frustration of those aims'.

There are, or course, many criticisms of the Rawlsian approach taken by both creditors' bargain and contractarian theorists. Principally, it is lacking in reality because it is impossible to 'strip the individual completely yet conclude that he or she would choose the difference principle'.[50] This assumption does not take into account whether some stakeholders might be more or less risk-averse than others and therefore willing to take the risk that they might find themselves in one of the positions of power once the veil has lifted. In such cases, they may bargain with a perceived self-interest that is not level with the lowest common denominator, which would distort the fairness envisaged by a Rawlsian approach. In addition, it is unclear to what extent diminutions in justice would be willingly traded off against gains in wealth, for example. Such an approach may actually be so protective as to create an uncertain result that would be catastrophic in terms of the effect that such a regime developed under Rawlsian principles would be on the cost of credit.[51]

While the contractarian approach does introduce a fairly robust framework within which a fair insolvency system could be created, it does not provide measurable tests to assess the most vulnerable. Therefore, it remains uncertain in the broad-based contractarian vision who should enjoy priority of protection over those in more powerful positions.[52] This is an issue that repeats itself in the next theoretical approach: the communitarian or traditionalist vision.

---

50 Finch (n 38) 235.
51 Ibid.
52 Ibid., 236.

Communitarian or Traditionalist Approaches

The communitarian vision developed by Elizabeth Warren eschews the contractarian approach while embracing a similar broad range of stakeholder interests that call for some redistribution of value so that high priority insolvency claims must give way to less powerful stakeholders.[53] It also embraces an aim that is in direct contrast to the creditors' bargain with its focus on the collective of contractual creditors. Communitarianism, instead, focuses on a fair distribution of the risk of insolvency by reference to relative power among the stakeholders rather than the fair distribution of wealth as a result of that insolvency.[54]

The communitarian approach also specifically takes into account non-entity stakeholders such as environmental cleaning costs that will affect a community should a corporation not have the ability to rectify such damages. In such circumstances, a communitarian vision would not only prioritise the less powerful involuntary creditors but would also redistribute the costs of environmental damage to be shared by both the debtor and its contractual creditors. These costs would be shared through a redistribution of value towards paying for those costs, which would reduce the pot for the collective of contractual creditors. However, such redistribution within the communitarian visions is not seen as an aberration from the protection of creditors' rights, but rather as a core function of insolvency law insofar as it should be a 'scheme designed to distribute the costs amongst those at risk.'[55] As Warren puts it:

> I see bankruptcy as an attempt to reckon with a debtor's multiple defaults and to distribute the consequences among a number of different actors. Bankruptcy encompasses a number of competing – and sometimes conflicting – values in this distribution. As I see it, no one value dominates, so that bankruptcy policy becomes a composite of factors that bear on a better answer to the question, 'How shall the losses be distributed?'[56]

The communitarian approach will also inevitably encourage the survival of viable but financially distressed companies in order to ensure those most

---

[53] E Warren, 'Bankruptcy Policy' (1987) 54(3) *University of Chicago Law Review* 775.

[54] Ibid., 777. See D Korobkin, 'Rehabilitating Values: A Jurisprudence of Bankruptcy' (1991) 91(4) *Columbia Law Review* 717 for an analysis of Warren's and Baird's argument between the creditors' bargain and a communitarian approach with detailed discussion of the strengths and weaknesses of both.

[55] Warren (n 53) 790.

[56] Ibid., 777.

vulnerable stakeholders are able to survive and recuperate their costs.[57] The rescue of viable businesses will also serve the distributional interests of many stakeholders who do not fall within the category of creditors but who do have an interest in the continuation of the business. These could include older employees who cannot realistically retrain, customers who would have to resort to alternative suppliers with less attractive goods and services, suppliers who will be losing current customers, nearby property owners who may suffer declining property values, and governments that may have shrinking tax bases that would otherwise benefit from a successful reorganisation. The provision of rescue options within insolvency frameworks acknowledges the potential losses of those who have depended upon the business by redistributing some of the risk of loss from the default.[58]

Although this approach embraces the UK Cork Committee's[59] vision that acknowledge that there are societal interests to be considered in insolvency as well as those of contractual creditors, it is also lacks a degree of focus that is present in both the creditors' bargain and broad-based contractarianism approaches, which at least provide a paradigm within which a framework can be developed.[60] Further, the communitarian approach embraced by Warren does not provide a means of weighing community interests. One of the principles upon which the communitarian visions rests is that it is possible and effective to entrust a bankruptcy judge with the discretion to balance the conflicting and competing interests of the various stakeholders.[61] Baird points out weaknesses among the other principles upon which the communitarian vision rests, but for the purpose of this chapter, an approach with vulnerability and resilience at its heart may well provide the missing measures. Finch asks, for example, 'How might a court balance the community's interests in maintaining employment against potential environmental damage?'[62]

Warren herself admits that she offers a 'dirty, complex, elastic and interconnected' view of insolvency law from which outcomes cannot be predicted nor are all the factors relevant to a decision on policy fully articulated. Certainly, an economic account such as that espoused by Thomas Jackson and

---

57 Finch (n 38) 237.

58 Warren (n 53) 788.

59 *The Report of the Review Committee on Insolvency Law and Practice* (Cmnd 8558) (1982).

60 B S Schermer, 'Response to Professor Gross: Taking the Interests of the Community into Account in Bankruptcy' (1994) 72(3) *Washington University Law Quarterly* 1049, 1051.

61 D G Baird, 'Loss Distribution, Forum Shopping, and Bankruptcy: A Reply to Warren' (1987) 54(3) *University of Chicago Law Review* 815, 816.

62 Finch (n 38) 237.

Douglas Baird in the creditors' bargain can justify its approach its approach empirically as a wealth maximisation mechanism benefitting the collective of legally connected stakeholders. However, a value-based account building on Warren's more socially conscious but philosophically fuzzy approach takes a step toward creating a measurable test that could be applied to the fairness of stakeholder treatment in insolvency and restructuring. Korobkin suggests a value-based approach founded on a deeper understanding of the concern to which bankruptcy law is addressed, which includes not just the economic, but also the moral, political, personal, and social problems that affect all stakeholders.[63] However, Korobkin slips back into a pseudo-Rawlsian standpoint insofar as he posits the worth of an insolvency law providing a forum for the representation of diverse values, adopting another social-contract style of approach: 'Under the value-based system, bankruptcy law has the distinct function of creating conditions for discourse in which values of participants may be rehabilitated into an informed and coherent visions of what the estate as enterprise shall exist to do.'[64]

This is in contrast to Warren's policy argument that simply focuses on the values to be protected in an insolvency distribution and the effective implementation of those values to assist decision makers even if, admittedly, there are no specific answers that can be derived from a testable set of criteria.[65] Whereas neither Warren or Korobkin dictates specific answers in relation to how interests should be assessed outside the pre-insolvency contractual entitlements, an approached based in vulnerability and resilience may offer a framework within which specific answers can be found by the application of a test.

VULNERABILITY THEORY AS A FAIRNESS PARADIGM IN INSOLVENCY AND RESTRUCTURING

A theoretical framework that considers the choices of all stakeholders affected by the decisions of a corporate entity is worth exploring given the somewhat recent shift from an emphasis on efficient liquidation outcomes to a preference for rescuing viable companies where possible. This shift raises a number of new issues that were not indicated in the collective processes used in traditional insolvency. Traditional approaches have tended to embrace the concept of creditor wealth maximisation, with fairness typically considered from a creditors' bargain perspective, which are generally drawn from a Law and Economics standpoint. However, Law and Economics considerations, and by

---

63 Korobkin (n 54) 762.

64 Ibid., 781.

65 Finch (n 38) 241.

extension the Jacksonian adherence to creditor wealth maximisation as the underpinning rational for insolvency procedures, is exclusionary, particularly in the more complex circumstances of business and company rescue.[66] It relies upon legal ties connected mostly to contract and property law. It typically does not allow for a balancing of the vulnerabilities caused by involuntary parties and information asymmetries inherent in processes instigated at the behest of a large or powerful creditors.

A socio-legal perspective, however, allows for an analysis of current legal structures in a way that is directly linked with the social situation to which the law applies,[67] thereby allowing for a focus on the impact on stakeholders who wield less power or who may be involuntary parties to an insolvency and unable to adjust their level of risk accordingly. Such stakeholders may also be less resilient to the financial impact of an insolvency or restructuring due to socio-economic dependencies resting on the debtor. Although both Korobkin's broad-based contractarianism and Warren's communitarian vision adopt an essentially socio-legal perspective, they do not succeed in creating a concrete paradigm within which a realistic corporate rescue framework can be designed that will be useful for the modern corporation in financial distress.

Although the theories mentioned in this chapter certainly have their place and provide useful frameworks for analysing and measuring the complex issues raised by the circumstances of financial distress, they do not necessarily cater to the shift in emphasis from efficient liquidation to the rescue of viable business that drives insolvency law policy today. In addition, current available theoretical frameworks either do not cater for the diverse needs of a rescue-based insolvency policy (creditors' bargain) or are not specific enough in terms of how to measure those diverse interest and introduce fairness between them (broad-based contractarianism and communitarianism). As such, there is a need for a new paradigm with vulnerability and resilience at its heart to meet the needs of the modern firm in financial distress. Such a paradigm will have a broader and more applicable set of measures for assessing the fairness of insolvency and rescue procedures, considering not only an economic and legal approach but also attempting to balance the social and moral issues that are also at play.

Martha Fineman's vulnerability theory provides a potential theoretical framework within which these conflicting areas can be viewed and balanced.

---

66 Jennifer L L Gant, 'Floating Charges and Moral Hazard: Finding Fairness for Involuntary and Vulnerable Stakeholders' in J Hardman and A McPherson (eds), *Floating Charges in Scotland: New Perspectives on Current Issues* (Edinburgh University Press 2022) 228, 241.

67 D Schiff, 'Socio-Legal Theory: Social Structure and Law' (1976) 39(3) *Modern Law Review* 287, 287.

Although Fineman's theory was constructed with human dependencies associated with social and cultural discrimination, with some adjustment it can also provide a new lens through which to view legitimately vulnerable stakeholders to a corporate insolvency or restructuring. Equality may even be an unjust measure when it is applied to 'situations of inescapable or inevitable inequality where differing levels of authority and power are appropriate',[68] such as in an employer/employee relationship or even the power imbalance between secured and unsecured creditors. A vulnerability approach applied to situations of financial distress may serve to recalibrate fairness between the clearly differential power structure among the various stakeholders due to rights attached to security and regulatory priorities. The resilience of a stakeholder will inevitably be linked to their ability to exercise power over a process which includes access to information, participation, and the notional ability to exercise control over their fate.[69]

What is Vulnerability Theory?

Vulnerability and resilience have been referred to multiple times in this chapter without a full explanation of what is meant by these terms. Before applying these concepts to assess and establish a new test of fairness, a brief description of Fineman's theory is necessary.

Vulnerability has been described as challenging the dominant conception of the universal legal subject as an autonomous, independent, and fully-functioning adult, a static figure that does not cater for the reality of humans who are socially and materially dynamic with varying levels of *resilience.* Fineman asserts that there should be political and legal implications for the fact that humans live within a fragile environment constantly subject to positive and negative change in both physical and social circumstances. Whereas vulnerability, according to Fineman, is a universal human constant, our relative resilience to that vulnerability varies over time. The inequality of human resilience is at the heart of vulnerability theory because it turns attention to society and social institutions. Resilience is produced, protected, or supported within and through institutions and relationships that confer privilege

---

[68] M Fineman, 'Vulnerability and Inevitable Inequality' (2017) 4(3) *Oslo Law Review* 133, 135.

[69] Material for this section was drawn from Gant (n 32); (n 66); and Guest Editorial: 'Optimising Fairness in Insolvency and Restructuring: a Spotlight on Vulnerable Stakeholders' (2022) 31(1) *International Insolvency Review* 1.

and power, and these relationships tend to be largely defined and reinforced by legal mechanisms.[70]

Legal institutions, as mechanisms of the social contract, have a responsibility in the structuring of societal relationships and institutions, which means that the state should bear some responsibility to ensure that these institutions and relationships are functioning fairly. Those involved in vulnerability theory as a policy project, predominately in the United States and within the orbit of Martha Fineman at Emory University in Atlanta, Georgia, aim to build an ethical framework for confronting neoliberalism with its emphasis on individual autonomy and personal responsibility. Whereas autonomy assumes independence and the possibility of a choice and that non-discriminatory access to opportunities exist, the reality is quite different when one considers the limitations affecting the human condition. Vulnerability theory recognises the many ways in which social relationships are shaped, reinforced, and modified by the law and argues that the state is always actively involved in the allocation, preservation, or maintenance of privilege and disadvantage. Therefore, the state also bears a responsibility through the introduction of fairness legislation to rectify the disadvantages and/or privileges that its institutions perpetuate.[71]

Institutions, as human creations, are also, though differently, vulnerable. They can be corrupted, captured and can decline and perish. They can cause harm and create situations that exacerbate or exploit human (or less powerful institutional) vulnerability. However, institutions, such as a fair corporate rescue and restructuring framework that accounts for the less resilient stakeholder, can also mediate, compensate, and mitigate vulnerability. As has been evident between 2020–2022 (at the time of writing), events such as the COVID-19 pandemic, the war in Ukraine, and the spike in energy prices can cause difficulties or even failure of institutions in the 'wake of market fluctuations, changing international policies, institutional and political compromises, or human prejudices'.[72] Given the human made nature of law and corporations and government, it is only sensible that these institutions should serve the human requirement for resilience. If the things humanity creates are not used to serve the needs of humanity, what is the point of having them at all?

---

70 See M Fineman, 'The Social Foundations of Law' (2005) 54(5) *Emory Law Journal* 201.

71 Ibid., 225.

72 M Fineman, 'The Vulnerable Subject: Anchoring Equality in the Human Condition' (2008) 20(1) *Yale Journal of Law and Feminism* 1, 12–15.

Equal Treatment is Not Always Fair Treatment

Fineman's vulnerability theory has been proposed as an alternative to 'traditional equal protection analysis' and has been described as a 'post-identity' enquiry focused not on discrimination against defined groups, but rather 'concerned with privilege and favour conferred on limited segments of the population by the state and broader society through their institutions'.[73] Traditional approaches to equality have been associated with John Locke's liberal subject which is based on the well-known ideal that human beings are by their nature free and endowed with the same inalienable rights.[74] However, these rights are not always accessible to all individuals due to differences in position and circumstance which affects the ability of those individuals to make use of their inalienable rights and freedoms. They begin from a starting line, for lack of a better analogy, that is behind more privileged groups or individuals. They must, therefore, 'work harder' to arrive at the same level of socio-economic success in the same time period. This incidental (or intentional) privilege that is enjoyed by some groups of people (in the traditional equal rights perspective) makes it difficult to rise above the original circumstances in which some find themselves. A similar paradigm could be applied to non-adjusting, involuntary, and non-traditional stakeholders in an insolvency or restructuring if one considers the power differentials inherent in these processes.

One of the key underlying precepts of collective insolvency procedures is that of equal treatment,[75] although there are so many priority carveouts that it is arguable whether this remains the case.[76] Martha Fineman notes, in respect to equality of treatment between individuals, that, where equality is 'reduced to sameness of treatment or a prohibition on discrimination, this has proved an inadequate tool to resist or upset persistent forms of subordination or domination'.[77] Furthermore: '[t]his version of equality is similarly weak in its ability to address and correct the disparities in economic and social wellbeing among various groups in our society. Formal equality leaves undisturbed - and may

---

[73] Ibid., 1.

[74] Ibid., 2.

[75] See A Keay and P Walton, 'The Preferential Debts Regime in Liquidation Law: In the Public Interest' (1999) 3(1) *Company Financial and Insolvency Law Review* 84, 85 as cited in R Mokal, 'Priority as Pathology: the Pari Passu Principle' (2001) 60(3) *Cambridge Law Journal* 581.

[76] For a full discussion on the realities of *pari passu* in the context of regulatory priorities, see Mokal (n 75).

[77] Fineman (n 72) 3.

even serve to validate – existing institutional arrangements that privilege some and disadvantage others'.[78]

Although the treatment of creditors already carries with it the obligations that were in place under a contract for the repayment of debts, the nature of debts for goods and services or for loans is different in nature from the obligations owed to employees under an employment contract or indeed the obligations owed to non-contractual, involuntary creditors, such as those who have suffered losses as a result of the company's activities. While there are certainly debts in terms of wages for work undertaken, the relationship is far more complex and far-reaching in terms of social implications, particularly when we consider the value of an employee's firm specific human capital contribution to the debtor company and the natural dependencies that employees have on their employment and job security. Equally, the damages owed to tort and environmental creditors tend to be treated as unsecured, so fall very low on the list of priorities.

With regard to environmental debts, the consequences of not paying out can be highly significant when the funds would be used to rectify certain environmental damage. The damage will still need to be rectified – in such circumstances who will ultimately pay? The obligation would likely fall upon society due to the necessity for governments to rectify the matter, which would inevitably have to be funded by the taxpayer.

Equal treatment in such circumstances is not necessarily fair treatment, given the varying degrees of power and resilience that different categories of stakeholders will have in an insolvency process, as well as the extensive impact that lack of funding can have on the wider society. This is also why so many carveouts already exist to this so-called fundamental principle, such as the categorisation of preferential debts that is often applied to employee claims.[79] These carveouts aim to some extent to redress the imbalance in power due to the greater vulnerability of less powerful stakeholders.

The Concept of Vulnerability in Corporate Insolvency

Fineman observes that the term 'vulnerable' can be used to describe:

> [...] a universal, inevitable, enduring aspect of the human condition that must be at the heart of our concept of social and state responsibility. Vulnerability thus freed from its limited and negative associations is a powerful conceptual tool with the

---

78 Ibid.
79 Keay and Walton (n 75) 85.

> potential to define an obligation for the state to ensure a richer and more robust guarantee of equality than is currently afforded under the equal protection model.[80]

Fineman goes on to explain that 'the concept of vulnerability can act as a heuristic device, pulling us back to examine hidden assumptions and biases that shaped its original social and cultural meanings'.[81] Vulnerability can then provide a valuable context within which critical perspectives on political, societal, and legal institutions can be constructed.[82] A focus on vulnerability goes beyond the normative claims for equality generally, whether formal or substantive, and suggests the interrogation of what may be 'just and appropriate mechanisms to structure the terms and practices of inequality'.[83]

Currently, insolvency procedures continue to be guided by economic paradigms, principally due to their association with corporate law, which are shielded to some extent in the UK, and to a larger extent in the US, by the continued reliance on the free market of Western capitalism.[84] However, given the social implications of corporate insolvency, an adjusted perspective that takes in these non-economic features is overdue.

By placing vulnerability and resilience at the centre of the social policies that have come to influence the preferences and entitlements for employees in insolvency law, a similar approach could be taken to assess the resilience of other less traditional stakeholders in order to determine their power status as well as the greater societal impact they may have without intervention in a corporate insolvency or restructuring situation. As has been evident in the age of COVID-19, some institutions will fail in the face of market fluctuations caused by sudden economic shocks such as lockdowns. By focusing on the ability for stakeholders to respond to a company's financial distress – their resilience – it may be possible to uncover the weaknesses of the institutions in place that were intended to respond to that vulnerability in terms of introducing and maintaining fairness according to the inherent needs of different stakeholders.[85] In so doing, those institutions can be adjusted to better account for the resilience of those affected by corporate distress.

80 Fineman (n 72) 8–9.
81 Ibid., 9.
82 Ibid.
83 Fineman (n 68) 134.
84 Fineman (n 72) 5.
85 Ibid., 12–13.

CONCLUSION

One of the first steps to introducing a new paradigm of assessing the fairness of insolvency and rescue frameworks must be to have a clear definition of who or what is a stakeholder for the purpose of that fairness assessment. This chapter has developed the stakeholder idea from the early days of stakeholder theory from the context of business theory and ethics and how that has influenced the identification of stakeholders in early forms of insolvency theory. The creditors' bargain took a narrow view in its exclusive concerns around contractual creditors' interests and its simplistic conception as the corporation as a pool of assets belonging to the collective of creditors when a corporation enters insolvency.

The broad-based contractarian approach widened this out to include any entity affected by the activities of a financially distressed company, insisting that all stakeholders should be party to the bargain behind the Rawlsian veil of ignorance. Whereas the communitarian vision adopts a similar broad premise, its indeterminate nature failed to create a measure of insolvency fairness that could effectively create a satisfactorily certain test.[86] A focus on vulnerability provides a baseline upon which tests of fairness can be built. It asks policy makers to look closely at the institutions that create fairness in insolvency and restructuring and ensure that they account for the impact that such process have on those stakeholders who may be less resilient in the process than others due to their non-adjusting or involuntary nature. The socio-legal approach based in vulnerability will also allow for an assessment of the dependency that stakeholders have on the institution of the corporation in financial distress, which will impact their relative resilience when it comes to ultimate failure or other dispositions of a company's assets.

Although this chapter has not introduced a concrete test based in vulnerability – that is yet to come in the research trajectory of this author – it has gone some distance to developing upon decades-old themes in insolvency theory that have previously failed to take hold in the context of insolvency policy in large part due to their uncertainty and indeterminacy. However, if one considers the broad base of stakeholders included in both the broad-based contractarian and communitarian approaches who have legitimate interests in the continuation of a financially distressed company, the theoretical paradigm becomes fully inclusive. In addition, if one considers the effect of power differentials among the insolvency or restructuring stakeholders and the concomitant need to mitigate to some extent the controlling economic power that

---

86 Finch (n 38) 242.

may be detrimental to the less powerful, one may be on the way to creating a fairness paradigm with resilience of stakeholders at its heart.

PART III

An outward-looking study of insolvency law

12. Insolvency law through the lens of human rights theories

Eugenio Vaccari and Tara Van Ho

INTRODUCTION

What would insolvency[1] look like if we imagined it behind a Rawlsian veil of ignorance?[2] Would it be a system designed to promote the common good at the expense of individual entitlements?[3] Or would it be a system where pre-insolvency entitlements are impaired only when strictly necessary to maximise net asset distributions to creditors?[4] Who would be protected by this system? Would it be creditors and workers only or would larger groups of stakeholders feature?

The purpose(s) of insolvency law has been debated for decades. Scholars have traditionally argued that in insolvency procedures, rational people would choose a course of action that promotes either efficiency and/or equality.[5] With

---

[1] The chapter covers literature and case law published before 1 November 2022. The authors are grateful to Drs Jennifer L L Gant (University of Derby), Dimitrios Kyritsis and Jessica Lawrence (both University of Essex), and participants in the Global Business and Human Rights Scholars Association 2023 workshop for their insightful comments on earlier drafts of this chapter. The final version of this chapter also reflects an INSOL Talk with Dr Gant and Chrystin Ondersma (Rutgers University) https://www.insol.org/Focus-Groups/Academic-Group/Events-and-Podcasts accessed 3 August 2023. The usual disclaimers apply. We use 'bankruptcy' to refer to procedures involving individuals, and 'insolvency' to corporate ones.

[2] J Rawls, *A Theory of Justice* (Harvard University Press 1971). Please see Chapter 7 of this book for a detailed discussion of 'A Rawlsian Approach to Insolvency Law' by Stathis Potamitis and Xenophon Paparrigopoulos.

[3] E Warren, 'Bankruptcy Policy' (1987) 54(3) *U Chi L Rev* 775; K Gross, 'Taking Community Interests into Account in Bankruptcy: An Essay' (1994) 72(3) *Wash U LQ* 1031.

[4] T H Jackson and R E Scott, 'On the Nature of Bankruptcy: An Essay on Bankruptcy Sharing and the Creditors' Bargain' (1989) 75(2) *Va L Rev* 155.

[5] Ibid., 178.

few notable exceptions,[6] the efficiency-equality dichotomy has never been challenged. In this chapter, we challenge that dichotomy by bringing together Fineman's vulnerability theory and the principles and tools of Business and Human Rights (BHR).[7] In doing so, we establish a stronger normative and practical argument for an equitable approach to insolvency law.

At the heart of the competing philosophies of insolvency is a concern over Jackson and Baird's 'common pool problem':[8] if a pool is commonly owned without a controlling mechanism, self-interested co-owners will fish without restraint. In doing so, they will deplete the pool to unsustainable levels and undermine the common interests in the lake. Applied to insolvency, this means that if individual creditors were allowed to act in their own self-interest, they would undermine the collective interest of the group.[9] In response, procedural collectivists argue that creditors should be treated as a singular class sharing rateably in the proceeds generated by the sale of a debtor's assets. In their view, the purpose of insolvency is to maximise creditors' returns, principally by means of the distribution of the debtor's assets.[10]

Collectivity denies a legal right to pursue individual remedies against the debtor. This is because all creditors – despite not being affected in the same manner – are faced with a 'common disaster': the fact that there is not enough money to repay creditors as a going concern.[11] This approach to collectivity is a 'central and seemingly indispensable feature' of insolvency law.[12]

Proceduralists argue that individual contracts (or pre-insolvency entitlements) should remain unaffected by the insolvency proceedings.[13] If this were not the case, parties would be incentivised to use insolvency law in a strategic manner.[14] It follows that a proceduralist system characterised by

---

6 B E Adler, 'A Theory of Corporate Insolvency' (1997) 72(2) *NYU L Rev* 343; A Schwartz, 'A Contract Theory Approach to Business Bankruptcy' (1998) 107(6) *Yale LJ* 1807.

7 K Udofia, 'Treatment of Employees in Corporate Insolvencies: An International Human Rights Law Perspective' (20 May 2019) https://www.pressreader.com/nigeria/thisday/20190416/282033328588071 accessed 1 November 2022.

8 T H Jackson, *The Logic and Limits of Bankruptcy Law* (Beardbooks 1986) 11–13; D G Baird and T H Jackson, *Cases, Problems and Materials on Bankruptcy* (Foundation Press 2020) 39–43.

9 Baird and Jackson (n 8).

10 K Gross, *Failure and Forgiveness: Rebalancing the Bankruptcy System* (Yale University Press 1997); C Frost, 'Bankruptcy Redistributive Policies and the Limits of the Judicial Process' (1995) 74(1) *NC L Rev* 75.

11 Report of the Review Committee, *Insolvency Law and Practice* (Cm 8558, June 1982) para [232].

12 RJ Mokal, *Corporate Insolvency Law: Theory and Application* (OUP 2005) 33.

13 Jackson and Scott (n 4) 161, 202.

14 Ibid., 161.

across-the-board redistributions is preferable to individualised distributional policies, as the former allows for the maximised net assets for distributions to creditors.[15] The issue with their theoretical approach – and much of the debate that followed[16] – has been an attempt to collectivise people's (and companies') thinking. In the proceduralist narrative, 'variation of insolvency rights is only justified when those rights interfere with group advantages associated with creditors acting in concert'.[17]

Jackson's approach to collectivity has stood the test of time as the most prominent mechanism within insolvency law. However, a case has been made for a more informed understanding of collectivity using path-dependency and historical institutionalism methods.[18] Other scholars have powerfully and convincingly argued that insolvency law is not and should not be a one-purpose system, meaning that it should serve interests other than simply maximising creditors' returns.[19] Those that espouse value-informed communitarian approaches suggest that high-priority creditors such as fixed and floating charge holders should share their entitlements with low-ranking creditors. In this chapter, we augment the current debates by bringing together a BHR-based critique with the socio-legal concept of vulnerability to suggest amendments to the proceduralist understanding of the purpose and limits of corporate insolvency law. In doing so, we call for expanding the concerns accounted for when seeking Pareto and Kaldor-Hicks efficiency in insolvency or restructuring procedures.[20]

This chapter's primary value lies in rephrasing the theoretical debate on the purpose(s) of corporate insolvency law by employing Fineman's vulnerability theory and international human rights law (IHRL) to challenge current approaches to collectivity. Scholars have considered the relevance of Fineman's vulnerability theory to corporate distress scenarios.[21] However,

---

15 Ibid., 202.

16 A Duggan, 'Contractarianism and the Law of Corporate Insolvency' (2005) 42(3) *Can Bus LJ* 463; R J Mokal, 'Contractarianism, Contractualism, and the Law of Corporate Insolvency' (2007) 1 *Sing J Legal Stud* 51.

17 V Finch and D Milman, *Corporate Insolvency Law: Perspectives and Principles* (3rd edn, CUP 2017) 29; Jackson (n 8); B E Adler, 'The Creditors' Bargain Revisited' (2018) 166(7) *U Pa L Rev* 1853.

18 E Vaccari, 'OW Bunker: A Common Law Perspective on Multi-lateral Co-operation in Insolvency-Related Cases' (2017) 28 ICCLR 245; E Vaccari, 'The Ammanati Affair: Seven Centuries Old, and not Feeling the Age' (2018) 93(3) *Chi-Kent L Rev* 831 (Vaccari, 'Ammanati').

19 Warren (n 3) 800.

20 See also Mokal (n 16) 54–57.

21 See J L L Gant, 'Optimising Fairness in Insolvency and Restructuring: A Spotlight on Vulnerable Stakeholders" (2022) 31(1) IIR 1; 'Floating Charges and Moral Hazard:

to date there have been no attempts to combine a human rights critique with Fineman's vulnerability theory within the context of a proceduralist understanding of the purpose of insolvency law. As we explain below, Fineman's theory can assist in challenging and deconstructing the underpinning assumptions in insolvency law, but it is not well-designed to offer an alternative reconstruction of the law. For that, we turn to IHRL and its subfield of BHR.

There have been attempts to apply a human rights approach to consumer bankruptcy situations, the proceduralist tenets of bankruptcy,[22] and occasionally insolvency law.[23] These attempts have principally drawn on the UK Human Rights Act 1998 (HRA 1998), the future of which is uncertain[24] and the focus of which was to regulate vertical relationships between the state and the individual.[25] This naturally limits the relevance of the HRA 1998 for insolvency law matters. In contrast, the 2011 United Nations Guiding Principles on Business and Human Rights (UNGPs) were specifically designed to consider the horizontal impacts on human rights stemming from conduct that might normally be considered a 'purely private' matter, like insolvency or employment contracts. The UNGPs are the most authoritative statement on the international obligations in relation to business impacts on human rights. Non-binding in their own right, the UNGPs reflect existing international law on state obli-

---

Searching for Fairness for Involuntary and Vulnerable Stakeholders' in J Hardman and A MacPherson (eds), *The Floating Charge in Scotland: New Perspectives and Current Issues* (EE Publishing 2022); 'Vulnerability, Resilience, and Employees: Can a Higher Degree of Fairness be Achieved by Looking Beyond Traditional Insolvency Norms?' in J Harris (ed), *Insolvency: A Research Agenda* (Edward Elgar 2023) (forthcoming); 'Reconsidering Fairness for Vulnerable and Involuntary Stakeholders in Insolvency and Restructuring' in E Vaccari and E Ghio (eds), *Insolvency Law: Back to the Future?* (INSOL Europe 2022) (Gant, 'Reconsidering Fairness') and Chapter 11 of this book on 'Vulnerability and Insolvency Law'.

[22] N Pike, 'The Human Rights Act 1998 and its Impact on Insolvency Practitioners' (2001) 1(Feb) *Insolv L* 25; W Trower, 'Human Rights: Article 6 – The Reality and the Myth' (2001) 2(May) *Insolv L* 48; M Simmons, 'Human Rights and Insolvency: An Update' (2001) 17 *IL & P* 203; P J Omar, 'Insolvency Law and Human Rights: An Update' (2009) 6 *Int CR* 369; C Ondersma, 'Overlooked Human Rights Concerns in the Restructuring and Insolvency Context' in P J Omar and J L L Gant (eds), *Research Handbook on Corporate Restructuring* (EE Publishing 2021) 466.

[23] J Ulph and T Allen, 'Transactions at an Undervalue, Purchasers and the Impact of the Human Rights Act 1998' (2004) *Jan JBL* 1; J De Lacy, 'Company Charge Avoidance and Human Rights' (2004) *Jul JBL* 448.

[24] Ondersma (n 22) 466; C Ondersma, 'A Human Rights Framework for Debt Relief' (2014) 36(1) *U Pa J Int'l L* 269; C Ondersma, 'A Human Rights Approach to Consumer Credit' (2015) 9(2) *Tul L Rev* 373.

[25] Human Rights Act 1998, Arts 6, 8–9.

gations[26] while their expectations for businesses have been incorporated into numerous international and domestic legal frameworks.[27] This chapter brings together insolvency and BHR expertise to draw attention to the distributional and allocative issues raised by insolvency cases and identifies alternative practices to address inequalities in insolvency scenarios.

In the remainder of the chapter, we first outline current competing narratives in insolvency law. After examining the concepts of procedural collectivity and natural egality, including a discussion of their theoretical and practical limitations, we consider calls for reform through the modular approach and the team production theory of insolvency and briefly examine how English courts have used the principles of equity and fairness to date. Finally, we introduce Fineman's vulnerability theory to deconstruct insolvency law, and IHRL and BHR to offer a means of reconstructing the legal framework.

THE DEBATE ON PROCEDURAL COLLECTIVISM, NATURAL EQUALITY, AND EQUITY

Collectivity is one of the defining factors of insolvency proceedings, providing for a singular or universal treatment of debtors in the name of Pareto efficiency and egality.[28] In this section, we explore the traditional understanding of collectivity as well as efforts to challenge or modify such vision through the modular approach and the team production theory. We explain the shortcomings of the current understanding of this notion, leading us to explore an IHRL-based approach in the remainder of the chapter.

Traditionalist Understandings of Collectivity

Proceduralist scholars view 'collectivity' in negative terms, as the absence of individual remedies.[29] These academics argue that should rational creditors be placed behind a Rawlsian veil of ignorance, they would not favour solutions

---

26 M Krajewski, 'The State Duty to Protect Against Human Rights Violations through Transnational Business Activities,' (2018) 23 *Deakin L Review* https://ojs.deakin.edu.au/index.php/dlr/article/view/804 accessed 1 November 2022.

27 UN Working Group on Business and Human Rights, 'Guiding Principles on Business and Human Rights at 10: Taking Stock of the First Decade,' UN Doc A/HRC/47/39 (2021).

28 H Eidenmüller, 'What is an Insolvency Proceeding?' (December 2016) Law Working Paper no 335/2016 https://papers.ssrn.com/sol3/papers.cfm?abstract_id=2712628# accessed 1 November 2022.

29 K van Zwieten, *Goode on Principles of Corporate Insolvency Law* (Sweet & Maxwell 2019).

that benefit the fastest, most skilled and most sophisticated of them.[30] Instead, they would opt for approaches that equally share the burden of the debtor's failure on all the debtor's creditors. As such, the proceduralist egalitarian notion of collectivism has developed with the following three tenets:

(1) insolvency proceedings must address the claims of all the company's creditors;
(2) creditors have *in lieu* rights in insolvency proceedings;
(3) creditors of equal standing have equal rights.[31]

Necessary corollaries to the proceduralist approach are cost-effective[32] and strictly rateable[33] distributions of debtors' assets (*pari passu* distribution) to minimise the 'common pool problem' by limiting individual, self-interested and value-destroying actions.[34] The common pool problem is seen as a multi-party version of the 'prisoner's dilemma'[35] where the rational involved parties realise that individual actions such as the enforcement of their claims against the debtor will deplete the pool of assets available for distribution while increasing procedural costs. Nevertheless, these creditors are pushed to betray the common good for a (potentially) individual larger gain. Proceduralism is a mechanism to limit individual, self-interested and value-destroying actions.

One of the main problems with this view of 'collectivity' lies in the exceptions recognised to its operation. For instance, there are frequent deviations from the absolute priority rule.[36] This rule mandates that lower ranking creditors are entitled to distribution only if higher ranking ones are paid in full.[37] Some of these exceptions are warranted by the law through the introduction of

---

[30] Jackson (n 8) 17.

[31] H Anderson, *The Framework of Corporate Insolvency Law* (OUP 2017) 20.

[32] T H Jackson, 'Bankruptcy, Non-Bankruptcy Entitlements, and the Creditors' Bargain' (1982) 91(5) *Yale LJ* 857, 862; Anderson (n 31) 3.

[33] R Mokal, 'The Authentic Consent Model: Contractarianism, Creditor's Bargain, and Corporate Liquidation' (2001) 21(3) *Legal Studies* 400, 421.

[34] Against: A Flessner, 'Philosophies of Business Bankruptcy Law: An International Overview' in J S Ziegel (ed), *Current Developments in International and Comparative Corporate Insolvency Law* (OUP 1994) 25–26.

[35] W Poundstone, *Prisoners' Dilemma* (OUP 1993); R C Picker, 'Security Interests, Misbehaviour, and Common Pools' (1992) 59(2) *U Chi L Rev* 645, 648.

[36] A Casey, 'The Creditors' Bargain and Option-Preservation Priority in Chapter 11' (2011) 78(3) *U Chi L Rev* 759; in contrast see D G Baird, 'Foreword: The Creditors' Bargain – Past, Present and Future' in B E Adler (ed), *Research Handbook on Corporate Bankruptcy Law* (EE Publishing 2020) xxiv.

[37] Bankruptcy, 11 US Code § 1129(b)(2)(B)(ii).

preferential treatments for categories of creditors.[38] Additionally, where a suspension of enforcement rights is offered as an option rather than as a necessary corollary of the statutory procedure,[39] parties seem reluctant to make use of it.[40] This behaviour impliedly dismisses the proceduralist argument that creditors behind a Rawlsian veil of ignorance would opt for collective procedures and reinstates the centrality of the prisoner's dilemma.

It may not always be necessary to depart from the collectivist narrative to protect pre-insolvency entitlements whilst promoting the public interest[41] or the preservation of value for selected creditors and the economy.[42] As stated elsewhere, 'equitable concepts could be employed to introduce a more nuanced understanding of the notion of "collectivity"'.[43] This approach would embrace collectivity while challenging the proceduralist, egalitarian notion of collectivism.

As noted above, the proceduralist egalitarian notion of collectivism rests on three tenets.[44] One outstanding point is to determine how essential it is that creditors have *in lieu* rights, and that creditors of equal standing have equal rights (points (2) and (3) above). English courts primarily focus on the first element, limiting the prominence of the other ones. In *Re 19 Entertainment*, the court was asked to recognise a foreign insolvency proceeding.[45] It determined that a foreign insolvency proceeding was one 'in which proceeding the assets and affairs of the debtor are subject to control or supervision by a foreign

---

38 With limited exceptions, pre-insolvency contractual preferential treatments are unaffected. The key provisions on preferences in liquidation procedures are ss 174A–176A IA 1986.

39 Part A1 moratorium, introduced by CIGA 2020.

40 Between 26 June 2020 and 31 May 2022, in England & Wales only 38 Part A1 moratoria were obtained, significantly lower than the government's expectations. Compare: The Insolvency Service, *Commentary – Monthly Insolvency Statistics May 2022* (17 June 2022) https://www.gov.uk/government/statistics/monthly-insolvency-statistics-may-2022/commentary-monthly-insolvency-statistics-may-2022; *Final Impact Assessment*, https://publications.parliament.uk/pa/bills/cbill/58-01/0146/SIGNED%20-%20IA%20Insolvency%20and%20Corporate%20Governance%20Enactment%20Stage.pdf both accessed 1 November 2022.

41 M Stubbins, 'What Kind of World Are We Living in? Creditor Wealth Maximisation, Contractarianism or Multiple Value in the Post-Enterprise Act 2002 Insolvency Regime' (2019) 32 *Insolv Int* 78, 79.

42 C Lamont, 'Re-structuring Leasehold Estates under Chapter 11 of the US Bankruptcy Code and in England and Wales – a Comparison' (2018) 31 *Insolv Int* 69, 70.

43 Vaccari, 'Ammanati' (n 18) 831.

44 Jackson (n 8).

45 *Re 19 Entertainment Ltd* [2016] EWHC (Ch) 1545, para [14].

court for the purpose of reorganisation or liquidation'.[46] As such, the court demonstrated a concern only for the first element of the English test, whether the proceedings address the concerns of all creditors.

This light-touch understanding of procedural collectivity has been advocated in other judgments,[47] although occasionally there have been instances where English courts have adopted more 'robust' views of the notion of collectivity.[48] The European Union's (EU) *Virgos-Schmit Report* also adopts a light-touch notion of 'collectivity' by stating that a 'collective action needs clearly determined legal positions to provide for an adequate bargaining power' for the affected creditors.[49] As such, the second and third tenets of procedural collectivity are left aside.

Unfortunately, in approaching the notion of collectivity, English courts adopt an unwarranted narrow focus on one specific category of stakeholders, the company's creditors. In *OGX*, albeit in an *obiter dictum*, the High Court clarified that the right to be heard cannot be invoked by any claimant.[50] For a procedure to be considered collective, only directly affected parties, meaning the company's creditors, should be included in a bankruptcy proceeding.[51] This is not and should not be the only possible approach.

The UNCITRAL Approach

The UNCITRAL Guide to Enactment of the Model Law on Cross-Border Insolvency (the Guide) expressly states that collectivity should result in coordinated, global solutions for all *stakeholders* of an insolvency proceeding.[52] Achieving collectivity may mean that classes of creditors are subject to differential treatments.[53] The same concept was later restated by the

---

46 Ibid.

47 *Re Lines Bros Ltd* [1983] Ch 1 at 20; *Re Stanford Int'l Bank Ltd* [2010] EWCA (Civ) 137.

48 *Rubin v Eurofinance SA* [2012] UKSC 46; *PricewaterhouseCoopers v Saad Investments Ltd* [2014] UKPC 35/5.

49 EU Council reference 6500/1/96, REV1, DRS 8 (CFC), 3 May 1996, para [8].

50 *Nordic Trustee ASA v OGX Petróleo e Gás SA (Re OGX Petróleo e Gás SA)* [2016] EWHC (Ch) 25.

51 Ibid., para [50].

52 UN Commission on Int'l Trade Law, *UNCITRAL Model Law on Cross-Border Insolvency with Guide to Enactment and Interpretation* (2014), [69] https://uncitral.un.org/sites/uncitral.un.org/files/media-documents/uncitral/en/1997-model-law-insol-2013-guide-enactment-e.pdf accessed 1 November 2022 (The Guide).

53 Ibid., [70].

European Preventive Restructuring Directive[54] and in the UK by the Corporate Insolvency and Governance Act 2020 (CIGA 2020). In other words, the notion of collectivity refers to the nature of the procedure.

Because (classes of) stakeholders can be treated differently to achieve collective outcomes, there is no need for procedures to be egalitarian. On the contrary, the Guide expressly allows affected 'creditors' – an unfortunate limitation – the right to submit claims, participate in the procedure and receive an equitable distribution.[55] As the Guide suggests, if collective procedures are simply those insolvency proceedings that address the claims of all the company's stakeholders, what is needed to make a collective framework individualist-maximiser and difference-enhancer?

Towards a Modular Approach

Insolvency scenarios raise challenges that go beyond traditional common pool problems. These include anti-common issues, occurring whenever the use of a resource for the stakeholders' best interest is prevented by a veto power exercised by a minority of players.[56] Anti-common practices may lead to underuse or sub-optimal use of the assets and have led to the adoption of mechanisms such as the cross-class cram-down.[57] There are also semi-common issues, described as 'encompassing the tragedies of both the commons and the anti-commons'[58] because the deflective behaviour of one party proportionately harms both that party and every other member in the group. Finally, there are free-rider issues whenever an interested stakeholder decides to 'wait-and-see', to reap the benefits from the interventionist approach of other stakeholders whilst not putting any efforts towards achieving a commonly beneficial goal.[59]

---

[54] Directive (EU) 2019/1023 of the European Parliament and of the Council of 20 June 2019 on preventive restructuring frameworks, on discharge of debt and disqualifications, and on measures to increase the efficiency of procedures concerning restructuring, insolvency and discharge of debt, and amending Directive (EU) 2017/1132 (Directive on restructuring and insolvency) [2019] OJ L 172/18.

[55] The Guide (n 52), [70].

[56] R J de Weijs, 'Harmonisation of European Insolvency Law and the Need to Tackle Two Common Problems: Common Pool and Anticommons' (2012) 21(2) *IIR* 67.

[57] This is when a restructuring plan is made binding on one or more dissenting classes of creditors.

[58] L A Fennel, 'Commons, Anticommons, Semicommons' in K Ayotte and HE Smith (eds), *Research Handbook on the Economics of Property Law* (EE Publishing 2011) 17.

[59] S Grossman and O Hart, 'Takeover Bids, the Free Rider Problem, and the Theory of the Firm' (1980) 11(1) *Bell Journal of Economics* 42.

The acknowledgment of what we call 'revised common pool dilemmas'[60] suggests the need for alternative principled approaches capable of being translated into corporate distress rules that results in less conflicting and more equitable deviations from proceduralist tenets. Drawing on broader scholarship advocating for contractualising social problems in a manner that avoids both statist and market-oriented approaches,[61] Schillig called for contractualising insolvency law.[62] For various reasons, attempts at doing this have failed,[63] making it even more pressing to develop a principled recalibration of insolvency law.

One such approach is the modular view of corporate insolvency law.[64] The proponents of a modular approach argue that the need for cost-effective and timely insolvency procedures requires deviating from 'one-size-fits-all' assumptions.[65] Insolvency frameworks should be flexibly and modularly designed to distinguish between viable and non-viable businesses; address the issues of cross-over of commercial and personal insolvency; and recognise different cultural, social, and economic norms.[66] Such an approach is especially promising when it comes to protecting the interests of 'vulnerable' categories of debtors, such as sole entrepreneurs and micro and small enterprises.[67] In fact, the procedures involving smaller enterprises may benefit from diminished procedural requirements and additional attention to unique issues, such as the personal implications of those corporate failures.[68]

---

[60] This taxonomy was first introduced by E Vaccari, 'Insolvency Statutory Rules and Contractual Freedom: A Study on the Limits of Corporate Insolvency Law in the Anglo/American Tradition' (PhD Thesis, City, University of London 2018).

[61] M Schillig, 'Corporate Insolvency Law in the Twenty-First Century: State Imposed or Market Based?' (2014) 14(1) *JCLS* 1.

[62] Ibid.

[63] D G Baird, 'A World Without Bankruptcy' (1987) 50(2) *Law & Contemp Probs* 173; B E Adler, 'A World Without Debt' (1994) 72(3) *Wash U LQ* 811; Schwartz (n 6).

[64] R B Davis et al, *Micro, Small and Medium Enterprise Insolvency: A Modular Approach* (OUP 2017).

[65] Ibid.; E Vaccari, 'A Modular Approach to Restructuring and Insolvency Law: Executory Contracts and Onerous Property in England and Italy' (2022) 31 *Norton Journal of Bankruptcy Law and Practice (West)* 534.

[66] Vaccari (n 65).

[67] See Davis (n 64).

[68] A successful example is the Small Business Reorganization Act of 2019. For an analysis of the approach taken by other jurisdictions, see (among others): E Vaccari, D Ehmke and F Burigo, 'MSMEs in Distress: Regulatory Costs and Efficiency Considerations in the Implementation of Preventive Restructuring Mechanisms. An Anglo-German-Italian Perspective' (2023) *J Int'l & Comp L* (forthcoming).

The Team Production Theory

Another complementary approach that builds on the 'team production theory of corporate law'[69] is to better value those who make company-specific commitments.[70] Many corporations often entail multiple internal and external actors involved in 'joint value creation'.[71] Similarly, LoPucki argues that corporations should be seen as production teams where their constituents or team members (creditors, managers, workers) delegate the board of directors to act for the benefit of the company and subordinate their legal rights to the preservation of the entity's going concern.[72] Because of their membership, these theorists claim that 'team members' such as employees are entitled to something more than compensation for their work.[73] As such, the corporation's representations should favour policies that respect worker's rights, such as prioritising reorganisations over pre-insolvency entitlements or asset distribution and creditor maximisation.[74] According to the managerialist underpinnings[75] of the team production conceptualisation, insolvency law should 'consider the value of an employee's firm specific human capital contribution to the debtor company and the natural dependencies that employees have on their employment and job security'.[76] As observed elsewhere, some salaried workers may contribute with 'more than just their labour for livelihood [in] service economies [and industries] requiring a high level of skill and intellect'.[77]

The team production theory shares similar underpinnings (that is, the law and economics background) with proceduralism. Despite being widely repli-

---

[69] M M Blair and L A Stout, 'A Team Production Theory of Corporate Law' (1999) 85(2) *Vand L Rev* 247.

[70] J L L Gant, 'The Role of Social Policy in Corporate Rescue and Restructuring: A Messy Business' in P J Omar and J L L Gant (eds), *Research Handbook on Corporate Restructuring* (EE Publishing 2021) 479.

[71] F Bridoux and J W Stoelhorst, 'Stakeholder Relationships and Social Welfare: A Behavioral Theory of Contributions to Joint Value Creation' (2015) 41(2) *Academy of Management Review* 229, 229.

[72] L M LoPucki, 'A Team Production Theory of Bankruptcy Reorganization' (2004) 57(3) *Vand L Rev* 741.

[73] A A Alchian and H Demsetz, 'Production, Information Costs, and Economic Organization' (1972) 62(5) *Am Econ Rev* 777; R Harris, 'The History of Team Production Theory' (2015) 38(2) *Seattle U L Rev* 537.

[74] LoPucki (n 72) 743. See also N D Martin, 'Noneconomic Interests in Bankruptcy: Standing on the Outside Looking In' (1998) 59(2) *Ohio State LJ* 429, 439.

[75] J Burnham, *The Managerial Revolution: What is Happening in the World* (John Day Co 1941).

[76] Gant, 'Reconsidering Fairness' (n 21).

[77] Gant (n 70) 479.

cable and applicable,[78] it has so far lacked a cross-border dimension, as it has been influential primarily in the US academic and policy debate.[79] Evidence persuasively demonstrates that the team production framework operates best in private companies, primarily those with independent boards.[80] In insolvency contexts, the team production theory may prove difficult to implement for large corporations with a dissatisfied workforce, because it is challenging to identify with sufficient accuracy the interests of the members of a production team and their individual contribution to the company.[81]

Furthermore, one of the major issues with the team-production approach is that it proves and assumes too much. The law should protect the constituents' interests to preserve the entity's going concern when there is evidence that those constituents worked towards that goal for a reasonably long period of time. When there is no such evidence, reliance on the team production approach lacks justification and corporations are better understood as pool of assets.[82] Additionally, corporations serve different purposes and address different issues in different times and contexts. Hence, a generalised approach based solely on the team production conceptualisation may be unwarranted.

The Need for a New Approach

Insolvency procedures continue to be guided by economic paradigms. However, scathing criticism of creditors' wealth maximisation led Parliament to empower insolvency judges to craft flexible remedies capable of achieving fair, equitable and just results for the parties involved, especially in restructuring scenarios.[83] If the judiciary and practitioners focus on the concepts of vulnerability, resilience, fairness[84] and team-effort in interpreting the law,

---

78 T Kuhn, *The Structure of Scientific Revolutions* (University of Chicago Press 1970) 23–24; 109–110.

79 Limited exceptions apply: B R Cheffins and R Williams, 'Team Production Theory across the Waves' (2021) 74(6) *Vand L Rev* 1583.

80 E Pollman, 'Team Production Theory and Private Company Boards' (2015) 38(2) *Seattle U L Rev* 619.

81 LoPucki (n 72).

82 For a comprehensive criticism, see A J Meese, 'The Team Production Theory of Corporate Law: A Critical Assessment' (2002) 43(4) *WM & Mary L Rev* 1629.

83 S Paterson, 'Judicial Discretion in Part 26A Restructuring Plan Procedures' (24 January 2022) https://ssrn.com/abstract=4016519 accessed 1 November 2022.

84 For the notion of fairness, see (among others): Gant, 'Reconsidering Fairness' in E Ghio and E Vaccari (eds), *The Emerging New Landscape of European Restructuring and Insolvency* (INSOL Europe 2022) and the further references listed in (n 21).

the law as practiced is sufficient to achieve equitable rather than egalitarian outcomes.[85]

An individualist-maximiser and difference-enhancer insolvency system would mitigate proceduralist tenets whenever this is needed to achieve substantially and procedurally fair outcomes for the benefit of vulnerable and firm-specific investors. This is only possible if achieving the stakeholders' interests and limiting their harm from the debtor's distress is viable.[86] Korobkin states that while an employee might have an interest in retaining their job, if the business is not viable the insolvency procedure cannot take a course of action that, ultimately, goes against the interests of many other claimants, including other vulnerable players.[87] Protecting nonviable interests by attempting to rescue unviable businesses is not a sound way of reducing stakeholders' vulnerability.[88]

While we agree with Korobkin's observation, we believe that it is possible to strengthen the case for a revised understanding of the procedural nature of insolvency law by conducting a critique of its collective foundations based in vulnerability theory and IHRL.

JUSTICE AND EQUITY IN ENGLISH LIQUIDATION PROCEDURES

Before turning to Fineman's vulnerability theory and IHRL, it is instructive to look at English courts' interpretation of the notion of justice and equity in liquidation procedures. The purpose of this exercise is to assess if and to what extent English courts depart from proceduralist tenets, as well as if and to what extent more detailed guidance is needed.

Pursuant to the Insolvency Act (IA 1986), companies can be wound up by a court if the judicial authority is of the opinion that it is just and equitable to do so.[89] Courts are required to balance competing reasons and identify public policy interests by making a winding up order,[90] particularly where companies

---

[85] On the limited validity of proceduralist theories in the 'real world', see D R Korobkin, 'The Role of Normative Theory in Bankruptcy Debates' (1996) 82(1) *Iowa L Rev* 75, 113.

[86] D R Korobkin, 'Vulnerability, Survival, and the Problem of Small Business Bankruptcy' (1994) 23(2) *Capital University L Rev* 419.

[87] Ibid.

[88] Ibid.

[89] IA 1986, s 123(1)(g) for registered companies, s 124A(1) for petitions on grounds of public interest by the Secretary of State and s 221(5)(c) for unregistered ones.

[90] *Re Walter L Jacob & Co Ltd* (1989) 5 BCC 244, [61].

are solvent.[91] Yet, we are still left in the dark as to the criteria pursuant to which these 'matters' are assessed. Are vulnerability, resilience, fairness and team-effort considered in the discretionary exercise of the courts' powers?[92]

Based on the principles outlined in *Re PAG Management*,[93] courts have used their discretionary powers when this was expedient to protect the public, and even in the absence of any claim that the company was acting illegally.[94] To assess if the public interest is at risk, courts consider:

> all the relevant interests against each other in order to arrive at the just and equitable result, considering both those matters which constitute reasons why a company should be wound up compulsorily and those which constitute reasons why it should not'.[95]

Overall, courts have been cautious in exercising their discretion. They have mainly relied on objectively ascertainable factors to employ their discretionary powers,[96] such as where it was proven that the debtor's actions lacked 'commercial probity'.[97]

Departures from strictly proceduralist approaches have occurred when the just and equitable winding up of a company was necessary to address a catastrophic loss of trust and confidence among the directors, such that the company's business could no longer be conducted.[98] In *Strathmore*, Newey J held that in exercising their discretion under the law, courts should consider the direct and indirect consequences arising from the conduct of the debtor, the respective sophistication and experience of the parties, and whether vulnerable parties were taken advantage of.[99] Equally, in *Yesilkaya*, the court implemented a team production view of managerial relationships, but refused

---

91 Ibid.

92 A first, affirmative answer was given by M Bruckner, 'The Virtue in Bankruptcy' (2013) 45(1) *Loy U Chi LJ* 233. See also E Vaccari, 'Broken Companies or Broken System? Charting the English Insolvency Valuation Framework in Search for Fairness' (2020) 35(4) *JIBLR* 135; E Vaccari, 'Promoting Fairness in English Insolvency Valuation Cases' (2020) 29(2) *IIR* 285.

93 *Re PAG Management Services Ltd* [2015] EWHC 2404 (Ch).

94 *Re Senator Hanseatische Verwaltungsgesellschaft GmbH* [1997] 1 WLR 515, 522(h).

95 *Secretary of State for BEIS v Vanguard Insolvency* [2022] EWHC 1589 (Ch).

96 *Secretary of State for BEIS v Celtic Consultancy & Enterprises Ltd* [2021] EWHC 1240 (Ch).

97 *Re Forcesun Ltd* [2002] EWHC 443 (Ch); *Secretary of State for BUS v PGMRS Ltd* [2011] BCC 368; *Re Abacrombie & Co* [2008] EWHC 250 (Ch).

98 *Il v Yesilkaya* [2021] EWHC 1695 (Ch). For a principled approach to the exercise of the court's discretion, see *Chu v Lau* [2020] UKPC 24.

99 *Helden v Strathmore Ltd* [2010] EWHC 2012.

to grant the order because the petitioner did not come with 'clean hands'.[100] On that occasion, Prentis J made use of team production and instrumental fairness concepts to reach an equitable decision on the dispute, even though that meant not ordering the just and equitable winding up of the business.

This does mean that there is space for alternative considerations in the exercise of the courts' discretion. As aptly stated by Cawson QC in *Celtic*:[101]

> [c]oncepts such as 'inherent objectionability' or 'want of commercial probity' are bound to have some moral content, though that content is not the subjective moral perception of the individual judge, but must be informed by any discernable policy of the law and guided by the view of other judges in other cases.

The balance between answering the moral questions inherent in the legislation and insolvency proceedings, and abusing one's discretionary power concerns English courts.[102] As such, English courts generally seek to employ their discretionary powers sparingly, cautiously and in exceptional and unusual circumstances.[103] In the next section, we utilise Fineman's vulnerability theory and BHR to address the 'common pool' question and suggest how courts might utilise the discretion given them without abusing their power.

VULNERABILITY AND A HUMAN RIGHTS BASED APPROACH TO INSOLVENCY

The rights to equal protection and non-discrimination and the right to a fair trial are among the most obvious human rights implicated in corporate insolvency procedures. Additional human rights can include employees' rights to work, to just and favourable conditions of work, to an adequate standard of living, and to social security.[104] Less obvious implications can be seen in areas such as the analysis of the socio-economic impacts on employees, their families, and local communities.[105] This can include the interests of those owed damages

---

[100] *Yesilkaya* (n 98).

[101] *Celtic Consultancy* (n 96) [122(i)].

[102] *Lancefield v Lancefield* [2004] 4 WLUK 467; *Rendle v Panelform Ltd* [2020] EWHC 2810 (Ch).

[103] See *Rendle*, ibid., [16].

[104] International Covenant on Economic, Social and Cultural Rights (1966) 993 UNTS 3, entered into force 1976, Arts 6–7; 9; 11.

[105] J L L Gant, 'Vulnerability, Resilience, and Employees: Can a Higher Degree of Fairness be Achieved by Looking Beyond Traditional Insolvency Norms?' in J Harris (ed), *Insolvency: A Research Agenda* (EE Publishing 2023). For the impact on local communities, see (among others): E Vaccari, L N Coordes and Y Marique, 'Global Trends in the Treatment of Local Public Entities in Distress: A Principled Approach' (2023) 32(1) *IIR* 93.

in tort for a company's negligence,[106] or communities whose rights to a clean and healthy environment or an adequate standard of living[107] were damaged by a company's pre-insolvency conduct. These individuals and communities do not enjoy the status of preferred creditors.[108]

The law does recognise and protect some human rights as IA 1986 modified the common law position that treated employees as unsecured creditors.[109] Accrued holiday pay and unpaid contributions to state and occupational pension schemes are treated as preferential debts.[110] However, the protections found in the law[111] only partially address the disruption, hardship, and human rights impact that can be experienced by employees when they are stripped of employment through corporate insolvency. This reality raises questions about the suitability of the proceduralist approach when proceedings touch upon or impact human rights.

Fineman's Vulnerability Theory and the Deconstruction of Insolvency Law

Understanding vulnerability theory

Fineman's vulnerability theory challenges a narrow, formalistic construction of equality premised on the belief that people should be treated the same without discrimination on the basis of enumerated, protected characteristics such as race, gender, and nationality.[112] Fineman understands 'vulnerability' as a natural human condition, both as a consequence of enjoying a human body that is inherently fragile and as a consequence of social institutions ranging from the family to political institutions and legal, cultural, and religious structures.[113] While these social institutions are designed to shield individuals from

---

106 See (n 104) Arts 11; 12.

107 Ibid.; UN Human Rights Council resolution 48/13 (2021).

108 IA 1986, Sch 6.

109 See *Re Welfab Engineers Ltd* [1990] BCC 600.

110 IA 1986, sch 6, Categories 3–5.

111 See, among others: IA 1986, Sch 6, Category 5; Insolvency Proceedings (Monetary Limits) Order 1986; Insolvency Proceedings (Monetary Limits) Order 2021; Insolvency Proceedings (Monetary Limits) Order 2015; Insolvency Proceedings (Monetary Limits) Order 2009; Insolvency Proceedings (Monetary Limits) Order 2004. Employees can also make a claim under the National Insurance Fund.

112 M A Fineman, 'The Vulnerable Subject: Anchoring Equality in the Human Condition' (2008) 20(1) *Yale JL & Feminism* 1, 2 ('Fineman, 'Vulnerable Subject'). See also J L L Gant, 'Vulnerability Theory and Insolvency Law' in E Ghio, J Wood, and J L L Gant (eds), *Rethinking Insolvency Law Theories in a Changing World: Perspectives for the 21st Century* (EE Publishing 2023).

113 Ibid.; M A Fineman, 'Vulnerability and Inevitable Inequality' (2017) 4(3) *Olso L Rev* 133, 142, 146 (Fineman, 'Inevitable Inequality').

the realities of their human vulnerability, they can create or institutionalise vulnerabilities through a distribution of costs and benefits.[114] Consequently, all people are vulnerable due to the human condition, but they experience vulnerability in different and unique ways.

Fineman's assertion that the state has substantive responsibilities for equality sits in contrast with a more traditional Western (and particularly, American) approach, in the vein of Locke's liberal individualism, to the state's role in securing rights.[115] A state focused on individual autonomy and non-discrimination, rather than substantive equality, is a 'restrained state', one that does not actively interfere in economic institutions or 'private' affairs.[116] Yet, these 'private' social institutions are codified and sometimes brought into existence by the state, whether discussing the protection of the family in law or the creation of corporations.[117]

The simultaneous universality and personal reality of human vulnerability requires addressing the role social institutions have in creating and combatting substantive inequality.[118] Institutions distribute the necessary resources for combatting vulnerability.[119] Those resources should be distributed in a manner that reflects the universal and unequal vulnerability of actors through a focus on building resilience, meaning an individual's ability to withstand disruptions to their security.[120] Unlike non-discrimination principles, building resilience requires treating people differently based on individual sets of circumstances.[121] To do this, the state must develop, adapt, and monitor even 'quasi-private' social institutions to ensure they alleviate, rather than exacerbate, vulnerability.[122] These institutions serve not only the private interests of individuals but also the public good and need of building resilience.[123] By understanding, adapting, and utilising the broader social purpose of these institutions, states can focus on securing physical, financial, spiritual, or social resilience for individuals.[124]

---

114 Fineman, 'Vulnerable Subject' (n 112) 9–11.
115 Ibid., 5.
116 Ibid.
117 Ibid., 6.
118 Fineman, 'Inevitable Inequality' (n 113) 146–148.
119 Ibid., 146.
120 M A Fineman, 'Beyond Equality and Discrimination' (2020) 73 *SMU Law Review Forum* 51; 52–53; 56–58 (Fineman, 'Beyond Equality').
121 Fineman, 'Inevitable Inequality' (n 113) 147; Fineman, 'Beyond Equality' (n 120) 52–53; 57–58.
122 Fineman, 'Inevitable Inequality' (n 113) 147.
123 Ibid.
124 Ibid., 146–148.

Deconstructing insolvency law

Fineman's vulnerability theory – developed in family law contexts but subsequently applied to company law and corporate interests[125] – challenges the assumptions underpinning insolvency law's proceduralist approach. First, vulnerability theory challenges the claim that equal and autonomous parties make private, pre-insolvency arrangements that should be honoured.[126] Instead, both parties are vulnerable but perhaps not *equally* vulnerable. The inequality of parties extends beyond the direct participants and can require different considerations for non-creditors impacted by insolvency, such as affected community members, employees, or consumers.

Second, vulnerability theory calls for understanding insolvency law as both an instrument of the state and a public good that can facilitate substantive equality and resilience. This suggests that pre-insolvency entitlements should not be assumed sacrosanct but must be questioned and adjusted in light of their impact on individual resilience. As such, not all parties to an insolvency proceeding can be or should be treated equally, challenging the insolvency law's focus on efficiency and egality. Instead, vulnerability concerns should guide practitioners to construct a distribution of the debtor's assets or to devise a restructuring plan that does the most to ensure resilience for all affected parties and mitigates any exacerbation of inequality that would arise in implementing a purely proceduralist and egalitarian approach.

The limits of vulnerability theory

A common critique of Fineman's theory[127] is that it does not offer a clear pathway on *how* to prioritise and distribute limited resources. As Kohn notes, vulnerability theory makes prioritising amongst individuals 'more problematic by emphasising the universality of vulnerability'.[128] As such, and perhaps ironically, when Fineman applied vulnerability theory to the interests of elderly persons, she ended up stripping individuals of their individuality and developing paternalistic responses in the law (although Fineman forcefully rejects the critique of paternalism).[129] Fineman asserted that age inevitably increases vul-

---

125 R Donyets-Kedar, 'Rethinking Responsibility in Private Law' in M A Fineman et al, *Privatization, Vulnerability, and Social Responsibility* (Routledge 2016) 34.

126 See also, J L L Gant, 'Editorial: Optimising Fairness in Insolvency and Restructuring: A Spotlight on Vulnerable Stakeholders' (2022) 31(1) *Intl Insolv Rev.* 3, 5.

127 N A Kohn, 'Vulnerability Theory and the Role of Government' (2014) 26(1) *Yale JL & Feminism* 1, 12–13; B P Davis and E Aldieri, 'Precarity and Resistance: A Critique of Martha Fineman's Vulnerability Theory' (2021) 36(2) *Hypatia* 321, 329.

128 Ibid.

129 M A Fineman, '"Elderly" as Vulnerable: Rethinking the Nature of the Individual and Societal Responsibility' (2012) 20(1) *Elder L Rev* 71, 92–93.

nerability such that there should be a presumption 'that older persons may not be able to bargain, contract, and protect their interests as wisely as or as well as those who are younger are presumed to'.[130] She called for 'age-sensitive rules' that protect elderly persons from unequal bargaining.[131] As Kohn explains, Fineman's prioritisation of security over autonomy – based on the belief that autonomy cannot be exercised absent security[132] – would upset many elderly people who value their autonomy at least as much as their security.[133] The result is an approach that ignores the interests of those the law seeks to protect and undermines their dignity.[134]

Kohn's concerns are also relevant to the application of vulnerability theory to insolvency law: absent a vague continuum of vulnerability, there is no clear criteria by which to divide limited assets or to assess the need for reorganisation of a business. Moreover, efforts to use vulnerability as a guiding principle can undermine the sense of agency needed to ensure smooth commercial transactions. The rules on honouring pre-insolvency entitlements are intended to ensure a functional economic structure that encourages investment and the flow of commerce to solvent companies.[135] Replacing that system with vague claims of vulnerability that are both universal and specific – absent clear rules for assessing vulnerability and prioritising resources – could, undermine practices necessary for building resilience within society and within affected individuals. As such, vulnerability theory fails to offer an alternative approach that simultaneously retains insolvency's purpose while ensuring resilience for affected individuals.

The shortcomings of the vulnerability theory may reflect Fineman's expressed reluctance to engage with IHRL because, she asserts, human rights 'tends to assume an ideally restrained or necessarily aloof state that may provide some basic essential services but is fundamentally uninvolved in orchestrating the mundane aspects of individual lives'.[136] As we explain in the next section, Fineman's critique of human rights is only partially correct. While IHRL presumes the state should not overreach into mundane aspects of individual lives, it has evolved generally, and the field of BHR specifically,

---

[130] Ibid., 92–94.

[131] Ibid.

[132] Ibid., 92.

[133] Kohn (n 127) 14–15.

[134] Ibid., 15.

[135] I Mevorach, *Insolvency within Multinational Enterprise Groups* (OUP 2009) 112.

[136] M A Fineman, 'Rights, Resilience, and Responsibility' (2022) 71(7) *Emory LJ* 1435, 1446 (Fineman, 'Rights'); M A Fineman, 'The Vulnerable Subject and the Responsive State' (2010) 60(2) *Emory LJ* 251, 254–255.

to call for exactly the kind of individualised assessment Fineman desires. As such, it is in IHRL and BHR that we find the tools and strategies for insolvency law to reconstruct itself.

BHR and the Reconstruction of Insolvency Law

Under IHRL, states have negative obligations to refrain from interfering in the realisation of rights as well as positive obligations to 'protect' rights and stop third parties from interfering in their realisation.[137] This requires states to, *inter alia*, regulate corporate activity to prevent harms to human rights.[138] Finally, states are obligated to 'fulfil' human rights by taking positive actions to facilitate the full realisation and enjoyment of the right.[139] The 'protect' and 'fulfil' standards require active and interventionist state conduct aimed at ensuring people can enjoy the full range of human rights. Attaching to all state actors, the protect and fulfil obligations include upholding socio-economic rights,[140] such as the rights to health, education, and an adequate standard of living.[141] Similar to the concept of 'vulnerability', this obligation could be considered too vague to be actionable: how should a state distribute an insolvent company's limited resources when faced with the variety of competing needs?

The International Covenant on Economic, Social and Cultural Rights (ICESCR) answers some of these concerns by identifying, within the treaty's text, priorities for the state.[142] Additionally, the independent, expert body entrusted with overseeing the implementation of the Covenant has provided further guidance for the implementation of the 'protect' and 'fulfil' approach. First it has identified 'minimum core obligations' – the bare minimum the state must provide even when constrained economically – for certain rights.[143]

---

[137] See generally, F Mégret, 'Nature of Obligations' in D Moeckli et al (eds), *International Human Rights Law* (OUP 2017) chapter 5.

[138] UN Guiding Principles on Business and Human Rights, UN Doc A/HRC/17/31 (2011) at Pillar 1; D Birchall, 'Reconstructing State Obligations to Protect and Fulfil Socio-Economic Rights in an Era of Marketization' (2021) 71(1) *ICLQ* 227; C Bettinger-López, 'Human Rights at Home: Domestic Violence as a Human Rights Violation' (2008) 40(1) *Colum Hum Rts L Rev* 19.

[139] Mégret (n 137) chapter 5.

[140] International Covenant on Economic, Social and Cultural Rights 1996, Arts 2(1), 11, 12, 13.

[141] Ibid., Art 2(1).

[142] Ibid., Art 11.

[143] See, e.g., Committee on Economic, Social and Cultural Rights, *General Comment No. 3: The Nature of States' Parties Obligations (art 2(1) of the Covenant*, (1990) UN Doc E/1991/23 [10]; Committee on Economic, Social and Cultural Rights, *General Comment No 14: The Right to the Highest Attainable Standard of Health (Art. 12)* (2000) UN Doc E/C.12/2000/4 [43]-[5].

Beyond the minimum priorities, the Committee's 'General Comments' identify what additional measures are needed to realise the right, and to measure progress towards their full implementation.[144] By articulating these priorities, the Committee identifies how states should think of their own limited resources. As explained below, these standards are not expected to guide business conduct as well.

Because ICESCR calls for 'progressively realizing' the rights,[145] the Committee has also recognised that measures that reduce the realisation of these rights constitute a breach of human rights.[146] Maintaining that status quo and building on it (or, in Fineman's words, building resilience through the further development of social institutions) is, therefore, part of the minimum expected conduct of states and a priority for the distribution of resources. If maintenance of the status quo is truly impossible, states can impair acquired rights only after a process that accounts for any impact on other human rights and the society's most vulnerable people.[147]

One might debate the particularities of a human rights' approach to the distribution of resources. Nevertheless, the treaty and its implementing guidance do offer a principled structure for measuring and evaluating a state's choice in the allocation of resources; and 171 states, including the UK, have agreed to be bound by these standards.

The traditional, binary nature of human rights law placed the primary obligation on the state to realise these rights. As a result, other social institutions – notably corporations – traditionally enjoyed impunity for actions that had negatively impacted human rights.[148] This gives credence to Fineman's concerns that human rights law offers a 'restrained' approach to state responsibility and intervention. Yet, human rights law has evolved. For more than a decade, the UNGPs have established a minimum expectation for businesses in understanding and responding to human rights.

The principles and pragmatics of BHR

Unlike Fineman's theory, the UNGPs offer very little that is serviceable for deconstructing the law. They offer a simple formulation for responsibility and

---

[144] See *General Comment No. 14* (n 143).

[145] International Covenant on Economic, Social and Cultural Rights, Art 2(1).

[146] *General Comment No. 3* (n 143) para [9]. This is absent a significant event that would truly preclude the ongoing realisation of the right.

[147] Ibid.

[148] See generally, T Van Ho, '"Band-Aids Don't Fix Bullet Holes": In Defence of a Traditional State-Centric Approach' in J Letnar Cernic and N Carrillo-Santarelli (eds), *The Future of Business and Human Rights: Theoretical and Practical Considerations for a UN Treaty* (Intersentia 2018) 111.

accountability: the state remains responsible for 'protecting' human rights, but all businesses (regardless of size, structure, industry, or operational context) must 'respect' human rights by not interfering in the realisation of rights.[149] Finally, both states and businesses must ensure those harmed by a business can access an adequate and effective 'remedy' meaning one that is, inter alia, rights-compatible, legitimate, and accessible.[150] While theoretically limited, the UNGPs were born of 'principled pragmatism' – what can be reasonably expected of businesses – and focus on the means of implementing these three 'pillars' of responsibility.[151]

Within the UNGPs, the business 'responsibility to respect' offers the richest material for insolvency law. The definition and content of human rights are to be defined in accordance with international treaties and consequently with authoritative guidance from expert 'treaty bodies' entrusted with each treaty's interpretation and oversight.[152] To realise their responsibility to respect, businesses are expected to undertake 'human rights due diligence' with reference to internationally defined human rights.[153] That process involves identifying the actual or likely harms to human rights a business can cause or contribute to.[154] Once harms are identified, businesses are supposed to take measures to mitigate and remediate those harms.[155] This responsibility exists throughout the life cycle of the businesses, and state actors have an existing obligation to ensure businesses fulfil these responsibilities.[156] Throughout the due diligence process, businesses are to engage in 'meaningful consultation' with affected individuals and groups.[157] It is presumed that a business cannot have an accurate or appropriate accounting of its likely human rights impacts, or of

---

149 UN Guiding Principles on Business and Human Rights (UNGPs), UN Doc. A/HRC/17/31 (2011) Pillar 1 and Pillar 2.

150 Ibid., Pillar 3.

151 J G Ruggie, 'The Past as Prologue? A Moment of Truth for UN Business and Human Rights Treaty' (IHBR Commentary 2014) 4 https://www.hks.harvard.edu/sites/default/files/centers/mrcbg/programs/cri/files/Treaty_Final.pdf accessed 1 November 2022.

152 UNGPs (n 149) , Principle 12.

153 Ibid., Principle 15. See also J Bonnitcha and R McCorquodale, 'The Concept of "Due Diligence" in the UN Guiding Principles on Business and Human Rights' (2017) 28(3) *Eur J Int L* 899; J G Ruggie and J F Sherman III, 'The Concept of "Due Diligence" in the UN Guiding Principles on Business and Human Rights: A Reply to Jonathan Bonnitcha and Robert McCorquodale' (2017) 28(3) *Eur J Int L* 921.

154 UNGPs (n 149) Principle 18(b).

155 Ibid., Principle 15(b).

156 Ibid., Principle 11.

157 Ibid., Principle 18.

developing appropriate mitigation techniques, without hearing from affected individuals.[158]

Ideally, businesses comply with all internationally recognised human rights at all times.[159] Where they face constraints, however, businesses can establish priorities by focusing on the 'most severe [impacts] or where delayed response would make them irremediable'.[160] Importantly, severity for BHR is not a static concept but is assessed within the context of the situation and 'relative to the other human rights impacts the business enterprise has identified'.[161] The severity of an impact can be understood both in terms of the nature of the right or in terms of the number of people it is likely to affect.[162] Because the nature of the right matters when prioritising limited resources or capacity, the minimum core obligations for rights in ICESCR are expected to be priorities.

If the vulnerability theory challenges insolvency's focus on 'efficiency', BHR provides the principles and tools for revising the law so that it reflects on and responds to its impacts on those unprotected and harmed by the current system. The principles of BHR require rethinking corporate insolvency as part of the business's fuller life cycle. As such, insolvency would not be a crisis to be expediently resolved in favour of those who could, and thought to, control their entitlements.[163] Instead, it is a consequence of the business's previous conduct and relationships and a next step in addressing those relationships with attention to their human rights impacts.

Reconceiving the law in this way refines the collectivist position that expects all creditors to equally bear the burden of a common disaster by recognising that the nature of the burdens being borne are different: not all financial harms are equal and as such merely seeking Pareto efficiency should not be defined narrowly. Instead, the efficiency and appropriateness of insolvency should be defined by how it impacts internationally recognised human rights. This narrows the potential of impacts and harms that insolvency must account for and recognises other concerns as legitimate policy choices that a state, or business, can pursue after addressing human rights. This inverts the current approach of insolvency, which privileges those creditors with the greatest means of controlling their relationship with the company. Instead, it calls for

158 Ibid.

159 Ibid., Principle 24.

160 Ibid.

161 Ibid., Principle 24, Commentary.

162 Ibid.

163 This language is borrowed from Dr Jennifer L Gant's comments during the INSOL Talk https://www.insol.org/Focus-Groups/Academic-Group/Events-and-Podcasts.

a focus on those with potentially the least power but who can suffer impacts to, *inter alia*, their housing, education, or living conditions.

This new approach to the purpose of insolvency law would require changing its practices. In the next sub-section, we offer the culmination of the theories of law outlined thus far – of insolvency law and of Fineman's vulnerability theory – and the practicalities of centring human rights within insolvency law. We briefly explain what it would mean to use the UNGPs to reconstruct insolvency law from the ground up.

Identifying a BHR approach to insolvency

Through its principles and standards for due diligence, BHR embodies many of the same concerns as Fineman. However, rather than proscribing actions, it promotes dialogue with affected stakeholders to identify appropriate responses. With its 'principled pragmatism', BHR also has the potential to unlock a new approach to insolvency law.

First, insolvency law can retain a presumption in favour of upholding pre-insolvency entitlements and the arrangements reached between parties in solvent times. These 'quasi-private' institutions still offer a legitimate foundation for starting any process and inquiry. Yet, the party seeking insolvency could be expected, as part of the proceedings, to undertake human rights due diligence and prepare a human rights impact assessment. Relying on internationally defined rights would allow the court and affected parties to identify key affected rights and interests. Conducting human rights due diligence would require the insolvent party to engage in a dialogue with affected stakeholders to evidence the impact of the insolvency or restructuring procedure on fundamental and internationally recognised human rights. It may also prompt new reflections on how best to approach the insolvency as stakeholders identify opportunities or impacts not previously considered. In affected procedures, this may result in additional complexities and delays. However, this would be justified by reconceiving how we define and measure Pareto efficiency.

Second, based on the reported human rights impacts, either the insolvent party, an independent expert, an affected party, or a court could make recommendations for alterations to pre-insolvency entitlements. A BHR approach to insolvency would not insist on the formalistic equality between parties but would allow flexibility to account for a proceeding's disparate impact on affected parties. Similarly, it would not treat all assets as of communal interest, to be distributed based on individual vulnerability. Instead, the presumption in favour of pre-insolvency entitlements would be upended only where necessary to redress impacts on internationally agreed upon and defined human rights. As such, the approach would primarily preserve the purpose of insolvency law and pre-insolvency entitlements while ensuring the insolvency proceedings respect, protect and fulfil human rights.

Finally, where an insolvency proceeding would trigger more human rights impacts than the court can address, BHR provides a means of prioritising the use of limited assets. Rather than utilising formalistic equality and 'sameness', the court would facilitate a modular approach based on the parties' vulnerability and the severity of to the impact of insolvency proceedings on other rights and interests. As the alternations would be undertaken in consultation with affected parties, the court would not paternalistically substitute its assessment of the parties' needs. Instead, the parties would enjoy an opportunity to participate in identifying priorities, mitigation strategies, and adequate remedies. In doing so, this modular process can enhance resilience and agency amongst the parties to the proceeding.

While these three changes to insolvency are more incremental than some might call for, they are still significant for the field. Rather than a focus on efficiency and egality, the revised framework would allow for additional flexibility to mandate a stronger understanding of the impacts of insolvency proceedings on vulnerable stakeholders. It would also broaden consideration of interests and allow parties to the proceedings to be active participants in their design. This may lead to more creative approaches to the distribution of assets while increasing a sense of agency within and through the law. Finally, it would identify alternative priorities for the court while relying on an internationally accepted legal framework. This would limit concerns about an abuse of the court's discretion.

CONCLUSION

This chapter opens a new dialogue within the scholarly literature on the purpose and principles of insolvency law. It posits a means of using BHR to redress the limitations of modern insolvency law. This use of BHR would upend the mainstream proceduralist nature of insolvency law. As such, whether insolvency law *should* adopt a BHR-focused approach is a normative question that needs to be more thoroughly debated. By explaining what could be, we offer the opening salvo in that discussion.

After outlining the principles and assumptions underpinning modern insolvency, we make three contributions to the literature. First, we use Fineman's vulnerability to deconstruct insolvency law. Fineman's theory challenges the underpinning assumptions that pre-insolvency entitlements are arranged through equal and autonomous parties. Instead, all parties to the proceedings (and perhaps some who are not party to it) are vulnerable and dependent on the social institutions in which they exist, including the economic arrangements at the heart of the proceeding. Additionally, the parties' dependence on the economic relation varies as does their vulnerability to the insolvency proceedings. Fineman's approach would identify insolvency law as only a 'quasi-private' endeavour that requires the distribution of assets, or the reorganisation of an entity, in a manner that enhances resilience. As such, pre-insolvency entitlements are no longer sacrosanct.

The second contribution we make is to reflect on the limitations of Fineman's approach as a practical solution to insolvency law's debates. While vulnerability theory offers an important tool for deconstructing erroneous assumptions in insolvency law, its simultaneous claims of universal and individual vulnerability effectively limit the pragmatic value of the theory. This reflection sets the foundation for a more robust and pragmatic approach to reconstructing insolvency law.

Finally, we utilise the field of BHR to call for a reimagining of insolvency law based on 'principled pragmatism'. In doing so, we articulate a novel yet revolutionary approach that would call into question the central assumptions to modern insolvency law and answer some of the practical limitations of vulnerability theory. We identify three principal changes that would be caused by applying BHR while seeking to preserve the purpose of insolvency law. In doing so, we open up the possibility of a new set of priorities for the law that could utilise limited flexibility to limit the harms that can arise from the application of the current approach to insolvency.

13. Insolvency law through the lens of company law theories

Jonathan Hardman

INTRODUCTION

Company law presents itself as an autonomous, discrete, universal subject of law.[1] I have argued elsewhere, though, that company law is predicated upon a number of descriptive factors.[2] The purpose of this chapter is to explore features of insolvency law that ostensibly autonomous, jurisdiction-neutral corporate law scholarship is predicated upon. These references are frequently tacit – embedded in the argumentation structure of corporate law. This chapter, then, opens a new front for insolvency law theory – implications from identifying that the structure of company law is built upon insolvency law's foundations. In identifying insolvency law as the 'dark matter' of company law, we open space for new linkages between the subjects. This opens the possibility for insolvency law theory to conceptualise more fully its effect on core company law considerations. To open this space, this chapter identifies the insolvency underpinnings of three areas of company law: separate legal personality, limited liability, and corporate purpose.

SEPARATE LEGAL PERSONALITY

Corporate law scholars have heavily debated the nature of separate legal personality.[3] A challenge, though, is to identify what we actually mean by stating that a company has separate legal personality. It has been called a 'convenient

[1] See J Hardman, 'Sevilleja v Marex Financial Ltd: Reflective Loss and the Autonomy of Company Law' (2022) 85(1) *Modern Law Review* 232.

[2] J Hardman, 'The Butterfly Effect: Theoretical Implications of an Apparently Minor Corporate Transparency Proposal' (2021) 50(4) *Common Law World Review* 180 and 'Atomising Corporate Law: A Battle Cry for Splitters' in C Bruner and M Moore (eds), *A Research Agenda for Corporate Law* (Elgar Edward Publishing 2023).

[3] See overviews in J Hardman, 'Looking Beyond Separate Legal Personality, or How Many Titles have Rangers Won?' [2022] (1) *Juridical Review* 1; J Hardman,

heuristic formula' for three basic concepts: the ability to owe and be owed obligations, the ability to sue and be sued, and the segregation of company assets from the assets of the shareholders.[4] This has been challenged on the grounds that legal entities which have separate legal personality do not always display such features.[5] Nonetheless, it remains the dominant conceptualisation.

Of these three features, the final one is considered the most important concept for company law – and organisational law more broadly – and is referred to as asset partitioning.[6] Asset partitioning separates the assets of the company from the assets of the individual shareholders. In doing so, it removes the assets of the company from claims of shareholder creditors. It therefore prevents the creditors of a shareholder in financial difficulty from enforcing against the assets of the company. This splitting of the corporate pool is seen as encouraging investment – I am more likely to invest in the project if the assets are effectively segregated into a separate fund.[7] The argument runs that this cannot be achieved purely by private ordering, and thus a discrete area of law – organisational law, or company law – is needed to achieve this.

The implicit pressure of insolvency is thus heavily present in this analysis. In a Panglossian world in which financial difficulty was not a concern, there would be no need for asset partitioning. This is because the assets of shareholders would always be sufficient to repay creditors of shareholders. They would then have no need to look for further recourse into the corporate vehicle itself. Accordingly, the risk of insolvency is what drives the pressure for asset partitioning, and with it the importance of separate legal personality.

That a company enjoys separate legal personality is one of the most foundational features of company law.[8] This foundation, though, is set in the shadow of insolvency and insolvency law. It is open to insolvency law to reduce the

---

'Fixing the Misalignment of the Concession of Corporate Legal Personality' (2023) *Legal Studies* doi:10.1017/lst.2022.44.

[4] See R Kraakman et al, *The Anatomy of Corporate Law* (3rd edn, Oxford University Press 2017) 5–8.

[5] L Macgregor, 'Partnerships and Legal Personality: Cautionary Tales from Scotland' (2020) 20(1) *Journal of Corporate Law Studies* 237; J Hardman, 'Reconceptualising Scottish Limited Partnership Law' (2021) 21(1) *Journal of Corporate Law Studies* 179.

[6] H Hansmann and R Kraakman, 'The Essential Role of Organizational Law' (2000) 110(3) *Yale Law Journal* 387; H Hansmann and R Kraakman, 'Organizational Law as Asset Partitioning' (2000) 44(4) *European Economic Review* 807.

[7] See discussion in S Watson, 'The Corporate Legal Entity as a Fund' [2018] *Journal of Business Law* 467.

[8] Established in *Salomon v Salomon & Co Ltd* [1897] AC 22. For discussion of the continuing importance of *Salomon*, see A Dignam and P B Oh, 'Disregarding the *Salomon* Principle: An Empirical Analysis, 1885–2014' (2019) 39(1) *Oxford Journal of Legal Studies* 16.

importance of a company's separate legal personality, and foreground itself into analysis, in two potential ways. First, it could provide an automatic ability for creditors of shareholders to 'look through' separate legal personality and obtain recourse to any investments that the company has undertaken. Different areas of legal taxonomy have tested the boundaries of separate legal personality in this way: from family law,[9] tort law,[10] to employment law,[11] different areas have explored methods to deviate from asset partitioning. The same is true within other business entities – e.g., the default partnership rule is that the insolvency of one of the partners brings the vehicle to an end.[12] This would undo the current approach of company law, which holds fast to its concept of asset partitioning.[13] Second, it could provide that any investment in any other legal entity automatically enjoys asset partitioning. This would reverse the position in respect of partnership law. Either approach would result in insolvency law providing a uniform response to investments in business entities. This would mean that there was a uniform insolvency law approach across all types of business entity. At the moment, different entities take different approaches, which results in differentials across business entities.[14] The lack of a uniform approach across business entities acts to make insolvency law appear to be more of a background consideration in the discussion of asset partitioning. However, the insolvency focus of these issues cannot be escaped – and a more muscular approach to insolvency law would foreground the importance of insolvency law in this theoretical construct.

LIMITED LIABILITY

The flip side of asset partitioning (where creditors of shareholders cannot proceed against assets of the company) is limited liability (where creditors of the company cannot proceed against assets of the shareholders). Limited

---

9 *Prest v Petrodel Resources Ltd* [2013] UKSC 34. See discussion in A Dignam and P B Oh, 'Rationalising Corporate Disregard' (2020) 40(2) *Legal Studies* 187.

10 E.g., *Vedanta Resources plc v Lungowe* [2019] UKSC 20; *HRH Okepabi v Royal Dutch Shell plc* [2021] UKSC 3. See discussion in C Witting, 'The Corporate Group: System, Design and Responsibility' (2021) 80(3) *Cambridge Law Journal* 581.

11 E.g., *Re MF Global UK Ltd (In Special Administration)* [2016] EWCA Civ 569.

12 Partnership Act 1890, s 33(1).

13 For a UK discussion, see D Cabrelli, 'The Case Against "Outsider Reverse" Veil Piercing' (2010) 10(2) *Journal of Corporate Law Studies* 343.

14 This is referred to as weak or strong forms of asset partitioning – see H Hansmann and R Kraakman, 'The Essential Role of Organizational Law' (2000) 110(3) *Yale Law Journal* 387, 403.

liability is stated to be a logical conclusion of separate legal personality,[15] and is a core concept in corporate law. More than this, it is one a few foundational attributes of being a company.[16] We cannot have capital markets without limited liability for investments[17] for two key reasons. First, it detaches the price of shares from the wealth of shareholders[18] (making the value of shares track, in theory, the value of underlying performance of the company). Second, it means that shares become fungible, so the identity of fellow shareholders does not matter,[19] which facilitates co-investment by those with different access to financial resources.[20] Whether the benefits of limited liability outweigh its costs is frequently debated within corporate law literature.[21] Nonetheless, it is not rooted in UK company law itself.

The Companies Act 2006 tells us that a company is a limited company if its constitution limits the liability of its members,[22] and that this can be limited by shares or by guarantee.[23] However, private declarations of limitation of liability have long been held to not have effect in respect of third parties.[24] Similarly,

---

[15] E.g., '[i]t follows from the fact that a corporation is a separate person that its members are not as such liable for its debts' – P L Davies, S Worthington and C Hare, *Gower Principles of Modern Company Law* (Sweet & Maxwell 2021) para 2-008. This is disputed in Hardman (n 5).

[16] Kraakman et al (n 4) chapter 1.

[17] J A Grundfest, 'The Limited Future of Unlimited Liability: A Capital Markets Perspective' (1992) 102(2) *Yale Law Journal* 387.

[18] R Gilson and R Kraakman, 'The Mechanisms of Market Efficiency' (1984) 70(4) *Virginia Law Review* 549.

[19] E.g., P Halpern et al, 'An Economic Analysis of Limited Liability in Corporation Law' (1980) 30(2) *University of Toronto Law Journal* 117; S E Woodward, 'Limited Liability in the Theory of the Firm' (1985) 141(4) *Journal of Institutional and Theoretical Economics* 601.

[20] C Mackie, 'From Privilege to Right – Themes in the Emergence in Limited Liability' [2011] 4 *Juridical Review* 294.

[21] For a recent discussion in the context of financial regulation, see C A E Goodhart and R M Lastra, 'Equity Finance: Matching Liability to Power' (2020) 6(1) *Journal of Financial Regulation* 1.

[22] Companies Act 2006, s 3(1).

[23] Companies Act 2006, s 3(2) and s 3(3).

[24] Limited liability has been expressly upheld if it was included in respect of a contract between a company and the relevant third party – see *Halket v The Merchant Traders' Ship, Loan and Insurance Association* (1849) 13 Queen's Bench Reports 960: 'We think, therefore, that by the contract itself (the policy) the plaintiff is precluded from taking any legal proceedings against the individual subscribers', 963 per Lord Denman CJ. Similarly, it has been upheld in respect of agreements between shareholders – *Hallett, Gooden, Clark, Allan and Hatfield v Dowdall* (1852) 18 Queen's Bench Reports 2. However, courts were very reticent to hold that third parties were bound by agreements that they were not party to – even if included in the company's prospectus: *Walburn v Ingilby* (1833) 39 ER 604 – 'The clause attempting to restrict the liability of

companies with members whose liability are limited by shares are expected to have the word 'limited' in their names.[25] These provisions, though, are not constitutive: the former does not state that law will recognise liability limits for shareholders provided in any constitution, and the latter is a consequence of limited liability rather than constitutive of it.

Prior to 1986, the UK's corporate law and insolvency law rules were contained within the same statute.[26] Since the two concepts were separated in 1986, the basis for limited liability of shareholders in the UK actually appears in the insolvency side, the Insolvency Act 1986. It is not even the default statutory provision – which is that 'every present and past member is liable to contribute to its assets to any amount sufficient for payment of its debts and liabilities, and the expenses of the winding up'.[27] There are a number of exceptions to this general position, though. The first three relate to past members who do not have to pay if they ceased to be a member one year before the winding up,[28] do not have to pay for any liability incurred after they ceased to be members,[29] and only have to contribute if existing members cannot satisfy any shortfall in corporate assets.[30]

The fourth exception is the one that actually provides for limited liability: if a company is limited by shares, members do not have to contribute in excess of the amount unpaid on their shares.[31] This, of course, represents the vast majority of companies.[32] Yet the doctrinal provision of limited liability under UK law is through insolvency law, and mainstream limited liability is halfway down a list of adjustments to the default legal position.

It is not, though, surprising that limited liability doctrinally appears as a result of insolvency law, as limited liability is (mostly) only relevant upon

the shareholders, till confirmed by Parliament, was of course only binding among themselves, and nugatory as to strangers', 609.

25 Companies Act 2006, s 58 for public companies, Companies Act 2006, s 59 for private companies.

26 See discussion in G Gretton, 'The Story of the Scots Law Floating Charge: 1961 to Date' in J Hardman and A MacPherson (eds), *Floating Charges in Scotland: New Perspectives and Current Issues* (Edinburgh University Press 2022).

27 Insolvency Act 1986, s 74(1).

28 Insolvency Act 1986, s 74(2)(a)

29 Insolvency Act 1986, s 74(2)(b).

30 Insolvency Act 1986, s 74(2)(c).

31 Insolvency Act 1986, s 74(2)(d). Companies limited by guarantee have a parallel limitation of liability – see Insolvency Act 1986, s74(3).

32 See J Hardman and G Ramírez Santos, 'Empirical Evidence for the Continuing Need to "Think Small First" in UK Company Law' (2023) 24(1) *European Business Organization Law Review* 117.

insolvency. Given that insolvency covers both cashflow[33] and balance sheet[34] aspects, for us to state that a company is solvent means that it has sufficient assets to meet its liabilities and sufficient liquidity to pay its debts as they fall due. It is thus irrelevant whether the shareholders have limited liability or not; all claims can be paid from the company's own funds. There is then nothing for the shareholders to be liable for. Limited liability is therefore predominantly an insolvency concept – it is primarily relevant when there are insufficient assets within the company to satisfy all claims.[35] This approach is primarily taken within conceptual company law discussions.[36]

It is, of course, possible to imagine unlimited liability for shareholders outside insolvency. It has been proposed that shareholders should become liable for corporate torts rather than recourse being taken to company assets.[37] Similarly, it has been proposed that specific matters – e.g., regulatory fines – be paid directly by directors or shareholders.[38] However, in a legal system that accepts the separate legal personality of a company, and thus asset partitioning, the segregated assets themselves will be expected to pay for any claims against the business run from such assets. It is therefore a logical extension of separate legal personality that the base-line rules of limited liability become an insolvency matter rather than a matter of general corporate law. Exceptions can be created to this – voluntarily[39] or by statute. These do not detract, though, from the general position that limited liability, a core aspect of company law, and a logical extension of separate legal personality, derives its relevance from insolvency law.

---

33 Insolvency Act 1986, s 123(1).

34 Insolvency Act 1986, s 123(2).

35 H Hansmann and R Kraakman, 'The End of History of Corporate Law' (2001) 89(2) *Georgetown Law Journal* 439, 442.

36 Thus, limited liability exists to 'to shift the costs of failure back towards those who have the responsibility for making these decisions' – Goodhart and Lastra, (n 21) 28. This is an assumption that underpins attempts to challenge caps on limited liability – e.g., J C Alexander, 'Unlimited Shareholder Liability through a Procedural Lens' (1992) 106(2) *Harvard Law Review* 387.

37 H Hansmann and R Kraakman, 'Toward Unlimited Shareholder Liability for Corporate Torts' (1991) 100(7) *Yale Law Journal* 1879; D W Leebron, 'Limited Liability, Tort Victims, and Creditors' (1991) 91 *Columbia Law Review* 1565.

38 See all sources cited at Goodhart and Lastra (n 21) 20.

39 Shareholders, especially in smaller companies, often give personal guarantees in respect of the debts of those companies – see J Armour, 'Legal Capital: An Outdated Concept?' (2006) 7(1) *European Business Organization Law Review* 5, 18–19. It has been argued that the rules of limited liability thus provide a default bargaining position and so make creditors *ask* for such guarantees rather than receiving them automatically – R A Booth, 'Limited Liability and the Efficient Allocation of Resources' (1994) 89(1) *Northwestern University Law Review* 140.

It is worth noting that this is not inevitable within the law of business organisations. Different organisations weaken limited liability approaches, for example, on the insolvency of a limited liability partnership, members are liable for any amount that they have withdrawn within two years of the insolvency of the LLP.[40] By contrast, shareholders are only liable for any dividend which was improperly declared and the shareholder knew of it.[41] Insolvency law design, then, thus has a strong influence on the outcome of a key area of company law – limited liability.

CORPORATE PURPOSE

The third area of company law to be explored is the purpose of the company. This is normally stated to be on a spectrum between the company existing purely as a vehicle for shareholders to maximise their wealth[42] to having a wider societal purpose.[43] The latter is returning to ascendency.[44]

This debate is relevant for our purposes due to the argumentation structure that tends to be deployed. Those arguing in favour of shareholder primacy tend to do so on the grounds that shareholders enjoy the 'residual claim' – that is that they receive the marginal profits of the company, therefore are the constituents who care whether the company makes £1 profit or £1m profit.[45] As such, they are the best guardians of the interests of the company as a whole.[46]

Those arguing in favour of stakeholder approaches tend to do so based on the harms that a company can cause. Thus the argument goes that a company who owns the only factory in a remote rural town should have a responsibility to that town to not relocate the factory and decimate the town.[47] The typical shareholder response is that there are other areas of the law that protect such

---

40 Insolvency Act 1986, s 214A.

41 Companies Act 2006, s 847. See discussion in S Robins, 'Knowledge, Ignorance, and Unlawful Dividends' (2007) 20 *Insolvency Intelligence* 33.

42 D G Smith, 'The Shareholder Primacy Norm' (1998) 23(2) *Journal of Corporation Law* 277.

43 R Phillips, R E Freeman and A Wicks, 'What Stakeholder Theory Is Not' (2003) 13(4) *Business Ethics Quarterly* 479.

44 E.g., C Mayer, 'Who's Responsible for Irresponsible Business? An Assessment' (2017) 33(2) *Oxford Review of Economic Policy* 157.

45 F H Easterbrook and D R R Fischel, 'Voting in Corporate Law' (1983) 26(2) *Journal of Law and Economics* 395.

46 J R Macey, 'An Economic Analysis of the Various Rationales for Making Shareholders the Exclusive Beneficiaries of Corporate Fiduciary Duties' (1991) 21(1) *Stetson Law Review* 23.

47 Of course, the interests here are not quite purely aligned – the town is interested in the factory continuing, not the legal vehicle.

stakeholders, so it is more appropriate to consider such protections as part of a different area of law than company law – so that worker considerations are treated as a matter of employment law, harms as a matter of tort law, etc.[48]

This argumentation structure, though, is once again predicated on a lack of insolvency. For such protections to be meaningful, we need to ensure that such obligations can be fulfilled by the corporate vehicle itself. The issue with the law outlined in the preceding two sections, though, is that legitimate corporate structuring can be used to minimise the possibility that the entities themselves have meaningful assets to meet such claims. Thus, companies can use the combination of limited liability and separate legal personality to set up corporate groups with segregated assets and liabilities.[49] Dividend rules allow for profits to be wicked away from the corporate group as soon as possible, and not be recoverable in the event of subsequent financial difficulty. The structuring of the group itself – whether to have multiple entities, and what should be in each one, is ultimately undertaken by the shareholders and directors – meaning that any such structuring will be self-serving rather than undertaken for the interests of the business more broadly.[50] This is coupled with managerial responsibilities being owed to the company, and ultimately captured by shareholders. Overall, then, we see the possibility for strategically under-capitalised companies ready to be jettisoned if an adverse claim is made against them. This, of course, becomes worse as we approach financial difficulty.

Insolvency law provides an insight into how we can square this circle. Duties of directors are owed to the company in the UK.[51] Breach of these duties can only be ratified by shareholders during solvency, providing effectual shareholder capture of such duties.[52] When the company heads towards insolvency, though, matters change considerably. This change does not come

---

48 A K Sundaram and A C Inkpen, 'The Corporate Objective Revisited' (2004) 15(3) *Organization Science* 350.

49 P Blumberg, 'The Corporate Entity in an Era of Multinational Corporations' (1990) 15(2) *Delaware Journal of Corporate Law* 283; P Blumberg, 'Limited Liability and Corporate Groups' (1986) 11(4) *Journal of Corporation Law* 573; M Petrin and B Choudhury, 'Group Company Liability' (2018) 19 *European Business Organization Law Review* 771; R Squire, 'Strategic Liability in the Corporate Group' (2011) 78(2) *University of Chicago Law Review* 605; C Witting, *Liability of Corporate Groups and Networks* (Cambridge University Press 2018); C Witting, 'The Corporate Group: System, Design and Responsibility' (2021) 80(3) *Cambridge Law Journal* 581.

50 See J Hardman, 'The Nexus of Contracts Revisited: Delineating the Business, the Firm, and the Legal Entity' (2022) 34(2) *Bond Law Review* 1.

51 Companies Act 2006, s 170. See discussion in P Hood, 'Directors' Duties Under The Companies Act 2006: Clarity or Confusion?' (2013) 13(1) *Journal of Corporate Law Studies* 1.

52 Companies Act 2006, s 239.

from company law, which merely acknowledges that this base company law position is subject to other enactments of law.[53] The relevant enactment of law comes from insolvency law – that the duties of directors as the company approaches insolvency switch from being exercised in the interests of shareholders to the interests of creditors.[54] This clearly has an important function in the wider insolvency law regime.[55] However, company law has traditionally struggled to rationalise it.[56] We can understand it better, though, through the lens of the corporate purpose. For other areas of the legal taxonomy to effectively bite in respect of a company, it cannot be possible for that company to entirely alienate its assets. There must be some restraint on the ability to utilise the corporate form to expose creditors to high risk. This is provided by this imperfect mechanism of company law. Indeed, the vagueness which company lawyers decry could be argued to provide further court discretion to ensure that other areas of the law are not stymied by the technical operation of company law. Thus, insolvency law facilitates the company law regime, and prevents abuse of a company law regime that would enable third party harm. Company law normally focuses on internal dynamics within the shareholder and director constituents of the company, mostly as a result of the mechanics and processes of company law being captured by those two constituents.[57] To keep company law societally palatable, then, we need insolvency law to mitigate its excesses.

Such an approach views this tool of insolvency law as a societal method to check company law. The reason for the need for this check becomes more evident if we view the corporate form's separate legal personality as a con-

---

[53] Companies Act 2006, s 172(3).

[54] *West Mercia Safetywear v Dodd* (1988) 4 BCC 30. See recent discussion in *BTI 2014 LLC v Sequana SA and others* [2022] UKSC 25. This chapter was written before the *Sequana* judgment was issued, but whilst some points of detail may have changed, the overall argument of the author remains valid.

[55] See K van Zwieten, 'Director Liability in Insolvency and its Vicinity' (2018) 38(2) *Oxford Journal of Legal Studies* 382.

[56] Sealy referred to 'phony jurisprudential antecedents' – L Sealy, 'Directors' Duties - An Unnecessary Gloss' (1988) 47(2) *Cambridge Law Journal* 175, 177. Similarly, the leading company law textbook states that

> there was and remains considerable uncertainty about the conceptual boundaries of this doctrine, leading to uncertainties about when the duty bites, about its concept, the remedies available and, to a lesser extent, the mechanisms for enforcing it [...] Only the most imprecise indications have been given by the courts as to when the duty is triggered.

Davies, Worthington and Hare (n 15) para 19-014. *Sequana* should provide clarity on this, but will take a while to be fully conceptualised by company law academics and textbooks.

[57] Hardman (n 50).

cession that the law provides to the business community.[58] Non-corporates do not receive the same state concessions.[59] The state provides these concessions to facilitate trade and maximise wealth.[60] However, it is logical in doing so to push for counter-concessions – that there should be limits on the untrammelled ability of companies to use corporate law techniques to the purely private advantage of its internal constituents. This perspective allows us to see the role of the shareholders as effectively delegated from the state, rather than a natural position in and of its own.[61] Thus, when shareholders fail in that role, then the state is justified in removing that particular concession.

As a result, the 'flip' in interests that insolvency law provides to company law should not be seen as an aberration but as a return to a more typical space. Company law exists to provide a set of rules when things are going well in a company. It is a mistake, though, to think of these as the base, underlying, or default rules. Instead, these should be seen as the exception – the concession provided to the business community. When financial difficulty approaches, then, the terms of this concession should be, and are, tightened. Internal constituencies are 'loaned' rights from the state, which are removed as financial difficulty approaches.

This analysis clarifies the interaction between insolvency law and company law. Insolvency law is not some rare aberration that amends the natural state of corporate interactions. Instead, it represents the default state, from which company law allows deviations whilst the company is solvent. In terms of corporate purpose, it means that shareholders are able to run the company (or set the direction of the company) *so long as* they do not do harm to the fixed

---

[58] For legal examples of such concession theory, see S Watson, 'The Corporate Legal Person' (2019) 19(1) *Journal of Corporate Law Studies* 137; S J Padfield, 'Rehabilitating Concession Theory' (2014) 66(2) *Oklahoma Law Review* 327. This approach has been further advanced in political sciences – R J G Claassen, 'Hobbes Meets the Modern Business Corporation' (2021) 53(1) *Polity* 101; D Ciepley, 'Beyond Public and Private: Toward a Political Theory of the Corporation' (2013) 107(1) *American Political Science Review* 139. This approach does not have universal acceptance – see E Micheler, *Company Law: A Real Entity Theory* (Oxford University Press 2021).

[59] E.g., H J Laski, 'The Personality of Associations' (1916) 29(4) *Harvard Law Review* 404; N MacCormick, *Institutions of Law* (Oxford University Press 2007) 84.

[60] See R J G Claassen, 'Wealth Creation without Domination: The Fiduciary Duties of Companies' (2022) *Critical Review of International Social and Political Philosophy* doi: 10.1080/13698230.2022.2113224.

[61] R Grantham, 'The Doctrinal Basis of the Rights of Company Shareholders' (1998) 57(3) *Cambridge Law Journal* 554, Part V. In particular '[r]ights are vested in shareholders so that they may perform tasks that would otherwise be undertaken by the state directly', 586.

claims of other creditors. Should they do so, then insolvency reverts the corporate form to its natural state.

This is a rather heterodox approach to company law analysis.[62] It provides considerable clarity, though, to the interaction between different theories and rules. It thus provides normative and descriptive answers to complex issues that we struggle to otherwise conceptualise. Most importantly, it demonstrates the interaction between insolvency law and company law: the former keeps the latter in check. The latter prioritises certain constituencies. This is fine so long as decisions can only benefit those constituencies and not harm the claims of others. Once other constituencies may be harmed, insolvency law provides a counterbalance. Insolvency law thus represents the societal base line, that company law is occasionally able to deviate from.

CONCLUSION

This chapter set out to explore the interactions between company law and insolvency law. It has demonstrated that two key debates – separate legal personality and limited liability – both arise due to insolvency concerns. A third issue, that of the corporate purpose, can be reconciled by bowing to insolvency law.

Thus, we see insolvency law acting in two different capacities. First, it is the important backdrop that frames corporate law issues; without the concern of insolvency there is no need for foundational aspects of company law. Company law therefore exists in the shadow of insolvency considerations. The comparative importance of these concepts depends on insolvency law. This should be a concern for corporate law. The current detachment from insolvency law is unsustainable, as it poses a conceptual weakness for company law. There are a number of ways in which insolvency law could reform to lower the importance of separate legal personality and limited liability. These need not be overt changes – company law risks being the victim of an unintended butterfly effect.[63]

Second, we can see insolvency law as acting as law's baseline for analysis, with company law providing deviations which apply so long as the venture is solvent. Thus, the analysis becomes the opposite to traditional approach. It is not that company law outlines the usual position and insolvency law deviates

---

[62] More orthodox approaches view the company as voluntarily established by shareholders and directors – F H Easterbrook and D R Fischel, 'The Corporate Contract' (1989) 89(7) *Columbia Law Review* 1416; Hansmann and Kraakman (n 35); R Romano, 'Answering the Wrong Question: the Tenuous Case for Mandatory Corporate Laws' (1989) 89(7) *Columbia Law Review* 1599.

[63] Hardman (n 2).

from it.[64] Instead, insolvency law sets out the default sets of rules and company law provides temporary deviations from it.

Insolvency law is the dark matter of company law. Company law is tacitly predicated upon insolvency law, and ultimately subject to it. Just don't tell any company lawyers that.

64 See discussion in A Keay, 'Financially Distressed Companies, Preferential Payments and the Director's Duty to Take Account of Creditors' Interests' (2020) 136 *Law Quarterly Review* 52.

14. Insolvency law through the lens of a contract theory of restructuring

Stephan Madaus

INTRODUCTION

The past decade has seen the introduction of court proceedings, which aim the completion of a restructuring of the capital structure of a debtor. Such introduction has taken the form of a straightforward law reform, most notably following the 2019 European Union (EU) Restructuring Directive.[1] Sometimes legal practices rediscovered existing means in their laws to achieve this, most notably with the rise of the use of English schemes of arrangements for debt restructurings since 2008.[2] The remarkable feature of these types of court proceedings is that they are deliberately separate from various types of insolvency proceedings that have pre-existed in these jurisdictions. In fact, these new procedural restructuring options ensue a widespread introduction of debt restructuring procedures in proceedings for insolvent debtors, often following the example of United States (US) Chapter 11. The German legislation provides a telling example. More than 20 years after the introduction of a Chapter 11-type restructuring plan option to uniform insolvency proceedings with a new Insolvency Code in 1999, a preventive restructuring framework, the 'German Scheme' was introduced in 2021 as an implementation of the 2019 EU Restructuring Directive.

Insolvency law theory has struggled with a normative answer to these new restructuring options. While a restructuring plan option in insolvency proceedings could be explained as an insolvency-only tool and hence fit under the

[1] Directive (EU) 2019/1023 of the European Parliament and of the Council of 20 June 2019 on preventive restructuring frameworks, on discharge of debt and disqualifications, and on measures to increase the efficiency of procedures concerning restructuring, insolvency and discharge of debt, and amending Directive (EU) 2017/1132 [2019] OJ L 172/18.

[2] J Payne, *Schemes of Arrangement* (Cambridge University Press 2021) 202 and 228.

umbrella of insolvency law rather flawlessly,[3] the rise of preventive restructuring or even company law restructuring tools challenged this conclusion. Based on the understanding that early restructurings are useful, the new tools move away from the moment in which a debtor is insolvent, or such an insolvency is imminent. Financial difficulties or a mere likelihood of a future insolvency is all that is required to access such procedural assistance if such a threshold exists at all. The idea to extend the umbrella of insolvency law to such proceedings necessarily leads to the conclusion that 'insolvency is a scalar attribute, that is, it is a matter of degree'.[4] The idea is further complicated by the assumption that the limits of insolvency law also define the ability of other law principles to become relevant. If a restructuring is achieved in the form of a workout or amicable settlement, contract law principles should apply instead of insolvency law.

This chapter develops an alternative normative approach to restructurings based on the insight that the realms of restructuring and insolvency laws are separate but may overlap. This approach is able to explain why the state of solvency or insolvency is less relevant with respect to the purpose and functioning of restructuring law while it remains a key threshold for the application of the full range of insolvency law tools. The approach also enables a differentiated application of frameworks designed for insolvency law tools to restructuring proceedings and their effects.

The chapter is structured as follows: first, a clear distinction between insolvency law, governing the tools needed to respond to a common pool problem and their cross-border effects, and restructuring law, governing any modification of the legal relationships of the debtor irrespective of a solvent or insolvent status in response to an anticommons problem and its cross-border effects, is described. Second, it is argued that these areas of law may well overlap where insolvent debtors are restructured in order to resolve their financial situation for the benefit of all parties, yet the cumulative application of tools and rules from two distinct areas of law does not dictate at all that all of the applied tools and rules shall be deemed to have the same doctrinal origin or character. The chapter concludes with an exercise on a new choice of law approach to identify the law applicable to restructuring proceedings in order to demonstrate the epistemic value of the alternative approach.

3 See e.g., Regulation (EU) 2015/848 of the European Parliament and of the Council of 20 May 2015 on insolvency proceedings (recast) [2015] OJ L 141/19, Art 7(2)(j) extending the application of the *lex fori concursus* to such plans. See also *UNCITRAL Legislative Guide on Insolvency Law* (UN Publication 2005) para 21 urging an inclusive approach to the scope of insolvency law.

4 R Mokal, 'What is an Insolvency Proceeding? *Gategroup* Lands in a Gated Community' (2022) 31(3) *International Insolvency Review* 418, 421.

THE SEPARATE REALMS OF RESTRUCTURING AND INSOLVENCY LAWS

The option for arrangements of creditors with the debtor has always been part of insolvency or bankruptcy law – from the times of the Roman law *cessio bonorum*[5] to the concordats and compositions of younger laws.[6] These tools granted the opportunity to mitigate or even avoid the liquidation of all the debtor's assets, usually with a purpose of enabling debtors to continue trading. These arrangements have been an integral and traditional part of insolvency statutes, which begs the question whether there is an actual need to reconsider the normative understanding of them. The answers follow from looking at the characteristics of insolvency proceedings first.

Understanding Any Court Restructuring Procedure as an Insolvency Proceeding?

Insolvency proceedings are a feature of any market economy. Where market participants are unable to service their debt, special rules apply. These rules are asset-focussed. An all-encompassing moratorium stays any debtor or creditor action aiming at a transfer of the remaining assets. Instead, the administration and liquidation of these assets is organised as a fair and transparent process, often a court procedure, with two aims: (1) maximising the value of the remaining assets, which includes a going-concern value if (parts of) the business can be sold; (2) a fair distribution of the generated value amongst all creditors according to a statutory ranking of claims (and equity). The treatment of unpaid debt is not a key issue in such a process. In the case of a corporate debtor, it disappears fairly automatically with the dissolution of the corporate entity. In case of an individual debtor, it could be paid from future income unless a statutory discharge provides for relief.

Faced with such dire consequences, debtors are able to avoid the liquidation of their assets (and business) by agreeing with their creditors about a different way to handle their failure to pay them on time. Provisions on a concordat or composition supported such a solution in many insolvency laws by introducing

---

5 Codex 7,71.

6 See, for instance, the French Code de Commerce, which included a composition since 1838. This inspired the regulation of the German version ('Zwangsvergleich') in the Konkursordnung of 1879; for earlier versions of a concordat or composition in local laws of Europe, see J Kohler, *Lehrbuch des Konkursrechts* (first published 1891, Wentworth Press 1891) 446–450. See also Mokal (n 4) 434–436. The US composition originated in §5103A of the 1867 Bankruptcy Act.

the consent of a majority of affected creditors if publicly confirmed by a court.[7] Often, such provisions would be accompanied by the ability to suspend payments for a negotiation period if the debtor feared enforcement actions or by a suspension of any liquidation if bankruptcy proceedings had already commenced. The (majority of) creditors would agree to a concordat if the debtor's offer seemed beneficial to them compared to a liquidation.

The specific features of such a concordat process became an integral part of insolvency laws in Europe and North America. An agreement supported by an accepting majority of creditors was binding on all creditors just as a supporting moratorium would stay all of them. Just like any bankruptcy liquidation, a concordat had (fully) collective effects and served as an option to avoid a potentially less beneficial bankruptcy liquidation. As part of insolvency law and insolvency proceedings, the confirmation of a concordat itself became an insolvency proceeding.

Interestingly, the logic or purpose underlying the concordat and a supporting moratorium – protecting a beneficial agreement from potentially value-destroying individual creditor action – is not only applicable to situations where the debtor is (already) unable to pay. It is even more urgent and true at an earlier stage when the debtor is still able to make payments but foresees a risk of insolvency. It seems conclusive and justified, therefore, to extend such procedural options to debtors who are not yet unable to pay but are already in an economic state of some form of financial difficulties.

Such an extension, however, raises two issues. First, a debtor with the ability to pay all debts today may not need a restructuring operation that involves all of their debt (and equity) on the balance sheet. Even more, it may indeed cause more harm than good if all creditors get involved at this stage, especially customers, employees or trade creditors, as it may prompt them to end the relationship and move to competitors.[8] Early debt restructuring negotiations may, therefore, benefit from a certain degree of claim selection and confidentiality. This is particularly important with regard to a supporting moratorium. A collective stay is often disruptive and harmful to the daily business of the debtor. A more selective stay may be useful if a stay is needed at all.

As a result of these considerations, restructuring options are widely available today for insolvent as well as for solvent debtors. Restructuring proceedings are also commonly selective in the sense that the restructuring plan does not need to affect all creditor rights. The more a legislator designates such procedural options to handle a preventive scenario, the more such options tend to

---

7 Ibid.

8 S Paterson, *Corporate Reorganization Law and Forces of Change?* (Oxford University Press 2020) 154.

become confidential and selective with a merely optional, often selective stay. In total, modern preventive proceedings lose key characteristics of insolvency proceedings. They are neither collective nor public nor addressing a situation of incapacity for payment exclusively or even characteristically. While this has led some scholars to doubt the characterisation of such proceedings as insolvency proceedings,[9] others remain committed by arguing that it suffices that restructuring proceedings are merely capable of responding to the needs of fully insolvent debtors as well and include a threshold to exclude perfectly solvent debtors.[10] Such a broad, more 'vague' concept of insolvency law is not able to provide a clear distinction between insolvency law and areas of law which are not insolvency law.[11] This is not only unsatisfying in terms of doctrine. It also invites an arbitrary construction of the scope of insolvency law frameworks.

The Caprice of Today's Purposive Definition of Insolvency Law

A broad normative concept of insolvency law is not only invasive to other areas of law when it aims to include all types of procedural options that are mere capable of assisting debtor in financial troubles. The focus on law governing specific procedural options produces a significant blind spot: informal restructurings or workouts.

If the scope of insolvency law was to be defined by the purpose of the undertaking regardless of the solvency of the debtor, any type of debt restructuring that is capable of curing a default would need to be considered a transaction under insolvency law. This is clearly not the case whenever such arrangements are negotiated and concluded out of court. The individual settlement with a tort creditor or the principal lender, vendor or landlord about a rescheduling of debt is not held to be an agreement under insolvency law even if negotiated in the likelihood of an inability to pay in time. Any coordinated out-of-court debt restructuring negotiation and agreement with a circle of creditors would even more constitute an action to avoid or overcome an inability to pay, yet it is not characterised as insolvency law governed. It is only the moment that the debtor decides to bring the debt settlement to court for homologation when insolvency law could apply, which would probably further depend on the condition that the agreed debt settlement is a workout involving several creditors, not just an individual settlement with an individual creditor. The latter, even if invoked

---

9 H Eidenmüller, 'What Is an Insolvency Proceeding?' (2018) 92(1) *American Bankruptcy Law Journal* 53, 56; 66 *et seq.*

10 Mokal (n 4) 425–429; 463.

11 Ibid., 421: 'Not only is insolvency metaphysically a scalar attribute, the concept of insolvency is also epistemically vague.'

with force under applicable rules to modify debt (*force majeure* clauses, etc.), would probably remain to be solely governed by contract law, company or commercial law or civil procedure law even pursuant to a vague and scalar insolvency concept as proposed above.

If this is true, however, it is neither the purpose of court involvement (preventing or overcoming the status of actual insolvency) nor the mere involvement of a court for such a purpose that defines insolvency proceedings and insolvency law today. Instead, the understanding of what should and should not be characterised as insolvency proceedings and insolvency law has been informed by the typical case (contract outside insolvency or composition as a part of insolvency).[12] Such an approach is not able to provide much guidance in cases where these prototypes converge.

The Law of Restructurings

This chapter argues that any approach to define the scope of modern insolvency law should start with a clear understanding of the phenomenon of restructurings.

The restructuring of debt, or more precisely the capital structure of an entity comprising of debt and equity, is not yet a fixed legal concept. It is a factual phenomenon.

Restructurings in the broadest sense

Any restructuring starts with the insight that the debtor is an entity, often an enterprise,[13] with a multitude of legal relationships to other entities or assets. The management of these relationships is the daily task of every person; in case of a business, the daily task of its management. Contracts are to be concluded, extended, or cancelled. Obligations under a contract or statute are to be performed. The adjustment of existing legal relationships to a new situation, new needs or abilities, is a key component of these management actions. Such adjustments are achieved by the use of respective legal options under the law governing contracts, taxes, companies, etc. The continuing 'restructuring' of existing legal rights and obligations can be understood as a 'restructuring in the broadest sense'. Such restructurings or adjustments occur on an individual

---

12 See, for instance, the Note by the Secretariat of UNCITRAL of 7 February 2022 on applicable law in insolvency proceedings, A_CN.9_WG.V_WP.179, para 11, arguing that the reason to exclude informal arrangements from the scope of insolvency law is solely that they are treated like this 'usually'.

13 Debt restructuring rules are commonly found in company law or corporate insolvency law or, historically, the insolvency law of merchants and traders. Yet payment plan options are a debt restructuring for individuals and consumers.

basis with each counterparty under the law applicable to their relationship including the ability of the parties to consensually modify a right/claim or to even unilaterally achieve such modifications under the applicable law, e.g., based on a price adjustment clause, a *force majeure* clause or a right to terminate a contract. All of these 'restructurings' bear relevance for the balance sheet of the debtor; they 'restructure' it on both the asset and the debt side. They also have the potential to cause or overcome an insolvency. Still, such acts are neither governed by insolvency law nor any special restructuring law. Such modifications remain in the realm of the law governing the original legal relationship, e.g., company law, tax law, labour law, or contract law, etc. This conclusion seems undisputed.

Coordinated restructurings of the capital structure

Things are different as soon as the means to modify legal relationships and obligations under their governing law become insufficient to address a situation in which one of the parties – the debtor – is potentially unable to pay all their debts as they fall due. As far as the law of obligations provides no remedy, the debtor is in need of an agreement with a subset of their creditors about a modification of the respective debt in order to prevent a default and insolvency proceedings, yet such an agreement may be difficult to achieve as each individual creditor may not be willing to finance the full payment of (some or even all) other creditors by agreeing to receive less than the full amount on behalf of their claims or at the agreed due date.

A specific collective action problem has arisen. It is rational for any creditor in this situation to bet that given the loss threatening every creditor in an insolvency of the debtor any other creditor might be more willing to accept the burden of a loss (or at least accept a (higher) share of the burden), thus giving our creditor a free ride in a restructuring. If every creditor behaves like this, the tragedy of the anticommons unfolds. The rational apathy of creditors results in a lack of cooperation that prevents all creditors from achieving a solution that is in their common interest – avoiding costly insolvency proceedings.[14]

In order to overcome rational creditor holdout behaviour, debtors can make use of certain strategies in order to build trust. This includes the sharing of financial information and coordinated debt restructuring renegotiations explaining the burden sharing scheme. Tools like mediation or conciliation can assist in overcoming holdouts and getting a 'yes'.[15] All of these strategies

---

[14] See further R de Weijs, 'Too Big to Fail as a Game of Chicken with the State: What Insolvency Law Theory Has to Say about TBTF and Vice Versa' (2013) 14(2) *European Business Organization Law Review* 201, 213.

[15] Mediation has become a tool in restructuring frameworks recently, see S Esendal, *Harmonizing the Rules of Mediation in Insolvency and Restructuring in*

have in common that they aim at the voluntary conclusion of a settlement about the proposed restructuring of debt (and equity) that reflects the general interest of the debtor and all creditors, even though not all of the debt may actually be affected. The burden sharing would nonetheless be negotiated with a view to other creditors (and shareholders) and the agreement would reflect the position, contribution and interests of these groups even if they do not directly participate in the agreement. Hence, a coordinated restructuring effort is obviously different from the individual 'restructuring' actions of a daily business management.

Procedures, or the role of courts

Policymakers are free to support such restructuring efforts by discouraging holdouts. One option is to reward cooperation. Creditors who agree to share the burden could be awarded by tax incentives or a preference in a potential future liquidation of the debtor's assets. Another option is to ban or punish holdouts. A statutory rule could provide that creditors could be legally obliged to agree to a restructuring of their claim if this is necessary in the general interest of creditors and the debtor as part of their obligation to recognise the interest of their counterparty in a legal relationship (duty of care). Where such a duty is not enforceable in court, it justifies claims for damages or the loss of privileges, for instance in the distribution in a potential future liquidation.

Only when policymakers decide to provide for an enforceable duty to cooperate do court proceedings come into play. These would be able to produce a judgment ordering cooperation in the form of agreeing to the proposed burden sharing. The court imposes a plan. As an interim measure, the court also imposes a stay of the enforcement of the litigated claim including any right to accelerate the due date.

The involvement of courts would suddenly trigger the broad definition of insolvency proceedings to apply. The proceedings aim at enforcing obligations regarding the prevention of losses due to the insolvency of the debtor based on relevant financial difficulties. While workouts are clearly contract law tools, workouts that are concluded based on an enforced duty to cooperate are suddenly considered insolvency law tools? The logic of such a delineation is not self-evident.

---

the EU. Comparative Study of Spanish, Portuguese and Dutch Laws (LLM Thesis, University of Leiden 2020). See also P Lucarelli and I Forestieri, 'The Three Targets of Insolvency Mediation: Dispute Resolution, Agreement Facilitation, Corporate Distress Management' (2017) 4 *TDM* 14–19.

Restructuring law as the law of all coordinated restructurings of the capital structure

A new definition could start by describing the realm of restructuring law first before discussing the relationship to insolvency law and the applicability of legal frameworks for insolvency proceedings.

Restructuring law should be understood as the set of legal rules that support or enable the conclusion of an agreement that concerns the adjustment of parts or all of the capital structure of the debtor according to a fair burden sharing scheme.[16] These rules are designed to address rational but illegitimate holdouts in a situation where cooperation is required in order to prevent the loss of value in a tragedy of the anticommons.[17] The fairness of the proposed burden sharing scheme would need to be agreed on by all parties bound to it in principle. The prototype of a restructuring agreement is a contract (workout). In a holdout situation, the fairness would nonetheless be indicated by a majority of parties agreeing to it; minority protection would be available in court based on a fairness review.[18] Restructuring law tools would comprise the sanctioning of such an agreement which can be understood as the enforcement of the statutory duty to cooperate against a party (holdout). Supportive measures like a temporary stay of enforcement rights, the involvement of a mediator or conciliator and the definition of cooperation benefits, for instance bankruptcy safe harbours or preferences, would be available for negotiating parties and could potentially be support by court orders if needed. Overall, restructuring law features a set of characteristic tools, tests and purposes. They work as a 'safety valve' in the background of workout negotiations.

These characteristics are different from those of insolvency proceedings, which are designed to provide remedies irrespective of any consent amongst affected stakeholders. The insolvency of the debtor has immediate effect on all creditors and other stakeholders that require fully collective legal responses in order to protect the remaining value (tragedy of the commons) as well as a statutory burden sharing scheme that applies regardless of any agreement. Insolvency law is asset-oriented and reflects the capital structure only when it applies a distribution scheme – the ranking of creditors (and equity holders) as provided by the law.

In comparison, restructuring law is not sensitive to the state of solvency or insolvency of the debtor. A fair burden sharing scheme may be developed

---

16 This definition reflects earlier work; see S Madaus, 'Leaving the Shadows of US Bankruptcy Law: A Proposal to Divide the Realms of Insolvency and Restructuring Law' (2018) 19 *European Business Organization Law Review* 615, 630.

17 Ibid., 633–639.

18 See, for instance, the 'fair and equitable' requirement in § 1129(b)(1) US Bankruptcy Code.

at any stage. The underlying fairness requirement is, however, very sensitive to the counterfactual scenario. Parties to the negotiations as well as judges will make their assessment of a scheme based on the position that the parties would fall back to if the proposed scheme is not adopted. This position would probably look significantly different in a preventive scenario compared to an insolvency because value could be distributed further down the capital structure in the early liquidation if a (still) solvent and trading company.

Restructuring law is also not susceptible to the degree of court involvement. While insolvency law is defined by the existence of court proceedings, restructuring law may well apply without any court involvement. In fact, the involvement of a court is only meant to be a backup for cases in which the parties are unable to agree in the shadow of an enforceable duty to cooperate. If needed, court involvement may range from a court-initiated mediation or a homologation of consensual agreements to the application of cross-class cramdown and interim stay provisions in a highly controversial case.

Finally, restructuring law is also not susceptible to the level of collectivity. Any fair burden sharing agreement is capable of support.

Restructuring agreements are contracts

Individual agreements between the debtor and a single creditor about the modification of a claim are contracts in nature (and a restructuring in the broadest sense). The coordinated modification of claims with several creditors or shareholders is a combination of such contracts or, if integrated and negotiated in one document (a restructuring plan), a multilateral contract – a workout. Where workout negotiations are supported by standstill agreements, another contract or set of contracts exists.

If the power of a court to sanction a contested restructuring agreement (or plan) is understood as the enforcement of a statutory obligation to cooperate against a holdout creditor or shareholder,[19] the need to enforce an act of cooperation does normally not modify the nature of the outcome: a contract concerning the coordinated modification of debt (and equity). A different mechanism produces the same result. The legitimacy of such an obligation to cooperate (and its enforceability) follows from the pre-existing relationship between the debtor and the creditor (or shareholder) and a duty of care thereof regarding the prevention of a tragedy of the anticommons. The underlying justification also explains why restructuring law is only capable of modifying pre-existing legal rights but unable to impose new obligations against the will of the individual.

---

19 Madaus (n 16) 626.

The contractual nature of the outcome of restructuring law tools is also consistent with the idea that the fair content of any coordinated modification of rights, the burden sharing scheme, is principally to be agreed on by those affected. Faced with a holdout, the actual consent of a significant majority of equally affected parties remains the key pillar of any fairness assessment.[20]

The proposition that a court-sanctioned restructuring plan is a contract by nature or at least to be construed as a contract is not new. It is reflected in the case law of relevant jurisdictions.[21] It is in line with the ability of contracts to modify pre-existing rights in principle. From a company law perspective, restructuring plans are able to implement the idea of a 'flexible capital structure'.[22] It provides a mechanism that enables the debtor to quickly adjust parts of the debt structure in a scenario when it becomes clear that the risk financing granted by 'sophisticated, informed, and strongly adjusting institutional financial creditors and investors'[23] will not be repaid. Restructuring law mechanism also enables the debtor to limit the effects of the adjustment to these very creditors.

The Relationship Between Insolvency and Restructuring Law

The ability to identify a specific type of rules as restructuring law prompts the question how this field of law fits with established fields of law, in particular insolvency law. The answer proposed is to abandon the concept exclusivity between contract (workout) and insolvency laws in favour of a concept that allows several fields of law to apply in parallel at a moment in time, especially when they complement each other. The history of restructuring law indicates that this is the case.

On a national level

The introduction of restructuring law rules has been a policy choice. It relies on the insight of policymakers whether they wish to actively support coordinated restructuring efforts (workouts) by introducing a support framework in order to save the economic value of a viable business or to avoid the social costs of a liquidation caused by a rational, freeriding holdout creditor.

---

20 Ibid., 636–638.

21 This includes the US (see e.g., *In re Dow Corning Corporation*, 456 F3d 668, 676 (6th Cir 2006): 'In interpreting a confirmed plan, courts use contract principles, since the plan is effectively a new contract between the debtor and its creditors.') as well as Germany (see e.g., Bundesgerichtshof, 7.5.2015, NZI 2015, 697 para 26).

22 Paterson (n 8) 71.

23 Ibid., 49.

The justification of a restructuring support framework (restructuring law) has been more obvious to policymakers in a scenario where the directly affected holdout creditor is held to be less protected anyway: the scenario of the insolvency of the debtor. A holdout position based on a nominal value of a claim that no longer exists is indeed difficult to accept. The justification of a restructuring support framework does, however, not depend on the insolvency of the debtor. It provides benefits for a society while protecting the economic value of dissenting stakeholder rights (claims or equity interest) where such stakeholder cannot be convinced (best interest test[24]).

This insight has led to the introduction of restructuring rules in insolvency law statutes first before lawmakers began to adopt preventive restructuring frameworks. This was, for instance, the case in Germany.[25] In other jurisdictions, in England in particular, practice started to use company law tools for debt restructurings (schemes of arrangements) before lawmakers formally adopted preventive restructuring frameworks ('Part 26A restructuring plans').[26] Only a few jurisdictions find constitutional barriers that strictly confine the use of coordinated restructuring tools to insolvency law.[27]

From a restructuring law perspective, the counterfactual of a currently solvent or insolvent debtor is (only) relevant for the fairness assessment of the proposed coordinated burden sharing. Its tools and principles apply regardless. Hence, restructuring law is not merely a part or even subchapter of insolvency law; it is also not merely a part of company law or contract law. Instead, it should be understood as a separate field of law fulfilling a specific function by offering a specific set of tools and guided by a specific set of principles. As a coordinated restructuring effort can be useful for companies as for individuals, for (still) solvent as for insolvent debtors, restructuring law is applicable at all stages of a company's or individual's lifecycle in theory. It can be added into an insolvency law statutory framework as it can be added to company law

---

24 See the 2019 Directive (n 1) Art 2(6). The idea originated in US bankruptcy law in the 1867 Bankruptcy Act, see J Hicks, 'Foxes Guarding the Henhouse: The Modern Best Interests of Creditors Test in Chapter 11 Reorganizations' (2005) 5(3) *Nev LJ* 820. It has become known as the 'no creditor worse of' test in Europe, see, for instance, § 901G (3) of the Companies Act 2006 or § 251 (1) no 2 InsO (German Insolvency Code).

25 The 1999 Insolvency Code (InsO) contained provisions on the content and conclusion of 'insolvency plans' in §§ 217–269.

26 The restructuring plan was added to the Companies Act 2006 in 2020 when the Corporate Insolvency and Governance Act 2020 was adopted.

27 A prominent example is the 'Contract Clause' in Art I, s 10, cl 1 of the US Constitution ('No State shall [...] pass any [...] Law impairing the Obligation of Contracts [...].'), which effectively limits the ability to provide for uniform federal restructuring law rules to bankruptcy law under the 'Bankruptcy Clause' in Article I, s 8, cl 4; see Madaus (n 17) 628.

or debt law statutes in general. Finally, restructuring law can be implemented as a stand-alone set of rules for both solvent and insolvent debtors. No matter where a lawyer finds its rules or where a lawmaker puts them, they should be understood as a coherent set of rules. It remains a policy decision whether to address holdout behaviour in a workout of (still) solvent debtors in the general interest of stakeholders.

There is another important aspect of separation. Restructuring law is not only formed by a separate set of rules regardless of the statute they are found in. It is further separate from the area of law that governs the legal rights which are meant to be restructured. The coordinated restructuring of labour law claims is not a labour law exercise; the restructuring of tax claims is not a matter of tax law. These areas of law may well provide for means to individually modify pre-existing claims or rights. The coordinated modification goes beyond such means and is only a matter of restructuring law. Hence, a separate policy choice is needed regarding the ability of restructuring laws to modify all pre-existing claims including politically sensitive claims of employees or public (tax) authorities. If restructuring law is applicable, both regulations to modify a right (individual and coordinated modification) overlap.

In a cross-border context

The autonomy of restructuring law from the law of insolvency and the laws governing the debt or rights to be modified would be relevant in a cross-border context as well.

Based on the insight that the restructuring agreement (plan) is a contract, the law governing the conclusion and validity of the contract would need to be found pursuant to the choice of the law principles developed for contracts until specific principles will be developed and agreed on for restructuring law. These principles provide for a prerogative of the parties to select the law applicable to their contract[28] and, if needed, the courts competent to issue a judgment.[29] If such a selection is not achievable, the law of the country with the closest connection to the restructuring needs to be identified.[30] For this assessment, all relevant facts are to be considered. In case of the restructuring of debt governed by the law of only one country, the applicable debt law may provide

[28] See, for instance, Regulation (EC) No 593/2008 of the European Parliament and of the Council of 17 June 2008 on the law applicable to contractual obligations (Rome I) [2008] OJ L 177/6, Art 3(1).

[29] See, for instance, Regulation (EU) No 1215/2012 of the European Parliament and of the Council of 12 December 2012 on jurisdiction and the recognition and enforcement of judgments in civil and commercial matters (recast) [2012] OJ L 351/1, Art 25.

[30] See, for instance, Rome I (n 28) Art 3(3).

for the closest connection also with regard to their restructuring. Where claims are to be restructured which are governed by the laws of multiple countries, the majority of debt in value or in numbers of creditors may indicate the closest connection. Where the restructuring effort is part of commenced (fully collective) insolvency proceedings, restructuring plans are commonly held to be ancillary to such proceedings[31] and hence are connected most closely to the country of these proceedings; the *lex fori concursus* applies to such restructuring plan proceedings. For stand-alone or preventive restructuring proceedings, however, the COMI of the debtor may not simply indicate a closest connection since such proceedings are debt-oriented, not debtor-oriented.[32] If the COMI concept is useful in this context at all, remains to be seen.[33]

The autonomous approach to restructuring law provides more flexibility and party autonomy where it is needed. It does relax the *vis attractiva concursus* in this respect without disregarding it in cases where restructuring support is a mere annex to insolvency proceedings.

HOW TO COVER AUTONOMOUS RESTRUCTURING LAW IN EXISTING INSOLVENCY LAW INSTRUMENTS?

The autonomous understanding of restructuring law is not yet covered in existing cross-border regulations, e.g., the European Insolvency Regulation or model laws like the UNCITRAL Model Law on Cross-Border Insolvency. The approach appears compatible with these instruments as far as restructuring cases are a mere annex to insolvency proceedings as defined by them. Restructuring law offers a restructuring solution and hence an outcome in insolvency proceedings, which is why the judgment confirming such an outcome can be understood as an 'insolvency-related judgement'[34] or as a 'composition approved by that court'.[35] Insolvency law superimposes restructuring law.

---

[31] See *UNCITRAL Model Law on Recognition and Enforcement of Insolvency-Related Judgments* (UN Publications 2019) Arts 2(d)(1) and 14(f)(i).

[32] For more see S Madaus, 'The Cross-border Effects of Restructurings' (2022) in *Festschrift Christoph Paulus* 479–482.

[33] The need to 'relax' the COMI requirement for restructurings is also conceded by I Mevorach and A Walters, 'The Characterization of Pre-insolvency Proceedings in Private International Law' (2020) 21 *European Business Organization Law Review* 855, 886–890.

[34] See UNCITRAL Model Law (n 31) Arts 2(d)(1) and 14(f)(i).

[35] See Regulation 2015/848 (n 3) Art 32(1).

Where such an annex is not given because the only court proceeding initiated is a procedure aiming at the use of restructuring law, things are more complex. Under a broad definition of insolvency proceedings, most of such restructuring proceedings would be brought under the scope of these instruments.[36] As a consequence, recognition abroad would strictly depend on the debtor's COMI in the country of the restructuring while the law governing the restructuring identified under a choice of law agreement or a closest connection assessment would be left irrelevant.[37] Parallel (secondary) proceedings could be commenced in other countries where the debtor has establishments, thereby limiting the effect of any restructuring agreement.[38] The recognition of any restructuring plan would not be facilitated even if carried by a consent of all creditors and instead depend on the assessment of the adequate protection of local creditors[39] or an unspecified public policy objection.[40] Overall, these frameworks barely meet the specific needs of a preventive restructuring.[41] In particular, they are blind to the needs of a more targeted restructuring, affecting only a particular bond, and more consensual restructurings, involving only a mediator or an act of homologation if a court is involved at all.

The autonomous understanding of restructuring law as the law of supporting the conclusion of a contract modifying pre-existing rights in a coordinated (planned) manner would indicate that any court involvement is merely reviewing the ability to overcome a holdout under the law. It is a judgment in a civil or commercial matter about the validity of a restructuring agreement or the application of other restructuring tools, such as the involvement of a mediator or expert. As the application of restructuring law is autonomous from the law of the restructured right, such judgments remain civil or commercial judgments even if they concern the restructuring of public law rights like, for instance, tax claims. In a cross-border context, judgments should be able to circulate pursuant to treaties or conventions on the recognition and enforcement of foreign judgments in civil or commercial matters, for instance the Lugano Convention

---

36 This is the core argument presented by Mokal (n 4) 31; 46.

37 See *UNCITRAL Model Law on Cross-Border Insolvency* (UN Publications 2014) Arts 2(b) and 17(2). See also Regulation 2015/848 (n 3) Arts 32(1) and 19(1).

38 See UNCITRAL Model Law ibid Art 2(c). See also Regulation 2015/848 (n 3) Arts 3(2) and 47(1).

39 See UNCITRAL Model Law (n 37) Art 22. See also UNCITRAL Model Law (n 31) Art 14(f)(i).

40 See UNCITRAL Model Law (n 37) Art 6. See also Regulation 2015/848 (n 3) Art 33.

41 See (for the European context) the assessment in the CERIL Report 2022-2 on Cross-Border Effects in European Preventive Restructuring, 6 July 2022 https://www.ceril.eu/news/ceril-report-2022-2-on-cross-border-effects-in-european-preventive-restructuring accessed 14 May 2023.

of 30 October 2007 on Jurisdiction and Enforcement of Judgments in Civil and Commercial Matters or, when in force, the Hague Convention of 2 July 2019 on the Recognition and Enforcement of Foreign Judgments in Civil or Commercial Matters. As these kinds of instruments have been designed with a view to two-party-litigation, they do not perfectly meet the specific characteristics of a restructuring. It is time to develop a set of rules to be adopted that is filling this gap.

CONCLUSION

This chapter developed the idea of restructuring law as an autonomous field of law. This includes any type of court procedures that aim at the support or completion of a coordinated restructuring of (parts of) the capital structure. The realms of restructuring and insolvency laws are separate and autonomous but may overlap. This approach is able to explain why the state of solvency or insolvency is less relevant with respect to the purpose and functioning of restructuring law while it remains a key threshold for the application of the full range of insolvency law tools. The approach also enables a differentiated application of frameworks designed for insolvency law tools to restructuring proceedings and their effects. A regulatory gap in existing cross-border instruments was exposed and should be addressed.

15. Insolvency law through the lens of property law theories

Alisdair MacPherson[1]

INTRODUCTION

Property is inescapably at the core of insolvency law. Much of the latter is concerned with property issues, namely: ascertaining the property within the insolvent debtor's estate; determining the property rights various parties hold; and regulating the use, realisation, and distribution of the insolvent's property. Property law provides a necessary foundation for each of these matters. Meanwhile, from the perspective of property law, insolvency law offers a 'litmus test' for distinguishing property rights (rights *in rem*/real rights) from mere personal rights (rights *in personam*)[2] and helps to determine what property is. There is thus mutual dependency between property law and insolvency law.

This chapter will examine how property features in insolvency law, with particular reference to the United Kingdom (UK) (principally English law). After demonstrating the interconnectedness of property and insolvency, attention will turn to considering insolvency in the context of property law theory, followed by consideration of the reverse, namely, how property features in insolvency law theory. It will become apparent that further consideration of theories from one domain could create new opportunities for rethinking law or theory in the other, or for achieving desired objectives.

It should be pointed out that this chapter does not offer a theory of property law or insolvency law or a unifying theory. It also does not provide a normative framework. Rather, it seeks to explore the extent to which property and insolvency law and theory are integrated or utilised together and how they may be better combined or used in tandem in future. Examining insolvency

1 I am grateful for the comments of Donna McKenzie Skene, Riz Mokal and Chris Odinet on an earlier draft of this chapter. Any errors or omissions are, however, mine alone.

2 These should not be conflated with real property and personal property.

through the lens of property, and vice versa, offers fresh insights in relation to both fields, enabling greater understanding of relevant law and the theories underpinning that law. Such an approach helps us to challenge those theories and to identify whether there is scope for their adaptation or expansion.

PROPERTY IN INSOLVENCY LAW

As stated by property law theorist Henry Smith, '[p]roperty is a platform for the rest of private law'.[3] Areas of law such as succession, trusts and, of course, insolvency, depend on property. Property and property law appear in insolvency in a variety of crucial ways and provide a body of rules with which insolvency law interacts. Indeed, it can be noted that insolvency law applies when the debtor's property cannot be used to pay debts due to creditors in full, either because the debtor's liabilities are greater than their assets or because the property is of a type that is not realisable in a way that enables debts to be paid as they fall due.

The significance of property law within insolvency law applies in legal systems generally, and is certainly true in the jurisdictions of the UK.[4] While in various respects property continues to exist in the same manner as before insolvency, there are divergences from the background law too.[5] Insolvency proceedings[6] often lead to a debtor losing control of their property. For processes that are not debtor-in-possession, an insolvency officeholder will seek to take custody or control of the debtor's property and will have powers in relation to that property.[7] And in some contexts the debtor's property will or can vest in the insolvency officeholder, for the purposes of preserving the estate and dealing with the property and realising it.[8]

---

[3] H E Smith, 'Property as the Law of Things' (2012) 125(7) *Harvard Law Review* 1691, 1691.

[4] The point is demonstrated by how many times 'property' is used in the Insolvency Act 1986.

[5] See R Calnan, *Proprietary Rights and Insolvency* (Oxford University Press 2016) para 1.130 for limits on proprietary rights in insolvency. In addition, property that is not ordinarily transferable may be subject to involuntary transfer to an insolvency officeholder.

[6] For what is meant by an insolvency proceeding (process), see R Mokal, 'What is an Insolvency Proceeding? Gategroup Lands in a Gated Community' (2022) 31(3) *International Insolvency Review* 418.

[7] See e.g., Insolvency Act 1986, ss 144; 234; 312 and Sch B1, paras 1(1) and 59(1). See Schs 1, 4 and 5 for the powers.

[8] This is possible but unusual for liquidation: Insolvency Act 1986, s 145. In bankruptcy, the bankrupt's estate vests in the trustee automatically, without any transfer: s 306.

The definition of property in the Insolvency Act 1986 is wide and non-exhaustive, stating that the term 'includes money, goods, things in action, land and every description of property wherever situated and also obligations and every description of interest, whether present or future or vested or contingent, arising out of, or incidental to, property'.[9] While some property may be separately excluded from the insolvent's estate,[10] non-excluded property is subject to existing property rights (including those of secured creditors).[11] Within both insolvency and property law, the distinction between personal rights and property rights is crucial,[12] and the effectiveness of a right notwithstanding insolvency helps to determine whether it is a property right. Parties frequently seek to contend that they have title to, or ownership of, property, thus removing it from the insolvent's estate.

Even where property is part of an insolvent's estate, some powers of parties with property rights may be suspended or lost. This could be the result of a moratorium, as exists in administration, which precludes enforcement of security over the company's property (which otherwise would be possible despite the insolvency procedure) and legal processes without the consent of the administrator or the court's permission.[13] An administrator even has the ability to obtain a court order to dispose of property subject to a (fixed) security as if it were not subject to the security, but only where the court thinks the disposal would be likely to promote the purpose of administration, and the security holder's interest is protected (as net proceeds are to be applied to discharging the sums secured by the security).[14] Insolvency law also allows for certain property earlier disposed of by the debtor to be returned to the estate (or its value paid), which would not be possible without insolvency. This is the case for challengeable transactions where property has been transferred under

[9] Insolvency Act 1986, s 436(1).

[10] E.g., property the insolvent holds on trust for another (see e.g., Insolvency Act 1986, s 283(3)(a); L Tucker et al, *Lewin on Trusts* (Sweet & Maxwell 2020) para 27-029; *Barclays Bank Ltd v Quistclose Investments Ltd* [1970] AC 567 and *Re Kayford Ltd* [1975] 1 WLR 279). Also, in bankruptcy, various property is excluded including tools, books, vehicles and other equipment necessary for personal or business use, and clothing, bedding, furniture, etc., 'necessary for satisfying the basic domestic needs of the bankrupt and his family': Insolvency Act 1986, s 283(2) and see also (3) and (3A).

[11] See e.g., Insolvency Act 1986, s 283(5) for bankruptcy.

[12] See e.g. S Mills (ed), *Goode on Proprietary Rights and Insolvency in Sales Transactions* (Sweet & Maxwell 2010) para 1.06; Calnan (n 4) para 1.89.

[13] Insolvency Act 1986, Sch B1, para 43. See also now the free-standing moratorium: Insolvency Act 1986, Part A1.

[14] Insolvency Act 1986, Sch B1, para 71. No such order is needed for property subject to a floating charge: para 70.

certain conditions (including at an undervalue) in particular time periods prior to insolvency procedures.[15] As well as such rules regarding the overall size of the estate and its constituent property, there are rules regarding (unfair) preferences, which challenge the priority that a party has illegitimately received in comparison to other creditors in the run up to an insolvency procedure.[16]

The examples so far should make it clear that property law provides a starting point for insolvency law, but that insolvency justifies the departure from normal rules of property in a number of ways. This is true in relation to the debtor's control over property, the powers available to other parties with property rights and the property which may fall within the insolvency estate. Consequently, it is important that theories of property take account of the effects that insolvency has on property rights, as this helps to explain the nature and features of property.[17] Meanwhile, insolvency law theories should adequately justify why normal rules of property are to be departed from.

INSOLVENCY IN PROPERTY LAW THEORY

Within property law theory, insolvency and insolvency law often only feature in a marginal way. This may be surprising given the variety of interactions between insolvency and property. Nevertheless, the uncertainty regarding what property actually is, means there is scope to consider how insolvency fits with or shapes different theories of property. It is indeed instructive that a concept as fundamental as 'property' in law is still so contested but its fundamentality may explain why it remains a subject of such debate. Much of property law theory revolves around questions such as: What is property? What does it mean to have a property right? Why does the law give effect to property rights? Whose interests does property law serve and whose interests should it serve? And against whom can a property right be exercised?[18]

---

[15] Insolvency Act 1986, s 238 for transactions at an undervalue in corporate insolvency; and s 339 for bankruptcy. See ss 423–425 for rules regarding transactions defrauding creditors, which do not require such time limits.

[16] Insolvency Act 1986, s 239 for corporate insolvency; and s 340 for bankruptcy. And see s 245 regarding the avoidance of certain floating charges.

[17] In this regard, at least some aspects of insolvency law may be considered components of property law.

[18] See e.g., the questions identified by A Bell and G Parchomovsky, 'A Theory of Property' (2005) 90(3) *Cornell Law Review* 531, 538 (see also 575–576).

Concepts of Property

Property refers to different concepts, depending on the context. In simple terms, property may refer to a 'thing'. A thing may or may not have a physical existence,[19] it could be land, a car, intellectual property, shares, a digital asset, a contractual claim against another party or something else recognised by the law.[20] A thing can be the object of a property right or interest, and that right is held by a legal person (whether natural or otherwise). Of particular significance for legal purposes, the relevant right or interest itself can be referred to as property.[21] Property in this context is sometimes considered (largely) synonymous with ownership; however, subordinate forms of property interest (or rights) are also within the domain of property law.[22] As Kenneth Reid succinctly states, 'property law is the law of things, and of rights in things (real rights)'.[23] The essence of property, particularly in the ownership sense, continues to interest and animate property law theorists.

The traditional view is that property is a right in relation to a thing that is enforceable against people generally (or the world). Blackstone stated that property is 'that sole and despotic dominion which one man claims and exercises over the external things of the world, in total exclusion of the right of any other individual in the universe'.[24] While there is often more recognition nowadays of the ways in which ownership is subject to, or affected by,

---

[19] However, some systems only recognise corporeal objects as part of property law, narrowly defined, and have a separate regime for incorporeal objects, e.g., in Germany BGB § 90.

[20] Yet there can be debate as to whether certain things should be recognised as property in a narrow sense, including digital assets, contractual rights and even shares. See e.g., A Pretto-Sakmann, *Boundaries of Personal Property: Shares and Sub-Shares* (Hart 2005), especially chapters 4 and 5; Law Commission, *Digital Assets: Consultation Paper* (Law Com No 256, 2022) chapter 2. See also J Toomey, 'Property's Boundaries' (2023) 109(1) *Virginia Law Review* 131.

[21] See e.g., A M Honoré, 'Ownership' in AG Guest (ed), *Oxford Essays in Jurisprudence* (Oxford University Press 1961) 128.

[22] The notion of 'ownership' in English law is contested, in part due to the existence of relativity of title. For a view that English law does allow for ownership, see L Rostill, *Possession, Relative Title, and Ownership in English Law* (Oxford University Press 2021) especially chapter 7. More broadly, some commentators contend that ownership and other property rights are not applicable to certain types of things, especially personal rights: e.g., G L Gretton, 'Ownership and its Objects' (2007) 71(4) Rabels Zeitschrift für ausländisches und internationales Privatrecht 802; Pretto-Sakmann (n 20) 106–107.

[23] K G C Reid, *The Law of Property in Scotland* (Butterworths Law 1996) para 11.

[24] W Blackstone, *Commentaries on the Laws of England* (1765–1769) II, 1, 2, yet subsequent passages identify a number of qualifications to this statement.

other rights and interests, the general approach still has significant support in many jurisdictions. Developments since the early twentieth century, particularly in the United States (US), have, however, led to a rival 'bundle of rights' approach. This was the product of the Hohfeldian atomisation of legal 'rights'[25] applied and developed by legal realists to challenge existing notions of property and the role(s) it serves.[26] The approach breaks property down into different components or incidents, including use, exclusivity, and transferability.[27] While this perspective has been dominant in the US (and in a number of other countries) for some time, recent decades have witnessed a reaction against it.[28] Henry Smith has stated 'it is the mediation of a thing that helps give property its *in rem* character – availing against persons generally' and he contends that the law of things approach is supported by law and economics analysis.[29] He has even sought to challenge the notion of bundle of rights as a theory and notes that what is still required 'is a theory of how the pieces fit together'.[30] Other recent property scholarship has sought to consider the purposes that property serves and there is a growing focus on sustainability and environmental protection.[31]

---

[25] Particularly in relation to property rights, see W N Hohfeld, 'Fundamental Legal Conceptions as Applied in Judicial Reasoning' (1916–17) 26(8) *Yale Law Journal* 710, 718ff, where there is discussion of property as a combination of rights, powers, privileges and immunities exercisable against a very wide class of persons.

[26] See e.g., T C Grey, 'The Disintegration of Property' in J R Pennock and J W Chapman (eds), *Ethics, Economics and the Law of Property* (New York University Press1980) 69; S R Munzer, *A Theory of Property* (Cambridge University Press 1990) 23; K Gray, 'Property in Thin Air' (1991) 50(2) *Cambridge Law Journal* 252. This development is discussed by J E Penner, 'The 'Bundle of Rights' Picture of Property' (1996) 43(3) *UCLA Law Review* 711, 724ff.

[27] Reference can be made to e.g. Honoré (n 20); M J Radin, 'The Liberal Conception of Property: Cross Currents in the Jurisprudence of Takings' (1988) 88(8) *Columbia Law Review* 1667.

[28] See e.g., J E Penner, *The Idea of Property in Law* (Oxford University Press 1997); T W Merrill, 'Property and the Right to Exclude' (1998) 77(4) *Nebraska Law Review* 730; Smith (n 3); S Douglas and B McFarlane, 'Defining Property Rights' in J Penner and H E Smith (eds), *Philosophical Foundations of Property Law* (Oxford University Press 2013); J E Penner, *Property Rights: A Re-Examination* (Oxford University Press 2020).

[29] Smith (n 3) 1691: 'For information-cost reasons, property is, after all, a law of things.' See also T W Merrill and H E Smith, 'Optimal Standardization in the Law of Property: The Numerus Clausus Principle' (2000) 110(1) *Yale Law Journal* 1, 8 where it is noted that standardisation of property rights reduces costs.

[30] Smith (n 3) 1709; 1725. For a defence of the bundle of rights approach, see J B Baron, 'Rescuing the Bundle-of-Rights Metaphor in Property Law' (2014) 82(1) *University of Cincinnati Law Review* 57.

[31] See below.

It is valuable to consider what viewing property law theories from the perspective of insolvency reveals and what this tells us about property itself. Any theory considering the nature or essence of property rights should give some regard to insolvency, as insolvency is often the context in which the existence of property rights (compared to mere personal rights) is most crucial. It can also, in some instances, represent a departure from 'normal' rules of property. Indeed, the way in which property is dealt with in insolvency may be considered as much an element of what property is as how it exists or functions in other contexts.

Property Rights and Personal Rights

The deconstruction and atomisation of property allows for a personalist approach to property, whereby property rights may simply be perceived as akin to personal rights but exercisable against an especially wide group of parties or as default contractual rules (in the sense that it is simply not possible for contracts to deal with all relevant situations and scenarios).[32] Yet this seems to undervalue the significance of property as a standalone concept and does not help to explain its distinctive character and the fact that various components, including its wider enforceability, serve to distinguish it from mere personal rights and require separate consideration. This is particularly true in insolvency where property rights continue to provide priorities of ranking and enforceability in relation to certain assets, as against all other parties, whereas personal rights do not. While it is true that rights (personal and real) are enforceable against other persons, the object of property is a key reference point and locus of property rights. Nevertheless, although there are often clear boundaries between personal rights and property rights, personal rights can give rise to property consequences in relation to debt enforcement and insolvency. A debtor's property can be the subject of enforcement to recoup payment and in insolvency their property may be sold off and proceeds distributed in an attempt to fulfil personal obligations to creditors. Thus, property is used to satisfy personal rights. In addition, from the perspective of the debtor's creditors, any claim the debtor has against another is an item of property (a thing/ chose in action), even though between the debtor and their claim debtor it is only a personal right.

Outside insolvency processes, a party may have many creditors and a range of obligations, but only inside insolvency is there likely to be direct competition between the creditors. An insolvency proceeding provides a forum in

---

[32] See e.g., R H Coase, 'The Problem of Social Cost' (1960) 3 *Journal of Law & Economics* 1; Bell and Parchomovsky (n 18) 535.

which such competing claims are assessed and ranked with distributions taking place accordingly. Related to this, insolvency is a testing ground for determining whether a right is a personal right or a property right. There is usually a clear delineation between the two in insolvency processes and different consequences arise dependent upon the determination. If a party has a property right, then one or more of the following applies: they are able to separate property from the insolvent estate;[33] they have the ability to independently enforce; they have special voting rights; they are unaffected (in legal terms) by the insolvency; and/or they receive a priority of distribution in comparison to those who only have personal rights. These features alone provide further support for the distinct importance of property and indicate that its essence involves a level of durability and non-disturbance that can survive the debtor entering insolvency, in a way that will often render a mere personal right ineffective or of significantly reduced utility (e.g., because its holder receives only a fraction of an amount due from the debtor). Insolvency therefore highlights the 'special' nature of property and underlines why it deserves to be considered separately from obligations.

Elements of Property

Accounts of property that seek to explain the key ingredients or elements of property must recognise insolvency's potential for shaping, or providing caveats to, or conditions for, those elements. For instance, if we consider the right to exclude to be a key or even decisive element of property,[34] it must be noted that in some insolvency processes even if the debtor retains property in a legal sense[35] they personally lose the ability to exclude, and that instead such power is exercised by an insolvency officeholder, who is acting in the interests of the creditors. The insolvency officeholder has the power to obtain possession or control of the property and may thereby exclude the debtor (as well as others), while the debtor is not able to exclude the officeholder from the property. In addition, in certain insolvency processes, the debtor can also no longer *include* and grant or transfer rights or apply their property in satisfaction of debts in the way they choose (subject to other property rights). Instead, the officeholder can grant and transfer rights, but this should only be done if it is in the interests of the creditors. While it can be contended that the insolvency

---

[33] When we refer to property in the debtor's estate, this can be conceptualised as encompassing all of a debtor's rights and powers subject to exceptions.

[34] Some writers consider it to be critical, e.g., Merrill (n 28) 731–734.

[35] In others the property may vest in an insolvency officeholder or the debtor may retain ownership and the ability to exclude.

officeholder is acting as agent of the debtor,[36] this is a form of agency in which the principal has no ability to deal with property itself and the agent is acting for the benefit of third parties, indicating that property in legal terms has been separated from its benefit or value. This all raises questions as to what is meant by property here and who holds it.

In the midst of a number of insolvency processes, the 'debtor's' property also receives special protections that do not always apply outside such a process, as other parties are not able to enforce and thereby obtain rights in the property without permission from a court or the officeholder.[37] As well as being able to transfer property to another party without the 'owner's' permission, some insolvency officeholders can disclaim onerous property.[38] A debtor will have lost the ability to transfer the property due to the insolvency process[39] and their earlier transactions may have become potentially challengeable transactions. Insolvency upholds the notion of property being formally held by the debtor (at least for a while) but disables the debtor (temporarily or permanently) in terms of dealing with the property and excluding others.

Some accounts of the elements or incidents of property give express regard to insolvency law. In his 11 standard incidents of ownership, Anthony Honoré includes liability to execution, which extends to insolvency, and involves the liability of an owner's interest to be taken away.[40] Yet liability to execution is clearly not a *necessary* element of property,[41] as various items are excluded from insolvency and execution but a debtor's interest in them is undeniably property. It can also be noted that until the property is formally transferred to another, other elements relating to ownership are compromised without the express agreement of the 'owner', such as the right to possess, the right to use, the right to manage and so on. The insolvency officeholder may exercise these and the property could be considered held on trust for the benefit of the creditors (e.g., in liquidation) but even in the strongest case there is an absence of incidents of ownership held by the creditors.[42] Can it really be said that the officeholder or creditors are 'owners' of the property, unless perhaps there is

---

36 Perhaps 'representative' is more accurate, despite the use of 'agent' in the Insolvency Act 1986.

37 The moratorium in administration is noted above. See also Insolvency Act 1986, s 130(2) (liquidation); s 285 (bankruptcy).

38 Insolvency Act 1986, s 178 (liquidator); s 315 (trustee in bankruptcy).

39 See e.g., Insolvency Act 1986, ss 127 and 284.

40 Honoré (n 21) 107.

41 Honoré himself acknowledges that none of the elements are individually necessary.

42 For discussion of the trust analysis and the status of creditors as beneficiaries, see R J Mokal, 'At the Intersection of Property and Insolvency: The Insolvent Company's Encumbered Assets' (2008) 20 (Special Edition) *Singapore Academy of Law Journal*

vesting? In any event, insolvency poses difficult questions for the notion of property.

If a debtor in an insolvency process may be considered the owner, or an owner, of property in the insolvent estate, it can support the view that property has an outer shell, which could contain various elements, but its existence does not necessarily depend on the presence of any such element(s) at a given time.[43] Once powers and rights relating to the property but held by others lapse or are exhausted, they return to the property owner. Property therefore provides that such powers/rights are reobtained, or the property interest is no longer encumbered by them. An insolvency process facilitates the transfer of property to another party, who, once they become owner, will not be burdened with various limitations faced by the debtor in the context of insolvency – incidents of property temporarily disapplied for the debtor as owner are 'restored' when another obtains the property interest.[44]

Purpose(s) of Property

Insolvency law can also help our understanding of the purpose of property and, in this regard, the extent to which insolvency law may take priority over 'normal' property rules is significant. Abraham Bell and Gideon Parchomovsky have noted that property's function 'as a device for capturing and retaining certain kinds of value–is almost completely absent from modern conceptual discussions of property'.[45] They contend that if 'defending value' is the 'overriding goal' involving property, then property 'must sometimes give way to a rule that protects value', and insolvency law can achieve this.[46] Of course, in an insolvency process, a debtor's property interest can be lost without their express consent, and other parties' property rights may be impinged upon, which may be viewed as insolvency law taking precedence over property law.[47] The preservation of value may be best served ordinarily by a party having the ability to protect their interest and having a wide array of powers in relation to an object. Upon insolvency, however, preserving the

495. The creditors are not ordinary beneficiaries as they merely have a right to receive proceeds in the relevant order of distribution.

43 There are some parallels here with the 'residuary character' incident of ownership identified by Honoré (n 21) 126–128. Honoré warns that his discussion is subject to the 'troubled waters of split ownership', which also has relevance here.

44 Likewise, if a debtor somehow manages to retain property upon exiting an insolvency process, they will no longer be subject to those same disabilities.

45 Bell and Parchomovsky (n 18) 536.

46 Ibid., 539.

47 See e.g., ibid., 608ff.

property's value becomes most important for the creditors and so protective measures intruding upon the debtor's property rights, and protecting creditors from one another as well as the actions of the debtor, may be necessary. In addition, not only does insolvency law seek to preserve value, but it must determine the allocation of the value arising from realisation of the debtor's property. It needs to provide a hierarchy for the entirety of a debtor's property (subject to some exceptions), which is unnecessary outside insolvency.

Of course, it is widely accepted that even in insolvency there is some property of which an individual debtor should not be deprived.[48] The protection of such property can be justified for the purposes of protecting human dignity, while also supporting human flourishing and future productivity. When determining the property which ought to be excluded from insolvency, the personal connection between the object and the individual may be considered an important factor. Margaret Radin draws a distinction between 'personal property' and 'fungible property', with the latter having a level of replaceability that does not apply to the former.[49] The removal of personal property, such as a wedding ring belonging to a devoted spouse, will cause distress because it is an important part of the individual's personhood or identity, and such property cannot adequately be replaced. While insolvency law does not tend to give regard to the sentimentality and personal connection that a person has in relation to a particular object,[50] it may validly be queried whether, in fact, it ought to do so to a greater extent than is currently the case.[51] For example, a war medal or a necklace that has been in a family for generations, even with a relatively low value, may have considerable personal significance to a party that will almost certainly not be true for a purchaser or indeed for creditors.[52] There is a contrast between a debtor's interest in such property and the fact that creditors do not wish to receive particular assets and instead would merely

---

48 Beyond protecting the property itself, there would of course be the potential for significant economic and social cost if the position were otherwise.

49 M J Radin, 'Property and Personhood' (1982) 34(5) *Stanford Law Review* 957, 959ff.

50 An exception is personal correspondence of a debtor, which has been held to be excluded from their estate in bankruptcy on the basis that it is 'of a nature peculiarly personal to him and his life as a human being': *Haig v Aitken* [2001] Ch 110 (Rattee J). In addition, in Scots law, in debt enforcement (diligence), an enforcing officer may not attach articles (under an exceptional attachment order), if they consider the items 'likely to be of sentimental value to the debtor' but only where the aggregate value does not exceed £150: Debt Arrangement and Attachment (Scotland) Act 2002, ss 51–52.

51 There would, however, need to be limits (monetary or otherwise), to achieve fairness for creditors.

52 Items with a low value might be uneconomical to sell and so in practice could be excluded from realisation of the estate.

like payment (thus fungible property). Consequently, there can be a transfer of property which may have significant personal value for an insolvent debtor, to a purchaser who is unlikely to have a personal connection to the property (at least initially) and for whom the property is fungible, while the proceeds distributed to creditors are also fungible.

A creditor's right to demand or receive payment of a debt, including within insolvency, can be considered as a property object and it has been suggested that this right is 'rooted in a sense of fidelity to property rights'.[53] However, while we consider that a party should ordinarily repay their debts, we may take a view that the repayment of some debts is more justifiable than others, whether because of the impact on wider society or public policy concerns.[54] In addition, the effects of insolvency law on property support the view that property rights may be limited or reformulated in the interests of a wider group,[55] whether that is creditors alone, as in insolvency, or potentially even a wider body of stakeholders. It may be contended that the importance of property rules as the default position, and the need for fairness to the owner, mean that a departure from these rules should only take place exceptionally and for highly significant policy purposes. Nevertheless, property already does give effect to community and public interests in various ways.[56]

For many progressive scholars, property's role is to serve underlying human values that are often community-focused and they consider that it should shape and reflect social relationships beyond merely being concerned with the protection of an individual's control of resources.[57] Within this field, there is a growing body of literature examining property theory through a critical lens focusing on protecting the environment and sustainability.[58] Insolvency may be considered a suitable forum in which to further similar policy goals, such

---

[53] C K Odinet, 'Of Progressive Property and Public Debt' (2016) 51(5) *Wake Forest Law Review* 1101, 1102.

[54] Ibid.

[55] It can be debated whether this involves limitation of property rights from outside property or, instead, reformulation of rights within property, taking account of wider interests.

[56] See e.g., K A Turčan, 'US Property Law: A Revised View' (2021) 45(2) *William & Mary Environmental Law & Policy Review* 319.

[57] See G S Alexander et al, 'A Statement of Progressive Property' (2009) 94(4) *Cornell Law Review* 743.

[58] For recent work, see e.g., J Fraley, 'Climate Change, Sustainability, and the Failure of Modern Property Theory' (2020) 104 *Marquette Law Review* 93; L L Butler, 'The Importance of Viewing Property as a System' (2021) 58 *San Diego Law Review* 73; B Akkermans, '(Normative) Models of Property Law. Using Van Erp's Framework to Advance Sustainable Property Law' in B Akkermans and A Berlee (eds), *Sjef-Sache – Essays in Honour of Prof mr dr JHM (Sjef) van Erp on the Occasion of his Retirement* (Eleven International Publishing 2021) 3.

as by not allowing for the disclaiming of contaminated property or by giving priority status to environmental claims in the debtor's estate. In addition, some theorists would suggest that employees or workers have special property entitlements,[59] which are often not formally realised in the legal system generally, but which insolvency law could facilitate through preferences and protections.[60]

PROPERTY IN INSOLVENCY LAW THEORY

On the basis of the above, descriptive and normative theories of insolvency ought to incorporate consideration of property and would benefit from paying regard to property theory. It must be acknowledged that much of the division within insolvency theory since the 1980s *has* revolved around the extent to which insolvency should, and does, give effect to pre-existing property entitlements (such as security rights), or whether it should, and does, allow for a departure from such entitlements in order to prefer other parties. Indeed, given the significance of property rights within legal systems, and the protected status of such rights generally, insolvency theories must justify not only the removal of property from a debtor but also why certain parties without property rights should receive priority status over those who do hold such rights.

As various theories and approaches to insolvency law are discussed elsewhere in this book, they will not be considered in detail here. Instead, property-focused aspects of some of those theories will be selectively drawn upon.

Respecting Property Entitlements

Thomas Jackson's well-known account of insolvency law in *The Logic and Limits of Bankruptcy* places particular importance on property rights.[61] One of his key points is that bankruptcy (in a wide sense of the term including corporate insolvency) should only be triggered if it is in the interests of creditors as a group, and that new entitlements in bankruptcy create incentives for certain parties to resort to it to gain advantages even where bankruptcy would not be

[59] The labour theory of property formulated by J Locke, *The Second Treatise of Government* (Awnsham Churchill 1689) §27 is influential in this area.

[60] See further below.

[61] T H Jackson, *The Logic and Limits of Bankruptcy* (Harvard University Press 1986) 1: he notes his departure from the notion that insolvency law has its own substantive goals that may require to be balanced with other areas of law, such as property law.

in the collective interest.[62] As such, pre-bankruptcy entitlements, particularly property rights, should not ordinarily be departed from. He also states that although bankruptcy law touches upon other areas of law, it is 'at its core [...] debt-collection law'.[63] Bankruptcy is considered a collective forum for dealing with the relative rights of 'owners' ('creditors and others with rights against a debtor's assets')[64] and gives 'protection against the destructive effects of an individual remedies system when there are not enough assets to go around'.[65] Insolvency law therefore stops parties from obtaining property rights for their own individual benefit over the debtor's property through debt enforcement. Jackson also asserts that a key question in insolvency is how to convert the ownership of assets from debtor to creditors and insolvency law is concerned with reducing conversion costs.[66]

In reality, insolvency law does pay significant regard to the sanctity of property entitlements and property serves as a default starting point, from which any departures must be forcefully justified. In the UK, for instance, even preferential claims do not give priority over fixed security, their priority status only applying against floating security, which is subordinated because of its wide-ranging scope and ability to cover all of a debtor's property, as this may leave little for other creditors. If insolvency law does not respect property entitlements, and gives priority to those without such rights, this blurs the distinction between property rights and personal rights.[67]

Overriding Property Rights

Property law's stability and certainty, and potential rigidity, may seem to favour more conservative approaches to insolvency law, such as creditors' wealth maximisation approaches. Yet given that insolvency does provide a forum to determine and rank the claims of different parties, this can open the question as to whether some parties are more deserving than others in terms

---

62 Ibid., 21. There may be some scepticism about the suggestion that a party will resort to pushing their debtor into an insolvency process to obtain a new entitlement, given that in many cases various negative consequences are likely to arise from this, including a diminution in the estate's value. However, some parties, including debtors, no doubt do use insolvency processes to obtain certain advantages: see e.g., Lindsey D Simon, 'Bankruptcy Grifters' (2022) 131(4) *Yale Law Journal* 1154.

63 Jackson (n 61) 3.

64 Jackson refers to creditors as owners in relation to the debtor's assets, which is justifiable in a broad sense, but not a strict legal sense.

65 Ibid., 20.

66 Ibid., 5.

67 See e.g., K van Zwieten, *Goode on Principles of Corporate Insolvency Law* (Sweet & Maxwell 2018) paras 2–29.

of dividing up proceeds from the realisation of the debtor's property. While security rights and other property rights continue to exist from outside the insolvency process, insolvency law does have the potential to override or to impinge upon such rights. In addition, given that the distribution can relate to the assets of the business as a whole, or a significant proportion of it, rather than just individual items, it may be contended that certain parties should have priority in relation to the overall business due to their contribution to it and its asset base. However, this can only be fulfilled through the proceeds arising from the sale of property. Related to this, it can be noted that the original justification for the prioritisation of the limited preferential claims of employees over floating charge holders, in English law, included that they had contributed to the production of the company's assets and that their relative loss would be greater if they did not rank ahead.[68] Preference rights may be considered to reflect the contributions that parties have made to the business, by reference to the whole asset base.[69] Yet if we accept that parties such as employees are deserving of a special level of priority, the current limitations on this in insolvency seem to undermine such an approach and should be revisited.[70] In a sense, insolvency collectivises property, as it can be viewed as giving all creditors an interest in the debtor's property, and therefore insolvency law must then rank their respective entitlements.[71]

Of course, a number of other writers have sought to use contractarian (and indeed Rawlsian) approaches to achieve more progressive outcomes than those supported by scholars such as Jackson, with less reverence for pre-existing property entitlements. Notably, Donald Korobkin contends that the parties behind the veil in a contractarian approach should be wider and include various different parties who would potentially be impacted by the failure of the company, such as employees and members of the wider community, as well as creditors.[72] This approach allows for favouring of such parties at the expense of those with pre-existing property entitlements, and may not even necessarily be limited to those with debts in the legal sense. Communitarian approaches

---

68 See HC Deb 10 Feb 1897, cols 70–87, regarding the Bill that became the Preferential Payments in Bankruptcy Amendment Act 1897.

69 But claims as preferential creditors for limited amounts are insufficient compensation for what employees may stand to lose if the company enters insolvency in terms of e.g., job losses, dislocation, fear and uncertainty.

70 Albeit that employees in the UK have the ability to claim unpaid wages and redundancy payments from the state: Employment Rights Act 1996, ss 166–170 and ss 182–190.

71 It may also be pointed out that the law is not necessarily determining who has the best title to the debtor's property, but who has the best claim to its value.

72 D R Korobkin, 'Contractarianism and the Normative Foundations of Bankruptcy Law' (1993) 71(3) *Texas Law Review* 541.

also involve consideration of a range of stakeholder parties and focus on disturbing property entitlements and redistribution to a significant degree.[73] These approaches can support the relegation or limitation of pre-existing property interests, to further progressive ends, such as environmental protection or safeguarding vulnerable stakeholders.[74] Additional support for these positions can be derived from the progressive theories of property law referred to above. Indeed, there are opportunities for collaboration between property and insolvency theorists in order to formulate approaches that advance mutual objectives.

Reconciling Property and Insolvency Theories?

In proposing his own contractualist model ('authentic consent model') Riz Mokal makes the point that if the goals being pursued are desirable in insolvency they ought to be pursued by the general (non-insolvency) law, unless the goals relate to circumstances peculiar to insolvency.[75] Otherwise, there can be 'arbitrary distinctions' between parties in formal insolvency processes and financially distressed companies outside these processes. Such an approach can also help to point towards a means of reconciling property and insolvency theories. Rather than merely focusing on insolvency law when trying to achieve progressive (or other) objectives, the reinterpretation or amendment of property law should also be focused on. This would blunt some of the objections about respecting pre-existing property entitlements and avoiding the incentivisation of insolvency procedures.

There are different ways in which property law could be adapted to give effect to particular policy objectives that are also of relevance in insolvency law. For instance, environmental liability could give rise to a form of high-ranking security right that would exist both outside and inside insolven-

[73] E.g., E Warren, 'Bankruptcy Policy' (1987) 54(3) *University Chicago Law Review* 775; E Warren, 'Bankruptcy Policymaking in an Imperfect World' (1993) 92(2) *Michigan Law Review* 336; K Gross, 'Taking Community Interests into Account in Bankruptcy: An Essay' (1994) 72(3) *Washington University Law Review* 1031. See also V Finch and D Milman, *Corporate Insolvency Law: Perspectives and Principles* (Oxford University Press 2017) for an excellent overview of various insolvency theories.

[74] E.g., B Mamutse and V Fogleman, 'Improving the Treatment of Environmental Claims in Insolvency' (2013) 5 *Journal of Business Law* 486; A Wardrop, 'Theorising About Insolvency Law and the Public Interest in the Context of Insolvent Utilities: An Australian Perspective' (2014) 29(3) *Banking and Finance Law Review* 435.

[75] R J Mokal, *Corporate Insolvency Law: Theory and Application* (Oxford University Press 2005) 66.

cy.[76] Such a security could be over a particular asset (or assets) or floating. Utilising this approach for more disparate groups such as employees or tort claimants is more difficult, particularly where there is no specific item(s) of property to which the claims relate. A radical overhaul of the law could, for example, provide that a company's assets are to be preserved by a trustee for the benefit of a company's stakeholders, which would help protect the interests of involuntary and non-adjusting creditors.[77] Yet such a change seems rather unlikely at the present time and would have to overcome a number of practical difficulties. It can also be contended that the issues certain parties, such as employees, have in voluntarily acquiring property rights under the current law and the problems inherent in providing these creditors with property rights automatically, mean that insolvency law is a suitable forum for addressing such unfairness. This is particularly so as the debtor's property is being (re-) allocated and priorities are being determined anyway. Furthermore, sometimes it is only in insolvency that vulnerable parties actually need special protection. Yet where the issues involved are broader and extend beyond insolvency, there may justification for utilising other areas of law, such as employment law, environmental law, and, indeed, property law, either alone or in tandem with insolvency law, to meet policy objectives.

CONCLUSION

This chapter has identified and discussed a number of aspects of the interrelationship between property and insolvency. There is certainly a significant level of circularity and mutual dependency between property and insolvency. Property is fundamental to insolvency and how it works, including with respect to management and realisation of the debtor's estate, and insolvency sets some of the parameters of property. Insolvency law and its effects raise questions for the meaning of property and need to be integrated into broader property theories. Theorists and policymakers in insolvency law would also benefit from acquiring greater familiarity with property theory and policy, as this would provide further assistance in achieving desired objectives. A more joined-up approach to property and insolvency theory would be of mutual benefit and could more effectively shape the law in both domains in future.

---

76 For some consideration of this, see e.g., C Mackie and M M Combe, 'Charges on Land for Environmental Liabilities: A Matter Of "Priority" For Scotland' (2019) 31(1) *Journal of Environmental Law* 83.

77 See e.g., Jennifer L L Gant, 'Floating Charges and Moral Hazard: Finding Fairness for Involuntary and Vulnerable Stakeholders' in J Hardman and A D J MacPherson (eds), *Floating Charges in Scotland: New Perspectives and Current Issues* (Edinburgh University Press 2022) 228, and the sources cited there.

On one view, much of insolvency law may be considered merely a branch of property law. It is a means of formally reallocating property resources and their value from one party to others. The management or control of the debtor's property may be passed to someone else, while the transfer of the debtor's property to others is facilitated, and the proceeds acquired in return (which are also property) are distributed in accordance with an order of priority, reflecting the perceived merits of different parties and their own rights in the debtor's property. Other parts of insolvency law can be viewed largely as the apparatus necessary to achieve these results. Yet while property is a fundamental component of insolvency law, insolvency does not simply involve a collection of property and how it should be allocated.[78] The increased focus on the rescue of companies in recent decades, as well as the discharge and protection of individual insolvent debtors, show that insolvency law has its own components and priorities separate from property law. In fact, given that normal rules of property sometimes give way to insolvency law, property may be viewed as subservient to insolvency in this regard. More broadly, insolvency law is also an intersection point for other areas of law such as obligations, persons, companies and actions. As with the relationship between property and insolvency, much further work can also be done to explore the relationship between these areas and insolvency law and theory.

---

[78] Related to this, Korobkin challenges the view that a company in insolvency is simply a pool of assets, stating: 'Unlike mere property, a corporation, whether in or out of bankruptcy, has potential': D R Korobkin, 'Rehabilitating Values: A Jurisprudence of Bankruptcy' (1991) 91(4) *Columbia Law Review* 717, 745. However, the suggestion that property does not have potential (at least in some hands) can be readily contested.

16. Insolvency law through the lens of psychology theories

Emilie Ghio[1]

INTRODUCTION

Over the years, the European Union (EU) has championed the creation of a European-wide body of rules in insolvency law for the benefit of the internal market and its actors. Against the integrationist objective of the EU, the harmonisation of insolvency law has been supported by the fact that:

> Insolvency matters have a strong Union dimension. An increasingly interconnected single market […] means that very few companies are purely national when aspects such as their client base, supply chain, scope of activities, investor and capital base (to mention a few) are considered.[2]
>
> Differences between domestic insolvency laws may hamper the establishment of an efficient internal market […] [T]he creation of a level playing field in these areas would lead to greater confidence in the systems of other Member States for companies, entrepreneurs and private individuals, and improve access to credit and encourage investment […] A higher degree of harmonisation in insolvency law is thus essential for a well-functioning single market.[3]

Legal harmonisation, generally, is about benefits, practicality and utility.[4] In an ideal world, in the words of Platsas, 'the legal harmonisation thesis [would be] a thesis which gives recognition to the nation-state but [would] equally posit[s]

[1] I am grateful for the insights and comments provided by Dr John Galvin (University of Warwick) on an earlier draft of this chapter.

[2] COM(2016) 723 final Proposal for a Directive of the European Parliament and of the Council on preventive restructuring frameworks, second chance and measures to increase the efficiency of restructuring, insolvency and discharge procedures and amending Directive 2012/30/EU [2016] (Proposal) 2.

[3] COM(2014) 1500 final Commission Recommendation of 12 March 2014 on a new approach to business failure and insolvency Text with EEA relevance [2014] OJ L 74/65 (Recommendation), Recital 8.

[4] For an in-depth exploration of the benefits of legal harmonisation, see e.g., G McCormack, *Secured Credit and the Harmonisation of Law: The UNCITRAL*

that national considerations subside when wider legal considerations proceed beyond the local, the domestic and the national'.[5] Therefore, '[h]armonization is a delightful notion. How could one possibly be so unsophisticated as to oppose it?'.[6]

Yet, the harmonisation of insolvency law has been slow and arduous. It took over 40 years for the first cross-border instrument to come into existence[7] and almost ten years for the Directive on Preventive Restructuring Frameworks 2019,[8] the first substantive harmonisation initiative, to be passed.

Familiar arguments explaining why the harmonisation of insolvency law in the EU has been challenging include the protection of national sovereignty,[9] path dependence,[10] the preservation of legal cultures,[11] and the superiority of regulatory competition.[12]

Experience (Edward Elgar Publishing 2011) Chapter 2; R La Porta et al, 'The Economic Consequences of Legal Origins' (2008) 46(2) *Journal of Economic Literature* 285.

[5] A Platsas, *The Harmonisation of National Legal Systems: Strategic Models and Factors* (Edward Elgar Publishing 2017) 2.

[6] S Weatherill, 'Why Object to the Harmonization of Private Law by the EC?' (2004) 12(5*) European Review of Private Law* 633, 633.

[7] Council Regulation (EC) No 1346/2000 of 29 May 2000 on insolvency proceedings [2000] OJ L 160/1 (Insolvency Regulation 2000).

[8] Directive (EU) 2019/1023 of the European Parliament and of the Council of 20 June 2019 on preventive restructuring frameworks, on discharge of debt and disqualification, and on measures to increase the efficiency of procedures concerning restructuring, insolvency and discharge of debt, and amending Directive (EU) 2017/1132 [2019] OJ L 172/18 (Restructuring Directive 2019).

[9] See e.g., G McCormack, 'International Organisations and the Search for Global Insolvency Standards' in Paul Omar and Jennifer L L Gant (eds), *Research Handbook on Corporate Restructuring* (Edward Elgar Publishing 2021). 31 *et seq*; McCormack (n 3) 30.

[10] I Lynch Fannon, 'Comparative Corporate Law Theory and Harmonisation of EU Insolvency Law: Understanding the Impact of Path Dependency' in M Veder and P Omar (eds), *Teaching and Research in International Insolvency Law: Challenges and Opportunities* (INSOL Europe 2015) 43; O Hathaway, 'Path Dependence in the Law: The Course and Pattern of Legal Change in a Common Law System' (2000) 86(2) *Iowa Law Review* 601.

[11] A Walters, 'Modified Universalisms and the Role of Local Legal Culture in the Making of Cross-border Insolvency Law' (2019) 93(1) *American Bankruptcy Law Journal* 47; P Legrand, 'European Legal Systems are Not Converging' (1996) 45(1) *International and Comparative Law Quarterly* 52; G Teubner, 'Legal Irritants: Good Faith in British Law or How Unifying Law Ends Up in New Divergencies' (1998) 61(1) *Modern Law Review* 11.

[12] H Eidenmüller, 'Free Choice in International Company Insolvency Law in Europe' (2005) 6(3) *European Business Organization Law Review* 423; A Ogus, 'Competition Between National Legal Systems: A Contribution of Economic Analysis to Comparative Law' (1999) 48(2) *International Comparative Law Quarterly* 405.

This chapter focuses on a new strand of emerging[13] scholarship: the application of psychology theories to insolvency law. Behavioural psychologists have long shown that decision-making is significantly bounded, and human actions are affected by various psychological factors.[14] In the legal world, Irit Mevorach notes that '[p]eople's preferences in making decisions systematically violate the axioms of expected utility theory as decision makers frequently deviate in predictable ways from economically optimal behaviour'.[15] Harmonisation decisions are ultimately made by people, who are susceptible to the same cognitive biases as any other individual and group making decision in other contexts.[16] This chapter discusses a number of key biases identified in decision-making, which could shed important light on harmonisation options.

This discussion is pertinent against the current Eurosceptic climate[17] triggered by a long-term polycrisis.[18] Questions about the future of the EU, its institutions, but also its policies and integration tools – such as harmonisation – lead to heated debates and generate strong conflict lines. Against this background, the 'seductive appeal of harmonisation is today tarnished [and its] role increasingly contested'.[19] Therefore, it is more important than ever for the European legislator to produce effective and efficient legislation. In the second part of this chapter, consideration will be given to the way psychological biases may affect the behaviour of Member States. The third part will consider how these biases could be overcome.

---

13 See I Mevorach, *The Future of Cross-Border Insolvency. Overcoming Biases and Closing Gaps* (Oxford University Press 2018).

14 F Parisi and V L Smith, 'Introduction' in F Parisi and V L Smith (eds), *The Law and Economics of Irrational Behaviour* (Stanford University Press 2005) 1–2.

15 Mevorach (n 13) 55.

16 However, it is noted that not all Member States will display the same biases towards harmonisation, and it is therefore difficult to predict exactly how biases operate in *all* Member States. As a result, this chapter adopts a holistic approach based on a selection of the psychological factors most influential to the decision-making of key actors.

17 See E Ghio, *Redefining Harmonisation: Lessons from EU Insolvency Law* (Edward Elgar Publishing 2022) 78 *et seq.*

18 Ibid., 75 *et seq.*

19 S Weatherill, 'Why Harmonise' in T Tridimas and P Nebbia (eds), *EU Law for the Twenty-First Century. Rethinking the New Legal Order* (Hart Publishing 2004) 31.

PSYCHOLOGICAL BIASES: LOSS AVERSION, STATUS QUO, BOUNDED WILLPOWER AND COGNITIVE DISSONANCE

Psychological biases are numerous. They range from selection bias to false consensus effect. For the purpose of this chapter, four main biases will be examined and applied to the Member States of the EU: loss aversion, status quo, bounded willpower and cognitive dissonance.

Loss aversion refers to the tendency for people to prefer avoiding losses rather than acquiring gains. It can be summarised by the popular phrase 'losses loom larger than gains'.[20] Losses are known for having a greater psychological impact than gains and are said to hurt twice as much as gains make us feel good.[21]

Status quo bias is a cognitive bias that favours decisions that maintain the current state of affairs, also known as the reference point.[22] Individuals affected by the status quo bias do not divert from established behaviours unless there is compelling evidence or incentives to change.

A reluctance to change and depart from the status quo can be exacerbated by bounded willpower, which refers to the fact that, as a result of cognitive discomfort, human beings make decisions that are not in their long-term interests.[23] This can occur when people are more focused on present concerns than future ones. Behaviours can be inconsistent with a person's best interests as people tend to discount future benefits.[24] One way in which the mind copes with the possibility of future regret is to place more value on what we have than what we do not have.[25]

The theory of cognitive dissonance argues that psychological discomfort occurs when two actions or ideas are not consistent with each other. According to this theory, discomfort arises when actions are taken that seem to conflict with the individual's starting attitude. The relationship between cognition and

---

[20] L Brenner et al., 'On the Psychology of Loss Aversion: Possession, Valence, and Reversals of the Endowment Effect' (2007) 34(3) *Journal of Consumer Research* 369.

[21] See generally D Kahneman, *Thinking, Fast and Slow* (Farrar, Straus & Giroux 2011).

[22] W Samuelson and R Zeckhauser, 'Status Quo Bias in Decision Making' (1998) 1(1) *Journal of Risk and Uncertainty* 7.

[23] D Kahneman et al., 'Anomalies: The Endowment Effect, Loss Aversion, and Status Quo Bias' (1991) 5(1) *Journal of Economic Perspectives* 193.

[24] T O'Donoghue and M Rabin, 'Doing it Now or Later' (1999) 89(1) *American Economic Review* 103.

[25] R Weaver, 'Three Essays in Decision-Making' (PhD Thesis, Massachusetts Institute of Technology 2008) https://dspace.mit.edu/handle/1721.1/44743 accessed 13 May 2023.

action can therefore be consonant (cognitions and actions are consistent) or dissonant (cognitions and actions are inconsistent). The degree of psychological discomfort is referred to as the 'magnitude of dissonance'.[26] When dissonance occurs, the psychological discomfort which arises can motivate the person to reduce the magnitude of dissonance. The tendency for people to attend to information likely to decrease the dissonance is known as confirmation bias. Confirmation bias influences how we collect, interpret and recall information, favouring the information that confirms previously held beliefs or biases. Thus, we seek out, and selectively attend to, information that confirms our prior beliefs. We interpret data and information so that they uphold our existing viewpoint; we remember information that reinforce our views and forget, or fail to attend to, information against them. As attitudes are often changed to align more closely with our actions, cognitive dissonance is an important source of attitude formation and change.[27]

KEY CHALLENGES AND TARGETING STRATEGIES FROM A PSYCHOLOGICAL PERSPECTIVE

While European harmonisation efforts have accomplished outstanding results in a previously complex and fragmented political environment, the limits of the top-down European harmonisation efforts[28] suggest that if the EU wants to pursue further harmonisation in insolvency law, it should be aware, and strategically adapt, to the challenges facing the legal harmonisation process.

Challenge 1: Speed of Change

Fundamentally, harmonising laws is about requesting Member States to implement changes within their legal systems. How, and how fast, change might be initiated is at the heart of harmonisation considerations because '[societies […] consist of webs of mutually supporting beliefs, behavioural customs, and technologies. Consequently, anyone who wants change has to overcome a massive inertia'.[29]

---

[26] L Festinger, 'Cognitive Dissonance' (1962) 207(4) *Scientific American* 93.

[27] R B Zajonc, 'Attitudinal Effects of Mere Exposure' (1968) 9(2 Pt 2) *Journal of Personalities and Social Psychology* 1.

[28] For a discussion of these limits, see E Ghio et al., 'Harmonising Insolvency Law in the EU: New Thoughts on Old Ideas in the Wake of the COVID-19 Pandemic' (2021) 30(3) *International Insolvency Review* 427.

[29] C Lindblom, 'Initiating Change: Modes of Social Inquiry' (1997) 40(3) *American Behavioral Scientist* 264.

Laws often develop incrementally.[30] This approach has been both praised and criticised, as will be discussed in the next section. Against the backdrop of psychological discussions, debates around incrementalism can be linked to the field of evolutionary biology, the discipline concerned with the origin of life and the adaptation of life forms over time. According to evolutionary biology, change can occur in two ways. First, organisms can change in a slow, incremental, fashion over long periods of time. This theory, known as incrementalism, was first put forward by Charles Darwin in his book *On the Origin of Species*.[31] Second, evolutionary change can also occur within shorter periods of rapid change, often in response to an environmental event that requires adaptation, followed by long periods of no, or very little, change. This theory, introduced by Gould and Eldredge, is known as punctuated equilibrium.[32] The incrementalism versus punctuated equilibrium debate has since been applied to a number of other fields, including psychology, with a view to exploring changes in psychological traits, tendencies, and behaviours.[33]

As far as the law is concerned, incrementalism has been championed where law reformers possess limited authority and where the subject is controversial or technical.[34] It is therefore not surprising that incrementalism has been a strategy of choice for the European institutions in insolvency law, an area which presents 'insoluble difficulties' for reaching an international agreement.[35]

---

[30] S Block-Lieb and T C Halliday, 'Incrementalism in Global Lawmaking' (2007) 32(3) *Brooklyn Journal of International Law* 851; E Ghio, 'The EU Incremental Approach to Cross-Border Insolvency Regulation: A Critical Analysis' (2017) 28(10) *International and Commercial Law Review* 369.

[31] C Darwin, *The Origin of Species* (first published 1859, Harper Collins 2011).

[32] J Gould and N Eldredge, 'Punctuated Equilibria: An Alternative to Phyletic Gradualism' in T J M Schopf (ed), *Models in Paleobiology* (Freeman, Cooper & Co 1972).

[33] S Stanley, *Macroevolution: Pattern and Process (*Freeman 1979); N Eldredge, *Reinventing Darwin: The Great Debate at the High Table of Evolutionary Theory* (Wiley 1995); A Chang, 'Punctuated Equilibrium and Linear Progression: Toward a New Understanding of Group Development' (2003) 46(1) *Academy of Management Journal* 106.

[34] Block-Lieb and Halliday (n 30) 852; P England, 'Book Review: Francis Botchway, 'International Encyclopaedia of Laws, Supplement 46: Ghana in *International Encyclopaedia of Laws: Environmental Law Volume 3*' (2005) 54(4) *International Comparative Law Quarterly* 1037, 1038, 'More sophisticated legal techniques are not necessarily the solution – realistic, feasible solutions driven by the political will of leaders, the general population and supported by the international community may offer a more incremental but ultimately more effective method of dealing with […] issues.'

[35] Block-Lieb and Halliday (n 30) 855.

The incremental approach in the field of European insolvency law dates back from the Istanbul Convention 1990.[36] Although the Convention did not come into force, its real significance was its ability to reach the stage of a final text agreed by all participants.[37] Following successive failed convention initiatives aimed at harmonising substantive insolvency law across all Member States,[38] the Istanbul Convention managed to gather the signatures of all participants – albeit not their ratification – by decreasing its scope and focusing on regulating procedural aspects of insolvency law only.[39] Despite the merits of conventions for the purpose of legal harmonisation, the EU finally opted for a regulation in 2000.[40] The Insolvency Regulation did not depart much from the status quo as it was almost identical to the Istanbul Convention. For example, both texts endorsed the linking of the main and optional territorial insolvency proceedings and provided for automatic recognition of insolvency proceedings. Commentators therefore argued that 'the EU Reg was virtually indistinguishable to the substance of the third draft convention'.[41]

The scope of European instruments harmonising insolvency law is also illustrative of the EU's incremental approach to harmonising insolvency law. None of the harmonisation instruments introduced by the EU over the years has been a full harmonisation measure. The 2012 Communication[42] and 2014 Recommendation[43] on a New European Approach to Business Failure were soft law instruments; the Insolvency Regulation 2000 and its 2015 recast version[44] are conflict-of-law instruments; and the Restructuring Directive

---

36 European Convention on Certain International Aspects of Bankruptcy, Council of Europe, Istanbul 5 June 1990, ETS No 136.

37 L S Sealy and D Milman, *Annotated Guide to the Insolvency Legislation 2022, Volume 2* (Sweet & Maxwell 2022) 85.

38 Report of the Advisory Committee on the EEC Preliminary Draft Convention on Bankruptcy, Winding-Up, Arrangements, Compositions and Similar Proceedings (1976) Cmnd 6602; Draft Convention on Insolvency Proceedings 1980, see Supplement 2/82, *Bulletin of the European Communities*; Convention on Insolvency Proceedings of 23 November 1995 (Council Document CONV/INSOL/X1).

39 For a discussion of the benefits of 'procedural incrementalism', see J Pottow's work on the UNCITRAL Model Law on Cross-Border Insolvency 1997: 'Procedural Incrementalism: A Model for International Bankruptcy' (2005) 45(4) *Virginia Journal of International Law* 935.

40 Insolvency Regulation 2000.

41 Susan Block-Lieb, 'The UK and EU Cross-Border Insolvency Recognition: From Empire to Europe to "Going It Alone"' (2017) 40(5) *Fordham International Law Journal* 1373, 1391.

42 Proposal (n 1).

43 Recommendation (n 2).

44 Regulation (EU) 2015/848 of the European Parliament and of the Council of 20 May 2015 on insolvency proceedings [2015] OJ L 141/19 (Insolvency Regulation Recast 2015).

2019 is a minimum standards instrument, focusing on a very narrow aspect of insolvency law, namely preventive restructuring.[45]

This preference for the status quo also prompted the European legislator to borrow from the templates used in previous instruments.[46] This is striking in the Insolvency Regulation Recast 2015 very few changes have been made to the structure, or even the wording, of its predecessor.[47] In fact, the entire framework of the Regulation is similar to the framework of its predecessor,[48] and several provisions are carbon copies of prior provisions contained in the Insolvency Regulation 2000.[49] The EU therefore shied away from overhauling the status quo and from departing from the reference point and it has been questioned whether the Insolvency Regulation Recast 2015 is a true reform instrument or a restatement of the status quo.[50]

Against this background, incrementalism can serve as a response to the cognitive limitations of decision-makers. First, bearing in mind Member States' tendency for inertia, harmonising measures should be drafted in a way that preserve maintenance of the status quo. Due to Member States' loss aversion and preference for the status quo, 'neither revolution, nor drastic policy change, nor even carefully planned big steps are ordinarily possible' when drafting policies or laws.[51] Instead, small, incremental steps – 'no more than muddling'[52] are to

45 On this point, see Ghio et al. (n 28) 448–450.

46 J Galbraith, 'Treaty Options: Towards a Behavioral Understanding of Treaty Design' (2013) 53(2) *Virginia Journal of International Law* 309, 359

47 Eidenmüller has described the European Insolvency Regulation Recast 2015 as a 'modest attempt to cautiously and carefully improve upon the status quo': 'A New Framework for Business Restructuring in Europe: The EU Commission's Proposals for a Reform of the European Insolvency Regulation and Beyond' (2013) European Corporate Governance Institute Law Working Paper N° 199/2013, 21.

48 On this point, see G McCormack, 'Reforming the European Insolvency Regulation: A Legal and Policy Perspective' (2014) 10(1) *Journal of Private International Law* 41, 65.

49 See e.g., Insolvency Regulation 2000, Article 4 and Insolvency Regulation Recast 2015, Art 7; Insolvency Regulation 2000 and Insolvency Regulation Recast 2015, Art 11; Insolvency Regulation 2000, Art 16 and Insolvency Regulation Recast 2015, Art 19.

50 F Mucciarelli, 'Private International Law Rules in the Insolvency Regulation Recast: A Reform or a Restatement of the Status Quo?' (2016) 13(1) *European Company and Financial Law Review* 1.

51 C Lindblom, 'Still Muddling, Not Yet Through' (1979) 39(6) *Public Administration Review* 517, 517.

52 Ibid.

be favoured. The idea behind incrementalism is that 'progress is best achieved by a series of small steps rather than by a great leap forward'[53] and that:

> [r]ather than confront states immediately with a legal regime that couples challenging goals with strong sanctions for failure to meet them, states can be gradually led toward stronger legal rules. This can be accomplished by starting with relatively weak international rules [...] that all states feel comfortable joining, but then gradually pushing states to accept successively stronger [...] requirements.[54]

In turn, this could help to circumvent obstacles such as strong national traditions and legal cultures, as well as psychological biases, because the 'repeated meeting of incremental improvements sets up expectations that its success will occur as a matter of course'.[55] This approach should help to lower policy failure and loss of Member States' support, because the European institutions only 'change from the status quo in many small and reversible steps'.[56]

However, just as European institutions should not go too far, too quickly, they should also act upon exogenous events to push the harmonisation agenda forward.

> Massive shifts in the velocity of policy occur when policy problems have been ignored during phases of stability. Moreover, institutional friction can present hurdles to policy change [...] Where more friction exists, then stability will be longer lasting. But once the momentum for change takes hold, then the punctuations will be larger.[57]

In the area of insolvency law, while law reform inertia was indeed long lasting due to the fact that insolvency law is a challenging field to harmonise across the EU, a momentum for change manifested in particular through the great

---

53 McCormack (n 48) 41.

54 O A Hathaway, 'Between Power and Principles: An Integrated Theory of International Law' (2005) 72(2) *University of Chicago Law Review* 469, 531. However, other scholars have criticised incrementalism in policy-making and have observed that European and international law-making tend to develop too slowly, following a 'two-steps forward, three steps back, three steps forward, two steps back' process leading to frustration and fragmentation of the law: Block-Lieb and Halliday (n 30) 851; J I Charney, 'Technology and International Negotiations' (1982) 76(1) *American Journal of International Law* 78, 79–80.

55 Block-Lieb and Halliday (n 30) 851.

56 J Dryzek and P Dunleavy, *Theories of the Democratic State* (Palgrave MacMillan 2009) 51.

57 D Benson, 'Patterns of EU Energy Policy Outputs: Incrementalism or Punctuated Equilibrium?' (2015) 38(1) *West European Politics* 185, 187; S Princen, 'Punctuated Equilibrium Theory and the European Union' (2013) 20(6) *Journal of European Public Policy* 854.

financial crisis of the late 2000s. Thus, external events made punctuated change possible, and the European institutions passed several harmonisation instruments in the course of a few years.

Therefore, it is argued that incrementalism can be a short-term strategy to tackle psychological resistance to change, while punctuated equilibrium is an opportunistic strategy when the legal, economic, policy or environmental conditions enable rapid change. Policy developments should thus exhibit both long-term incremental growth involving periods of relative stability, as well as interruptions by short phases of rapid changes.[58]

Challenge 2: Governance

Another key challenge in the harmonisation process is governance. The concept of 'governance' derives from economics and administrative studies and is described as a mixture of the terms 'government', 'control', 'management' and 'coordination'.[59] These elements apply to the complexity of a pluralistic entity which 'leads to a functional and territorial border-crossing in the national realm of competency'.[60] Governance is comprised of three specific elements: (i) it is a network-like structure which differs from typical forms of a nation-state top-down government; (ii) it has a transnational nature in that governance arrangements happen between nation-states and; (iii) it includes a variety of actors on various levels that are directly and indirectly involved in the governance structures.[61]

The third element of governance refers to the involvement of actors into the policy- and decision-making processes. This is commonly referred to as participation, which in turn, leads to the empowerment of actors.[62]

---

[58] F Baumgartner and J Bryan, *Agendas and Instability in American Politics* (University of Chicago Press 1993); see also F Baumgartner et al., 'Punctuated Equilibrium in French Budgeting Processes' (2006) 13(7) *Journal of European Public Policy* 1086.

[59] A Benz and N Dose, *Governance – Regieren in komplexen Regelsystemen* (VS Verlag für Sozialwissenschaften 2010) 22.

[60] P Ulrich, 'Participatory Governance in the Europe of the (Cross-Border) Regions: The Example of the European Grouping of Territorial Cooperation (EGTC)' (2016) Centre International de Formation Européenne, 2016/1 n 379, 160.

[61] P Ulrich, 'Institutionalizing (Cross-border) Citizenship on Subnational Level – The European Groupings of Territorial Cooperation (EGTC) as a New Administrative Space for Participatory and Functional Governance in Europe' (2016) 13(1) *Federal Governance* 11.

[62] Dempsey and Foreman have defined empowerment as a psychological construct which enables actors to exert maximal power: I Dempsey and P Foreman, 'Toward a Clarification of Empowerment as an Outcome of Disability Service Provision' (1997) 44(4) *International Journal of Disability Development and Education* 287.

In the psychological literature on empowerment, studies have predominantly looked at the workplace relationship between employees and their employers. In particular, studies have found that empowering employees through participation leads to increased cooperation and smoother relationships between actors.[63] Empowerment in workplace settings can therefore be defined as a 'social exchange-driven process which requires [superiors] to relinquish dependence on power and control and instead use cooperation and facilitation in relating with their subordinates'.[64] Altogether, empowerment strategies involve the transmission of power in organisations and include efforts to increase employees' participation in the decision-making process, in addition to encouraging more active participation in the whole organisation.[65]

As far as the EU is concerned, although it may be argued that Member States are not subordinates in the harmonisation process in the same way as employees are in their relationship with employers, the psychological process of empowerment can nonetheless be applied in the case of top-down harmonisation measures due to the power/control dynamics involved. The EU is a multilevel polity which encompasses different kinds of actors working on different levels, with the supranational layer as an agenda-setter and the national level as an empowered and participating layer, which are mutually interacting for decision-making and problem-solving.

Empowerment has taken place in two ways in insolvency law. The first is through participatory governance. Schmitter defines participatory governance as 'regular and guaranteed presence when making binding decisions of representatives of those collectivities that will be affected by the policy adopted'.[66] In the field of insolvency law, the EU has first relied on participatory governance when designing the Restructuring Directive 2019, which was influenced by 422 different inputs from a range of sources.[67] From March to June 2016, the European Commission released an online public consultation and more

---

[63] M Moye and A Henkin, 'Exploring Associations between Employee Empowerment and Interpersonal Trust in Managers' (2006) 25(2) *Journal of Management Development* 101.

[64] Y Chan et al., 'The Role of Subordinates' Trust in a Social Exchange Driven Psychological Empowerment Process' (2008) 20(4) *Journal of Managerial Issues* 444.

[65] W Bennis, 'Why Leaders Can't Lead' (1989) 43(4) *Training & Development Journal* 35; J A Conger, 'Leadership: The Art of Empowering Others' (1989) 3(1) *Academy of Management Executive* 17.

[66] P Schmitter, 'Participation in Governance Arrangements: Is there any Reason to Expect it will Achieve Sustainable an Innovative Policies in a Multilevel Context?' in J Grote and B Gbikpi (eds), *Participatory Governance. Political and Societal Implications* (Leske + Budrich 2002) 56.

[67] For information on working groups, see the webpage on 'Transparency' (European Commission 2019).

than 250 national stakeholders from 27 Member States sent their contributions.[68] Dedicated meetings were also organised, involving Member States' governmental experts and an informal group on debt restructuring, insolvency and second chance was created.[69] Finally, the Commission commissioned a study on national substantive insolvency laws identifying areas where differences in national laws may raise obstacles to the internal market,[70] as well as an economic study on the impact of minimum standards in restructuring and insolvency law,[71] while a conference on the convergence of insolvency frameworks within the EU was organised in July 2016. Compliance outcomes can be improved thanks to the satisfaction of endowment needs which, in turn, may increase policy acceptance. Compliance outcomes will be improved as the EU has satisfied the needs for endowment, which ultimately should encourage policy acceptance.[72]

Second, over the last two decades, a phenomenon of legal emulation has occurred amongst EU Member States. Two decades ago, liquidation was often the only option for financially distressed companies in many Member States. From the 1990s onward, European countries initiated major reforms in this area, introducing more rescue-oriented procedures. The result of these reforms is interesting. Although national insolvency regimes across the EU continue to show differences in their substance, the revisions have introduced greater similarity among the domestic policies. Some Member States have borrowed their neighbours' restructuring practices, such as the debtor-in-possession feature, the stay on enforcement actions, the priority given to fresh money providers, and cram-down provisions. There has been an 'almost feverish sense among most of European States to outdo the others in amending their laws'.[73]

---

[68] For the data and numbers, see the 'Public Consultation: Building a Capital Markets Union' (European Commission: Banking and Finance 2015) https://ec.europa.eu/finance/consultations/2015/capital-markets-union/index_en.htm accessed 13 May 2023.

[69] The main participants were BusinessEurope, AFME, EBF, ACCA, UEAPME, ESBA, Independent Retail Europe, EuroChambers, ETUC, EFIN, FEE, INSOL Europe, FDC, The Council of Bars and Law Societies of Europe, European Law Institute. The group met three times in 2016.

[70] Gerard MacCormack, Andrew R Keay, Sarah Brown, Judith Dahlgreen, *Study on a New Approach to Business Failure and Insolvency: Comparative Legal Analysis of the Member States' Relevant Provisions and Practices* Tender No JUST/2014/JCOO/PR/CIVI/0075 (European Commission DG Justice Publications Office 2015).

[71] Ibid.

[72] W D Leach and P A Sabatier, 'To Trust an Adversary: Integrating Rational and Psychological Models of Collaborative Policymaking' (2005) 99(4) *American Political Science Review* 491.

[73] C Paulus, 'A Vision of the European Insolvency Law' (2008) 17(5) *Norton Journal of Bankruptcy Law and Practice* 607, 611.

Additionally, during the recent COVID-19 crisis, in the absence of top-down harmonisation from the EU, national, state-centric initiatives resulted in significant degrees of legal alignment and, ultimately, a phenomenon of natural convergence.[74]

Participatory governance through legal emulation and convergence would support the case for further harmonisation across the EU, as it would most likely be better accepted by national governments. To accommodate diverse national policies and domestic interests, it is important that the EU acknowledges and gives weight to natural convergence stemming from the Member States' level. Rather than merely pushing for top-down harmonisation that has, arguably, failed to create a truly harmonised framework, recognising the more nuanced and multi-layered approach that allows for legal evolution and emulation within the EU could be the most promising path for future European law-making in this area. This would mean allowing Member States to directly participate in the shaping of policies through:

1. granting Member States some leeway in the formulation of their domestic insolvency and restructuring policies;
2. the sharing of best practices across Member States (facilitated by the EU institutions);
3. the codification, at the EU level, of these provisions and mechanisms which have proven efficient and innovative.[75]

Those features which prove successful end up forming a body of minimum standards that no competitor can afford to go below.[76] This process of codification leads to the elevation of domestic best practices into Union-wide standards,[77] which results in indirect participation of the Member States in the European law-making process. It allows for a strong involvement by the Member States in shaping supranational measures and reveals that the harmonisation process can happen through learning and exchange of information between the national and supranational levels. Ultimately, empowerment

[74] See Ghio (n 30) 436 *et seq.*

[75] See Ghio et al. (n 28) 447.

[76] Paulus (n 74) 611.

[77] For an example of how this process has occurred when the Restructuring Directive 2019 was created, see D Ehmke et al., 'The EU Preventive Restructuring Framework: a Hole in One?' (2019) 28(2) International Insolvency Review 184, 209; SWD(2016) 358 final Commission Staff Working Document Executive Summary of the Impact Assessment Accompanying the document Proposal for a Directive of the European Parliament and of the Council on preventive restructuring frameworks, second chance and measures to increase the efficiency of restructuring, insolvency and discharge procedures and amending Directive 2012/30/EU [2016] 55.

through either participatory governance or legal emulation, contributes to a 'Europe bottom-up.'[78]

Challenge 3: Linguistic Factors

The final challenge to be discussed is related to linguistic factors. Psycholinguistics is the scientific study of the relationships between linguistic behaviour and psychological processes.[79] Certain features of language produced (speaking or writing) will influence the processing of that information for the receiver (listening or reading). One of the most important psycholinguistic features influencing decision-making is salience.[80]

The salience bias is the finding that people are more likely to focus on the most prominent items of information and ignore those that are less so.[81] It also influences fixation order, with more salient features being fixed on earlier than those that are less obvious or perceptible. For instance, making one object salient is always done at the expense of making all other objects in the environment relatively less salient.

The salience bias is influential within decision-making[82] as it can be used to nudge individuals towards certain behaviours,[83] since the salience with which information is presented affects the extent to which individuals make use of it.[84] For example, it has been argued that:

> emphasizing the 'newness' of a harmonisation measure may not be prudent, insofar as it forces actors to confront the differences between the new rule and the psychological default. Assuming that they have been using a particular rule for a settled period of time and therefore have a favourable view of the old rule, dissonance by

[78] N Bucker, *Europe Bottom-Up: How Eastern Germans and Poles Frame the European Union* (Nomos 2012).

[79] J Field, *Psycholinguistics: The Key Concepts* (Psychology Press 2004).

[80] T F Jaeger and K Weatherholtz. 'What the Heck is Salience? How Predictive Language Processing Contributes to Sociolinguistic Perception' (2016) 7 *Frontiers in Psychology* 1115.

[81] D Kahneman et al., *Judgment Under Uncertainty: Heuristics and Biases* (Cambridge University Press 1982).

[82] P Bordalo et al., 'Salience Theory of Choice under Risk' (2012) 127(3) T*he Quarterly Journal of Economics* 1243.

[83] F Kehr, 'Feeling and Thinking: On the Role of Intuitive Processes in Shaping Decisions about Privacy' (PhD Thesis, University of St Gallen School of Management, Economics, Law, Social Sciences and Internal Affairs 2015).

[84] S Taylor, 'The Availability Bias in Social Perception and Interaction', in D Kahneman et al (eds), *Judgment under Uncertainty: Heuristics and Biases* (Cambridge University Press 1982) 192.

> confrontation will force actors to take steps to reach a state of comfort. Most can be counted on to stick to their long-held views and thus opt-out of [...] the new rule.[85]

Similarly, and more specifically, the European institutions should be aware of the receptiveness of certain words by Member States. Different words are often used interchangeably by the EU. In the English versions of the Treaty establishing the European Community (TEC), Treaty on the Functioning of the European Union (TFEU) and the Treaty on the European Union (TEU), for example, the words 'approximation', 'convergence' and 'harmonisation' are used without clear distinction or definition, each of them referring to the process of creating similar rules in fields considered essential for the integration and functioning of the internal market. However, these words do not have the same meaning and therefore, do not confer the same mandate on the European institutions. Depending upon how one defines the task, harmonisation may 'present only minimal intrusions upon national legislation, involving the identification of common approaches among existing domestic laws',[86] or it may represent a stronger encroachment on the national sovereignty of Member States.[87] The salience of some words in harmonisation measures within certain settings will therefore impact Member States' perceptions of and receptiveness toward top-down harmonisation measures.

Being attentive to linguistics by acting upon the salience bias means being mindful of the way information is presented to the Member States, particularly in legal spheres that require attitude change towards top-down legal harmonisation measures such as insolvency law.

The EU institutions should be mindful of their harmonisation rhetoric. For example, the European institutions have tasked themselves with 'harmonising'[88] the field, as well as with 'modernising'[89] rules on insolvency proceedings.

---

[85] G Low, 'The (Ir)Relevance of Harmonization and Legal Diversity to European Contract Law – A Perspective from Psychology' (2010) 38(2) *European Review of Private Law* 285, 304.

[86] S Block-Lieb and T Halliday, 'Harmonization and Modernization in UNCITRAL's Legislative Guide on Insolvency Law' (2007) 42(3) *Texas International Law Journal* 475, 476-77.

[87] For a discussion of linguistic issues around the concept of harmonisation in the EU, see Ghio (n 17) Chapter 2.

[88] Restructuring Directive 2019 (n 8) Recital 2; European Parliament Resolution of 15 November 2011 with recommendations to the Commission on insolvency proceedings in the context of EU company law (2011/2006(INI)).

[89] Proposal (n 2) 2 and 8; COM(2012) 573 final Communication from the Commission to the European Parliament, the Council, The European Economic and Social Committee and the Committee of the Regions Single Market Act II Together for new growth [2012] 11.

Based on the salience bias, it would be best to avoid the word 'modernisation' as the most salient word. The European institutions should hew to the word 'harmonisation', which can be clearly defined.[90] Indeed, while the notion of 'modernity' implies an element of progress and advancement, its paradox lies in its vacuity. It 'could mean something temporal ([...] different from something older); it could mean something comparative ([...] in comparison to [a] country which is not); or it could functional (i.e. it achieves a "modern" function hitherto missing in a legal or economic system)'.[91] Modernisation in the context of insolvency can mean several things, such as filling a gap in domestic law ('in with the new') or replacing domestic laws by a supranational standard ('out with the old').[92]

The difference between the words 'harmonisation' and 'modernisation' is thus important.

> Depending upon how one defines the task, harmonization may present only minimal intrusions upon national legislation, involving the identification of common approaches among existing domestic laws [while] with ... modernization, the global actor purports to speak authoritatively to national legislatures about both the need for and content of law. Modernization may threaten national legislatures' sovereignty more acutely than an 'in with the new' reform agenda where national law exists on a topic, but is viewed by the international community as out-of-date. This 'out with the old' method of modernization requires the international organization both to reject existing legislation and create new law.[93]

In terms of the content of the harmonisation rules, consideration should also be given to specific insolvency words such as 'rescue', 'reorganisation' and 'restructuring'. Although there may be little difference between these terms at first sight, it is interesting to note that in the UK, discussions have tended to avoid reference to words such as 'insolvent', 'insolvency' and 'bankruptcy' when describing business rehabilitation. Commentators have argued that:

> avoiding the use of such words helps to remove a stigma that might otherwise attach to those associated with the insolvent business that is likely to benefit from the regime. If it is indeed the case that a business rehabilitation regime might be shunned, despite its potential for beneficial use, on account of the terminology used, then clearly it would be desirable to avoid the off-putting terms.[94]

---

[90] For a definition of the word 'harmonisation', see Ghio (n 17) Chapter 6.

[91] Block-Lieb and Halliday (n 30) 513.

[92] Ibid.

[93] Ibid., 476–77.

[94] J L Westbrook (ed), *View of Business Insolvency Systems* (Martinus Nijhoff Publishers 2010) 124. For a discussion of the stigma around insolvency, see E Ghio and D Thomson, 'Corporate Insolvency: Why are Directors Afraid of Help? Preliminary

Finally, the European institutions should also ensure that they match their harmonisation narrative with the harmonisation instruments adopted. The wording in various instruments has not always quite matched the content of these initiatives. Inconsistencies between language and regulatory content can be spotted, first, in the Recommendation 2014, which heralded itself as introducing a 'new approach' to insolvency. While some provisions within the Recommendation were new to some Member States, even some with mature insolvency systems, the overall rhetoric of the Recommendation was rather disproportionate and did not match its content, which was merely a variation on a very familiar process, i.e., Chapter 11 of the United States Bankruptcy Code. The Recommendation mainly laid down best practices in preventive restructuring already known or in place in several Member States.[95] Another example of inconsistency in the wording can be spotted in the Insolvency Regulation Recast 2015. Although the Commission used the word 'recast' in its title, which is defined as 'to change the form of something',[96] commentators have argued that the measure was 'modest and unambitious'[97] and that the rhetoric was 'overblown and far divorced from the quite modest changes proposed in the revised Insolvency Regulation'.[98] As stated by McCormack, '[w]hile the modern tendency may be to hype everything and to herald eagerly rafts of new initiatives, this approach sows the seed of disillusionment and disappointed expectations'.[99]

Proposed Strategic Analysis

This chapter has argued that in addition to discussions around known obstacles to European legal harmonisation such as national sovereignty, legal culture and regulatory competition, psychological biases also play a role in the resistance which the harmonisation process can be met with. The chapter has provided an analysis on how to overcome some of these key challenges using psychological theory.

Study on the Stigma Associated with Corporate Insolvency' (*Chicago-Kent Law Review*, 2023) (forthcoming).

95 Ray Warner, e.g., noted that the Commission's invitation that Member States align their laws 'may have arrived a little late […] [M]ost of the EU member states already had laws incorporating major features of rescue before the Recommendation was formally issued': 'Reimagining Rescue: The View from the United States' in R Parry and P Omar (eds), *Reimagining Rescue* (INSOL Europe 2016) 177.

96 See the definition of the word 'recast' in the *Cambridge Dictionary*.

97 Eidenmüller (n 47) 150.

98 McCormack (n 48) 67.

99 Ibid.

The three strategies proposed are focused on change, governance and linguistics, themselves based on the psychological theories of incrementalism and punctuated equilibrium, empowerment and salience.

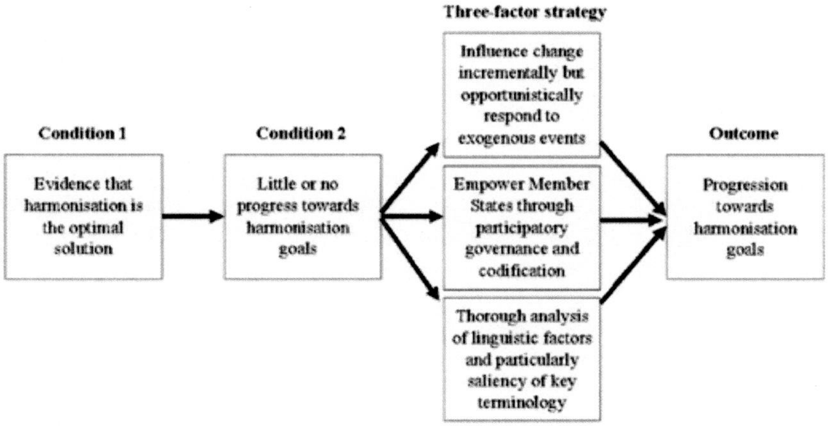

Source: Author's own depiction.

Figure 16.1 *If conditions 1 and 2 are met, then apply the three-factor strategy to achieve the outcome*

As depicted in Figure 16.1 above, first, when harmonisation is met with resistance by the Member States, the European Union should influence policy and legal change incrementally overall, while also responding to exogenous events opportunistically, with punctuated change. Second, empowered Member States are more willing to engage and comply with the harmonisation process as they directly, or indirectly, participate in the decision-making process. Successful empowerment can take several forms, but legal bottom-up codification and participatory governance are adequate governance tools leading to the empowerment of Member States. Finally, the EU should be mindful of the language and wording of its harmonisation measures, by analysing the salience of key terminology.

The above analysis could be applied to other fields of law when two conditions are met:

i. evidence shows that legal harmonisation is an optimal solution in a given field to achieve a specific objective at European level; and
ii. little or no progress towards harmonisation goals have been achieved (see Figure 16.1 above for the full strategic model).

While it is likely that these strategies apply to other areas of law which are also subject to harmonisation, more pressing challenges and therefore strategies may emerge in other fields. It would therefore be useful that further research investigates the influence that the biases studied in this chapter have on the harmonisation process in other fields of law and/or on specific Member States.

CONCLUSION

This chapter has provided a new perspective on the challenges facing European harmonisation. The literature has traditionally focused on issues of national sovereignty, legal cultures and the regulatory competition/harmonisation dichotomy but social psychology theories support a deeper understanding of bounds on decision-making and the (often unconscious) biases present in the law-making process. This chapter's findings from the field of social psychology, with its focus on psychological processes and group behaviours, provide a new perspective on how and why the challenges of legal harmonisation are difficult to overcome. Therefore, it is important that policymakers and scholars be aware of psychological biases in order to consider ways to address or circumvent them when designing or implementing harmonisation measures.[100]

This discussion around the concept and process of legal harmonisation is particularly relevant at this point in time, when globalisation seems to have lost certain of its shine and the European Union is experiencing some 'integrational panic'.[101] Indeed, the EU has been faced with a multifaceted crisis over the last decade, which culminated in the Brexit vote on 23 June 2016. This has led to a politicisation of European integration and an increase in Euroscepticism across the Member States. In this context, harmonisation initiatives are more and more contested for not respecting the diversity of the Union and domestic policies are preferred to address domestic concerns. It is therefore more important than ever for the European legislator to produce effective and efficient legislation and theoretical considerations in the law and psychology sphere can assist in this regard. When choosing amongst harmonisation options, consideration should be given to psychological biases and how they may affect the behaviour of Member States in the implementation of the chosen instrument, as well as how to best overcome them.

---

[100] L C Fentiman, 'Guilty but Mentally Ill': the Real Verdict is Guilty' (1985) 26(3) *Boston College Law Review* 601 (n 63) (quoting Professor Ernest Roberts).

[101] M Davis Cross and X Ma, 'EU Crises and Integrational Panic: the Role of the Media' (2015) 22(8) *Journal of European Public Policy* 1053, 1056.

17. Concluding remarks: new ways to theorise about insolvency and rescue

Jennifer L. L. Gant, Emilie Ghio and John M. Wood

Theory has often been an *ex post* development in the area of insolvency law, deliberated upon and extrapolated against pre-existing approaches and procedures. Insolvency law has changed with socio-political and economic shifts in culture while theory has arguably become stagnant, failing to keep pace with changes in policy and the law, and continuing an approach that aims to explain the law after, and as, it is being used, rather than creating frameworks that could be relied upon to instigate and implement reform that responds to social and economic policy and the shifts in culture that continues to gain pace.

This volume has provided an opportunity for eminent academics from a variety of perspectives and jurisdictions to provide a new approach to theorising about insolvency law that could pave the way for an *ex ante* development of theories which, it is hoped, will promote further developments in this area that will better serve the needs of companies, their stakeholders, and society at large.

HISTORICAL, MORAL, PHILOSOPHICAL INFLUENCES

In Part I of this book, the philosophical influences on insolvency law were examined from a modern perspective.

Law and Morality in Insolvency

The laws we create as a society are an accretion of the choices that we make which are of course influenced by the moral, political, and social preferences of the day. These preferences can easily become embedded and create path dependent forces that delineate a jurisdiction's legal characteristics and culture. From a global insolvency law perspective, the starting point must be the historic and moral nature of debt in society, as Paul Omar discusses in his chapter of this volume. Debt introduces inequality to a relationship that should otherwise be on an equal footing. The need to repay is related to the need or desire to redress the inequality in the relationship. That inequality also historically has given rise to a stigmatisation of the debtor resulting in a punitive approach to debt resolution, which is later reflected in the chapter authored by John Tribe.

Omar notes that the personal and moral nature of debt has been considered and dealt with in different ways in two particular cultural contexts: the three Abrahamic religions and the Roman framework. The former tempers indebtedness by limiting it to seven years, whether that is the duration of the debt itself or a period of debt bondage. There is also an emphasis on being charitable to the debtor (or the poor) which is present in all of the religious texts of the three Abrahamic religions. Debt discharge and debtor-friendly insolvency systems are undoubtedly influenced by these cultural characteristics. However, the Roman approach was entirely opposed and, arguably, a clear creditor-friendly approach. Indebtedness attracted, instead, an obligatory response from authority which often carried an extremely punitive outcome ranging from physical slavery, dismemberment and later a more commercially oriented 'civil death'.

The potential for discharge is a recent invention, historically speaking. The stigma remains associated with debt and insolvency, and given its long history based in morality and religion, it continues to be difficult to dislodge. However, the influence of the Abrahamic religions is also present in medieval times, which did provide some elements of relief in certain circumstances, thus the two approaches merge, which largely reflects the systems in place today – a mix of creditor- and debtor- friendly provisions and procedures. There also remains a requirement of trust and confidence, echoing the morality aspect of debt present in both of these approaches. Given the current shifts in theoretical approaches, for which this volume provides a snapshot, understanding the historical and moral underpinnings of debt and debt resolution provides a point of reference for future reform.

Reflections on the Liberalisation of Bankruptcy Law

Following on from Paul Omar's exploration of historical morality and insolvency, David Milman interrogates the liberalisation of bankruptcy law over time by seeking to demonstrate why there is a recurrent tendency in the evolution of English bankruptcy law to be liberal and whether the process of liberalisation has finished or is on-going. Acknowledging that although legislating on bankruptcy law includes a close connection between theory policy and practice, that link is not always easily seen or defined. By acknowledging influences beyond judicial precedent to include theory and policy, it is possible to permit a softer approach to the adjudication of bankruptcy or insolvency – a more liberal approach, as it were.

Milman, like Omar, concedes to the influence of religion and morality on the development of bankruptcy systems over time as well as the liberal approach taken by Abrahamic religions. The importance of kindness toward debtors is equally present in Judaism, Hinduism, and Buddhism, in one way or another. These approaches can be seen as being at odds with our largely capitalist society, with communists and socialists seeing debt as a way of oppressing the masses. However, the nineteenth century, as exemplified in literature by Dickens, was a pivotal moment in the liberalisation of bankruptcy and views of indebtedness despite the competing Victorian values that contractual obligations should be met. This question continues to challenge the balance between the honest debtor and the creditor who is legitimately owed money under a contract.

The further liberalisation of bankruptcy law and debt relief options is arguably continuing despite the entrenched conservatism since 2010. There has been a growing acceptance of the need to consider the socio-economic context of debt and provide alternatives to draconian insolvency procedures, such as debt restructuring options, moratoria, and the opportunity for debt discharge. These changes are policy led and demonstrate a clear liberalisation in this area, focused on providing a kinder and more understanding approach to debt resolution. However, a balanced approach is still needed in order to ensure that by catering to the vagaries of life and economic uncertainty, liberal policies and rules relating to debt resolution and discharge do not deter lending in general.

Insolvency Theory and the Legal Feminist Movement

Milman, in the previous chapter, noted that aspects of liberalisation can be demonstrated in the extension of autonomy in financial matters to women in 1935. Lezelle Jacobs takes a large leap forward to discuss insolvency law in the context of the legal feminist movement. By its very nature, the feminist approach to law, theory, and jurisprudence is not static. It changes and adapts to the shifts in society and legal culture in order to best accommodate the needs of the day. Insolvency law, however, has historically been, by its nature, framed in terms of categorisation and hierarchies of rights and obligation. This 'masculist' approach is diametrically opposed to the feminist approach, which eschews concrete categorisation. In addition, the feminist approach would also adopt compassion and connection as important considerations in legal development generally. This is contrary to the basic premise of insolvency law's core principles of creditor wealth maximisation, which continues to be the primary guiding principle in its fundamental aims in most jurisdictions.

Extending the feminist approach to insolvency law frameworks and theory, most traditional approaches such as the creditors' bargain (discussed in detail by Jason Harris) and other approaches that adopt a contractarian view, including those of a proceduralist persuasion, tend toward categorisation and fragmentation of stakeholders, assets, rights, and entitlements. However, not all contractarian approaches are absolute in their masculist character. The team production theory is predicated on a *social* contract that recognises that a company's success relies on a vast array of stakeholders, all of whom are affected by an insolvency, but not all of whom will be creditors in the traditional contractual sense. Communitarianism takes this a step further and extends to include the community at large, which is also affected by a company's insolvency.

The underpinning feature of a more feminist approach to insolvency theory is remembering that humans are the bedrock of the body corporate and that depersonalisation of the company loses sight of the purpose of the corporate form: to serve the humanity for which it was created. Jacobs, in her inimitable style, introduced a new theoretical approach, the Enlightened Creditor Value Approach, which aims to strike a balance between the competing interests of the different stakeholders, ultimately to benefit creditors. This approach combines both masculist hierarchical approaches and feminist connectivity and compassion acknowledging that not all stakeholders affected will have the same power in the process. Such an approach would be able to adapt more effectively to the changing social needs of the world, including sudden shocks such as the Coronavirus Pandemic of 2020–21 and issues associated with the cost of living crisis at the time of writing.

A Dworkinian Approach to the Priority of Tax in Insolvency

While Jacobs explored fairness and equality within insolvency law frameworks from a feminist perspective geared towards shifting perspectives towards connection and compassion, Catherine Brown and Colin Anderson explore the fairness of priorities generally and in particular in relation to a specific stakeholder, which has clear broader social implications: the national tax authority. Tax will of course impact essentially every corporate insolvency as it is one of those universal certainties. Brown and Anderson approach the question of fairness in the taxation priority shared by many international jurisdictions through Ronald Dworkin's equality theories as a potential cohesive and unifying policy approach toward future law reform.

Although a shallow consideration of the national taxation authorities' rights in insolvency might instigate a knee-jerk response challenging the fairness of priority for debts owed to the state, the question is far more complex if one considers the existential quality of those debts. Where taxes are not collected from one place, the money will have to come from somewhere and will therefore have a potential impact on other taxpayers. Does this mean that tax should be accorded a priority in repayment given the potential social impact and the fact that it is technically an involuntary creditor? Or is the standard *pari passu* adequate to ensure equality, simplicity and certainty in insolvency and taxation?

Brown and Anderson argue that Ronald Dworkin's equality theories should provide a cohesive and unifying approach through which tax debts can be considered and treated during the financial distress of a corporation. The question is how to balance the conflicting views of the tax authority, given its statutory position, legislative power, and overall resilience in an insolvency compared to other involuntary creditors against the position of other involuntary creditors, such as employees, who tend to be undiversified, unlike the taxation authority as their debtors are legion. With two competing principles to resolve issues relating to priority of tax authorities (*pari passu* and public policy arguments relating to revenue retention and moral obligation to pay taxes), the authors find a normative conflict between justice or fairness and communitarian values. However, in applying Dworkinian principles, the authors conclude that any departure from *pari passu* should be guided by the preferences of participants within the insolvency process. Although communitarian values are clearly connected to taxation matters, these are external factors that should be disregarded, according to the authors, in favour of adhering to the purpose for which the legislation has been drafted, retaining certainty in the process in the absence of legislative intervention to adjust the principles underlying that process.

A Nietzchean Approach to Debt and Human Thought

John Tribe takes us on a philosophical and historical tour through the relationship between the human psyche, in particular guilt, and the debtor-creditor relationship. This chapter explores another moralistic aspect of debt and insolvency, broadening out the discussion of the moral obligations to pay tax in Brown and Anderson, to the deep underlying impulse of human beings to achieve equality of power between each other. Although there have been many discussions about moral aspects of debt repayment and fairness in insolvency, this theoretical discussion draws from psychology and philosophy to explore and explain fundamental connections between debt and the human condition.

Nietzche begins with pre-history with a hypothesis that this is logically where human beings first began to seek balance – equivalencies between injury and compensation. Whereas pre-history may have very much meant injury was essentially physical in one way or another, this need for equivalence feeds into the modern views of debt and credit. It is also within this human need for balance that such imbalances took on a moral, spiritual, or faith-based aspect. These aspects are evident in the early treatments for debtors and bankrupts through physical punishment and severe civil sanctions. However, as Tribe and other authors acknowledge, the assessment of our pre-historical ancestors on this topic is conjectural history and although modern authors, such as David Graeber, have approached this topic scientifically, it remains an essentially unknowable past, although there are certainly logical connections between the assumptions made about the past and the present state of affairs.

Nietzsche's interrogation of legal texts ranging from commentary by eminent legal minds at the time, such as Sir Henry Maine and Josef Kohler as well as his study of ancient, Roman, and Medieval law were fundamental to his exploration of the relationship between debt and guilt. This is related to the moral obligation to keep promises – to honour debts. Where one fails to do so, there must be guilt because of the dishonour of failing to keep that promise. For Nietzsche, and indeed for many modern insolvency theorists, the debtor-creditor relationship offers a commentary on the human condition. It explains why those in debt often suffer from anxiety and stress with an accompanying relief when that debt has been paid or discharged. With these concepts in mind, it becomes all the more clear why it is important to examine insolvency law and theory within the context of the human influence and impact of debt and guilt.

A Rawlsian Approach to Preventive Restructuring

The subsequent chapter takes a fairness approach. Building on the need for moral balance in Tribe's discussion, Stathis Potamitis and Xenophon Paparrigopoulos examine the modern concept of preventive restructuring as introduced legislatively through the EU Preventive Restructuring Directive in 2019, and how a Rawlsian approach to justice and fairness may assist jurisdictions in achieving a fair implementation of its provisions. Rawls' classic approach to justice from his *Theory of Justice* is derived from a hypothetical original agreement among equal individuals operating in their own self-interest from behind a 'veil of ignorance'. Behind this veil, the principles of justice are chosen upon which an ostensibly fair society can be built. This hypothetical bargaining is of course not unknown within insolvency theory, given that the creditors' bargain itself is very much a similar approach.

Although an *ex ante* agreement of the Rawlsian or creditors' bargain sort is impossible in practice, the law has been used to create procedures globally that attempt to permit a *post facto* agreement among stakeholders of a company in financial distress. The nature of these frameworks will depend on a jurisdiction's perspective of fairness and equality/equity and how these should be considered when it comes to bargaining in the shadow of insolvency. The authors aim this perspective at the new Restructuring Directive insofar as it creates negotiating conditions like an *ex ante* bargain, setting conditions for a fair and efficient response to the insolvency threat, while maximising outcomes for the least privileged stakeholders.

The Restructuring Directive could be seen to apply Rawls' 'difference principle' insofar as it tries to ensure that sacrifices imposed on weaker parties are proportionate to the benefit obtained by the same group. It derogates from corporate law rules in order to protect the more vulnerable parties. The authors acknowledge that although the binding of dissenting creditors to a plan may be controversial, the Directive is set up in such a way that fairness and equal treatment of all classes of creditors, inclusive negotiations towards a restructuring agreement, the preference towards unanimity, combined with the availability of majoritarian solutions as well as the protective treatment of all stakeholders, are also important aspects which aim, beyond efficiency, to fairness and equal treatment. The authors conclude that the Rawlsian theory finds direct application to a situation where the interests of creditors, shareholders and other stakeholders are in conflict, by the application of a restructuring solution with the main features introduced by the Restructuring Directive.

PART II: AN INWARD-LOOKING STUDY OF INSOLVENCY LAW

The second part of this volume explored insolvency law from an inward-looking approach, examining theories which have emerged from within the field of insolvency law over the years.

Decision Theory and Insolvency Law

John Wood begins the second part of this volume with an exploration of decision theory and its presence within judicial and professional approaches to the application of insolvency law frameworks. Insolvency and restructuring require decisions to be made by a wide range of stakeholders. The law is set up to facilitate flexibility and discretion, so expertise and interpretation is necessary in order to construct the best possible outcome for individual insolvency or restructuring matters, whether that is by the debtor, practitioners, or the judiciary. However, the shift toward corporate rescue has brought new questions and challenges as to the decision-making that takes place under such circumstances, leading the author to as firstly how theories have choice have influenced decision-making and secondly, and perhaps more importantly, whether because there is a desirability to achieve certain outcomes there has been a relaxation of rationality in order to achieve the objectives of corporate rescue.

Classical decision theory relies on a rational model that seeks to explain how decisions can be made in order to achieve a desired outcome, which is done through interdisciplinary rationalisation to achieve the greatest advantage in an uncertain environment. Despite its broad interdisciplinarity, decision theory is fundamentally concerned with human behaviour and judgement. Through the lens of decision theory, Wood considers procedures within corporate rescue frameworks to illustrate how failure and rescue are assessed and resolved by its human actors. The wide discretions available to practitioners and judges can, however, lead to deviations from expected norms.

Establishing the purpose of rescue requires outcomes and trade-offs to be assessed, which means decisions are rationalised on what produces a favourable result given an uncertain environment. The decisions that can be made by the various actors within a corporate rescue process are numerous and varied, demonstrating a perhaps less than rational approach based on the individual biases associated with each case, which can lead to uncertainty when subsequent decisions on similar facts do not necessarily align, regardless of the pragmatism employed when arriving at decisions. The inherent flexibility in insolvency and rescue – which is needed in order to meet the variety of needs of different companies and stakeholders – and the discretion of human actors to exercise their decision-making within that flexibility, means that today it is not always easy to rationalise decisions made with prior cases. Although difficult to rationalise, Wood submits that such decisions are not in and of themselves irrational, particularly when rescue is the goal.

Competing Goals Theory and Insolvency Law

Like Wood, Jason Harris also discusses how to best determine the goals of insolvency law and their beneficiaries. He examines this question from the context of competing goals theory. On the face of it, there is clear conflict internal to corporate insolvency (and rescue) when we consider the competing interests of the many stakeholders affected, whether they are contractual or not – whether they are public or private in nature. Harris examines the debate around the importance that should be given to creditors (secured or otherwise) in modern insolvency law frameworks. Beginning with Jackson's Creditors' Bargain Theory, which reflects many Rawlsian attributes as discussed in Chapter 7, such as the hypothetical bargain agreed behind a veil of ignorance. The difference is who has been invited to the bargaining table. In the case of the creditors' bargain, the clue is in the title, and will traditionally only extend to actual contractual creditors, rather than those of an involuntary nature.

The creditors' bargain, however, cannot easily justify corporate rescue as a goal of insolvency as to do so contradicts the connection between resolution and pre-contractual entitlements. As rescue regimes will generally include involuntary creditors such as employees and accord them some level of preference or priority, they are antithetical to the norms of the creditors' bargain.

In addition, practitioners also will be doing more than simply satisfying the private bargains of parties. They will also be fulfilling certain public interest goals that often will contribute little to the objective of creditor wealth maximisation.

Harris argues that insolvency law should not be seen as fitting squarely within the realm of private law because in most insolvency cases, there are no returns to creditors and the majority of insolvency procedures serve a broader public interest rather than supporting economic returns to creditors. Insolvency law is not a collective extension of debtor/creditor enforcement law, but rather serves a variety of public interest goals that are pursued using public law tools operating through administrative processes that are either state controlled or exhibit extensive state intervention. Put simply, the Creditors Bargain Model is an inadequate theoretical justification for modern insolvency law because insolvency law is no longer focused solely on creditor interests. Rather, the shift to corporate rescue and the socio-economic issues that it aims to address calls for something far more flexible. This aligns well with all of the discussions preceding this chapter, acknowledging that modern insolvency law is not just about achieving maximum distributions to contractual creditors anymore.

Successor Liability Theory and Insolvency Law

Successor liability law seeks to balance the need for finality in the conclusion of business transactions with the policy of allowing injured parties to seek redress. The doctrine allows a court to hold a purchaser of a business liable for the seller's liabilities or tortious conduct. Laura Coordes considers successor liability theory within the context of insolvency law frameworks and the tension this causes with the concept of a 'fresh start' for a debtor in the American system. The 'fresh start' that forms such an important part of American bankruptcy law is difficult to achieve if parties are able to bring claims against the debtor's successor for conduct of the debtor prior to bankruptcy and, indeed, it has been held on many occasions that the Bankruptcy Code itself pre-empts these rights. Coordes challenges the value of the successor liability doctrine and its relevance in terms of its functionality within reorganisation processes in satisfying its claimants within that set of circumstances as well as the frustration it can cause to a reorganisation process.

Sales under Section 363 of the US bankruptcy code have been interpreted by some American judges as circumventing successor liability claims despite the fact that the code is not clear. The Code provides that a Chapter 11 plan can be confirmed free and clear from claims and interests of creditors, which has been interpreted or extended to include successor liability claims. However, not all courts have agreed on the extent of the definition of 'interest' which is not defined in the code. It is perhaps not surprising then that there is controversy around this position, particularly given the involuntary position of claimants in this area, who will often be tort claimants that have suffered damage due to the actions of the company. To date, American judges have been reluctant to put a limit on the definition of interests, keeping flexibility in their interpretation, which has been used to benefit tort victims in some cases while throwing them to the wolves in others.

Coordes concludes by questioning the place of bankruptcy as a means of resolving mass tort liability, which is clearly not a fundamental purpose of insolvency law generally and raises any number of ethical questions. If bankruptcy, at least in the US context, is being used to circumvent liabilities to vulnerable stakeholders who have been adversely affected by the actions of a company, Coordes asks if it is not then perhaps time to reconsider not only successor liability within bankruptcy, but the true role of bankruptcy law as well. Coordes raises an important ethical question that is reflected in a number of the previous chapters relating to the extent to which insolvency and restructuring frameworks are constructed and used in a way that is fair to those they affect.

Vulnerability Theory and Insolvency Law

Coordes touches on certain ethical issues subtly in her chapter that relate to claimants or involuntary creditors who are affected by the financial distress of a company. Tort victims, like environmental claimants and to a lesser extent, employees, have no choice in their involvement in the company. In addition, there is a higher level of vulnerability that can be ascribed to their position in an insolvency. Employees, for example, are less capable of recovering from the loss of their job and livelihood as (usually) undiversified creditors than are secured or even unsecured creditors who will likely have a number of contracts that they can rely on for income. Adopting a stakeholder approach to insolvency that goes beyond traditional stakeholder theories, Jennifer Gant applies an approach to fairness that adopts vulnerability and resilience to explain the need for greater care in insolvency and restructuring frameworks when coordinating solutions that affect involuntary and non-adjusting stakeholders.

Moving beyond traditional stakeholder theory paradigms, Gant questions the internal mechanism that measures and applies fairness in insolvency and restructuring frameworks. Starting from a point of view that draws the reader's attention back to the purpose of the company as a tool for humanity to utilise to serve its needs, she encourages a shift that considers the social obligations owed between human beings, which should include how businesses are run and how their financial distress is resolved to the benefit of the human beings that they should serve. However, Gant acknowledges the tendency toward greed and recommends Martha Fineman's vulnerability theory as a means of creating measures to encourage a more humane approach to resolving financial distress.

Stakeholder resilience as a measure of introducing greater fairness in the resolution of corporate financial distress is a socio-legal perspective on a complex problem with many competing points of view. A fundamental premise of feminism, previously discussed by Jacobs, and from which vulnerability theory is derived, is the concept that equality of treatment does not always lead to equitable treatment. Turning to equity, an approach that embraces vulnerability could create a progressive paradigm shift that introduces ethical considerations into insolvency and rescue that could naturally include non-adjusting and involuntary creditors, beyond employees who are often already preferred in some way. This approach could provide a platform for tort claimants and environmental claims and other stakeholders who would otherwise have no say in the internal processes associated with insolvency and rescue. Such an approach would fill a gap in the traditionalist ideals of Warren to develop a functional mechanism that could be used to test and apply fairness to all stakeholder affected by the financial distress of a company, placing humans back at the centre of the corporate entity.

PART III: EXTERNAL LOOKING INVESTIGATION OF INSOLVENCY LAW

The last part adopted an outward-looking perspective, guided by the belief that external elements, including other legal fields, can enhance our understanding of insolvency law.

Insolvency Law Through the Lens of Human Rights Theories

While Gant takes a magnifying glass to how fairness is assessed and applied within insolvency frameworks and challenges the paradigm, Eugenio Vaccari and Tara Van Ho build on the concept of vulnerability drawing from international human rights law and business human rights. Reflecting the equality versus equity argument discussed by Gant, Vaccari and Van Ho provide a discussion predicated on human rights matters, which has an inherently equitable foundation. For decades, law and economics ideals have underpinned insolvency law and theory based on the assumption that humans are rational and will choose a course of action that promotes their self-interest, which in insolvency frameworks would inevitably reflect efficiency and equality. Vaccari and Van Ho take a shot over the bow of these classic paradigms, in particular the fallacy of society's desire for equality while what it actually needs is equity.

Equity means celebrating differences. Equity means taking differences into account so that everyone has a chance to succeed. Equity means recognising that Joe is not the same as Jack. That Brembo is not Faurecia. That Airbus is not Boeing, even if they are all unsecured creditors of Monarch Airlines. In their seminal piece on the nature of bankruptcy, Jackson and Scott rightly argued that pre-insolvency entitlements should remain unimpaired. The issue with their theoretical approach – and much of the theoretical debate that followed – has been an attempt to collectivise people's (and companies') thinking. We are unique. We are different. Insolvency should celebrate differences rather than promote collective values for a questionable common good.

Vaccari and Van Ho investigate how a true, individualist-maximiser and difference-enhancer insolvency system would look like by analysing the treatment of selected creditors, not categories of them, reflecting a feminist approach similar to Jacobs. The main argument is that a business and human rights approach to insolvency suggests that collective (but not collectivist) procedures could not, and ought not, depart from the individual pre-bankruptcy entitlements negotiated by the parties in solvent times. While there is a presumption that parties freely and individually negotiated such entitlements to their best interest, this presumption is rebuttable and arguably a fallacy in many cases. Departures from this basic premise are possible and necessary for the purpose of promoting equity rather than equality. This should happen when it is demonstrated that parties have not taken differences in stakeholder resilience into account in their negotiations, with the result that not everyone was given a truly fair and equitable (rather than egalitarian) chance to succeed.

Insolvency Law Through the Lens of Company Law Theories

Company law and insolvency law are inextricably linked and although company law is considered an autonomous, discrete, universal subject of law, it is rather predicated upon a number of descriptive and doctrinal factors. Jonathan Hardman takes a hard look at insolvency law through important principles of company law: separate legal personality, limited liability, and the corporate purpose.

Separate legal personality is, of course, one of the most foundational features of company law. A recurring debate in corporate law is from whence the company obtains its separate legal personality. Does it arise by way of private arrangement, or as a gift from the state? Hardman explores what is meant by separate legal personality, and argues that the core, irreducible part of separate legal personality arises on insolvency: the partition of the corporate fund from the assets of, and claims of the creditors of, the shareholders. As such, separate legal personality is mostly relevant, and is conceptually predicated, upon insolvency because it is only at that time that the protection really matters and comes into play. Limited liability is also a function of insolvency law, rather than company law. Evidence for this proposition can be seen from the source of limited liability (in the Insolvency Act 1986), and a counterfactual exploration of shareholder unlimited liability. Here, the question is the timing of any potential shareholder liability, and the answer from most theorists is upon financial difficulty – that is, the insolvency of the company. Without insolvency, and insolvency law, limited liability reduces in theoretical importance.

Finally, Hardman explores the corporate purpose. It is frequently argued that the corporate purpose is shareholder wealth maximisation, until corporate financial difficulty, at which point the purpose 'flips' to be that of the creditors. Hardman argues that the 'flip' should be seen as a return of powers to its correct and natural home, rather than a peculiar exception driven by insolvency. As such, insolvency features provide a core insight into the correct operation of corporate law theory. By reviewing these features this way, Hardman challenges orthodox company law theories and argues that, ultimately, insolvency (and avoiding it) is what the law cares about in a corporate context. As such, rather than thinking of insolvency as the exception to corporate law, we should consider insolvency as the basis for corporate law, with solvent companies providing the theoretical outlier. With these shifts in perspective in mind, it drives home the point that insolvency and debt are core issues in life and in the law. Company and commercial law are constructed around how to protect shareholders and creditors from insolvency at various points on the corporate life cycle.

Insolvency Through the Lens of a Contract Theory of Restructuring

Retaining an external view of insolvency through the perspective of theory, Stephan Madaus follows by considering modern restructuring, which has become prevalent in the past decade in particular, through a consideration of contract theory. As previously noted, the best-known insolvency law theories have struggled to provide a normative basis for restructuring within insolvency frameworks, as acknowledged by Harris. As theories such as the creditors' bargain and even the more flexible and socially oriented theories of Korobkin and Warren cannot seem to accommodate all of the various outcomes of a corporate restructuring comfortably, Madaus suggests that it may be preferable to make a clear distinction between insolvency law and restructuring. This would allow for separate goals and purposes underpinned by their own theories that will not consistently conflict.

Although restructuring proceedings conceived within an insolvency procedure would fit well within a discussion of insolvency proceedings, the same cannot be said for *preventive* restructuring procedures. Madaus argues that it may not be possible to understand such proceedings in the same way, and therefore be included in frameworks of insolvency and cross-border insolvency, perhaps requiring different mechanisms of enforcement. As court proceedings, preventive restructuring within the aegis of the EU Preventive Restructuring Directive relate to insolvency law insofar as they aim to prevent the need to use conventional insolvency procedures. However, they are fundamentally different.

Madaus argues that workouts are restructurings just like preventive restructuring plans or insolvency plans and that they all form a distinct set of legal instruments governed by a special area of law: restructuring law. Doctrinally, these instruments originate from contract law. The separation of restructuring and insolvency law allows a better understanding of the relationship between them. Madaus further argues that this relationship should be understood as a partial overlap. This approach is able to explain why the state of solvency or insolvency is less relevant with respect to the purpose and functioning of restructuring law while it remains a key threshold for the application of the full range of insolvency law tools. The overlap idea also enables a differentiated application of frameworks designed for insolvency law tools to restructuring proceedings and their effects. Madaus' innovative thinking in this chapter provides an excellent view on the shift that has occurred in the resolution of financial distress over the last several decades and suggests a logical means by which legislation and commentary can come to an agreement that will not be continually fraught with semantic challenges.

Insolvency Law Through the Lens of Property Law Theories

Insolvency is arguably all about property and Alisdair MacPherson provides a property lawyer's and academic's perspective on the integration and relationship between these two important areas of law. This view offers a fresh insight that facilitates a greater understanding of the law and underpinning theories, providing fuel to challenge these theories, and identifying ways in which they can be changed to better accommodate the modern realities of insolvency and property law. Insofar as these ideas intersect with concepts discussed previously in this volume, it should be remembered that the right to property has historically been one of the foundational rights that play out within human rights. Thus, the treatment of property is equally important when one considers how external theories help to inform progressive approaches to insolvency and restructuring law.

The resolution of financial distress through insolvency and restructuring involves many property issues, such as ascertaining the assets within the insolvent debtor's estate; determining the property rights that various parties hold in those assets; and regulating the use and realisation of the insolvent party's property. Insolvency law is also relevant to property law insofar as it offers a 'litmus test' for distinguishing property rights (rights *in rem*) from mere personal rights (rights *in personam*). There is thus mutual dependency between property law and insolvency law. Despite this, the significance of insolvency is frequently neglected in property theory and, similarly, property theory is often overlooked in the context of insolvency theory.

MacPherson demonstrates that insolvency plays a defining role in property law and should therefore also be more integrated into formulations of property theory. Insolvency and its relationship with property are used to examine and challenge existing theories regarding the nature of property rights and to explore how theories focused on the purpose(s) of property could be applied in the insolvency context. In turn, MacPherson considers the extent to which insolvency theories adequately incorporate property and property theory. He highlights that some theories are more respectful of property rights than others (with the latter being more likely to allow for such rights to be overridden), but that many approaches to insolvency law would benefit from drawing upon property theory in order to achieve their key objectives. A more joined-up approach to property and insolvency theory would be of mutual benefit and could more effectively shape both areas of law in the future to the overall benefit of humanity. Given that insolvency law is increasingly aiming to promote financial distress resolution that provides wider benefit to stakeholders including the survival of viable business enterprises, a more cohesive approach among the intersecting areas of law could only be a good thing.

Insolvency Law Through the Lens of Psychology Theories

Emilie Ghio completes the third part and this volume, which imparts significant updates to insolvency and restructuring law theory, by examining insolvency law from the perspective of psychological theories and the impact of human decision-making on the progress of harmonisation in Europe. This approach logically follows early chapters discussing the historical, moral, and anthropological underpinning of our views on debt and credit by Omar and Milman as well as the guilt issues extrapolated in Nietzche's work by Tribe. As noted by Ghio, harmonisation decisions are ultimately made by people, who are susceptible to the same cognitive biases as any other individual and group making decisions in other contexts. For these reasons – among many others – the harmonisation of insolvency law, and indeed generally, legal harmonisation in the European Union has proven challenging. These considerations are important and relevant at the time of writing, if harmonisation is to continue, due to a certain dispassion felt toward globalisation and a certain level of integrational panic in the EU post-Brexit.

Harmonisation is met by a variety of cultural, socio-political, and institutional obstacles. Ghio examines these obstacles to harmonisation from the perspective of the field of social psychology to provide a perspective that will further our understanding of the challenges to insolvency law harmonisation in the EU. In particular, Ghio examines the harmonisation process with psychological biases in mind such as loss aversion in terms of the integrity of state sovereignty; status quo bias which sees people and institutions prefer what they know rather than risk change; bounded willpower resulting in cognitive discomfort when faced with decisions that may not be in their long-term interests; and cognitive dissonance in terms of how our attitudes toward change are affected by information that conflicts with previously held beliefs. All of these psychological factors affect our willingness, as human beings, to accept and promote change and as EU law and harmonisation thereof is a matter of human decision making, such biases will inevitably affect the pace of change.

Further complicating these biases are institutional challenges such as the speed of change, governance, and linguistic factors. The pace of change can be difficult to sell if it appears to be faster than institutions, policies, and attitudes can maintain. Law is a path dependent entity and is difficult to change rapidly because it is embedded in culture and society. Harmonisation requires changing the law to align it centrally, which is difficult when cultures can vary significantly between EU member states. Ghio recommends an incremental approach to circumvent the resistance to a faster pace of change, which also helps to get around status quo bias, for example. Hesitations around governance and loss of sovereignty could be combatted, Ghio suggests, but adopting an empowerment approach that allows member state participation in legislative process. The EU Preventive Restructuring Directive and its flexible implementation options arguably reflects an approach of empowerment in EU legislation while natural convergence among member states supports a flexible approach as it aligns with the natural impulses of member state legislative activity in areas like insolvency law. Finally, linguistic bias due to preconceptions and bias against certain words should also be considered when drafting and presenting legislation aimed to harmonise law among member states. Given the foregoing challenges, it is important for harmonisation initiatives pursued by the European legislator to produce effective and efficient legislation and theoretical considerations in the law and psychology sphere can assist in this regard.

CONCLUSION

Insolvency and restructuring law are legal areas that sit at a crossroads of many other areas of law. These other areas of law can be external forces that exert an influence on the formulation of insolvency law frameworks due to the need of collective resolution to meet the competing demands of a variety of stakeholders.

How does a financially focused legal area such as insolvency law incorporate the human element of business and the fact that it should logically be in the service of humanity? Should this enter into the theoretical frameworks within which legislative provisions are formulated? Does it matter that commercialism and companies were created by human beings to serve their needs and wants? The true conceptual nature of corporatism seems to have been lost somewhat over time; however, the contents of this volume have largely brought these ideas back into focus as a matter of importance to consider going forward when reforming insolvency and restructuring law frameworks throughout the world. Although the authors have discussed a myriad of perspectives and old fan favourites have found their voice as well, the discussion progresses theory in insolvency law beyond law and economics approaches. Every chapter takes a broader perspective, embracing the current progressive nature of academic commentary in this area and offering an alternative to the arguably outdated paradigms that have informed insolvency theory since the 1980s and before. The time has come for a change in the way we think about the corporation and how we create frameworks that provide fair mechanisms to resolve financial distress.

Index